# PAYMENT SYSTEMS
## In Eleven Developed Countries

Third Edition

Prepared under the aegis of the
Bank for International Settlements
by the
Central Banks of the Group of
Ten Countries and Switzerland

Published by
Bank Administration Institute

*Published May 1989.*
*Printed in the United States of America.*

No. 679                                                    ISBN: 1-55520-116-4

# CONTENTS

# FOREWORD

This is the third edition of what has come to be known as the "Red Book" on payment systems. The previous editions have been translated in whole or in part into French, German, and Japanese, which can be taken as a fair indication of the extent of interest in the subject matter. The Group of Experts on Payment Systems of the central banks of the Group of Ten Countries* first attempted to identify the growing areas of mutual interest in developments in the field of payment systems in 1978. These initial efforts not only served to highlight the increasing similarities in the different national environments by showing that payment systems were developing along common lines, but also convinced the central banks of the need to publish their findings. The central banks' principal reason for undertaking studies in this field is, of course, the fact that money, in the broadest sense of the term, is one of their main objects of concern and an area of prime responsibility.

Much has happened in the field of payment systems since the 1985 edition appeared, and, when one looks at what is being done today to promote electronic funds transfers (EFT), a certain perspective is called for to enable the reader to appreciate the magnitude and speed of changes in this area. It is hoped, in particular, that the third edition of the "Red Book" will enable the reader to monitor and compare the ever-increasing number of interrelationships arising from the use of electronic systems for the transfer of the ownership of money in the eleven countries.

In 1978, when the initial work was being done for the first edition, EFT POS was a subject for academic and sometimes esoteric debate. Today EFT POS is an economic reality, with regional and nationwide systems in place. It is predicted that by the mid-1990s there will be over 200,000 EFT POS terminals in the United Kingdom alone.

Moreover, in 1978, S.W.I.F.T. electronically linked about 500 banks in 16 countries and was considered successful because it had achieved an annual traffic volume of almost 25 million messages. Today S.W.I.F.T. handles almost the same number of messages each month. Domestic electronic networks for interbank payments are witnessing a similar growth in traffic.

Like its predecessors, this edition presents the findings essentially in the form of a descriptive manual for consultation and comparison. It is based on 1987 data and is divided into two distinct parts.

After an introductory chapter that highlights the major developments since the last study was completed and identifies the forces behind these changes, the first part provides detailed descriptions of the payment systems of the eleven countries. While

---

*The Group of Ten Countries are those that participate in the General Arrangements to Borrow within the IMF, namely, Belgium, Canada, France, Germany, Italy, Japan, the Netherlands, Sweden, Switzerland, the United Kingdom, and the United States.

in this edition a more rigorous attempt has been made to follow a common framework so as to facilitate comparisons, there are inevitably differences of emphasis reflecting the relative importance of different aspects of the various national payment systems.

The second part of the book presents a series of comparative and country tables as a statistical addendum. The reader is warned that, although considerable improvements have been made in the quality of the statistical data, they are not in all cases complete or uniform and there may be a margin of error where estimates have had to be made. It is hoped, however, that the margin of error is small enough to allow an accurate picture to be given of trends in the various countries taken individually or as a group. Given the rapid pace of change, the Group of Experts on Payment Systems plans to update the statistical addendum annually.

In view of the wide readership expected for this edition and the fact that only a limited number of copies of the last edition are available, every effort has been made to ensure that this edition should serve as a reference work complete in itself and independent of its predecessors.

In addition to preparing the "Red Book" for publication, the central banks of the Group of Ten Countries have addressed the question of security and reliability in electronic systems for payments and have published three manuals on the subject since 1975. These studies, known as the "Yellow Books," have been translated into French, German, Italian, Japanese, and Spanish, with the objective of promoting greater awareness of the need for safe and reliable electronic payment mechanisms. It is, after all, one of the overriding interests of all central banks to ensure a smoothly functioning, reliable, and efficient payment system in each of their countries. It is with this in mind that the reader is encouraged to compare the progress being made in the various countries towards achieving this goal.

# INTRODUCTION

The principal aim of the third edition of this book on payment systems in eleven developed countries is to facilitate comparisons between what on the surface might strike the reader as quite different payment systems. One is still tempted to group the eleven countries into two camps in this respect, the "giro," or credit transfer, and the "cheque," or debit transfer countries, even if this is no longer so evident as it was in 1980 when the first edition was published.

A common theme running through the various country reports is the recognition that cooperation between banks is essential for setting up sophisticated electronic networks. While there had already been a marked increase in interbank cooperation at various levels, particularly in payment system standards, the large investments required to introduce and operate electronic funds transfer (EFT) systems, whether intended for use between banks at an international level or by bank customers at the point-of-sale (EFT POS), have helped to focus the banks' attention on the need to cooperate in establishing the basic infrastructure required for such systems and to share the costs involved, often with a view to ultimately competing more effectively for customers.

This recognition of the need for increased cooperation in the development of infrastructures has led a growing number of countries, both within and outside the Group of Ten, to follow the Canadian example and establish permanent public coordinating bodies for this purpose or to create ad hoc inter-industry groups as forums for discussion. In some countries the benefits are already being felt by both corporate and personal customers. One central bank, the Bank of Italy, published a "White Paper on the Payment System in Italy" in 1987 with a view to formulating an integrated plan of action in this regard in collaboration with the banking sector, and another, the Nederlandsche Bank, formally issued a memorandum describing the basic principles to be followed in the development of the payment system.

It was natural that various banks in a number of countries should have wished to create their own large, and in some cases nationwide, automated teller machine (ATM) and cash dispenser networks, but experience showed the wisdom of giving customers access to a wider range of networks and of sharing what had originally been proprietary systems. Indeed, the advent of network-sharing is a major theme in most of the eleven chapters. The statistical data underline the phenomenon that network-sharing has itself promoted wider and more frequent use of these card-based systems by the participating banks' customers. If one of the goals of the expanded and interconnected networks was to support new payment practices through the convenient siting of large numbers of machines, then this goal has been achieved in a number of countries. This is the case, for instance, in France, where most of the banks have joined to issue a single bank card that can be used in 11,500 cash dispensers and which is accepted at 415,000 points-of-sale.

With all the emphasis on electronic payment systems throughout the chapters that follow, the reader will not be surprised that the relative importance of cash in the money supply ($M_3$) of the eleven countries under review has decreased in almost all of the countries. Despite this trend, cash appears to play an important role in payment systems both at the retail level and in the so-called gray or underground economy. The convenience, universal acceptability, and anonymity of cash will secure the bank note's role in payment systems for some time to come.

As first noted in the 1985 edition, there is growing attention regarding the relative costs of the various payment instruments, particularly in view of the continued use of paper-based and hence labour-intensive instruments. This has resulted in more widespread specific pricing of particular payment services and the promotion of direct depositing of wage and pension payments, as well as the automation of the traditional clearing house mechanisms, and the growing use of cheque truncation in a number of countries. However, costs alone are not the primary force working towards change.

As mentioned previously, parallel to the growth in the use of electronic systems for domestic payments there has been a dramatic expansion in the use of sophisticated switching systems for internationally related payment networks. The increasing use of these systems continues to give rise to a noticeable growth in the netting of positions within groups of users. This is particularly true in the so-called offshore netting centers, such as the Tokyo-based U.S. dollar clearing system and the Private ECU (European Currency Unit) Clearing and Settlement System. While it could be said that the offshore netting schemes are an electronic extension of domestic netting schemes made possible by telematic technology, they do raise questions regarding the finality of payments given the time-zone differences and about new aspects of the central banks' role as lenders of last resort.*

While it is the conventional wisdom that electronic banking brings with it both factor economies and economies of scale not available in a paper-based system, it is not for this reason alone that banks have forged ahead with the development of complex electronic systems. There is a growing awareness of the ability of third parties, such as value-added network suppliers, to meet the payment demands of a public that finds itself increasingly at ease in the use of terminals, ATMs, and cash dispensers. The advent of home-banking schemes sponsored by postal authorities in some countries has placed further emphasis on the pioneering efforts of certain banks and has highlighted the need for banks to cater to a section of the market that is both affluent and familiar with the advantages of electronic communication over the traditional paper-based means.

Another force bringing about change is the growing dependence on credit and debit cards by an ever more mobile population for personal transactions. This "popularisation" of international payment transactions has led to greater coopera-tion in establishing means of detecting and preventing the fraudulent use of plastic credit or debit cards on an international basis. Further steps must be taken in this respect.

The new systems have also brought with them a new phenomenon, the con-sequences of which remain to be seen. This is the possibility of transmitting payment messages at electronic speeds in times of crisis. The increased interdependence of the

---

*Renato De Mattia, former Central Manager of the Bank of Italy and former adviser to the Bank for International Settlements, was one of the first persons to state that the traditional constraints of time, distance, and volume on the transfer of large amounts of money are not valid when applied to the use of electronic means for the transfer of funds.

securities markets and the various payment systems, coupled with the globalisation of the securities markets, raises the issue of the growing danger of systemic risk in payment systems. This is the risk that one or more participants in a payment system will be unable to meet their obligations when due and thus cause other participants to be subsequently unable to meet theirs. Of the various kinds of risk to which banks may become exposed through the accelerated use of the new technology, it is this systemic risk that is the greatest cause for concern. The central banks of the Group of Ten Countries are aware of this danger and are currently examining the question with a view to minimising its potential impact on the sound functioning of the payment systems in their respective countries via work on finality, netting, and reducing the probability of purely technical problems.

# GLOSSARY

**ACH.** Automated clearing house.

**Automated teller machine (ATM).** Electromechanical device allowing the authorised user not only to withdraw cash from his account but also to access a varying range of other services such as balance inquiry, transfer of funds, and acceptance of deposits.

**Cash dispenser.** Electromechanical device allowing the authorised user to withdraw bank notes and, in some cases, also coins.

**Chip or IC card.** Card into which have been inserted one or more integrated circuits (ISO definition).

**Credit card.** Card indicating that the holder has been granted a line of credit. It enables the holder to make purchases and/or draw cash up to a prearranged ceiling; the credit granted can be settled in full by the end of a specific period, or it can be settled in part, with the balance taken as extended credit. The holder is not always charged an annual fee, but interest is charged on the amount of any extended credit.

**Debit card.** Card enabling the holder to draw cash from a retail outlet, an ATM, or a cash dispenser and also, in some cases, to have his purchases directly charged to funds on his account at a deposit-taking institution.

**Home banking.** Services that a customer of a financial institution can access using a telephone, a television set, or a terminal as a telecommunication link to the institution's computer center.

**MICR.** Magnetic ink character recognition.

**OCR.** Optical character recognition.

**Off-line.** Pertaining to equipment or a procedure that is operating under local rather than remote central control.

**On-line.** Pertaining to equipment or a procedure that is operating under remote central control.

**PIN.** Personal identification number. The code or password the cardholder possesses for verification of identity (ISO definition).

**Point-of-sale terminal for electronic funds transfer (EFT POS).** A terminal at a retail location that is designed to capture, and in some cases also transmit, payment information by electronic means.

**S.W.I.F.T. (Society for Worldwide Interbank Financial Telecommunication).** An international financial transaction processing network through which more than 2,300 institutions in 56 countries exchanged on the average of more than 900,000 messages per day in 1987. Created and owned by banks, the network is also available now to the following categories of nonbank institutions: securities brokers and dealers, clearing and depositary institutions, and recognised exchanges for securities.

**Telematics.** Combined use of data-processing and data-transmission techniques.

**Travel and entertainment (charge) card.** Card indicating that the holder has been granted a line of credit. It enables him to make purchases without any expenditure limit, but does not offer extended credit, the full amount of the debt incurred being settled at the end of a specified period. The holder is usually charged an annual fee.

**Truncation.** A procedure in which the physical movement of paper items is curtailed, being replaced by the transmission of all or part of their content in electronic form.

**Videotex (Viewdata).** A two-way interactive computer system capable of displaying centrally stored pages of text and graphics on adapted television screens using simplified commands.

# PAYMENT SYSTEMS
## In Eleven Developed Countries

# PART I

# PAYMENT SYSTEMS
# IN THE
# ELEVEN COUNTRIES
# REVIEWED

# 1 BELGIUM

# Belgium

## I  INTRODUCTION

The main features of payment systems in Belgium can be summarised in the following points:

▶ The relative importance of the share of cash in the money supply ($M_1$), although it has been clearly declining for many years.

▶ The large proportion of the population holding bank accounts and the large number of bank offices.

▶ Among cashless payment instruments, the predominance of the credit transfer and its derivatives over the cheque.

▶ The increasingly rapid deployment of electronic technology, reflected both in the appearance and spread of new payment systems and instruments available to customers of financial institutions (e.g., ATMs, POS terminals) and in the rationalisation of the processing of traditional payment media within the banking system (e.g., truncation, automated clearing).

▶ The fact that payment services are, to a very large extent, free, in spite of recent moves towards charging.

▶ A balance between competition and cooperation, with cooperation in the form of sharing joint technical infrastructure and drawing up interbank standards.

▶ The growing involvement of nonbanks, such as issuers of credit and travel and entertainment cards, large retail chains, and issuers of luncheon vouchers.

Briefly, the "traditional" payment instruments and systems are facing growing competition from new instruments and systems relying on electronic technology and/or offered by nonbank institutions.

## II  INSTITUTIONAL FRAMEWORK

As the issuing authority, the central bank—the National Bank of Belgium—issues notes on its own behalf and coin on behalf of the Treasury.[1] While it carries out the production of notes, the minting of coin is the prerogative of the Royal Mint of Belgium, responsible to the Ministry of Finance.

In the payment system field, the only other areas of explicit central bank intervention are those of the interbank clearing mechanisms, both traditional (the clearing houses, located at the branches and agencies of the central bank and chaired by it) and automated (the CEC), and—partly connected—of standardisation within the financial system. Neither the central bank nor any other authority exercises real powers of specific supervision regarding payment systems.

The banking system comprises three broad categories of financial intermediaries:

▶ The commercial banks                    (86 at year-end 1987)
▶ The savings banks                       (32 at year-end 1987)
▶ The public credit institutions          ( 5 at year-end 1987)

---

[1]Within the framework of the Belgium-Luxembourg Economic Union (BLEU), Belgian coin and notes are legal tender in the Grand Duchy of Luxembourg, but the reverse is not the case.

To these three broad categories must be added the Postal Cheque Office, which constitutes the financial department of the Postal Administration.

Although each of these types of financial institution was originally fairly specialised in terms of markets and products, these distinctions have become progressively blurred since the mid-1970s. Only the Postal Cheque Office, owing to strict legal constraints, continues to be restricted in the range of services offered.

Three main interbank institutions are operating in the payment system field:

▶ The nonprofit-making association of CEC (Clearing Center for the Belgian Financial System), founded in 1974 by the banking sector as a whole, the object of which is the automated exchange of payment transactions for clearing and which is chaired by the National Bank of Belgium, which also takes care of the management of day-to-day operations.

▶ The Mister Cash consortium (32 members at year-end 1987), without separate legal status, which since year-end 1978 has operated a shared network of ATMs and POS terminals.

▶ The Bancontact cooperative society (29 members at year-end 1987), which since mid-1979 has managed a shared network of ATMs and POS terminals.

Nonbank institutions are also represented on the payment media market:

▶ Companies issuing credit and travel and entertainment cards (numbering four, only one of which, in fact, has no connection with the banking sector).

▶ Commercial companies issuing in-house cards, these being essentially either petrol companies or large retailers.

▶ Companies issuing luncheon vouchers.

Monetary policy is decided by the National Bank of Belgium in consultation with the Minister of Finance.

Prudential supervision of the financial institutions—with the exception of four of the five public credit institutions[2] and the Postal Cheque Office, which are supervised by various ministries — is the responsibility of the Banking Commission, a body independent of the central bank.

## III   PAYMENT SYSTEMS

### 1. Payment Systems Available to Customers

*(a) Cash*

Cash comprises notes in denominations of B.fr. 100, 500, 1,000 and 5,000 and coin in denominations of B.fr. 0.50, 1, 5, 20, 50, and 500.[3] There has been a shift between notes and coin in recent years, in the form of a substitution of coins for notes of B.fr. 20 and 50.[4] Among the notes, the B.fr. 5,000 denomination represents an ever-larger share of the total stock of notes in circulation (69.3 percent by value at year-end 1987), despite the growing success of ATMs. These, in fact, only deliver notes of B.fr. 1,000, which accounted for 25.1 percent of notes in circulation (by value) at December 31, 1987. Bank notes constitute 97.2 percent of total cash in circulation and coins 2.8 percent.

It is impossible to estimate the value or number of payments made using cash. The only indication available—although very inconclusive—lies in the share of cash in $M_1$, which has recorded a marked decline over a number of years. It amounted to 34.7 percent at year-end 1987, compared with 42.4 percent at year-end 1978. The

---

[2]There are plans to make these also subject to supervision by the Banking Commission.
[3]This coin cannot be said to be "in circulation" because it is hoarded by the public.
[4]This note, issued on behalf of the Treasury, will finally be replaced in the spring of 1989 by a coin of the same value.

average cash holding per inhabitant stood at close to B.fr. 42,000 at year-end 1987,[5] after deducting the share of cash in circulation held by the financial intermediaries (6.5 percent). The total stock of cash in circulation on December 31, 1987, amounted to B.fr. 440.3 billion.[6]

In spite of the rise of payment media in competition with the bank note, developments over the last two years show that its use has begun to gain ground again, also in real terms (for the first time this decade). This movement seems, however, to have slowed down again recently.

### (b) Deposit money

#### General

*Deposit money* comprises sight deposits held by nonfinancial economic agents, with financial intermediaries legally entitled to receive such deposits (banks, savings banks, public credit institutions, and the Postal Cheque Office).[7]

A few figures illustrate the importance that deposit money has acquired:
▶ The share of deposit money in $M_1$ amounted to 65.3 percent at year-end 1987, compared with 57.6 percent at year-end 1978.
▶ The number of sight accounts in Belgian francs open as of December 31, 1987, stood at 9.49 million, representing a theoretical average of 96 sight accounts per 100 inhabitants (compared with 58 in 1978).
▶ The stock of deposit money amounted to B.fr. 775.9 billion at year-end 1987, representing an average of about B.fr. 78,500 per inhabitant.

These data illustrate, at least theoretically, the large banking propensity and the preference for liquidity of the Belgian population.

#### Payment instruments

Various payment instruments are associated with sight accounts:
▶ The credit transfer and its variants, such as the standing order and variable standing order.
▶ The cheque and its corollary, the cheque guarantee card.
▶ The direct debit.
▶ The debit card.

The most commonly used payment medium is the credit transfer, which is an order to transfer a given amount from the sight account of the initiator of the payment to the account of the payee. The order is given by the customer making the payment to his bank either in paper form—handed in at his bank branch or sent by post—or in automated form (diskette, magnetic tape, telecommunications). An estimated 304.9 million credit transfers were made in 1987.

The standing order or variable standing order is a form of credit transfer created to rationalise the system for recurring payments (e.g., payment of rent, salaries). Instead of setting a credit transfer in motion each time the payment falls due, the customer instructs his bank to make a regular, automatic transfer of a given sum, at specified intervals, to a named account (standing order). In the case of a variable standing order, some of the data are variable and the customer must communicate them before each payment falls due to his financial institution by means of a list (paper-based or automated). In 1987, an estimated 34.7 million payments were made in the form of standing or variable standing orders.

---

[5]There is some bias in this figure as a result of the circulation of Belgian cash in Luxembourg and vice versa.
[6]Although not legal tender in Belgium, the Luxembourg coin and—to a very limited extent—notes also circulate within the country; however, except in border regions, they represent a tiny proportion of the total circulation.
[7]Combined cash and deposit money holdings stood at about B.fr. 120,000 per inhabitant at year-end 1987.

One development of significance is certainly the growing "dematerialisation" of payment orders transmitted by customers. In point of fact, more and more firms are communicating their payment orders via magnetic media or via telecommunications, which obviates the need to capture the data within the financial system. For 1987, it is estimated that 87.3 million payment orders—or 21.9 percent of total credit transfers and payments made in the form of standing and variable standing orders—were submitted in paperless form.

There is also a hybrid payment instrument offered chiefly by the Postal Cheque Office, *viz.*, the *inpayment transfer.* This enables a payment to be made to a holder of a (bank or postal) sight account on the basis of a cash inpayment at a post office. This instrument is primarily intended for payers who do not have a sight account. In 1987, 94.3 million inpayment transfers were made for a total value of B.fr. 6,097 billion, giving an average of B.fr. 64,623 per transaction.

After the credit transfer, the *cheque* is the most used cashless payment instrument. The Eurocheque is the most common type of cheque in Belgium; approximately 50 percent of the cheques issued in 1987 in Belgium were Eurocheques. To promote the use of the cheque, financial institutions increased its acceptability to creditors by supplying creditworthy customers with cheque guarantee cards. This card serves as a guarantee that any cheque drawn will be honoured up to an amount of B.fr. 7,000, whether or not the drawer's sight account is covered with sufficient funds. To make the guarantee effective, the number of the cheque guarantee card must be indicated on the back of the cheque. It is the duty of the payee to check the validity of the card and whether the information on the card corresponds with what is written on the cheque. The cheque guarantee card carries an automatic (interest-bearing) overdraft facility of B.fr. 25,000 (B.fr. 30,000 or 50,000 with some institutions). The only restriction is that it is prohibited to have a permanent debit balance for more than three consecutive months. In all, 205.2 million cheques, including 11.3 million postal cheques, were issued in 1987. On December 31, 1987, there were 4.47 million cheque guarantee cards in circulation (3.01 million of them Eurocheque cards), equivalent to a theoretical average of 47 cards per 100 sight accounts. Unlike other cashless payment instruments, the cheque can be used for several successive payments, by means of endorsement. This practice is, however, still relatively limited.

A special category of cheque is the *postal draft.* As its name implies, this instrument is issued by the Postal Cheque Office. It makes it possible to send by post a payment order that the recipient can cash at a post office or at a financial institution of which he is a customer. This payment medium enables a payment to be made to a payee who has no sight account or whose sight account number is not known by whoever initiates the transaction. The draft is drawn on a postal current account, possibly with a financial institution other than the Postal Cheque Office acting as intermediary. The government and its various services make extended use of the postal draft system. In 1987, 38.6 million postal drafts were issued for a value of B.fr. 563.1 billion, equivalent, on average, to B.fr. 14,591 per draft.

The direct debit is a mechanism created in 1980 whose purpose, like that of the standing order and variable standing order, is to simplify the execution of payments that are regular in certain respects. However, it differs from both these instruments in two ways:

▶ It is based on a formal four-cornered procedure involving a supplier of goods or services, his customer, and their respective banks. The customer must give authorisation for the supplier automatically to draw on his sight account, through the intermediary of the two financial institutions concerned, an amount equivalent to the bills for which he is liable regarding the services he has received.

▶ The payment is initiated by the supplier, who notifies his bank, generally in automated form, of the amount to be collected from those of his customers who have accepted the direct debiting of bills.

In 1987, 49.1 million payments[8] were executed under direct debit agreements, including 0.56[8] million refunds.[9]

*Debit cards* issued by financial institutions to their customers with sight accounts are dealt with in the following section, which is devoted exclusively to this topic.

### Pricing and value dates

Gross interest of 0.5 percent per annum is paid by the deposit-taking institutions on credit balances on the sight accounts of "ordinary" customers. To compensate for this virtual absence of remuneration, payment services offered to holders of sight accounts are, as a rule, free of charge. This principle of no charge, which is still valid, applies both to the issue of cheques and to the execution of payment orders. There are two exceptions:

▶ The cheque guarantee card is issued for a fee, set at B.fr. 300 for 1988.

▶ Foreign transactions are subject to a commission.

In addition, the postal charges for the mailing of statements of account are also, as a general rule, borne by the customers.

Regarding value dates, the practice concerning "ordinary" customers is as follows:

▶ Value the previous working day when an account is debited.

▶ Value the following working day when an account is credited (in the case of cheques for collection, credit under reserve).

There are no regulations governing these practices or setting maximum time limits for crediting counterparties.

### (c) Bank cards

Apart from cheque guarantee cards, which are not, strictly speaking and as their name indeed indicates, a payment medium, the financial institutions issue debit cards that can be used at ATMs and, usually, at POS terminals.

Two recent developments are under way in this field:

▶ The gradual amalgamation of the debit card and cheque guarantee card, with the magnetic stripes that characterise the debit card being affixed to the cheque guarantee card so as to create a single multifunctional card.

▶ The increasing promotion of the logo of the issuing financial institution, whereas, in the early years of their development, debit cards primarily bore the trademark of the interbank network to which they provided access (Bancontact or Mister Cash).

With the exception of the debit cards issued by the Postal Cheque Office (Postomat), which can only be used in the ATMs installed by this institution and solely for withdrawals, bank debit cards can be used at both ATMs and POS terminals. All the debit cards have magnetic stripes[10] and require a personal identification number (PIN) to be keyed in on the keyboard of the terminal before the services can be accessed. If a wrong number is keyed in three times, the card is invalidated; this can be reversed by the issuing financial institution.

The trader who is paid by means of a debit card is guaranteed payment, with no limit on the amount.

On December 31, 1987, approximately 4 million debit cards were in circulation, 3.9

---

[8]An estimate.

[9]A refund in connection with a direct debit could, for example, be made by an electricity company for an overpayment.

[10]The networks do not plan to use microprocessor cards in the short term for the following main reasons: the high cost of the microprocessor card; existing on-line networks; the need to break even on the heavy investments made.

million of them with access to both ATMs and POS terminals. This represents a ratio of 42 cards per 100 sight accounts, or 40 cards per 100 inhabitants. These figures have to be put into perspective, given the rates of utilisation of these cards; it seems, in fact, that up to 40 percent of them are never used.

In the last few years, the use of debit cards has started to become internationalised. Hitherto this trend has only been in evidence at the ATM level, with the following tangible results to date:

▶ There is a reciprocal agreement between the Postal Cheque Office and its counterpart organisations in the Grand Duchy of Luxembourg and France.

▶ Holders of Bancontact and Mister Cash cards have access, within the framework of the Eurocheque community, to ATMs in an increasing number of European countries (currently 10), but reciprocity will only materialise in 1989.

The volume and the value of transactions concluded by means of debit cards have increased tremendously since their introduction, in tandem with the number of cards in circulation and terminals installed.

In 1987, the following results were recorded for transactions concluded in Belgium by holders of Belgian cards:

▶ 47.3 million withdrawals—for a total value of B.fr. 165.6 billion—at ATMs, or, on average, 14 withdrawals per card and B.fr. 3,500 per withdrawal.

▶ 0.45 million deposits—for a total value of B.fr. 4.9 billion—at ATMs, or, on average, 0.14 deposit per card and B.fr. 10,890 per deposit.

▶ Approximately 32 million electronic payments at POS terminals for a total value of some B.fr. 34 billion, or, on average, 9.6 transactions per card and B.fr. 1,063 per payment.

As terminals have been installed in sectors other than that of petrol distribution, the share of the latter in total transactions concluded electronically declined to only 80 percent in 1987. The share of transactions concluded in the large retailer sector thus rose to 11 percent in 1987.

As far as "international" transactions are concerned, they are still fairly marginal since:

▶ Authorised holders of foreign cards (i.e., those from Luxembourg and France) made slightly more than 21,000 withdrawals at Belgian ATMs in 1987, for a total of approximately B.fr. 88 million, or an average of B.fr. 4,190 per transaction.

▶ Holders of Belgian cards executed approximately 75,500 withdrawals at ATMs abroad in 1987, for a total value equivalent to B.fr. 427 million, or an average of B.fr. 5,650 per operation.

The cost to the consumer of using debit cards—at ATMs and POS terminals—consists in theory only of an annual fee, set at B.fr. 165 for 1988. However, the large retailer sector decided in November 1987, to make consumers pay the fee of B.fr. 2 per transaction that the interbank networks wanted to impose on it and which traders belonging to the other sectors have themselves already been paying.

*(d) Nonbank cards*

There are two distinct types of nonbank cards:

▶ Credit cards and travel and entertainment cards issued by American Express, Diners Club, Eurocard (a consortium of Belgian banks, affiliated to MasterCard) and Crédit Européen[11] (VISA).

---

[11]This institution has recently been taken over by a large Belgian bank, and its VISA franchise will be shared with other Belgian financial institutions as from 1989. The Belgian subsidiary of a large U.S. bank has just started to issue its own VISA cards to its customers, independently of this scheme.

▶ In-house cards issued by petrol companies (e.g., Esso, Shell, and Texaco) and large retailers (principally GB-Inno-BM, Colruyt, and Trois Suisses[12]).

*Credit cards and travel and entertainment cards* are, by definition, widely accepted in Belgium and abroad. They can be used at a large number of businesses. These cards, however, were long the prerogative of an elite minority of Belgians and foreign visitors. But as a result of vigorous promotion efforts by the companies concerned, the number of cards in circulation has shown a considerable increase: from some 70,000 at year-end 1978 to approximately 466,000 at year-end 1987.[13] Some months ago these cards were joined by the AirPlus card, launched by a group of European airlines and represented in Belgium by Sabena (the Belgian airline). This card is intended for use in other sectors, not just that of air transport proper.

Traders enjoy the advantage of guaranteed payment, for an unlimited amount, subject to compliance with the procedures prescribed by the issuers of the cards and the payment of a variable fee per transaction.

In 1987, credit cards and travel and entertainment cards accounted for a transactions volume that may be illustrated by the following figures[13]:

▶ 7.4 million transactions were effected in Belgium for a total of B.fr. 32.7 billion, 3.1 million of which were payments by foreign cards (for B.fr. 12.2 billion).

▶ Approximately 3 million transactions were effected abroad by Belgian cardholders for a total value of B.fr. 16.3 billion.

In 1987, the average value of a transaction was as follows[13]:

▶ Transactions in Belgium using Belgian cards:    B.fr. 4,768
▶ Transactions in Belgium using foreign cards:    B.fr. 3,958
▶ Transactions abroad using Belgian cards:    B.fr. 5,498

Naturally, these average values vary considerably according to the type of sector where the purchases are made. However, the preceding figures suggest that, on average, each Belgian card was used 17.2 times in 1987 (in Belgium and abroad).

With the exception of customers of American Express—which, in 1986, installed two ATMs in Brussels to dispense notes and travellers' cheques—holders of credit cards and travel and entertainment cards have no access to ATMs—whether owned by banks or card issuers—in Belgium, whereas Belgian cardholders are largely able to take advantage of this facility abroad.

A growing number of issuers have recently begun automating their payment procedures. At a (still relatively limited) number of points-of-sale not only does authorisation take place electronically on-line, but details of the transaction are immediately recorded by the issuing company's computer system. A slip evidencing the transaction is automatically printed out on the spot.

*In-house cards* can, by their nature, only be used at points-of-sale controlled by their issuers. A distinction can be made between in-house cards that use the issuers' own infrastructure and those that are, in fact, managed at the strictly operational level by another commercial card issuer (interbank network or credit card issuer). The latter category comprises cards issued by petrol companies.

Some of these in-house cards, moreover, are linked with POS terminals, whereas others can only be used "manually."

The most striking example of an in-house card is certainly that issued by the largest Belgian retail group, GB-Inno-BM, which has launched itself vigorously onto the payment cards market (and, at one and the same time, onto the consumer credit market), with its "Shopping" card (new name). This card can be used either as a debit

---

[12]Strictly speaking, Trois Suisses does not belong to the large retailer sector.
[13]The data relating to credit cards and travel and entertainment cards partially include the Grand Duchy of Luxembourg owing to the impossibility of eliminating a proportion of the Luxembourg figures.

card (through the direct debiting technique) or as a credit card, the choice being made by the cardholder at the moment of each purchase. Only some of the POS terminals installed by GB-Inno-BM can be accessed by the cards issued by the interbank networks and then only on payment by the consumers of the B.fr. 2 fee per transaction that GB-Inno-BM would normally have to pay to these networks.

The main features of the in-house card market in 1987 may be summarised as follows:

▶ 577,000 cards in circulation on December 31, 1987.

▶ 8.7 million transactions for a value of B.fr. 14.7 billion, making an average of B.fr. 1,690 per payment.

▶ Payments at POS terminals alone represented 94.3 percent of the total volume and 92.2 percent of the overall turnover effected by means of in-house cards.

*(e) Other instruments*

Other instruments are also used in Belgium, the main ones being:

▶ The luncheon voucher.

▶ The traveller's cheque.

▶ The commercial bill.[14]

In addition, barter, clearing operations outside the financial system, and foreign bank notes also constitute means of settling debts. It is, however, impossible to quantify the significance of these, although this should not be underestimated.

The only instrument for which data are available is the *luncheon voucher,* which theoretically may only be used for the payment of a restaurant bill or for the purchase of food products. These vouchers are issued by two French-owned companies (Le Chèque-Repas CR and Ticket Restaurant) to any other firm wishing to distribute them to its employees as part of its compensation package. For reasons of an essentially fiscal nature,[15] use of the luncheon voucher has increased very considerably in the course of the last few years, as is illustrated by the following statistics:

▶ Number of vouchers issued in 1987: 48.3 million (1978: 6.1 million).

▶ Total value of vouchers issued in 1987: B.fr. 9.4 billion (1978: B.fr. 0.55 billion).

▶ Number of firms issuing luncheon vouchers to their staff in 1987: approximately 8,660 (roughly 500 in 1978).

*(f) Interbank networks available to consumers*

Two interbank networks are aimed at consumers:

▶ Mister Cash, which has been operational since the end of 1978.

▶ Bancontact, which commenced operations in mid-1979.

These two networks manage ATM and POS terminals on-line, access being by means of magnetic stripe cards and secret PIN numbers.

The transactions possible at ATMs are withdrawals, inpayments, consultation of balances (sight accounts, savings accounts), ordering of documents (cheques, credit transfer forms), and transfers from sight accounts to savings accounts.

Each transaction triggers various immediate checks:

▶ Blacklist (e.g., stolen cards).

▶ Balance on current account, on the basis of the balance at the previous day's close, taking into account the total of the day's operations effected by means of the card and the amount of the credit line.

---

[14]It is not totally incontestable that the commercial bill and its variants possess the characteristics of a payment instrument. In any case, final settlement of the transaction underlying the bill will have to be in the form of another payment medium (cash or deposit money). The commercial bill, however, can be passed to a third party by means of endorsement.

[15]The tax advantages accruing to the employer and the employee under the luncheon voucher system, however, have been progressively reduced recently.

▶ Margin available *vis-à-vis* the authorised limit—per day or per week—set, for security reasons, on the cumulative value of electronic transactions.

Since mid-November 1987, all terminals installed in Belgium can be accessed by all cards (Mister Cash or Bancontact) regardless of which network manages the terminal. The computer centers of the two networks are interconnected to ensure that all transactions can be processed instantaneously and completely.

On December 31, 1987, 732 ATMs[16] and 13,518 POS terminals[17] had been installed by the two interbank networks. Of a total of 800 ATMs,[18] only 31 had been installed at nonbank sites. The estimated percentage distribution of the 13,868 POS terminals[19] between the main commercial sectors at year-end 1987 was as follows:

▶ Filling stations:         17.59%
▶ Large retail outlets:      6.31%
▶ Small retail outlets:     60.84%
▶ Hotels:                    1.15%
▶ Restaurants/bars:          9.47%
▶ Other:                     4.64%

While the POS terminals installed at filling stations and large retail outlets are, like ATMs, heavyweight terminals linked via leased lines to the networks' computer centers, those installed at small retail outlets and in the other sectors are of the "teledataphone" type, which involves the use of the switched telephone network. Although they represent more than three-quarters of the terminals in service, machines located at sites other than filling stations and large retail outlets only account for some 8 percent of operations, which is attributable to a number of factors (e.g., recent installation, greater competition from other payment instruments, opening hours).

The rate of use of all these terminals varies, as evidenced by the following figures, calculated for all of 1987:

**Average Number of Transactions
per Terminal, per Month**

| ATMs[20] | | POS Terminals | |
|---|---|---|---|
| Withdrawals | 5,194 | Total[21,22] | 262 |
| Withdrawals + deposits | 5,244 | of which, at filling stations[21] | 1,072 |

The apparent relatively sparse coverage of ATM networks[23]—approximately one ATM for every 12,350 inhabitants at year-end 1987—is attributable to the following factors that are peculiar to Belgium:

▶ The creation of two interbank networks in 1978-79, which has from the outset restricted competition.

▶ The compatibility of the two networks since June 1987.

▶ The heavy concentration of the population in the urban zones.

By way of comparison, likewise at year-end 1987 the coverage of bank branch offices worked out at an estimated ratio of one branch for every 808 inhabitants.

---

[16]Together with the 68 ATMs of the in-house Postomat network of the Postal Cheque Office, the total number of machines is 800.

[17]Plus 350 terminals installed at large retail outlets on sites already equipped by GB-Inno-BM.

[18]Bancontact, Mister Cash, and Postomat.

[19]Including the 350 terminals installed in the large retailer sector to which reference is made in footnote 17.

[20]Bancontact, Mister Cash, and Postomat.

[21]Including transactions effected by means of in-house cards issued by petrol companies that have entered into agreements with Bancontact or Mister Cash.

[22]Including the terminals to which reference is made in footnotes 16 and 18.

[23]Bancontact, Mister Cash, and Postomat.

By contrast, the number of POS terminals is considerable, which testifies to the great importance already attached to electronic payments in Belgium. Two statistics support this assertion: There is—estimates as of year-end 1987—one terminal for every 712 inhabitants and more than one point-of-sale in 10 is already equipped (for filling stations alone the proportion is even 4.5 in 10).

The compatibility between the two interbank networks brought about gradually in 1987 should stimulate the expansion of the interbank networks and the volume of transactions. Clearly, it is difficult to determine the magnitude of any such impact at this stage. Nevertheless, it appears that the increase in the number of withdrawals at ATMs accelerated rapidly in the second half of 1987, i.e., precisely after the entry into force of the agreement on ATM compatibility, the rise between the first half of 1986 and the first half of 1987 having been 9.5 percent, while that between the second half of 1986 and the second half of 1987 amounted to 40.2 percent. In the case of POS terminals, where the number installed and the volume of operations had already been increasing considerably before 1987, the figures do not, at first glance, suggest that the compatibility agreement had any pronounced effect. The rates of increase recorded in 1987 do not differ as markedly from those observed in the preceding years, although a slight acceleration is perceptible. However, data for the first nine months of 1988 show a marked decline in the rate of growth of both ATM and POS transactions (23.1 percent and 34.4 percent, respectively).

The interbank networks can be accessed not only by bank debit cards but also by a range of in-house cards issued by petrol companies that can be used exclusively at filling stations selling each company's particular brand. These companies make use of the whole infrastructure of the interbank networks, but offer additional services aimed at attracting corporate customers with fleets of vehicles.

Alongside these two interbank networks, other networks exist, operated by firms competing with the banking sector, from the large retailer sector or from the credit card and travel and entertainment card sector. The total number of POS terminals installed or used (teledataphones) by these other networks amounted to an estimated 1,920 at year-end 1987. In addition, two ATMs are owned by American Express.

### 2. Exchange Circuits Within the Banking System

*(a) In-house networks*

All the major banks—including the central brank—have automated the activities of their branch and agency networks, and the links between these and the head offices. As a result, a whole range of data pass through their respective telecommunication networks, including messages relating to payment operations for the account of customers.

*(b) Networks between banks and their customers*

With a view toward reducing the costs of processing operations originating from their corporate customers, on the one hand, and improving the services they offer these clients, on the other, the largest financial institutions have set up procedures for exchanging information between themselves and their corporate customers by means of telecommunications.

The information exchanged is of various kinds: general economic and financial information (exchange rates, data concerning firms), statements of account, payment orders, cash management, and tools to assist decision-making.

Although Belgian banks do not, at present, offer any real banking services to their private customers on the videotex network,[24] some of them are installing multipurpose ATMs within their branches solely for their customers' use. These multipurpose machines are not integrated into the interbank ATM networks. They can generally also be accessed outside the branches' normal opening hours. However, access to these "automatic banks"—premises and machine—is by means of the same debit card as that used for the interbank network terminals. In addition, in September 1984, one major public credit institution set up a network of several hundred terminals that deliver statements of account to its customers. These machines, located in the outside walls of its branches, can be accessed by means of debit cards.

All the recent developments point to the reappearance of some competition among banks based on proprietary technical infrastructures and systems, whereas the trend since the late 1960s had been towards devising common infrastructures and standards (automated clearing, EFT).

*(c) Interbank networks and circuits*

Payment operations involving two parties who are both customers of the same financial institution are settled within that institution, without any need for recourse to the interbank exchange and clearing mechanisms. It is estimated that approximately 40 percent of all payment operations are carried out by simple internal transfers in the books of the financial institutions. As for transactions that cannot be settled within a single institution, a number of different systems—varying considerably in significance—exist at the interbank level, as is shown in the following table. The interbank exchange and clearing mechanisms are fundamentally multilateral in nature.

|  | Share of Number of Items Cleared[25] (1987) | Share of Funds Cleared (1987) |
|---|---|---|
| "Traditional" paper clearing | 5.16% | 94.90% |
| CEC | 93.00% | 4.92% |
| Bilateral exchanges | 1.84% | 0.18% |

On December 31, 1987, there were 21 *"traditional" clearing houses* in Belgium, located in Brussels and in 20 provincial towns, where they occupy premises placed at their disposal by the National Bank of Belgium, which is a member and, in fact, acts as chairman of the clearing. Items are exchanged between clearing houses by post or, in the case of cheques and bills of exchange, by special same-day-delivery courier. The main characteristic of "traditional" clearing is that only paper-based media are exchanged. Items passing through, therefore, are those that have not been processed by the CEC because they are ineligible (e.g., cheques for amounts in excess of B.fr. 250,000, bills of exchange, securities and coupons) or because the persons/bodies remitting them are not full members of the CEC, or for some other, more or less fortuitous reason (urgency, for instance). With the expansion of the CEC, the relative importance of this channel, in terms of the number of items exchanged, has been significantly reduced. However, in terms of the value of the funds cleared, the "traditional" clearing houses still account for the great bulk of exchanges.

The aim of the CEC, set up in 1974, is the automated exchange of items to be cleared. Before its foundation, a good deal of essential standardisation work was carried out within the financial sector under the auspices of the central bank. The

---

[24]There are, in fact, only few banking videotex applications specifically aimed at certain sections of the corporate customer sector. More generally, videotex is still in an early stage of development in Belgium. One large bank has recently started introducing banking services by telephone (so far for balance inquiries only).

[25]Excluding securities and coupons exchanged, the number of which is unknown.

CEC processes cheques (for amount of up to B.fr. 250,000[26]), credit transfers (including standing orders and variable standing orders), payment operations related to direct debits, and transactions at the ATMs and POS terminals of the two interbank networks (Mister Cash and Bancontact). The main characteristics of the CEC are as follows:

▶ "Truncation," with no physical exchange between banks of the payment instruments to be cleared, which are retained by the institution that received them from their customers in the first place.

▶ The existence of three different generic EDP applications: "cheques," "credit transfers," and "direct debits."

▶ The use of several types of medium (magnetic tapes, diskettes, telecommunications)[27] for transmitting data on items to be cleared to the CEC and receiving data on items cleared from it; the availability since early 1987 of a telecommunication network that allows on-line access to the CEC and that carried about one-third of the data by the end of 1988.

▶ Voluntary participation, except in the "credit transfers" application, whose output cannot be refused.

▶ Centralisation in Brussels, which obliges the provincial financial institutions to send their data to the capital (by telecommunications, post, or special courier).

▶ Management of the CEC by the central bank, which recovers all the relative costs from the members on the basis of volumes exchanged.

▶ Equal sharing of the costs of capturing payment operations between payer and payee members.

▶ Continuous operation, i.e., the system receives, processes, and delivers data 21 hours a day, five days a week.

On December 31, 1987, of a potential total of 133 financial institutions,[28] 75 participated "actively" and "passively"[29] in the "credit transfers" application, 68 in the "cheques" application, and 49 in the "direct debits" application.

*Bilateral exchanges,* in principle, concern only flows of tax payments and social security contributions intended for the public authorities and passing through the Postal Cheque Office.

The fact that such exchanges — on magnetic tape — continue to exist is the consequence of a value-date problem, extremely crucial in that it involves payments of large sums that have to be effected by a given date and which those concerned only execute at the last moment.

In 1987, taking all systems together, a total of 494.2 million items[30] were cleared, for a value of B.fr. 134,750 billion. The automated clearing house (CEC) handled, respectively, 93 percent and 5 percent of these totals. The provincial clearing houses accounted for 2.1 percent of the total volume and 5.9 percent of the total value.

The final individual balances are determined and settled daily at "traditional" clearing houses, either in Brussels or in the provinces depending on where the head office of the financial institution is located. Each participant's final balance is calculated manually at the end of the day by adding together:

---

[26]Or the equivalent of B.fr. 30,000 in the case of Eurocheques made out in a foreign currency. For security reasons, cheques for large amounts (in excess of B.fr. 250,000 or 30,000, respectively) are still exchanged manually at "traditional" clearing houses.

[27]It is possible to obtain paper-based data as output, but this latitude does not extend to input data for processing by the CEC, which has to be in an automated form.

[28]This number includes, in addition to the institutions referred to in Section II, banks affiliated to public credit institutions together with a number of special institutions (including the central bank).

[29]To participate "actively" and "passively" means that the financial institution concerned submits data to and receives data from the CEC.

[30]Excluding securities and coupons exchanged, the number of which is unknown.

▶ Its balances with respect to each of the CEC applications (positions at 1.30 P.M. at the latest).

▶ Its (provisional) balance at the "traditional" clearing house corresponding to its "home" clearing house.

▶ Its balances (as transmitted by telecommunications) at other "traditional" clearing houses where it is also represented.

The final (creditor or debtor) balances are settled by open outcry in the call-money market held after the final clearing session (at around 4 P.M.) in Brussels, or by varying recourse to central bank credit. Clearing is not finally over until the close of the session of the call-money market. Any borrowing, whether on the call-money market or from the central bank, has to be covered by depositing securities with the central bank. Moreover, a financial institution may not be a net debtor on the call-money market on a quarterly average.

The net claims and liabilities—calculated on a multilateral basis—arising from operations between stock exchange members are settled directly in the books of the central bank, where each participant has a current account that must not show a debtor balance at the end of the day.

Finally, Belgian banks use the international S.W.I.F.T. network for some national traffic, *viz.*, transfers of funds received through S.W.I.F.T. from correspondents abroad where the final beneficiaries hold accounts with other Belgian banks. In 1987, 1.5 million messages were exchanged between Belgian banks in this way via S.W.I.F.T.

## IV   GENERAL REMARKS

Five — in some ways related — major issues are, in varying degrees, in the foreground of current thinking:

▶ The pricing by the financial institutions of payment services used by customers.

▶ The sharing of electronic payment costs among the financial, commercial, and consumer sectors.

▶ The accessing by credit cards and travel and entertainment cards of the terminals run by the interbank networks.

▶ The regulation of electronic payment systems.

▶ The extension of the CEC to other types of operation.

### 1.  The Pricing of Payment Services

In an increasingly competitive environment, and faced with a number of paper-based transactions that show no sign of decreasing in spite of the marked expansion of the Bancontact and Mister Cash networks, an objective of the financial system would be to introduce certain charges for the payment services it offers its customers.

The objective would be twofold: to reduce the net costs of processing "traditional" payment media, and to encourage consumers to make still greater use of electronic payment systems, in which considerable sums have been invested.

After an unsuccessful attempt in 1988 to establish a pricing scheme for cheques, which provoked accusations of cartelisation, the banking sector is apparently now considering other ways of pricing payment services.

### 2.  Sharing the Costs of Electronic Payment

The debate is principally between the banking sector and the large retailers, the other commercial sectors having so far accepted the conditions proposed by the interbank networks.

The large retailers are, in fact, refusing to pay the banks a fee of B.fr. 2 per transaction, arguing that it is the banks that gain most from electronic payment, on the one hand, and, on the other, that they charge nothing at present for processing "traditional" payment media. In the absence of an agreement, in November 1987, the large retailer sector therefore decided, unilaterally, to pass on the B.fr. 2 fee direct to the customer. However, any real expansion of electronic payments in the large retailer sector will depend on the conclusion of a genuine compromise between it and the financial institutions. Any such agreement might have an impact on the relationships between the interbank networks and the other commercial sectors.

### 3. Access via Credit Cards and Travel and Entertainment Cards to Interbank Terminals

With the exception of American Express, which has recently installed two ATMs (distributing bank notes and travellers' cheques) in Brussels, the issuers of credit cards and travel and entertainment cards have no such terminals. Furthermore, no credit card or travel and entertainment card has access to the ATMs belonging to the interbank networks.

Primarily with the aim of offering an additional service to their foreign customers visiting Belgium, the issuing companies would like to be able to obtain access for their cards to these interbank ATMs. That solution seems to them preferable to the comparatively costly alternative of setting up their own networks. It implies, however, finding some common ground with the banking sector—precisely the sector with which, to varying degrees, issuers of credit cards and travel and entertainment cards are in competition. Such agreements could be brought into force in 1989.

The situation is different regarding POS terminals, since, first, they are located in places where issuers of credit cards and travel and entertainment cards are, by definition, traditionally present and, second, they represent a markedly lower investment cost. Moreover, a growing number of credit card issuers have recently started using electronic payment terminals (teledataphones) at a—still relatively limited— number of points-of-sale.

### 4. Regulation of Electronic Payment Systems

Currently there is no specific legal provision governing electronic payment systems. Relations among financial institutions, consumers, and retailers are, therefore, governed by private contracts drawn up by the financial sector. Thus, these are, to a large extent, so-called membership contracts. In more general terms, the problem of proof, under systems not involving manual signature, is not covered by positive legislation.

It appears that this legal vacuum, a cause of regret to various parties, is to be filled only at the European level. The Commission of the European Communities has been studying these issues for several years.

### 5. Extension of the CEC

With the aim of reducing paper-based interbank exchanges to the minimum, the sphere currently covered by the CEC (cheques, credit transfers, transactions at electronic terminals, direct debits) could be extended. A new application (unpaid direct debits) was successfully introduced in September 1988. Other applications are already envisaged such as urgent and large-amount credit transfer orders, unpaid cheques, and so on.

A number of initiatives might also be taken to increase the rate of participation in existing applications. Such efforts would be targeted primarily at the smaller financial institutions.

Furthermore, although only seven financial institutions—including the two largest banks — (mid-October 1988) have full recourse to the CEC's telecommunication network for their exchanges with it, it is foreseeable that a growing number of members will gradually abandon the system of magnetic media (which will thus be gradually relegated to the status of backup). In the future, this network might also be used for other types of application not connected with clearing but involving the exchange of data between the central bank and the financial system (e.g., central office for consumer credit, accounting data).

The ultimate aim is the total automation of clearing, the attainment of which can only be envisaged in the long term because of a multitude of technical, legal, and security-related difficulties.

# V  CONCLUSIONS

Although until the early 1970s payment systems in Belgium were characterised by their traditional nature, they have undergone major changes during the past 15 years. These changes, which are still going on, have led, in particular, to Belgium being in the avant-garde in a number of fields, both in regard to electronic payment systems and to automated interbank clearing mechanisms.

These fundamental changes are of several types:
▶ The growing trend towards cashless payment systems.
▶ The spread of electronic payment instruments (magnetic cards, automated media).
▶ The automation of interbank clearing mechanisms.
▶ The marked involvement of nonbanks in payment systems (issuers of credit cards and travel and entertainment cards, major retailers, issuers of luncheon vouchers).
▶ The increasing internationalisation of payment systems.

The scale of these movements and the length of time they have been under way differ from case to case.

The major forces behind these phenomena—forces that may have been interacting to a varying extent—include:
▶ The socioeconomic development of the population.
▶ The spectacular growth in the costs of running the payment system for the banking sector.
▶ Technological progress (data processing, telecommunications).
▶ The compromise between cooperation and competition within the financial system.
▶ The internationalisation of economies.
▶ The growth and diversification strategies pursued by firms (banks and nonbanks).

As for the future, while it seems certain that payment systems are going to go yet much farther in the direction of automation and internationalisation, other trends—although probable—do not yet seem to be established:
▶ The further "disintermediation" of banks in payment systems.
▶ The systematic pricing of payment services.

On the other hand, the hypothesis that all paper-based payment media (including cash) will disappear completely does not seem to be realistic, for a number of reasons.

In any case, today's new breed of payment systems raises new problems for which solutions need to be found in order to safeguard the integrity, the security, the reliability, and the equity of payment systems.

# 2 CANADA

# Canada

## I INTRODUCTION

As in other countries, the payment system in Canada is in the process of evolving from almost exclusive reliance upon cash and paper transactions toward a significant use of electronic media. Although Canada is still at an earlier stage in this process than some other countries, the share of electronic transactions in total is now growing rapidly, and there has been mounting activity in the planning and testing of new electronic payment mechanisms. Nevertheless, since the paper-based payment system is highly automated and efficient and minimises clearing float, its cost disadvantage *vis-à-vis* paperless technologies is not as extreme as in some countries. So the role of paper in the payment system, while declining in relative terms, is likely to remain significant for the foreseeable future. The application of electronic technology at the point-of-sale is still at an early stage, and there has been little displacement of cash by electronic media; as yet, indeed, there is some evidence of an opposite trend.

A number of recent key developments are currently shaping the evolution of the Canadian system.

The first was the emergence of the generalised sharing of automated teller machine (ATM) networks. Regional shared networks had been operating since the late 1970s, linking the ATMs of local cooperative credit institutions. Most of the rapid increase in the total number of ATMs installed in Canada during the late 1970s and early 1980s, however, was still attributable to the expansion of the proprietary ATM networks of the larger banks and trust companies. However, it subsequently became apparent to these larger institutions that, even with their nationwide branch systems, there would be sharply diminished returns from further expansion of their proprietary networks, while customer convenience and institutional presence could be enhanced through the nationwide sharing of networks. Accordingly, Interac Association was established in November 1984, to create a national shared ATM network by linking various proprietary systems. The interchange of transactions began in April 1986. Membership of the Canadian Payments Association (CPA) is a condition for participation, and the technical standards for network sharing have been established by the CPA. Interac is, however, a distinct entity having no structural link with the CPA. An indication of the technical success of ATM sharing in Canada and of the rapid acceptance of shared ATMs by the public is that the number of cash withdrawals through network interchanges, beginning at 4 million in 1986, rose to 34 million in 1987 and an annual rate of 52 million in the early months of 1988.

Another strong motive for ATM sharing has been provided by the spread of ATMs to locations away from the branches of deposit-taking institutions, for example at airports, department stores, and shopping malls.

An important development aimed at enhancing the integrity of the payment system as a whole has been an initiative taken by the CPA to strengthen the prudential basis for the acceptability of different types of payment instruments for interinstitutional clearing. In addition to cheques drawn on banks and other CPA members, a variety of other types of payment orders have, over the years, been introduced into the clearings. The principal examples of these are the orders drawn by the federal government on itself, and cleared through the central bank, for transfer payments. There are also, however, some orders drawn upon financial institutions that are not eligible for CPA membership and upon nonfinancial corporations.

In May 1987, the CPA established the basic criteria for acceptable items. These must be drawn on member institutions or on institutions that are eligible for membership. For the payment system in Canada to deliver the high level of service that the user expects, including immediate credit for deposits, and to do so at reasonable cost, the participating institutions must be able to have a high degree of trust in each other. They can do so only if items delivered into the clearings will be settled with a very high degree of certainty in the ensuing settlement process. By the definition of acceptability now established, the participants in the national clearing and settlement system and the public at large can take comfort from the fact that the requirement for prudential supervision that applies as a statutory criterion for CPA membership stands behind the payments passing through the system.

At the same time, the CPA made it clear that it fully intends to continue operating the national clearing and settlement system for the public benefit, by properly identifying and defining as acceptable for clearing a number of other types of payment, such as government warrants, grain elevator receipts, and postal money orders. Such items will continue to be processed through the national clearing and settlement system, and so will new ones as they are developed, provided that they meet the same criteria; but some payment services hitherto offered by entities that are not eligible for CPA membership are likely to have to be modified to bring them within the new definition of acceptability. While this is probably a somewhat more restrictive delimitation of access to the clearing system than applies in some other countries, it is fully in line with the express intention of the federal government that the deregulation of the financial services industry in Canada should be based on a sound prudential structure.

A third significant development relates to the planning process itself. Recognising that the nontechnical issues relating to the payment system in general and to electronic payment mechanisms in particular are important, and that nonmember organisations that use the system have a valid interest in its development, the CPA has taken steps in recent years to establish means by which those issues can be identified, addressed, and resolved, especially electronic funds transfer at the point-of-sale (EFT POS). The Senior Planning Committee of the association's board of directors is the most important of these means. It acts as the principal channel through which the various sectors of the Canadian economy not represented within the CPA can, by consulting members, express their views in the payment system planning process. In addition to its other activities, the committee has carried out extensive and effective liaison with a wide range of interest-group organisations. The association has also developed a discussion-draft process as a systematic means of disseminating proposed procedures and standards to interested parties for comment.

In the particular field of EFT POS, a number of pilot projects are in place. Until recently, these have been essentially bilateral in character, usually involving one deposit-taking institution or group (such as a credit union central) and one retail organisation. Projects are now in operation that involve, or will shortly involve, a number of institutions and organisations on one side or both, thus requiring the interinstitutional clearing of EFT POS transactions.

The CPA has been laying the groundwork for the exchange and settlement of such payments where access to deposit accounts at member institutions is required. In early 1986, it published its analysis of the necessary parameters for the evolution of the Canadian payment system in the direction of generalised EFT POS. Central to this analysis is the proposition that, if the deposit-taking institutions are to fulfill the obligations imposed on them by law, custom, and practice, namely, to safeguard the funds entrusted to them and to make payments out of them only when properly authorised to do so by account holders, they must be in a position to verify the authenticity of every debit card transaction, just as they can with every cheque.

Having prepared a discussion draft on "The Fundamental Elements of EFT POS," the CPA has now convened a number of Operational Planning Teams, including organisations representing the full range of interested parties—consumers, retailers, corporate treasurers, communications common carriers, equipment manufacturers, and other suppliers — to discuss such topics as inquiry and complaint handling, technical standards, interface requirements, and privacy and security. The next phase of the work will be the development of the guidelines, procedures, and minimum common standards needed to facilitate the generalised expansion of EFT POS in Canada.

Improvements to existing payment mechanisms have also played an important role in the development of the Canadian payment system in recent years. Among the more noteworthy are the modernisation of the procedures for preauthorised payments; the implementation on a large scale of systems for the electronic authorisation of credit card transactions and draft capture; and the introduction of retroactive settlement. The last, which involves value-dating participants' net clearing gains and losses on the books of the central bank as of the date on which the underlying payment items are exchanged, has greatly simplified the banking arrangements between CPA members and their larger customers. Significant resources were being devoted to the calculation, pricing, and management of settlement float, without any resulting increase in economic efficiency. Retroactive settlement, which came into effect on July 16, 1986, has largely eliminated this misuse of resources. Moreover, it has placed the paper and electronic streams within the payment system on the same effectively same-day settlement basis.

Finally, work is in progress within the CPA to develop an electronic system for large-value transactions. It may well be able to rely to a significant extent on the existing automated infrastructure developed for the paper-based system, such as the CPA's Automated Clearing Settlement System, and it is likely to involve timely and irrevocable settlement.

## II   THE INSTITUTIONAL FRAMEWORK

The financial system in Canada comprises a number of different types of institutions — deposit-taking institutions, insurance companies, investment dealers, sales finance companies, and so forth. Those that typically accept deposits transferable by order to a third party are the most important institutions in the context of the Canadian payment system.

Although continuing change, partly achieved by sunset laws, is characteristic of the Canadian financial system, 1987 marked the beginning of a major reshaping. In December 1986, the federal government had set out the general principles for its revision of statutes governing the powers and ownership of federally incorporated financial institutions. In 1987, it began to give concrete form to those principles.

In June 1987, the government consolidated the various federal agencies responsible for supervising federally incorporated financial institutions under the authority of one official, to be known as the Superintendent of Financial Institutions. It also established a committee composed of the Superintendent of Financial Institutions, the Governor of the Bank of Canada, the Chairman of the Canada Deposit Insurance Corporation, and the Deputy Minister of Finance. This committee will ensure the exchange of information and consultation among the members on matters that have implications for solvency, last-resort lending, and potential disbursements under the deposit insurance scheme.

In December 1987, the government published draft legislation applicable to trust and mortgage loan companies, intended also to be the model for the revision during 1988 of the legislation governing chartered banks, insurance companies, and cooperative credit associations.

### 1. Deposit-Taking Institutions

This group includes chartered banks, cooperative credit institutions, trust and mortgage loan companies, and governmental savings institutions.

#### (a) Chartered banks

As of December 31, 1987, there were 72 chartered banks. The six largest Canadian-owned banks operate both nationwide and internationally and serve the business, household, and government sectors. The other banks typically concentrate on serving the financial needs of a particular region of the country or of a particular sector of the economy. Most of these others are wholly owned by foreign banks.

All chartered banks are incorporated and operate under the provisions of the *Bank Act*. This federal act regulates certain internal aspects of the banks' operations, such as the auditing of accounts, corporate powers, and the issuing of stock, and certain aspects of the banks' relationships with the public, the federal government, and the Bank of Canada. The *Bank Act* has been revised at approximately 10-year intervals since 1871; the most recent revision was enacted by Parliament late in 1980 and came into effect on December 1 of that year.

Chartered banks accept various types of deposit from the public, including accounts payable on demand, personal savings deposits (both chequable and nonchequable), nonpersonal notice deposits, and fixed-term deposits. In addition to holding a portfolio of securities, banks make loans under a variety of conditions for agricultural, commercial, consumer, and industrial purposes. Banks also deal in foreign exchange, provide safekeeping facilities, and perform various other services. As of April 30, 1988, there were 7,135 chartered bank branches in Canada and 234 branches in more than 40 foreign countries.

#### (b) Cooperative credit institutions

The cooperative movement plays a significant role in the Canadian economy. Its contributions are most notable in agriculture, housing, and household finance. Indeed, among the most important institutions within the Canadian cooperative movement are local credit unions and caisses populaires.

##### Local credit unions and caisses populaires

Local credit unions and caisses populaires are deposit-taking institutions that provide savings, loan, and other financial services to their member-owners, including deposit facilities, chequing services, loans and guarantees, safekeeping, and automated teller machines. Locals were originally established in the early 1900s to encourage saving and to provide loans to members who could obtain credit only at prohibitive interest rates or not at all. They range in size from small, community-based institutions to large, multibranch operations.

As of December 31, 1987, there were 2,947 local credit unions and caisses populaires in Canada, with some 8.9 million members.

Membership in a local is based on a common bond of association, such as residence in a community or parish, employment in an industry or profession, or affiliation with an ethnic group. Membership is available through the purchase of a share (usually a minimum Can.$ 5 savings share), democratic control being retained by allocating only one vote to each member, regardless of the number of shares held.

### Credit union centrals and caisse populaire fédérations

Local credit unions and caisses populaires have established centrals and fédérations, respectively, at the provincial and regional level. These second-tier organisations provide technical and financial assistance to their member locals, including communications, market intelligence, management and programme development, and liquidity support. The latter function involves, *inter alia,* the investment of surplus funds of locals and the lending of funds to these institutions when they cannot meet the local demand for loans. Locals are permitted to invest and deposit their statutory liquidity reserves and other surplus funds with their central or fédération, and many do so. To accommodate these funds, centrals maintain a range of demand and fixed-term deposit accounts.

Centrals and fédérations are incorporated or registered under provincial legislation, typically a credit union act, although the federal *Co-operative Credit Associations Act* also applies in the case of credit union centrals, which are owned by their member locals. Each central or fédération is also an independent entity, although it may have operational links with others.

As of December 31, 1987, there were 23 centrals in Canada.

### Third-tier organisations of centrals

With the establishment of centrals and fédérations, a need arose for third-tier organisations that could provide them and other cooperative organisations with coordinated financial and support services similar to those offered by centrals and fédérations themselves to their member locals.

The Canadian Co-operative Credit Society Limited (CCCS) was incorporated in 1953 under the federal *Co-operative Credit Associations Act,* which is now administered by the Office of the Superintendent of Financial Institutions. Membership in the CCCS is open to centrals and to other cooperative organisations that can meet the criteria established by the Office of the Superintendent of Financial Institutions. At present the CCCS has 47 member shareholders, of which eight are centrals representing locals in as many provinces; the remainder are other types of cooperative organisations. The CCCS also acts as group clearer for a number of its member centrals.

La Confédération des caisses populaires et d'économie Desjardins du Québec is incorporated under a law of that province. It provides financial and support services, similar to those provided by the CCCS, to its 11-member fédérations as well as to a number of other member cooperative organisations and acts, through an operating subsidiary, as group clearer for the fédérations.

### (c) Trust and mortgage loan companies

Trust companies perform financial intermediary as well as fiduciary functions. As intermediaries, trust companies offer a range of deposit instruments similar to those offered by the chartered banks. They are, at present, the only corporations empowered to conduct fiduciary business. In this capacity they act as executors, trustees, and administrators under wills or by appointment, as transfer agents for stock and bond issues, as trustees for bond issues, and in a variety of other agency and trustee functions.

Mortgage loan companies may also accept deposits from the public and may issue both short- and long-term debentures. The largest among them are in fact subsidiaries of chartered banks.

The Superintendent of Financial Institutions regulates federally incorporated trust and mortgage loan companies and also, by arrangement with the provinces concerned, trust and mortgage loan companies incorporated in a number of provinces. Trust and mortgage loan companies, whether federally or provincially incorporated, must be licensed by each province in which they operate.

Although there are some differences between the applicable federal and provincial acts, the broad lines of the legislation are common. In their business as financial intermediaries, trust and mortgage loan companies have the power to borrow funds, subject to maximum permitted ratios of these funds to shareholder equity. The funds may be invested, with some quantitative restrictions, in specified assets, which include first mortgages secured by real property; government securities, and the bonds and stocks of corporations that have established earnings records; loans on the security of such bonds and stocks; and unsecured commercial and personal loans. Trust and mortgage loan companies are not required to hold specified cash reserves, but there are broadly defined liquid asset requirements in most of the applicable acts.

As of December 31, 1987, there were approximately 80 trust companies and at least 35 mortgage loan companies in Canada.

*(d) Governmental savings institutions*

There are two governmental savings institutions in Canada: the Province of Alberta Treasury Branches, and the Province of Ontario Savings Office.

### Province of Alberta Treasury Branches

The Alberta Treasury Branches organisation is a division of the provincial Treasury Department. However, the operations of the Treasury Branches are kept separate from the other operations of the department. The provincial government can establish and operate Treasury Branches anywhere in Alberta.

They now provide a wide range of financial services to their customers. These services include current and savings accounts; loans; safekeeping facilities; travellers' cheques; money orders and drafts; foreign remittances and money transfers; and the sale and purchase of securities.

### Province of Ontario Savings Office

Deposit-taking is the principal service offered to the public by the Savings Office. It offers three types of account: a daily-interest chequing account, a more traditional chequable savings account and, since April 1988, term deposits. The Savings Office provides a limited range of other services, including safekeeping facilities, travellers' cheques, and money orders.

The Savings Office does not lend money to the public. All funds in excess of day-to-day requirements are deposited in the provincial Consolidated Revenue Fund. The Treasurer of Ontario pays interest on these funds to the Savings Office to meet the interest payable on public deposits and all other expenses. Any surplus on operations is credited to the Treasurer at the end of the year.

## 2. Bank of Canada

The Bank of Canada, Canada's central bank, began operations on March 11, 1935, under the provisions of the federal *Bank of Canada Act* of 1934, which charged the bank with responsibility for regulating "credit and currency in the best interests of the economic life of the nation" and which conferred upon it specific powers for discharging this responsibility. The act also vested in the bank the sole right to issue paper money for circulation.

The role played by the bank in the payment system is central, but narrow in scope. The bank does not accept deposits from individuals or nonfinancial business corporations. It does, however, effect the final settlement of balances for the national clearing and settlement system; it lends to direct participants in that system that have liquidity needs; and government receipts and disbursements are cleared through it.

The bank's operational role in the payment system has not expanded significantly as a result of the introduction of electronic payment mechanisms. The bank nevertheless has an obvious interest in the efficiency and equity of the operations of the national payment system, and it plays an important role in the Canadian Payments Association. This role has been conferred upon it by the Association's Act, which requires the bank to appoint one of its officers to be the chairman of the association's board of directors.

The establishment of the CPA has also led to a new and direct relationship between the bank, in its role as the provider of the final means of settlement between participants in the national clearing and settlement system, and a number of large nonbank deposit-taking institutions. Nonbank deposit-taking institutions that participate directly in the clearing and settlement process maintain settlement accounts at the bank through which their daily net clearing gains and losses *vis-à-vis* the other participants are settled. Each such institution is granted, on essentially the same basis as a chartered bank, a line of credit under which an unforeseen overdraft on its settlement account may be met by a temporary advance from the Bank of Canada. This direct access to central bank credit, although not intended to be frequently used, provides a useful additional source of liquidity to banks and nonbank deposit-taking institutions alike.

The proposals of the federal government for restructuring the financial sector envisage the abolition of the statutory requirement on chartered banks to hold reserves at the bank against their deposit liabilities. This reform will not affect the ability of the bank to implement monetary policy, because the bank will still be able to determine the availability of settlement balances to those deposit-taking institutions that participate directly in the clearing and settlement process. However, the new provisions may require some technical changes in the implementation of monetary policy. The bank has been discussing these matters with the major financial institutions.

The head office of the Bank of Canada is in Ottawa. The bank has agencies in Halifax, Saint John, Montreal, Ottawa, Toronto, Winnipeg, Regina, Calgary, and Vancouver.

## 3. Canadian Payments Association

The *Canadian Payments Association Act* came into effect on December 1, 1980. The objectives of the Canadian Payments Association, as stipulated in the act, are "to establish and operate a national clearing and settlement system and to plan the evolution of the national payment system."

The management and operation of the CPA are the responsibility of a board of directors, the members of which are, with the exception of the director appointed by the Bank of Canada, elected by the CPA's four different classes of member institution.

As of May 31, 1988, the membership of the CPA included, in addition to the Bank of Canada, 72 chartered banks, 26 credit union centrals, caisse populaire fédérations and third-tier organisations, 35 trust and mortgage loan companies, and eight other deposit-taking institutions, which include the Alberta Treasury Branches and local credit unions and caisses populaires that are not members of a central, for a total of 142 members. Taken together, the CPA's member institutions account for well over 95 percent of the transferable deposit liabilities of all Canadian deposit-taking institutions. (For more detailed information about the Canadian Payments Association, see Appendix I.)

# III  PAYMENT SYSTEMS

## 1. Cash Payments

### (a) Background

#### Coinage

The Ottawa Mint, established as a branch of the Royal Mint under the *United Kingdom Coinage Act* of 1870, opened on January 2, 1908. On December 1, 1931, by an act of the Canadian Parliament, it became the Royal Canadian Mint and operated as a branch of the Department of Finance. The mint was established as a Crown corporation, i.e., a government-owned corporation, in 1969 by the *Government Reorganisation Act* of that year to provide greater organisational flexibility. The mint reports to Parliament through the Minister of Supply and Services.

#### Currency

The *Bank Act* of 1871 laid the foundation for the coordinated issue of currency by chartered banks, and this system continued in effect until 1934. In 1934, with the creation of the Bank of Canada, the sole responsibility for the issue of paper currency was transferred to the new institution, although the withdrawal of chartered bank currency was spread over a 15-year period. The bank assumed the liability for the chartered bank note issue on December 31, 1949, and the chartered banks paid over to the Bank of Canada the final balances outstanding in their note circulation accounts as of that date.

### (b) Distribution and Handling

#### Coin

Deposit-taking financial institutions generally provide the public with all the Canadian coin it requires. Branches that find that their holdings of coin are insufficient replenish their supplies directly from the mint, which maintains stocks of new coin in depots in major cities across the country.

The government will neither buy back nor take back coin that is still fit for circulation. However, the mint will assist in the exchange of coin between surplus and deficit Direct Clearers, since this is more efficient than having the deficit Direct Clearers order more coin. Although coin is not a liability of the Bank of Canada, the bank will, on behalf of the government, redeem coin that is no longer fit for circulation.

A new one-dollar coin was introduced into general circulation on June 30, 1987.

#### Bank of Canada notes

Direct Clearers are also the main distributors of Bank of Canada notes. Notes that are surplus to the public's needs are deposited with deposit-taking institutions, which may redeposit them with the Direct Clearers. Unlike coin, surplus notes, even if fit for reissuing, may be returned by the Direct Clearers to the Bank of Canada, either in exchange for other denominations or for immediate credit to their accounts.

The Bank of Canada also redeems unissuable notes, i.e., notes that are too soiled or worn or otherwise unfit for further circulation. Financial institutions, in handling notes, are expected to sort out the unissuable notes and ship them directly to the nearest Bank of Canada agency.

Notes still fit for circulation that are turned in to the Bank of Canada are held and reissued as the need arises. The bank also arranges for the supply of new notes, buying them from two privately owned printing companies and issuing them in response to orders received from the central branches of the Direct Clearers.

The one-dollar Bank of Canada note will no longer be issued after June 30, 1989.

*(c) Usage*

Although there is a wide variety of payment media available to Canadians, notes and coin continue to be the most frequently used means of effecting everyday transactions. Unfortunately, there are no data or other information on either the number or the value of cash payments; however, it is not unreasonable to suppose that the use of notes and coin in Canada is similar to that in many other countries.

## 2. Cheques

*(a) Background*

The legal framework for cheques in Canada is provided by the federal *Bills of Exchange Act,* the common law, the *CPA Rules Manual* (devolving from the *CPA Act* and the CPA By-laws), and the agreements between deposit-taking institutions and their customers.

### The Bills of Exchange Act

The federal *Bills of Exchange Act* is the principal statute governing cheques. It was passed by Parliament in 1890, is derived from the British *Bills of Exchange Act* of 1882, and has remained substantially unchanged since its enactment.

### The common law

The common law represents the judicially developed part of the legal framework and is specifically incorporated by reference in the *Bills of Exchange Act.* Some of the fundamental principles that govern the use of bills of exchange and cheques are derived from cases decided by the courts, including those in the United Kingdom, dating back hundreds of years.

### The CPA Rules Manual

In the context provided by the CPA Act and the CPA By-laws, particularly the clearing by-law, the *CPA Rules Manual* sets forth the procedures and standards that govern the daily operations of the deposit-taking institutions in the national clearing and settlement system. The rules, too, are thus part of the legal framework governing the use of cheques and other payment media.

The rules facilitate the exchange of cheques and other payment items between deposit-taking institutions by defining the procedures to be followed and the rights and obligations of the parties involved. They touch upon many aspects that affect the treatment of cheques and other payment items and include provisions that:

▶ Determine which items may be entered into the national clearing and settlement system.

▶ Set forth the basis on which, and the time limits within which, items may be returned by branches or by data centers.

▶ Govern the participation of Indirect Clearers, i.e., deposit-taking institutions that do not participate directly in the clearing and settlement process.

▶ Apply in the event that a data center ceases operating because of the breakdown or failure of a deposit-taking institution's internal computer communications network or a component part thereof.

### The agreements between a deposit-taking institution and a customer

Most deposit-taking institutions require a customer, on opening an account, to sign a standardised agreement. The exact nature of the agreement will vary depending on the nature of the account. For example, customers agree to verify, within a specified time, the entries in the statement of account or authorise the deposit-taking institution to levy service charges. For most businesses that maintain current accounts, the agreement covers a variety of subjects, including:

▶ The authority to charge accounts.

► Service charges.
► Lost instruments.
► Agency for collection.
► Waiver of certain rights.
► Cheque forms.
► The authority to return an item.
► Verification of the statement of account.

### 3. Direct Debit and Credit Payments

Both direct debit arrangements (typically referred to as preauthorised debits) and direct credit arrangements (usually referred to as direct deposit or direct funds transfer systems) are being increasingly used in Canada. They are confined mainly to recurring, fixed-amount payments such as insurance premiums, mortgage payments, utility bills, and rent in the case of debits, and salaries, annuities, and certain governmental payments in the case of credits.

Direct debit and credit payments may be effected by the clearing of paper vouchers or by exchanging magnetic tapes. Paper vouchers are still frequently used for debits, while magnetic tapes are generally used for direct credit payments.

Preauthorised debits began in Canada with the introduction of the original Pre-Authorised Payments (PAP) Plan by chartered banks during the 1950s. The plan was designed to collect contractual and recurring payments for a company from its clients. The plan was to be used exclusively for fixed-amount and fixed-period payments such as insurance premiums and mortgage instalments.

With the establishment of the Canadian Payments Association in 1980, it became necessary to adapt the PAP mechanism, which was founded on an interbank indemnity agreement, to the statute-founded environment of the CPA and, at the same time, to address certain anomalies. The PAP mechanism was beginning to be used for the interchange of transactions of types that would not normally have been expected to fall under the procedures, such as the debiting to consumer accounts of transactions through ATMs and POS terminals and corporate cash management transactions. The CPA's Board of Directors issued a policy statement in March 1985, clarifying the scope of the PAP Plan, and subsequently approved new procedures for preauthorised debit payments. The key modifications included:

► Bringing the plan under the umbrella of the CPA, enabling all CPA member institutions to enter preauthorised debits into the national clearing and settlement system.
► Limiting the amount of individual debits (with a separate facility for higher-value payments).
► Requiring authorisation from the customer to cover debits for a specified amount, with reasonable latitude for normal adjustments.
► Protecting the customer and the system as a whole through standardised documentation and conditions governing the dispute of an item by a payer.

The Direct Funds Transfer System (DFTS) is the computerised preauthorised credit transfer system. Until 1983, the system was operated in accordance with operating rules that were agreed on between the banks and the federal government on the basis of more general procedures and standards for the exchange of financial data on magnetic tape. Since 1983, however, the system has continued to operate using the equivalent rules of the CPA and has been open to participation by all Direct Clearers.

Each Direct Clearer that participates in the preauthorised debit and direct deposit systems registers with the CPA those of its data centers at which it is prepared to receive computer-readable files. There are six tape exchange points in Canada, each located in a major center and serving the surrounding area. Virtually every branch of every deposit-taking institution in Canada may receive files addressed to it through one of the tape exchange points. Each such branch has been allocated a distinguishing number in the CPA's Financial Institutions File, the computer data base of all branches and offices of deposit-taking institutions in Canada. The value transferred by the direct deposit system is customarily collected through the exchange of an offsetting debit voucher in the ordinary clearing.

## 4. Credit Cards

It has been estimated that, at the end of 1987, there were approximately 25 million credit cards, including bank credit cards, proprietary retail cards, and travel and entertainment cards, in circulation in Canada and some 40 different issuers. VISA and MasterCard, with 17.6 million cards in circulation, had a dominant presence in the market and were also the most widely accepted cards; most merchants that accept them accept both issuers' cards. Although they are now issued by nine nonbank deposit-taking institutions in Canada as well as by seven chartered banks, they are customarily referred to as "bank credit cards." They are administered by private contract, not under the procedures and standards of the CPA.

### (a) Operations

The bank credit card plans permit cardholders to obtain cash advances at the branches of all members of each plan and to charge purchases at the outlets of all participating merchants. Cardholders are billed once a month and have the option of paying the whole amount or an installment. It has been estimated that over half of Canadian cardholders pay their bills in full each month, while the remainder make monthly payments. The plans offered by individual institutions differ: Usually, if the entire amount is paid within the grace period, the length of which varies, no interest charge is made, except for cash advances. Interest on cash advances is charged from the moment the advance is posted to the cardholder's credit card account. User fees are now charged by most card-issuing institutions.

### (b) Usage

Bank credit cards are used extensively by consumers both as a means of payment and as a form of credit. A further indication of the widespread use of credit cards is that more than two-thirds of all adult Canadians carry at least one card and that fully 8 percent carry five or more. The growth in the amounts charged on bank credit cards has also been substantial. The gross dollar volume of transactions and cash advances increased from Can.$ 3.6 billion during the 12-month period ended October 31, 1977, to Can.$ 26.9 billion during the 12-month period ended October 31, 1987. Approximately 451 million sales drafts were processed during the latter period for an average dollar value of about Can.$ 57. These trends attest to the growing importance of bank credit cards in personal finance.

### (c) Recent developments

In Canada, bank credit cards, and credit cards generally, can be considered a "mature" product. Accordingly, the main thrust of marketing efforts by deposit-taking institutions is to gain market share. This intensely competitive environment helps to explain the following four important recent developments:

▶ The installation of terminals at a growing number of merchant outlets to speed up the authorisation process and to reduce credit card fraud, by eliminating merchant floor limits and providing more timely information on lost or stolen cards.

▶ The move to electronic draft capture to contain the direct operating costs of card-issuing deposit-taking institutions by increasing processing efficiency.

▶ The introduction of premium cards to meet the needs of the up-scale and business markets.

▶ Affinity group marketing.

### 5. Cash Dispensers and Automated Teller Machines

*(a) Background*

As of January 31, 1988, there were some 5,400 cash dispensers and ATMs installed in Canada, compared with approximately 250 at the end of 1977.

Most large and several medium-sized deposit-taking institutions have proprietary cash dispenser/ATM networks. As of year-end 1987, in addition to the shared ATM networks operated by credit union centrals and fédérations of caisses populaires, there were 13 other such networks operating in Canada. (Shared ATM networks and the factors that led to their emergence in Canada are discussed in Section I of the present report.)

*(b) Operations*

The ATMs in current use permit a customer who has an access card and a personal identification number to withdraw notes either from an account or as a cash advance against a credit card line of credit. The customer can also make deposits, verify the status of an account, effect a number of types of transfer between accounts, and pay bills. Cash dispensers are simpler devices used only to withdraw notes and, in some instances, to make balance inquiries.

Although most ATMs have been installed either in the banking halls or lobbies or in the outside walls at branches of deposit-taking institutions, the installation of ATMs at off-site locations, e.g., at airports and shopping malls, has become increasingly common. Cash dispensers have been installed almost exclusively at off-site locations.

*(c) Usage*

Customer acceptance of both cash dispensers and ATMs has developed quite rapidly in Canada since the early 1980s. Not only are more customers of deposit-taking institutions using the machines, but customers are also using them more frequently and for a wider range of transactions.

It has been estimated that between 600 and 650 million transactions were effected at cash dispensers and ATMs in 1987, compared with 150 million during 1983. Moreover, between 30 and 35 percent of the customers of deposit-taking institutions currently use the machines and of these fully one-third use the machines regularly.

That ATMs are also being used to effect a wider range of transactions is shown by changes in the so-called transactions mix. For example, it has been estimated that, during the early 1980s, cash withdrawals accounted for between 80 and 85 percent of all ATM transactions; that proportion had dropped to little more than 60 percent by 1987.

*(d) Recent developments*

Although the emphasis of the cash dispenser and ATM programs of deposit-taking institutions will remain on providing customers with convenient access to cash and other commonly used services, more sophisticated services are being studied. These new services include passbook updating, statement printing, the purchase of securities, and making loan applications.

### 6. Electronic Funds Transfer at the Point-of-Sale

After many years of discussion and planning, electronic funds transfer at the point-of-sale (EFT POS) became a reality in Canada in mid-1985 with the inauguration of the first of several pilot projects.

Six EFT POS pilot projects were begun in Canada between mid-1985 and late 1988. Of these, the first one became fully operational in the autumn of 1987 and another in

January 1988; two have concluded, and the two most recently inaugurated projects will continue as pilots for the time being. Each project so far has been bilateral, in the sense of involving one deposit-taking institution, the customers of that institution, and one or more merchants.

Over time, the pilot projects have become increasingly ambitious. The earliest projects usually involved only one or two merchants and a small number of terminals in a single city or town; the most recent project is intended to involve approximately 300 different merchants and some 500 terminals in one of Canada's larger cities.

Several additional bilateral pilot projects are in the planning stage. The expansion of existing projects to include more deposit-taking institutions and merchants is being discussed. In that regard, the shared ATM network organisation, Interac, has announced a year-long, three-location project involving a number of deposit-taking institutions for either late 1989 or early 1990.

The objective of the CPA's work in this area is to define a basis for EFT POS in Canada that preserves the soundness, equity, and integrity of the national payment system; that maximises the system's efficiency, accuracy, and reliability; that recognises the interests of consumers and other users; and that provides for effective competition in the marketplace.

For practical reasons, the CPA has initially limited the scope of its work to an environment in which debit cards, issued under the control of CPA members and using magnetic-stripe technology and personal identification numbers, are used to initiate on-line authorisation and real-time data capture. In this context, the association has developed its analysis of the fundamental elements that must guide the evolution of EFT POS in Canada, addressing such issues as access and identification methods, message formats, security, and the interface between EFT POS networks and the national clearing and settlement system.

The second phase of the CPA's work has been one of consultation with organisations representing the full range of interested parties: consumers, retailers, corporate treasurers, communications common carriers, equipment manufacturers, and other suppliers. This work was carried out between January and June 1988. Three Operational Planning Teams were established to serve as the forums in which all potential participants could express their views. The CPA's analysis of the fundamental elements of EFT POS provided the basis for discussion within the OPTs, and each team addressed a particular topic or group of topics: inquiry and complaint handling; cardholder and acceptor interface requirements; and security, auditability, and control.

The detailed reports by the OPTs will provide valuable input for the third phase of the work, which will be devoted to the development of the guidelines, procedures, and minimum common standards needed to achieve the underlying objective of the CPA's work.

### 7. Home Banking

Two home-banking pilot projects in Canada have recently been concluded. Each project involved between 100 and 200 Canadian households and the core set of home-banking services. Three of the principal conclusions that have been drawn from both projects are first, that security is a major concern for customers; second, that home banking is unlikely to emerge in Canada on a large scale before the early 1990s; and third, that at least until that time affluent customers and small businesses are the most promising potential users of home-banking services. Two further pilot projects have been announced for late 1988 and early 1989. These projects will, however, involve a larger population of terminals than the two earlier ones. Based on the experience of other countries, a large population of terminals would appear to be one of the prerequisites for the success of home banking.

## 8. Cash Management Systems

Reporting services (e.g., account balances, deposit details) were the banks' original initiatives in electronic cash management. Recently, however, they have concentrated more of their development efforts on creating or improving electronic interfaces for transaction-initiation services, such as payroll services, recurring debits and credits, and cheque reconciliation. These services have evolved from paper to magnetic-tape input and now permit direct input from a company's own computer. Similar developments have taken place for cheque-reconciliation services, with some banks offering features such as initiating stop-payments from the customer's office and, for high-volume customers, on-line "look-up" facilities for all cheques passing through their accounts. Banks also offer a service corporate customers can use to initiate large-value, nonrecurring third-party payments from a terminal. The specific features that are offered by each bank vary, but typically include the ability to generate both recurring and nonrecurring payments in multiple currencies and to store the payments for up to a month.

With the changes now taking place within the Canadian financial environment, it is possible to expect new electronic banking services. Already, some banks are offering customers the capability for issuing short-term debt instruments or applying for letters of credit electronically. Other banks have focused on building electronic interfaces for securities processing systems.

Two other trends are currently influencing the development of electronic banking services. The first is a push by some corporate customers of chartered banks to have their banks' reporting systems supply more detailed information, thus facilitating a direct link with the companies' own internal accounting systems. The second trend is electronic data interchange (EDI), which is gaining momentum in Canada. As more companies trade with each other electronically, not only will they make more payments by electronic means, but they will also expect deposit-taking institutions to provide more electronic interfaces with them.

## 9. Clearing and Settlement Systems

### (a) The national clearing and settlement system

Canada's national clearing and settlement system is, in the opinion of many observers, one of the most effective and efficient paper-based systems in the world. One indicator of the system's reliability is the universal practice among Canadian deposit-taking institutions of giving most customers immediate credit for cheques and other payment items deposited with them.

### Background

Direct Clearers represent themselves directly in the clearing and settlement process and act as clearing agents for other deposit-taking institutions. To be eligible to be a Direct Clearer, a CPA member institution must account for one half of 1 percent of the total volume of cheques and other payment items exchanged in the Canadian clearing system. Taken together, the eligible institutions, including the Bank of Canada, account for nearly 97 percent of this total, which in 1987 amounted to nearly 1.9 billion individual items.

As of December 31, 1987, there were 15 Direct Clearers: the Bank of Canada, nine chartered banks, and five nonbank deposit-taking institutions, including the two that act as Group Clearers on behalf of centrals and fédérations.

The shares of the total clearings accounted for by the different classes of institution were: banks, 76.6 percent; centrals and fédérations, 11.8 percent; trust and mortgage loan companies, 5.5 percent; Bank of Canada, 4.7 percent; and other financial institutions, 1.4 percent; (figures for nonmember institutions, probably amounting to less than 1 percent, are included in those of their clearing agents, which are mainly banks).

*Operations*

*(i) The paper-based clearing system*

The paper-based clearing system performs two functions: first, it transmits negotiable instruments from the institution where they are deposited to the institution on which they are drawn — in some cases, over great distances; second, by calculating the net amounts due to and from each institution, it facilitates the settlement of these transactions at the Bank of Canada. The clearing by-law of the association and the rules that have been approved by the CPA's board of directors govern how the various deposit-taking institutions that offer transferable deposits cooperate to achieve these objectives.

*(ii) The Automated Clearing Settlement System*

On November 19, 1984, for the first time in almost a hundred years, clerks did not meet at clearing houses across the country to strike the "due-to" and "due-from" balances for each Direct Clearer. Instead, the CPA's Automated Clearing Settlement System (ACSS) began to perform the tasks of logging each Direct Clearer's deliveries of payment items to and receipts from other Direct Clearers, determining and where necessary reconciling the "due-to" and "due-from" balances, and communicating these balances to the Bank of Canada by means of an on-line, interactive computer communication network. Each Direct Clearer has access to the network via microcomputers that are used as intelligent terminals to prepare and to transmit messages to other Direct Clearers describing its shipments of items to them. Other microcomputers located in the cash-management areas of each Direct Clearer institution display its net clearing gains or losses and, thus, timely and accurate information about the day's movements in its account at the Bank of Canada.

*(iii) The clearing and settlement process*

The clearing process begins when a payment item acceptable for clearing is deposited at a branch of a deposit-taking institution. Starting around midday, the items are bundled and totalled, collected by courier and delivered to the institution's nearest processing center if the institution is itself a Direct Clearer or to its agent's if it is not. There the items are checked, amount-encoded with magnetic ink (if not already so encoded at the branch), and sorted into "on-us" items, including those drawn on Indirect Clearers for which the Direct Clearer is the agent, and items drawn on other Direct Clearers, including items drawn on Indirect Clearers for which those Direct Clearers are agents. At this stage, as many items as possible are microfilmed for tracing and security purposes. Items drawn on other Direct Clearers are bundled together with control listings, picked up by courier, and delivered to the processing centers of the other Direct Clearers. This exchange of items begins at around 6 P.M. each day, rises to a peak late in the evening and, depending on the distances to be covered by the courier runs, slows down again around midnight. The ACSS records the net clearing gains and losses resulting from the exchange of items after each delivery of items is logged on the ACSS terminal of the delivering Direct Clearer. Direct Clearers that are receiving items verify the contents of the deliveries and may contest them.

A cut-off time for the exchange of payment items is established for each Regional Settlement Point; the time may vary from RSP to RSP and by type of item, but is generally around midnight, local time. After the cut-off time, items exchanged between Direct Clearers are not, with certain exceptions, included in the figures for settlement at the Bank of Canada until the following clearing cycle.

Payment items received by a processing center that are drawn on branches of the same Direct Clearer in areas served by other centers are, wherever possible, also moved by air courier that evening. However, most Direct Clearers have implemented automated systems enabling information on "on-us" items deposited in one region to be stripped from them and transmitted via high-speed communication lines to processing centers in the regions serving the branches on which the items are drawn; this allows the physical items to follow later without affecting the float time. After midnight, the processing center will fine-sort "on-us" items drawn on branches within its own region, post these items to the customers' accounts, and produce updated branch reports.

The settlement process begins at approximately 8.30 A.M. (Ottawa time) on the following day, when certain regular and mutually agreed transactions affecting Direct Clearers are carried out via the ACSS. These include especially the drawdown or redeposit of balances of the federal government by the Bank of Canada from or to each Direct Clearer. These transactions are carried out by the bank in its role as the government's fiscal agent and are at the same time a key element in the day-to-day implementation of monetary policy. At 9.30 A.M. the preliminary net clearing gain or loss of each Direct Clearer is available to the institution from the ACSS. Between 9.30 A.M. and 11.00 A.M. bilateral reopenings of the clearings may take place, via the ACSS, to handle corrections, provided that both Direct Clearers concerned agree. Shortly after 11.00 A.M., the final net gains and losses are available from the ACSS. At 1.30 P.M. (Ottawa time) the Bank of Canada obtains each Direct Clearer's "national standing," i.e., net gain or loss, from the ACSS in the form of a printed statement and adjusts the balances of the Direct Clearers on its own books, as of the previous day's date, thus effecting the ultimate transfer of funds between Direct Clearers. At approximately 4.00 P.M. (Ottawa time), following any final adjustments and any necessary central bank advances, the bank establishes the closing balances of each Direct Clearer as at the end of the previous day. Final settlement, therefore, takes place retroactively.

*Usage*

On a typical weekday evening some 9 million payment items, including on-us items, are processed by the data centers of Direct Clearers. In 1987, approximately 2.4 billion items were posted to over 40 million demand deposit and chequable savings accounts at deposit-taking institutions across the country. Of these items, approximately 1.9 billion had been exchanged and settled for between Direct Clearers, the remainder being "on-us" items. There are two specialised markets that contribute significantly to the magnitude of the flow of payment items through the national clearing and settlement system: the foreign exchange market and the money market. The number of payment items issued as a result of large transactions in these markets and for large corporate transactions is relatively small. On a typical day less than 1 percent of the items exchanged between Direct Clearers have an individual value in excess of Can.$ 50,000. Those items that do, however, are large, with an average value of Can.$ 1.9 million, and these items account for about 92 percent of the total value of the items cleared on a typical day.

The national clearing and settlement system also handles a range of payment items that are not drawn on accounts maintained at deposit-taking institutions. These items include federal government payments, which are cleared and settled through the Bank of Canada and which account for about 10 percent by volume of all the items handled by the system; postal and other money orders; grain elevator receipts, and travellers' cheques. Finally, about 20 percent of the items deposited at the branches of deposit-taking institutions are drawn on their own customers' accounts and can, therefore, be processed internally without being entered into the national clearing and settlement system.

### Recent developments

#### (i) Retroactive settlement

On July 16, 1986, the national clearing and settlement system became, effectively, a "same-day" system. From that date on, the entries in the books of the Bank of Canada that reflect the previous day's net clearing gain or loss by each Direct Clearer have been dated retroactively, i.e., value has been transferred between the Direct Clearers to be effective on the same business day that the underlying transactions took place rather than, as in the past, on the following day. The important consideration for both the CPA and its member institutions was not to speed up the processing of large-value payment items, which the national clearing and settlement system already handled very efficiently; rather, it was to eliminate the float associated with them—and, indeed, all paper items—as a result of the one-day delay in effecting settlement. Corporate customers might well, like individual customers, obtain immediate credit for items deposited, but they also had to pay charges to compensate the institution for crediting the funds to the customer's account before receiving value itself the next day. The resources that were being expended both by deposit-taking institutions and by their corporate customers to calculate and to negotiate these charges and the efforts by the customers to minimise them by manipulating their payment flows—all essentially unproductive activities in social terms—were already large and clearly increasing.

The major objective of eliminating settlement float was achieved by completing the clearing and settlement cycle in the normal manner, with adequate time for corrections and adjustments, and then giving settlement value retroactively. This brings the settlement dating for paper payment items into line with that for electronic items: magnetic tapes are exchanged between the Direct Clearers days ahead of the due date, and settlement vouchers representing their value had previously been cleared one day prior to the due date for settlement on the due date. These vouchers are now being cleared on the due date, since they are being settled retroactively the next day.

With the effective elimination of any difference in the timing of settlement between various payment mechanisms, the Canadian payment system is well positioned for the orderly and rational development of both traditional and newer mechanisms. In addition, the customer is able to choose between alternatives on the basis of cost and convenience and in a manner undistorted by float considerations.

#### (ii) A large-value system

Of approximately 7.3 million payment items that are exchanged through the national clearing and settlement system on a typical day, only 25,000, or 0.3 percent, are large-value items, i.e., items that have an individual value in excess of Can.\$ 50,000. Although small in number, they have a value of some Can.\$ 47 billion, or about 92 percent of the total daily value of all items cleared.

All these large-value payments are paper items; they are not electronic as in several other countries, although in some cases, the payment instructions are sent and received electronically.

The CPA is now beginning work to replace the paper payment items that are used for large-value transfers with electronic items.

### (b) The Canadian Depository for Securities (CDS)

*Background*

CDS was federally incorporated in 1970. It is a private company owned by the principal institutions in the Canadian financial community Representatives of Canada's major banks, trust companies, and investment dealers each hold one-third of the CDS equity shares.

The depository's business is to provide reliable and efficient services for the clearing and settlement of securities transactions. Currently, the principal use of these services involves equity (share) transactions. CDS receives and processes information on these transactions and sends reports to participants on their delivery and payment obligations, as calculated by CDS. Each participant makes a net payment to, or receives a net payment from, CDS in each settlement cycle. Participants can make book-entry deliveries without the physical movement of certificates. Deliveries between participants can also be made on a certificated basis, using CDS as a clearing house for physically receiving and delivering envelopes containing security certificates.

Participants wishing to make book-entry deliveries deposit their securities certificates with CDS. The securities are then registered in the name of a CDS nominee, and CDS credits the amount deposited to an account maintained for the participant. Participants with a credit securities balance can deliver or pledge them to another participant by giving the appropriate instructions to CDS. This contributes significantly to the efficiency of participants' operations. It reduces their need for a physical stock of security certificates and therefore cuts the costs of safekeeping and recordkeeping, as well as the messenger and banking costs of certificated deliveries.

The value of securities held on December 31, 1987, was Can.$ 87.7 billion. There were 9.2 million equity trades reported to CDS in 1987, representing all the trading on the Montreal and Toronto stock exchanges, together with a growing number of nonexchange trades.

The cost advantages and simplified recordkeeping services offered by CDS are of prime importance to participants. This was especially evident during the unprecedented market activity in October 1987. CDS systems were able to cope efficiently with the high transaction volumes, clearing a record number of trades that exceeded by 40 percent the typical daily volume for 1987. There is, consequently, considerable interest in expanding services to include all other types of securities.

For example, to facilitate the inclusion of debt securities in the CDS clearing and settlement systems, a number of new activities are under way. The existing system to clear equities works on a five-day clearing and settlement convention. Money market transaction processing, which is not currently handled by CDS, involves same-day settlement. A new money market system is under development that will provide a centralised facility for clearing and settling these transactions. The service will be an on-line, real-time computer system that will link the CDS participants who are the buyers, sellers, agents, lenders, borrowers, and issuers within the system. Securities will enter the system by being issued directly into the service or by certificate deposit. Custodial services will also be provided by CDS in support of the immobilisation of these instruments.

The types of security to be included in the new money market system are Treasury bills, bankers' acceptances, bearer deposit notes, commercial paper, provincial and municipal notes, term deposits, and guaranteed investment certificates.

An initiative to immobilise Government of Canada marketable debt in the depository, in order to facilitate clearing and settlement, was initiated in 1986, and CDS plans to immobilise Government of Canada bonds during 1989. It is estimated that the value of eligible outstanding bond issues will be more than Can.$ 50 billion.

As the first step in the process of immobilising Government of Canada marketable securities in the debt clearing system of CDS, a new CDS service, the New Issue Distribution Service for Government of Canada Bonds, has recently been developed. This service facilitates the primary distribution of new Government of Canada marketable bond issues by permitting trading transactions that occur before delivery of a new issue to be settled among participants.

Furthermore, these new developments, and the rapidly changing market and regulatory environment in Canada and abroad, have necessitated a re-examination of CDS security, internal controls, and organisational structure. One major step in the minimising of risk is the planned transfer of all operational data processing from a service bureau environment to CDS's own dedicated data center. The new money market service will be run at the new CDS Data Center as well.

## IV  GENERAL REMARKS AND CONCLUSION

As in most countries with highly developed financial markets, the link between the payment system and the securities and foreign exchange markets is important because of the significant proportion of the total value of payment traffic that is accounted for by transactions in those markets. Securities market payments in Canada in particular are currently effected mainly by the use of certified cheques. In the context of the work described earlier on a proposed electronic transfer system for large-value payments, and of work by the Canadian Depository for Securities to terminate the physical movement both of securities and of the related payments, new and more efficient mechanisms are in the process of development to link the financial markets to the clearing and settlement system.

Appendix I

## CANADIAN PAYMENTS ASSOCIATION

The approach to developing the payment system of the future embodied in the CPA was the first of its kind in the world, although comparable organisations have now been set up in other countries. The essence of this approach lies in the fact that responsibility for planning the evolution of the system has been entrusted to a private association of interested financial institutions—some of them private, some cooperative, and some governmental—with a legislated public purpose.

### The Association's First Objective

The first objective of the association was to bring nonbank deposit-taking institutions into partnership with the chartered banks in the management of the clearing and settlement system.

The Association's Act provides that it may "...arrange the exchange of payment items at such places in Canada as the Association considers appropriate...." and that the CPA's Board of Directors may "...make by-laws respecting clearing arrangements and related matters...respecting settlements and related matters,...(and) subject to the by-laws...such rules respecting clearing arrangements and the settlement of payment items as it considers necessary." By-laws become effective only when approved by the Federal Cabinet.

On February 1, 1983, following approval of the association's clearing by-law by the Federal Cabinet, the CPA assumed responsibility for the operation of the system.

The contents of the clearing by-law cover include: the organisational structure of the clearing system; the general procedures for exchanging payment items and settling the claims thereby created; and the definition of the rights and obligations of member institutions and the provisions for default, either on the part of a Direct Clearer or on the part of a deposit-taking institution that uses a Direct Clearer as clearing agent.

Important as the clearing by-law and rules are, unquestioned mutual trust and confidence among Direct Clearers and among CPA member institutions in general are vital to the smooth functioning of the national clearing and settlement system. First and foremost among the means of developing and maintaining trust is the section of the Association's Act regarding financial stability, which stipulates that every member institution be subject to prudential regulation and supervision. Second, both bank and nonbank Direct Clearers now have operational relationships with the Bank of Canada and direct access to central bank credit. Third, there is a formal link between the day-to-day operations of the national clearing and settlement system and the prudential context within which that system operates, in that Direct Clearers are required by the clearing by-law to report to the relevant regulatory authority all instances in which an Indirect Clearer needs to make sizable and repeated borrowings for the purposes of settlement.

The success of the operational partnership that has developed between the Direct Clearers is reflected in three accomplishments in particular: the automation of the clearings in 1984; the introduction of retroactive settlement in 1986; and the implementation of an automated system for the bulk exchange of U.S. dollar items among Canadian deposit-taking institutions in 1987. Each of these initiatives resulted in improvements to the national clearing and settlement system as a whole, with benefits accruing to clearing and corporate clients as well as to the Direct Clearers themselves. Each initiative required the Direct Clearers to modify internal procedures. In the instance of the Automated Clearing Settlement System, significant investments were required to bring into being the first interactive computer communication system linking Canadian deposit-taking institutions.

The National Clearings Committee of the CPA (NCC) maintains an ongoing review of the inter-member procedures, standards, and practices contained in the *CPA Rules Manual* for the exchange of paper-based and electronic data within the national clearing and settlement system and recommends changes to the rules to the board. The NCC also coordinates efforts to resolve operational problems and to increase the efficiency of the national clearing and settlement system. Every Direct Clearer is entitled to representation on the NCC.

### The Association's Second Objective

In the coming years the CPA will be continuing the work it has begun on:

▶ Promoting and extending the use of direct funds transfer for recurring credit payments and electronic preauthorised credits in general.

▶ Modernising and automating the long-established system for the preauthorised debiting of recurring payments.

▶ Developing procedures for the automated transfer of large-value payments.

▶ Developing more cost-effective ways for processing household bill payments.

▶ Developing the framework for electronic funds transfer at the point-of-sale.

None of these initiatives concerns the Direct Clearers alone or, indeed, CPA members alone. The needs and preferences of a wide variety of other financial institutions and nonfinancial corporations are involved, as are those of consumers. The necessary processes of consultation, reconciliation, and allocation of responsibility are in progress under CPA auspices.

The Senior Planning Committee, a standing committee of the CPA's Board of

Directors, has the general responsibility for advising the board on all matters relating to the planning of the evolution of the national payment system. Its terms of reference include:

▶ Identifying specific systems development projects.

▶ Acting as the principal channel through which the various sectors of the Canadian economy not represented within the CPA — e.g., consumers, retailers, communications common carriers, and equipment manufacturers — may express their views in the planning process.

▶ Identifying subjects requiring research by the CPA.

▶ Developing policy concerning the national payment system for approval by the board.

The board decided early in 1988 that, in addition to regular liaison with a wide range of individual nonmember institutions and organisations on particular issues or subjects, the Senior Planning Committee should hold two plenary meetings every year. The purposes of these plenary meetings are, first, to provide the representatives of nonmember institutions and organisations with an opportunity to express their groups' views in the planning process and, second, to provide the Senior Planning Committee with an opportunity to discuss with the representatives, in a complete and comprehensive way, the issues currently facing the Committee. The first plenary meeting was held in April 1988.

The work of the Senior Planning Committee is complemented by that of *ad hoc* committees on matters such as EFT POS and a large-value transfer system.

Member institutions, through their participation in association work and meetings, have been able to gain a greater appreciation of the nature and scope of each other's business activities, practices, and philosophies. The CPA is not, however, a guarantor of its member institutions and does not have a mandate concerning the liquidity or solvency of its members or other prudential matters.

Appendix 2

## Table 1
### Total Assets of Canadian Deposit-Taking Institutions, 1983-87
(in millions of Canadian dollars, at end of period)[1]

|  | 1983 | 1984 | 1985 | 1986 | 1987 |
|---|---|---|---|---|---|
| Chartered banks[2] | 368,628 | 405,560 | 443,761 | 467,972 | 486,384 |
| Local credit unions and caisses populaires | 37,111 | 40,625 | 44,045 | 48,780 | 55,060 |
| Trust and mortgage loan companies[3] | 61,588 | 67,377 | 74,114 | 84,805 | 94,456 |
| Quebec savings banks[4] | 5,255 | 5,664 | 6,239 | 3,896 | |
| Governmental savings institutions[5] | 3,422 | 4,232 | 4,521 | 5,520 | 6,153 |

[1]December 31, except in the instance of governmental savings institutions, where end of period is March 31 of the following year.
[2]Including assets of wholly- and majority-owned subsidiaries.
[3]Excluding chartered-bank mortgage loan subsidiaries.
[4]The Montreal City and District Savings Bank became a chartered bank in September 1987.
[5]Province of Alberta Treasury Branches only.

## Table 2
### Domestic Branches of Canadian Deposit-Taking Institutions, 1983-87
(as of December 31)

|  | 1983 | 1984 | 1985 | 1986 | 1987 |
|---|---|---|---|---|---|
| Chartered banks | 7,091 | 7,057 | 7,016 | 6,971 | 7,148 |
| Local credit unions and caisses populaires | 4,186 | 4,059 | 4,173 | 4,156 | 4,129 |
| Trust and mortgage loan companies | 1,135 | 1,189 | 1,279 | 1,513 | 1,523 |
| Quebec savings banks[1] | 117 | 122 | 131 | 129 | |
| Governmental savings institutions | 151 | 151 | 155 | 157 | 156 |
| Total | 12,680 | 12,578 | 12,754 | 12,926 | 12,956 |
| Population per branch | 1,963 | 1,995 | 1,982 | 1,973 | 1,991 |

[1]The Montreal City and District Savings Bank became a chartered bank in September 1987.

Appendix 2

**Table 3**
**Currency Outside Banks, 1983-87[1]**
**(in millions of Canadian dollars, average of Wednesdays during December)**

|  | 1983 | 1984 | 1985 | 1986 | 1987 |
|---|---|---|---|---|---|
| Notes | 11,212 | 12,117 | 13,073 | 14,079 | 15,170 |
| Coin | 1,189 | 1,247 | 1,273 | 1,305 | 1,374 |
| Total | 12,401 | 13,364 | 14,345 | 15,384 | 16.544 |
| Currency per capital (dollars) | 498 | 532 | 567 | 603 | 641 |

[1]Owing to the rounding of figures, components may not always add to the total shown.

**Table 4**
**Transferable Deposits, 1983-87[1]**
**(in millions of Canadian dollars, at end of period)[2]**

|  | 1983 | 1984 | 1985 | 1986 | 1987 |
|---|---|---|---|---|---|
| Chartered banks[3]: |  |  |  |  |  |
| Demand deposits (less private-sector float) | 17,768 | 16,826 | 18,513 | 19,454 | 21,136 |
| Chequable savings deposits | 12,269 | 20,037 | 34,702 | 43,623 | 45,007 |
| Local credit unions and caisses populaires: |  |  |  |  |  |
| Demand and chequable savings deposits | 4,751 | 5,030 | 5,684 | 6,644 | 7,414 |
| Trust and mortgage loan companies: |  |  |  |  |  |
| Demand and chequable savings deposits | 3,663 | 5,218 | 7,765 | 8,479 | 8,848 |
| Quebec savings banks[4]: |  |  |  |  |  |
| Demand and chequable savings deposits | 324 | 330 | 472 | 724 |  |
| Governmental savings institutions: |  |  |  |  |  |
| Demand and chequable savings deposits | 1,175 | 1,277 | 1,346 | 1,707 | 844[5] |
| Total | 39,950 | 48,718 | 68,482 | 80,631 | 83,249 |
| Transferable deposits per capita (dollars) | 1,604 | 1,941 | 2,707 | 3,162 | 3,227 |
| Transferable deposits and currency per capita (dollars) | 2,102 | 2,473 | 3,274 | 3,765 | 3,868 |

[1]Owing to the rounding of figures, components may not always add to the total shown.
[2]December 31, except in the instance of governmental savings institutions, where end of period is March 31 of the following year.
[3]Average-of-Wednesday data.
[4]The Montreal City and District Savings Bank became a chartered bank in September 1987.
[5]Province of Alberta Treasury Branches only.

Appendix 2

**Table 5**
**Selected Data on Bank Credit Cards, 1977-87**
**(as of October 31 or for 12-month period ending October 31)**

| | 1977 | 1978 | 1979 | 1980 | 1981 | 1982 | 1983 | 1984 | 1985 | 1986 | 1987 |
|---|---|---|---|---|---|---|---|---|---|---|---|
| Number of cards in circulation (millions) | 8.18 | 8.99 | 9.85 | 10.76 | 11.98 | 11.58 | 12.13 | 13.05 | 13.97 | 15.50 | 17.62 |
| Dollar sales (billions) | 3.61 | 4.90 | 6.64 | 8.82 | 10.59 | 13.83 | 14.84 | 16.92 | 19.35 | 23.01 | 26.37 |
| Gross dollar volume[1] (billions) | 4.04 | 5.44 | 7.32 | 9.44 | 11.51 | 13.38 | 14.85 | 17.10 | 20.42 | 23.57 | 26.90 |
| Sales drafts processed (millions) | 118.82 | 150.76 | 185.83 | 218.42 | 249.64 | 274.90 | 297.55 | 325.16 | 372.91 | 417.21 | 450.65 |
| Average sale (dollars) | 30.46 | 32.50 | 35.72 | 39.47 | 42.43 | 50.53 | 49.88 | 52.05 | 51.90 | 55.15 | 56.79 |
| Merchant accounts[2] | 271,150 | 290,692 | 322,115 | 347,845 | 371,831 | 382,206 | 419,610 | 442,928 | 527,042 | 571,771 | 642,429 |

Source: The Canadian Bankers' Association.
[1]Equals the total of dollar sales and cash advances.
[2]Merchants accepting VISA or MasterCard or both. Duplication may occur since merchants accepting both cards have been reported by each plan.

Appendix 2

## Table 6
### Distribution of Cash Dispensers and ATMs, 1984-88
(as of January 31)

| | By Classes of CPA Member Institution | | | | |
|---|---|---|---|---|---|
| | 1984 | 1985 | 1986 | 1987 | 1988[1] |
| Chartered banks | 1,670 | 2,399 | 2,775 | 3,222[2] | 3,874[2] |
| Local credit unions and caisses populaires | 251 | 437 | 545 | 759 | 864 |
| Trust and mortgage loan companies | 39 | 170 | 238 | 344 | 467 |
| Other deposit-taking institutions[3] | | 66 | 70 | 89 | 64 |
| Total | 1,960 | 3,072 | 3,628 | 4,512 | 5,269 |

| | By Province or Territory | | | | |
|---|---|---|---|---|---|
| | 1984 | 1985 | 1986 | 1987 | 1988 |
| British Columbia | 334 | 444 | 574 | 721 | 738 |
| Alberta | 294 | 428 | 462 | 532 | 593 |
| Saskatchewan | 98 | 120 | 147 | 178 | 212 |
| Manitoba | 66 | 86 | 125 | 162 | 207 |
| Ontario | 874 | 1,357 | 1,564 | 1,876 | 2,160 |
| Quebec | 249 | 539 | 614 | 867 | 1,123 |
| New Brunswick | 11 | 30 | 37 | 51 | 80 |
| Nova Scotia | 25 | 44 | 72 | 83 | 102 |
| Prince Edward Island | — | 5 | 7 | 7 | 11 |
| Newfoundland | 9 | 19 | 25 | 33 | 40 |
| Yukon and North West Territories | — | — | 1 | 2 | 3 |
| Total | 1,960 | 3,072 | 3,628 | 4,512 | 5,269 |
| Population per machine | 12,702 | 8,167 | 6,966 | 5,652 | 4,896 |

Source: Canadian Payments Association.
[1]Figures for 1987 and 1988 include ATMs located in branch lobbies that are available for use only during normal branch hours.
[2]Estimate.
[3]The Montreal City and District Savings Bank became a chartered bank in September 1987.

Appendix 2

Table 7

**Annual Flows of Payment Items Through the National Clearing and Settlement System, 1983-87**
(Canadian dollars)

| | 1983 | 1984 | 1985 | 1986 | 1987 |
|---|---|---|---|---|---|
| **SMALL CHEQUES** | | | | | |
| Volume | 1,174,305,298 | 1,524,083,442 | 1,602,374,053 | 1,678,415,247 | 1,714,869,978 |
| Value ($000) | 536,235,044 | 697,476,005 | 747,839,188 | 814,590,225 | 912,364,627 |
| Avg/Trans($) | 457 | 458 | 467 | 485 | 532 |
| **LARGE CHEQUES** (over $50,000) | | | | | |
| Volume | 3,171,677 | 4,166,570 | 4,991,617 | 6,076,890 | 6,274,692 |
| Value ($000) | 4,562,527,661 | 6,407,108,620 | 7,609,418,149 | 9,850,555,122 | 11,894,427,478 |
| Avg/Trans ($) | 1,438,522 | 1,537,742 | 1,524,440 | 1,620,986 | 1,895,619 |
| **RETURNS**[1] | | | | | |
| Volume | 1,617,543 | 1,455,352 | 1,388,567 | 1,338,842 | 1,291,971 |
| Value ($000) | 1,076,251 | 1,040,675 | 805,270 | 1,104,223 | 980,609 |
| Avg/Trans ($) | 665 | 715 | 580 | 825 | 759 |
| **UNQUALIFIED**[2] | | | | | |
| Volume | 12,385,522 | 13,909,539 | 11,740,872 | 11,216,430 | 10,286,768 |
| Value ($000) | 16,870,859 | 15,918,531 | 11,145,181 | 10,791,763 | 9,628,219 |
| Avg/Trans ($) | 1,362 | 1,144 | 949 | 962 | 936 |
| **MAGNETIC TAPE DEBITS** | | | | | |
| Volume | — | — | — | 24,334,011 | 35,869,440 |
| Value ($000) | — | — | — | 13,496,168 | 9,809,270 |
| Avg/Trans ($) | — | — | — | 555 | 273 |
| **MAGNETIC TAPE CREDITS** | | | | | |
| Volume | 14,620,430 | 25,176,165 | 40,025,833 | 31,255,586 | 44,317,957 |
| Value ($000) | 12,827,154 | 24,919,704 | 35,397,821 | 28,116,256 | 41,255,563 |
| Avg/Trans ($) | 877 | 990 | 884 | 900 | 931 |
| **SHARED ATM NETWORKS** | | | | | |
| Volume | — | — | — | 4,176,773 | 34,096,429 |
| Value ($000) | — | — | — | 368,350 | 2,098,477 |
| Avg/Trans ($) | — | — | — | 88 | 62 |
| **TOTAL** | | | | | |
| Volume | 1,206,100,470 | 1,568,790,068 | 1,660,520,942 | 1,756,813,779 | 1,847,007,235 |
| Value ($000) | 5,129,536,969 | 7,146,463,535 | 8,404,605,609 | 10,719,022,107 | 12,870,564,243 |
| Avg/Trans ($) | 4,253 | 4,555 | 5,061 | 6,101 | 6,968 |

Source: Canadian Payments Association.
[1]Payment items that have been returned principally because of insufficient funds in the payor's account or because of stop-payment-orders.
[2]Payment items that do not meet the standards and specifications for MICR-encoded documents of the Canadian Payments Association.

# 3  FRANCE

# France

## I  INTRODUCTION

The main features of the French payment system are as follows:

*At the institutional level:*

▶ A uniform legal framework (the Banking Law of January 24, 1984), which regards the issue and administration of payment instruments as banking operations.

▶ A high degree of concentration.

▶ Substantial state involvement.

▶ A high percentage of the population holds bank accounts.

▶ The important position of the Postal Administration's financial sector, which belongs to what may be termed the "French banking community" in the broad sense.

▶ The relationships of competition and cooperation between the various networks that make up this "community" (including that of the Postal Administration).

*In the field of payment media:*

▶ The important role of cash, especially for low-value, routine payments (according to the latest estimates, in 1987, 15.6 billion direct payments to retail businesses and market services alone—as opposed to payments over distances—were settled in bank notes and coin, representing almost 70 percent of the total of such payments).

▶ By contrast, the supremacy of deposit money over cash when payments are expressed in value terms; at the end of 1987, sight deposits in francs made up 84.7 percent of $M_1$ (or Fr.fr. 1,244 billion).

*Regarding deposit money media:*

▶ The variety of instruments used, dominated by the cheque (65.4 percent of the total number of settlements in deposit money).

▶ The rapid expansion in transactions by bank card and the significant proportion of book-entry payments for which they now account (7.9 percent of the number of transactions); the replacement of the cheque, the traditional paper-based instrument, by a new automated instrument is tending to gather pace.

▶ The growing share of other automated instruments, such as credit transfers and direct debits (respectively, 15.4 and 9.4 percent of the total number of instruments).

*Regarding interbank exchange circuits:*

▶ A situation reflecting the state of affairs regarding deposit money instruments, namely, the coexistence of exchanges of paper-based media in the clearing houses and automated circuits (computer clearing centers, regional cheque record exchange centers, bank card processing centers, and the SAGITTAIRE system[1]), with paper-based exchanges outnumbering automated exchanges (respectively, 62.8 and 37.2 percent by number).

*Regarding concrete modernisation measures:*

▶ Application of the new EFT technologies to establish:

—The Interbank Teleclearing System (Système Interbancaire de Télécompensa-

---

[1]The automated system for the integral handling of transactions by telecommunication means and the settlement of "foreign" operations.

tion, SIT), a national telecommunications-based system, a pilot scheme that came into operation in mid-May 1988.

—A single national electronic payment system based on the use of the Cartc Bancaire, which was the result of the agreements signed in July 1984, on the use of a single card in various institutions' networks.

—Cards containing microprocessors for security reasons (2 million such cards are expected to be in circulation by the end of 1988).

## II  INSTITUTIONAL FRAMEWORK

The description of the banking system is followed by an outline of the main institutions involved in the development of payment media.

### 1. The Banking System

Banking activities and the terms by which they may be carried out are defined by legislation (the Banking Law of January 24, 1984). The law stipulates that only credit institutions may customarily engage in banking business, which includes the issue and administration of payment instruments as well as the taking of deposits from the public and the granting of loans.

A number of institutions not subject to the Banking Law (primarily state networks) may also carry out banking operations and hence offer payment services.

*(a)  Credit institutions*

These fall into the following main categories:

*(i)  Banks in the sense of commercial banks*

These institutions, which may engage in a highly varied range of activities, have a universal role, in that they may carry out all types of banking operation; in particular, they may accept deposits of all kinds and perform associated operations, such as foreign exchange transactions and the marketing of transferable securities and financial products.

Among the 222 banks under French majority control,[2] three institutions stand out on account of their size: Banque Nationale de Paris (BNP), Crédit Lyonnais, and Société Générale, which alone operate more than half of all the permanent branches of the banks as a whole and accept more than 50 percent of the funds gathered by this category of institution; at the end of 1987, 19 banks were in public ownership, including BNP and Crédit Lyonnais.[3]

Foreign banks have a significant presence in France; 155 institutions are under foreign control,[4] more than 40 percent of all the banks established in France.

*(ii)  A group of networks* comprising the mutual banks, the cooperatives, the ordinary savings banks (as opposed to the National Savings Bank), and the municipal credit banks, which are also authorised to take deposits for any term but whose business is restricted in certain respects by the specific legislation or regulations governing them.

These networks are grouped together at the national level under central bodies performing mainly promotional and organisational functions and administrative, technical, and financial supervision.

---

[2]Banks established in metropolitan France and Monaco; 216 have their head office in France and are governed by Franch law, six have their head office in the Principality of Monaco and are governed by Monegasque law. The 17 banks established in the overseas departments and territories are not covered by the statistics contained in this study.
[3]Of the 38 banks that had previously belonged to the public sector, 19 were privatised under a law promulgated on August 6, 1986. They included Société Générale, which had been nationalised in 1945.
[4]Five of these are established in Monaco and governed by Monegasque law.

*(iii) Finance companies,* which may not accept funds from the public for terms of less than two years unless an exception has been granted and whose activities are further limited by their statutes. They comprise in particular the institutions known previously as financial establishments (établissements financiers), whose business includes lending and securities transactions.

*(iv) Specialised financial institutions* to which the state has entrusted permanent tasks in the public interest; they may not carry out banking operations other than those relating to these tasks except in an ancillary capacity.

### *(v) Organisation and supervision of the banking industry*

The credit institutions are represented collectively *vis-à-vis* the public authorities at two levels:

▶ At the first level, the institutions not belonging to a network with a special legal status are required to be members of a professional body performing functions in the general interest, e.g., the French Bankers' Association in the case of banks or the Professional Association of Financial Establishments in that of certain finance companies. In the case of networks, this function is entrusted to their central bodies.

▶ At the second level, the central bodies and professional associations are affiliated to the French Association of Credit Institutions representing the banking industry as a whole.

Credit institutions come under the supervision of the Banking Commission; all credit institutions come under the jurisdiction of the National Credit Council and two special committees:

### *The National Credit Council*

The council, which has as its chairman the Minister of the Economy, Finance and the Budget and as its vice-chairman the Governor of the Bank of France, discusses and deliberates on the direction of monetary and credit policy and examines the conditions in which the banking and financial system operates. It is a forum for wide-ranging consultation among representatives from all sections of economic and financial life. In the field of payment instruments, its deliberations have concerned the new electronic payment media and especially the legal and international aspects of payment cards.[5]

### *The special committees*

There are two such committees, whose regular members are chosen from the National Credit Council.

▶ The main function of the Banking Regulations Committee is to lay down general rules applicable to credit institutions (credit policy), security standards to be observed, the interest rates and terms for financial operations, and rules governing the establishment of networks.

▶ The Committee of Credit Institutions is responsible primarily for all decisions, authorisations and exceptions of an individual nature.

Although autonomous, these two committees maintain close links with the National Credit Council.

### *The Banking Commission*

The Banking Commission, which is chaired by the Governor of the Bank of France and was previously called the Banking Control Commission, is responsible for monitoring the credit institutions' compliance with banking regulations, scrutinising

---

[5]The council's work has led to the production of two reports, entitled, respectively, "Legal Aspects of the New Payment Media" (July 1986) and "European and International Aspects of Payment Cards" (March 1988).

their operating conditions, and verifying the adequacy of their financial structure and their compliance with the rules of sound banking practice. The Bank of France organises and carries out on-the-spot inspections on behalf of the Commission.

*(b)  The state networks*

A number of networks operated by the Treasury and the financial departments of the Postal Administration perform banking operations broadly comparable with those carried out by credit institutions.

The financial departments of the Postal Administration, which make up the largest of the networks, perform an important role within the French financial system; their 8.2 million sight accounts (most of which are opened with the Postal Cheque Centers) and 19.8 million time accounts (administered by the National Savings Bank) represented 18.7 percent of the total number of accounts and 15 percent of total account balances at the end of 1987.

The Treasury's branch offices also accept deposits from individuals, holding 641,000 sight accounts.

The state networks and the Deposit and Consignment Office, which, among its numerous activities, uses funds collected by the savings banks to finance local authorities, are not directly subject to the Banking Law of January 1984. However, they form part of the French banking community, within which they compete and cooperate.

## 2.  The Main Bodies Involved in the Development of Payment Media

The problems raised by the evolution of the payment system have led to a process of wide-ranging and almost continuous consultation in which the Bank of France takes an active part. It plays a particularly important role through the Working Party on Payment Media, which sets forth broad guidelines. The banking industry also cooperates on a more technical level in a number of other bodies.

*(a)  The Bank of France[6]*

The actions taken by the central bank with regard to payment media are based primarily on legal requirements:

▶  Under its statutes (the Law of January 3, 1973 and the Decree of January 30, 1973) it is vested with the general task of overseeing the currency, credit, and the banking system.

▶  Under the Banking Law of January 24, 1984, only credit institutions subject to regulation and supervision in which the central bank plays an essential role may administer payment media and make them available to customers.

Its role is strengthened by the important position the bank occupies in its capacity as a provider of collective services, such as the provincial clearing houses, the computer clearing centers, and the regional cheque record exchange centers (CREIC, SAGITTAIRE, Joint Collection Service), and as a participant in payment exchanges.

It has few private and business customers, but it is one of the largest payment collection institutions by virtue of being the sole banker to the Treasury and the fact that its customers include public bodies such as French Railways and the banks, which tend to entrust it with the collection of items payable at centers in which they themselves are not represented.

Although the Bank of France has always paid the utmost attention to the smooth operation of the payment system, the acceleration in the pace of technological

---

[6]The responsibilities of the Bank of France with regard to bank notes and coin are described in Section III, 1.*(a)* dealing with this issue.

change and especially the prospects it has opened up with regard to payment media led the bank to initiate and develop a more decisive plan of action from the end of the 1970s onwards.

### (b) The Working Party on Payment Media

The forecasting studies undertaken by the Bank of France at the end of the 1970s for its own internal purposes coincided with the public authorities' concern about the consequences of the increasing computerisation of society; in 1979, they therefore charged the bank with setting up the Working Party to promote the rational and coherent development of payment media.

The group, which includes representatives of all interested parties (banking institutions, mutual and cooperative networks, public-sector financial agencies and the public authorities), was instructed:

▶ To determine the policy that should be preferred with regard to payment instruments.

▶ To define the general rules the banks should apply to interbank exchanges of deposit money.

▶ To act as a forum for investigating problems relating to internetwork exchange conditions.

▶ To organise pilot schemes for new electronic payment systems and monitor their results.

The Working Party on Payment Media has worked actively since its inception and has set up several sub-working parties. Its discussions have led to a consensus that has allowed important decisions to be taken on matters such as the construction of the Interbank Teleclearing System and the creation of a National System for Card Payments, the development of which will permit the gradual implementation of the chip card.

### (c) Other bodies

The other bodies play a key role by providing a forum for consultation on technical issues and standardisation among banking and quasi-banking institutions. The main ones are:

▶ The French Committee for the Organisation and Standardisation of Banking Practice, chaired by the Bank of France; through its numerous working groups this committee is responsible for studying issues of mutual interest concerning the simplification of bank work, and rationalising and codifying the methods or documents used by banking institutions. The aforementioned working groups include the Clearing Computer Commission, which deals with all the aspects of exchanges executed via the clearing computer.

▶ Several economic interest groupings whose task it is, *inter alia,* to manage the major exchange systems; particular mention may be made of the economic interest grouping of S.W.I.F.T. users in France, the Interbank Teleclearing System Group, or the Cartes Bancaires Group, which is more specifically responsible for promoting a national system for payments by card.

## III  PAYMENT SYSTEMS

### 1. Payment Media Available to Customers

### (a) Cash payments

At the end of 1987, the amount of currency in circulation in the metropolitan territory (France and Monaco) stood at Fr.fr. 223.8 billion, with bank notes accounting for Fr.fr. 210.2 billion and coin for Fr.fr. 13.6 billion. Both are legal tender, although the acceptance of coin is compulsory only within certain limits. Responsibility for the minting of coin is vested by law in the Treasury, while the Bank of France has the sole right to issue bank notes. The bank puts bank notes and coin into circulation via its 234 branches and ensures that the needs of the public are met as regards both quantity and quality.

At the end of 1987, the currency in circulation was made up of five denominations of note (20, 50, 100, 200, and 500 francs) and nine denominations of coin (5, 10, 20, and 50 centimes and 1, 2, 5, 10, and 100 francs).[7] In view of the sole right of issue it possesses, the Bank of France itself undertakes the design and printing of bank notes, the replacement of worn or damaged notes, and the detection of forgeries.

Bank notes and coin have tended to stabilise at around 15.2 percent of the monetary aggregate $M_1$ (15.22 percent in 1986 and 15.25 percent in 1987), while the proportion of $M_3$ for which they account is continuing to decline very slowly (6.46 percent in 1986 and 6.20 percent in 1987), but will probably reach an equilibrium level shortly.

Cash is still the payment medium most used by individuals, mainly because of its great convenience for local, routine transactions of low value. The number of cash transactions effected each year is not known exactly; according to the latest estimates, approximately 15.6 billion were made with retail businesses and market services alone (excluding tolls and administrative payments). Cash therefore accounts for a large majority of payments in terms of numbers (more than 80 percent), whereas in value terms it only represented slightly less than 2 percent in 1987).

The prevalence of this method of payment varies according to the type of shop; as an indication, it is estimated that 42 percent of the volume of transactions is carried out in retail food shops, 6 percent in stores and supermarkets, and 11 percent in hotels and restaurants.

To improve the quality of bank notes in circulation and prevent the issue of forgeries, the Bank of France has begun to update the various denominations, a process that should be completed during the 1990s.

There are two main ways in which customers can make cash withdrawals:

▶ By using a card at one of the 11,500 cash dispensers or ATMs. In 1987, 432 million operations involving a total of Fr. fr. 197 billion were carried out; the average value per transaction came to Fr.fr. 456. Cards bearing the logo of the Cartes Bancaires Group (see (c) below), indicating that they can be used at machines other than those of the customer's bank, accounted for 370 million of these transactions, with a value of Fr.fr. 167 billion. All the cash dispensers installed outside banks can be accessed with any of the 16.5 million cards issued under the Group's scheme[8] (statistics as of year-end 1987). For security reasons, withdrawals are limited to a weekly maximum of Fr.fr. 1,800, and there are plans to connect all payment machines on-line (at present one in two operates in this way). Other cards issued by banks to permit exclusive access to their services enable customers to withdraw cash from the bank's own cash dispensers and ATMs. The number of transactions effected using cards of this kind is estimated at 62 million.

▶ By writing a cheque to the order of the drawer, approximately 523 million cheques of this kind were issued in 1987, with an average value of approximately Fr.fr. 1,548.[9]

---

[7]The silver 100-franc coins are not used for payments but hoarded by households.
[8]In all, 16.4 million payment cards and 8 million cards that can be used solely for cash withdrawals at the cash dispensers or ATMs of the issuing network.
[9]These figures also include cash withdrawals over the counter using bank cards ("emergency" withdrawals).

The volume of cash in circulation seems unlikely to change significantly in the near future; barring unforeseen circumstances, it can be predicted that the use of bank notes is likely to be encouraged by the growing use of cards in an extensive network of cash dispensers and ATMs; on the other hand, the foreseeable development of prepaid or stored-unit cards will slightly reduce the use of coin for payments such as car parking fees, motor-way tolls, and telephone charges; the average value of transactions effected using cards is decreasing, and this type of payment may begin to compete with notes and coin.

### (b) Payments in deposit money (excluding cards)

In many cases, deposit money media are preferred to notes and coin in view of their convenience for the user, especially if large sums are involved, if payments are to be made over distances, or if the customer wishes to have evidence of the transaction. Moreover, payments made in the intermediate stages of production and marketing are executed almost entirely in deposit money.

The customers of banks and quasi-banking institutions can choose from a wide range of instruments, among which the cheque predominates despite the rising importance of automated forms of payment instruments at the expense of the traditional paper-based forms.

The statistics on which the remarks regarding book-entry payment instruments are based take account not only of transactions passing through official exchange circuits,[10] but also of those that do not follow this route,[11] whether issued by banks or quasi-banking institutions, such as postal cheques. Data on the latter type of transaction have been obtained from a sample survey; the figures given should therefore be considered approximate.

### (i) Cheques

The cheque is the most widely used payment instrument in France; approximately 4.4 billion were issued in 1987,[12] accounting for 65.4 percent of the total number of book-entry payments. This situation is nevertheless the result of a slowdown in the growth of cheque transactions between 1982 and 1986, followed in 1987 by a decline in absolute value terms for the first time in the history of this instrument. Small though it is, the decrease signals the change that is beginning to emerge in French payment habits. The success traditionally enjoyed by this instrument, which still meets with widespread favor among bank[13] customers, is due essentially to its ease of use, versatility, and the fact that it is free of charge.

Cheques are thus used both by individuals and by businesses and authorities. Although it is impossible to say exactly how many cheques are written by each category, it is estimated that approximately 900 million were issued by businesses and authorities and 3.5 billion by individuals in 1987. Individuals with bank accounts write about 120 cheques per year, of which more than half (around 54 percent) are for amounts of less than Fr.fr. 250.

Cheques are used for two main purposes, apart from cash withdrawals: direct

---

[10]Clearing House of Bankers of Paris, provincial clearing houses, computer clearing centers, regional cheque record exchange centers, the Bank of France, and the processing center operated by the Cartes Bancaires Group.

[11]Instruments exchanged directly between networks or within the same group or instruments relating to customers and beneficiaries of the same institution.

[12]To arrive at the total number of cheques issued, account should also be taken of the 523 million cash withdrawals over the counter, most of which are made using cheques written to the order of the account holder.

[13]The adjectives "bank" and "banking" will be used throughout the remainder of the chapter on France to describe the banking industry as a whole, comprising both banks in the strict sense and quasi-banking institutions.

hand-to-hand payments and payments over distances, which are estimated to have given rise to 2.9 and 1.5 billion transactions, respectively.

The efforts made by the banking industry have enabled the cost of cheques to be reduced significantly:

▶ Processing and routing procedures have been modernised by using magnetic character reading techniques and reader/sorter machines.

▶ The major networks have adopted internal cheque truncation, with only the cheque details being transmitted in computerised form; in the field of interbank exchanges, by contrast, this procedure for the circulation of "cheque records" continues to be of only marginal importance (see Section 2 below on exchange circuits).

▶ The administrative organisation of interbank exchange circuits has been simplified (see Section 2 below on exchange circuits).

When exchanged via official interbank channels, cheques may be:

▶ Presented physically at the clearing house; interbank settlement then occurs on day D + 1 for cheques presented at the main clearing house to which the drawn branch belongs (joint procedure established in October 1980), and on D + 3 for cheques not presented in the clearing house with territorial jurisdiction (optional exchange procedure for "outside-area" cheques instituted in February 1984).

▶ "Dematerialised," the data record of the cheque being exchanged in the regional cheque record exchange centers and the interbank settlement date being set by agreement between members of the center.

Cheques can also be presented directly to the drawn institution or via an intermediary (a third bank or the Bank of France), which collects them via the clearing.

In principle, cheques are free of charge for the drawer and the beneficiary, although specific fees are charged in certain circumstances, such as the use of a cheque to obtain emergency funds. An attempt by the banks in 1987 to bill account holders for the use of cheques could not be put into effect to any significant degree, in particular because of opposition from consumer associations.

Despite the substantial increase in the number of payment incidents in recent years (notifications of unpaid cheques, which banks are required by law to make to the Central Cheque Register at the Bank of France, increased by almost 23 percent in 1987), rubber cheques rejected and notified to the Central Cheque Register accounted for 0.11 percent of the total number of cheques exchanged. Moreover, a determination to combat the theft of cheques—220,000 cheque books are stolen each year, containing 1.3 million cheques worth Fr.fr. 1.5 billion—gave rise to the plan to establish a National Register of Stolen Cheques, which would be administered by the Bank of France.

The banking industry's efforts to promote the use of alternatives to the cheque has already led to changes in consumers' payment habits. It is reasonable to assume that the use of cards will increasingly take the place of cheques for local payments, given the speed at which it is developing, and that the current large disparity between these two payment methods in volume terms (4,400 million cheques a year, 530 million card payments) will tend to narrow.

For payments over distances, direct debits, and interbank payment orders (titres interbancaires de paiement) will play a larger role, although it is not possible to predict the rate at which their use will grow or the scale of the substitution effect.

*(ii) Commercial bills*

Approximately 130 million commercial bills are officially exchanged between banks each year; the use of this instrument as a medium for payments between firms and its popularity among them is due, in particular, to the role played in France by suppliers' credit.

Commercial bills are issued in the form of bill of exchange statements (46.2 percent in 1987), for larger enterprises, or in conventional form (53.8 percent in 1987), particularly for small and medium-sized enterprises.

The system of bill of exchange statements (lettres de change-relevés-LCRs) and truncated promissory notes (billets à ordre-relevés-BORs) was designed to rationalise and automate the management of commercial bills. In addition to the usual features of the conventional bill of exchange or promissory note, these instruments include the debtor's banking identity; they are exchanged between banks not in paper-based form but on data media via the clearing computer. The debtor receives, in advance of each maturity, a list of the bills that he is required to pay. He issues his instructions by completing the statement and returning it to the bank at which payment is to be effected.

Furthermore, since November 3, 1987, conventional commercial bills bearing the debtor's banking identity can, if the jointly liable parties have no objection, be dematerialised. The instruments are then collected in the same manner as LCRs. As a result of this reform, the number of bills exchanged on data media rose from 46.2 percent in 1987 to 74 percent in 1988.

Commercial bills are settled between banks two days after exchange in the clearing house and five days after exchange via the computer clearing center; the period for presentation via the clearing computer will be reduced when the Interbank Teleclearing System comes into operation (see Section 2 below on exchange circuits).

In principle, operations are free for the drawee of a bill of exchange or the maker of a promissory note unless the paying bank provides additional services. Commission is charged to the collector, however; this is set at a level that will favor the automated forms.

### (iii) Credit transfers

Credit transfers are second only to cheques in terms of the number of transactions to which they give rise, which totaled 1.2 billion in 1987; they accounted for 16.8 percent of exchanges. These figures relate to both bank and postal credit transfers.[14] This instrument is used mainly by businesses, public bodies, and public authorities.

When credit transfers are used on a one-off basis—e.g., by businesses to pay their suppliers, by the Treasury's branch offices or when they are of a financial nature—paper-based media are the most frequently used. However, credit transfers of a recurring nature are largely automated; this applies particularly to the payment of salaries and pensions, for which businesses frequently submit their instructions on a magnetic medium obtained as a by-product of their accounting.

The trend towards the ever greater automation of credit transfers that has prevailed for several years is continuing. At present almost 90 percent of transactions are automated.

Whether exchanged in paper or automated form, credit transfers are settled on the day on which they are presented, with the exception, however, of fixed-date credit transfers, which may be presented two or three days prior to interbank settlement.

Ordinary credit transfers, whether bank or postal, are free of charge for the beneficiary and the ordering customer, although the latter may have to bear any ancillary costs, such as the cost of transmission by telex or telegram. A commission payable to the destination bank is levied on fixed-date credit transfers when they pass through the clearing computer.

---

[14]Credit transfers account for a large proportion of all deposit money instruments in value terms (63.4 percent), but this figure is hardly representative since it has not always been possible to separate commercial transactions clearly from cash management operations, which are substantial in value terms.

To encourage the use of automated credit transfers, the banking industry is taking steps to improve the service for both issuers and beneficiaries. At the beginning of 1987, it created the fixed-date credit transfer, which is designed to guarantee execution within a maximum period from the date of exchange in the computer clearing center; this makes it possible to reduce the uncertainty currently surrounding other credit transfers as regards the time of execution.

As of January 3, 1989, the guarantee of availability of funds for the account of beneficiaries on the first working day after interbank settlement will be extended to cover all automated credit transfers; i.e., the beneficiary's bank will make the information available to its customer and take the corresponding operation into account.

The automation of credit transfers is also tending to involve telecommunications, thereby giving birth to new forms of "teletransfer," which can be initiated by a business or from terminals accessible to the general public, such as ATMs or videotex; the use of transfers of this kind is likely to expand significantly.

### (iv) Direct debits and interbank payment orders

Created in 1967, the *direct debit* still occupies a relatively modest position, accounting for no more than 8.2 percent of the total number of transactions in deposit money. Direct debits are used by organisations with recurring claims to collect (electricity, gas, telephone, and water bills) and for the payment of monthly income tax, for instance.

In spite of the advantages of this instrument for the banks (the processing cost is low because the instrument is fully automated), for the businesses issuing it (ease of accounting) and even for individuals (considerable simplification of the actual act of payment), its use has not spread as rapidly as had been expected at the outset. It is for this reason that various measures were taken in October 1985, to stimulate the use of this instrument, such as the creation of "accelerated" direct debits that are settled more quickly than ordinary ones and the banking system's adoption of a post-debit regularisation procedure, which in certain circumstances allows account holders who contest the validity of the payment to have the account entry reversed.

Before sending the direct debit to his bank for collection, the issuer sends the debtor an invoice notifying him of the amount of the debit and the date on which it will be executed so that he can ensure that sufficient funds are in the account or object, as appropriate.

Direct debits are channeled via the computer clearing centers if they are the subject of "official" interbank exchanges, but they may also be exchanged between banks direct. Settlement occurs two or four days after exchange at the computer clearing center, depending whether they are "accelerated" or ordinary items. The collection of most ordinary direct debits gives rise to the payment of commission by the issuing creditor to the presenting bank, which passes part on to the paying bank. "Accelerated" direct debits are subject to a specific commission at a higher rate than that levied on ordinary items.

The *interbank payment order* (titre interbancaire de paiement—TIP), which was created in February 1988 to replace universal payment orders, differs from the direct debit insofar as the debtor is expected, as in the case of cheques, to consent to the funding of each operation. To do so, he must sign the TIP form sent to him by his creditor, which is then processed automatically at an authorised center.

The OCR records of the data appearing on the interbank payment orders are subsequently presented to the clearing computer. The records are channeled to the debtors' banks to enable them to debit their customers' accounts automatically without having to check the payment orders, which are kept by the authorised centers.

This new instrument is practical from the point of view of the debtor, who maintains complete control over the operation, simple and efficient from that of the creditor because it enables collections to be rationalised and optimised, and productive for the banks because it is suited to complete automation. A modern payment medium, the interbank payment order combines the advantages of the direct debit and cheque without having any of their drawbacks; it is expected gradually to replace certain payments made using cheques over distances, and it is likely to become totally paperless with the development of telepayment techniques.

*(c) Transactions by card*

*(i) Main types of card in use*

Three main types of card are used in France:

▶ *Bank cards,* issued by credit institutions individually or under the auspices of an interbank organisation (the Cartes Bancaires Group) to holders of accounts with the issuing bank. At the end of 1987, a total of 16.4 million interbank cards, called Cartes Bancaires, were in circulation.[15]

▶ *International credit cards* issued by bodies that do not manage deposits but theoretically have the status of banks (within the meaning of the Banking Law of 1984), which authorises them, *ipso facto,* to issue payment media.

▶ In-house cards (18 million in 1988) issued by retailers or providers of services to offer credit facilities to their customers, who arrange for repayment through the debiting of their bank accounts, to which the card issuer does not have direct access. They also have a commercial function and serve to gain customer loyalty.

In France, if in-house cards are not intended for exclusive use with the organisation issuing them, they are subject to the Banking Law, i.e., their issuers must have the status of credit institutions—or use the services of a credit institution—as they alone are authorised to issue payment media.

The remarks that follow relate only to bank cards, which are used for the bulk of payments by card and most withdrawals from cash dispensers.

*(ii) National System for Payments by Card*

Banks affiliated with the two major bank card networks (Carte Bleue and Crédit Agricole Group, Crédit Mutuel) signed an agreement in July 1984, to develop a National System for Payments by Card.

The work of designing the system has been carried out by an economic interest grouping (the Cartes Bancaires Group established in December 1984) and is still under way.

*Card characteristics*

Most of the cards distributed are of the conventional type with magnetic stripes; the remainder (around 1.1 million at the end of the first half of 1988) also contain a microprocessor (chip cards).

Mixed cards are already in use in some regions (all of Brittany and parts of Provence Côte d'Azur) and will become more widespread. By the end of 1988, there should be 2 million in circulation, the magnetic stripe card being replaced by the mixed card at the time of annual renewal in the priority areas.

*Payments at retail outlets* (statistics as of year-end 1987)

In 1987, a total of 530 million payments were made by bank card, 7.9 percent of the number of transactions in deposit money. There are 16.4 million cards in circulation that can be used to pay for purchases at 420,000 French retail outlets affiliated to the

---

[15]The number of bank cards giving customers exclusive access to the services of a particular institution is estimated at approximately 8 million.

system. Approximately 7.5 million of these cards[16] are affiliated to VISA or Master-Card, thereby also enabling their use abroad.

Businesses affiliated to the system are guaranteed payment on certain conditions (verification that the card has not been stopped and prior authorisation from an authorisation center in the case of payments above a set threshold).

Collections are currently the responsibility of interbank processing centers.

Cardholders' accounts are debited either immediately after each transaction or "off-line," in which case they are summarised at the end of each month.[17]

Cardholders pay the issuing institution an annual subscription, which varies according to the functions the card can perform (simple cash withdrawals, national payments, international payments). Retailers, for their part, are charged a commission in proportion to the value of the transaction. It is negotiated freely between the bank and the customer.

An interbank scale of charges has been introduced that is independent of the foregoing commission. It consists of a commission paid by the retailer's bank to the cardholder's bank that provides the payment guarantee. This so-called interchange commission is shortly to be graduated in such a way that in principle it takes account of the level of equipment security.

### Electronic payments

In the main, these consist of payments effected by means of a Carte Bancaire (with a stripe or microprocessor) issued by a bank belonging to the Cartes Bancaires Group. The corresponding network comprises 70,000 electronic payment terminals, which gave rise to 292 million transactions in 1987. Under the terms of individual agreements concluded between the Cartes Bancaires Group and the issuers of in-house cards, a number of these terminals allow payments to be made by both Cartes Bancaires and in-house cards.

Finally, there are also some terminals specifically designed only to accept in-house cards issued in particular by large retailers.

### Future developments

Motivated primarily by a desire to reduce card fraud, the main work being undertaken by the banks within the Cartes Bancaires Group is currently directed towards introducing the chip card nationwide (between 5 and 6 million cards should have been issued by the end of 1989 and nationwide coverage completed by the end of 1990); designing a network for routing authorisation requests and responses; graduating the guarantee level in proportion to the fraud; the use of techniques enabling the confidential code to be checked (chip cards or magnetic-stripe cards checked with the aid of hybrid circuits).

### (d) Intrabank networks accessible to customers

They relate primarily to:

▶ Services offered by ATMs; requests for cheque books, teletransfers between two accounts of the same customer at the same bank, account inquiries, and so forth, which are generally available only to customers of the particular bank (or network or group).

▶ Cash withdrawals by means of cards that are not of an interbank kind.

▶ Telematic services (see the following section).

---

[16]Of the 7.5 million international cards, 120,000 are "top of the range" cards.

[17]French bank cards were designed from the outset as debit cards, not credit cards. This characteristic is tending to become blurred, in that banks are increasingly offering customers credit lines on accounts debited by means of bank card transactions.

*(e) New payment methods*

The main innovations concern:

▶ Calls from public payphones. Almost a quarter of the public telephone boxes are operated exclusively by means of memory cards,[18] cards issued by the Postal Administration (prepaid cards or subscriber cards, where call charges are added to the subscriber's telephone bill) or Cartes Bancaires.

▶ *Telematic services to individuals and enterprises.* The 3.4 million Minitel videotex terminals currently installed (as of year-end 1987) enable their users to access the home-banking services offered by most of the large banks. There were 300,000 individual and professional subscribers to "banking and financial" services at the beginning of 1987. Services aimed at the mass public mainly allow users to consult account balances and review recent movements, to consolidate different accounts, and to obtain financial and stock exchange information. Services for businesses cover a wider field, including treasury management aids (remote loading of banking transactions onto the bank treasurer's data-processing equipment, execution of interbank movements between predetermined accounts of the same company).

Whether intended for individuals or businesses, these services are charged according to the length of connection time and are also subject to a monthly subscription charge.

Some retailers or creditors have combined videotex and the payment card to foster the development of "teletransactions."

The use of the Minitel terminal in combination with the magnetic-stripe bank card to effect a debit is accepted by some organisations such as mail order companies, but it is not satisfactory from the point of view of security. The chip card, on the other hand, is likely to open up an entire range of new operations, provided it is read in a card reader connected to the Minitel terminal. This question is currently the subject of a number of studies, in particular regarding the introduction of "telepayment" based on a secure telematic system using a microprocessor card.

## 2. Exchange Circuits Within the Banking System

*(a) Intrabank or group networks*

Most of the large and medium-sized banking institutions have telecommunication networks, which, in the case of groups or federations, often consist of two levels: one local and intrabank, the other national linking the various member institutions. The networks generally handle the computerised records of cheques drawn on the branches of the bank or group because most of the large banks have adopted internal cheque truncation procedures. The networks also carry accounting data on payments to the bank or group as a result of interbank exchanges and automated instruments internal to the bank or group.

By way of indication, the proportion of instruments involving two accounts (that of the payer and that of the payee) in the books of the same bank is far from negligible, being estimated to account for 17 percent of cheques and direct debits and 31 percent of credit transfers in terms of the number of instruments issued.

By contrast, automated exchanges between banks in the same group concern a relatively small number of payments, approximately 2.5 percent of automated credit transfers and less than 4 percent of direct debits.

---

[18]A large proportion of these cards are technologically specific to the payphone equipment. The eventual aim is to permit the use of "bank memory cards" in public payphones; this is already possible in some parts of the country.

*(b) Interbank circuits and networks*

The general organisation of funds transfers is based on two types of exchange: those using and those not using official circuits.

The first type use the clearing houses, the computer clearing centers, the regional cheque record exchange centers, the processing centers of the Cartes Bancaires Group, the SAGITTAIRE system, and the Interbank Teleclearing System; these handle the bulk of the instruments exchanged among the banks (75.1 percent in terms of the number of operations). On the other hand, a smaller, but by no means negligible, proportion of operations (24.9 percent) is not channeled over the official circuits; 43.3 percent of the total number of credit transfers exchanged, 38.8 percent of commercial bills, 28 percent of direct debits, and 21 percent of cheques are involved in these nonofficial exchanges.

A diagram of exchange circuits is appended to this chapter, which deals only with "official" exchanges.

These are of three types:

▶ Traditional paper-based exchanges via the clearing houses.

▶ Conventional automated exchanges on magnetic media; these involve the computer clearing centers and the regional cheque record exchange centers.

▶ Exchanges based on the use of telecommunications via the SAGITTAIRE system and the Interbank Teleclearing System.

*(i) Clearing houses*

Following a number of reforms to simplify administrative procedures, official exchanges of paper-based instruments—mainly cheques, credit transfers, and commercial bills—take place via the 104 principal clearing houses:

▶ Clearing House of the Bankers of Paris (Paris and adjacent départements).

▶ 102 provincial clearing houses in the capitals of départements and certain other important towns where a branch of the Bank of France is located.

▶ Monaco.

A total of 3.5 billion items with an aggregate value of Fr.fr. 39,654 billion were presented in 1987.

Any institution on which cheques are drawn or at which commercial bills are domiciled is, in accordance with regulatory provisions, bound to participate in the clearing houses, if necessary through the intermediary of a representative. In practice this means the banks and savings banks, the Treasury, the Postal Cheque Centers, and the Bank of France.

The clearing house sessions are held each bank working day, between 11 A.M. and 12 noon for the provincial clearing houses, and between 9:15 A.M. and 4 P.M. for the Clearing House of the Bankers of Paris.

Some transactions (credit transfers) are settled the same day; others (cheques and commercial bills) are only settled at the end of an agreed period.

At each clearing house the members' debit or credit balances, calculated at the end of each session, are entered each day in the accounts administered locally by the Bank of France. The sums accruing from credit balances do not become the property of the members until the end of the day and then only if the debtor members can cover their debtor position the same day.

In practice, all payment instruments must be presented to a specific clearing house, depending on the catchment area. However, in the case of cheques, which constitute 97.4 percent of the instruments exchanged, a specific procedure has been in operation since 1984.

By virtue of this agreed procedure, known as the "agreement on the exchange of outside-area cheques," the bank presenting the outside-area cheque can exchange it at the clearing house of its choice, irrespective of the place of payment; this procedure enables cheques to be presented closest to their point of encashment; it leaves the drawee bank to decide on the best way to route them to the paying bank, for instance, by truncation of the cheque forms between its own services.

Naturally, the period allowed for settlement has been designed to offset this shifting of the administrative burden to the drawee bank (settlement within three days instead of one).

Where a bank is a signatory to the agreement on the exchange of outside-area cheques but is not represented at any of the 104 clearing houses, it can ask the Bank of France to receive cheques on its behalf and to forward them to it. This service is performed by the Joint Collection Service, which acts as a simple intermediary between the presenting bank and the drawee bank and does not guarantee the finality of the payment.

The major credit institutions participate in the exchange of outside-area cheques; in 1987, 613 million cheques were exchanged in this way, equal to 18 percent of all cheques cleared.

### (ii) Computer clearing centers

The computer clearing centers, which have a nationwide coverage, are operating in nine cities: Paris, Lyon, Strasbourg, Rennes, Nantes, Lille, Marseille, Bordeaux, and Toulouse. The first entered service in January 1969, and the last in May 1985. Apart from cheque records, all types of instruments for which interbank exchanges have been automated are eligible (credit transfers, direct debits, interbank payment orders, automated commercial bills, bank card transactions). The first two account for 80 percent of the number of transactions exchanged.

In 1987, the centers handled almost 1.3 billion items with a total value of Fr.fr. 3,596 billion, equivalent to 22.6 percent of all official interbank exchanges in terms of number and 8.3 percent in terms of value.

In recent years, the clearing computers have been interconnected by telecommunication links for the transmission of certain specific operations (out-of-town transactions whose settlement has thus been accelerated); nevertheless, the overall design of the system is that of a central interbank organisation receiving magnetic media from presenters, sorting data according to destination bank, and forwarding them to the latter on magnetic media.

In March 1988, the 990 participants fell into two categories: direct members (50 institutions), which present and receive operations directly, and sub-participants (940 institutions), which present and receive operations via a direct member. A number of institutions (432) are not affiliated owing to their low level of operations and do not participate in exchanges; the Bank of France handles operations on their behalf.

The Bank of France operates the computer clearing centers.

In Paris two daily sessions are held:

▶ The first session, called the "anticipated session," is held between 8.30 and 10 P.M. on the day preceding settlement day.

▶ The session on settlement day itself, called the "supplementary session," takes place from 11 A.M. to 1.30 P.M. on the day in question.

The "anticipated session" enables non-urgent bulk transactions to be cleared, whereas the "supplementary session" is designed to deal with small quantities of urgent transactions (credit transfers in particular).

In the provinces a single session is held at 7.30 A.M.

The balance resulting from operations is settled via members' accounts at the Bank of France, either the same day, in the case of so-called sight operations, or at the scheduled settlement date, in that of so-called term operations (which are presented several days in advance of their settlement date). The operations presented or received by sub-participants are not itemised for accounting purposes; they are included in the settlements recorded on behalf of the members representing them, it being up to the latter to pass on the amounts accruing from such operations to their sub-participants.

### (iii) Regional cheque record exchange centers

Situated in nine cities, of which eight have a computer clearing center,[19] the regional cheque record exchange centers enable members to exchange cheque data on magnetic media, the cheque forms being retained by the presenting bank. Apart from the Bank of France, only banks with a regional or local structure are members of these centers, which handled only 2.6 percent of the number of cheque payments exchanged by the banks via official circuits in 1987.

The Bank of France operates the regional centers.

### (iv) SAGITTAIRE

Relying entirely on the use of telecommunications, SAGITTAIRE is a national interbank settlement system designed to complete, in francs, operations connected with international transfers. In the final stage, the Bank of France undertakes the daily clearing of transactions, on completion of which it credits or debits the accounts opened in its books on behalf of the institutions concerned.

As with the other clearing systems, the transactions, which are irrevocable from the moment they are received by the bank, are deemed final only at the end of the accounting day and may be canceled in the event of default by a participant. Having come into operation on October 16, 1984, the system is managed by the Bank of France and had 58 members in December 1988. The service is open five days a week, from 8 A.M. to 5.30 P.M.

In 1988, 1,381,041 SAGITTAIRE messages were received involving a total of Fr.fr. 12,800 billion.

Payments effected via SAGITTAIRE take the form of messages conforming to S.W.I.F.T. standards; they also meet specific requirements aimed at permitting the complete automation of processing by the system manager and facilitating automated processing by recipient member banks.

Payments are booked at various times. Data are received from members in real time, with the accounting entry itself being made on the value date; this appears on debit orders and credit advices and may be day D, D + 1, or D + 2.

In all, 75 percent of messages relate to bank transfers and the remainder to customer transactions. Although 41 banks are linked up to receive payment messages and 34 to issue them, four institutions alone account for 65 percent of payments issued and 50 percent of those received.

### (v) Interbank Teleclearing System

In 1983, the Working Party on Payment Media approved a proposal from the Bank of France to establish a national automated clearing system based on telematic exchanges. Until then, automated exchanges had been based mainly on the exchange of magnetic media; by reason of its centralised nature the arrangement precluded direct links between members.

The main objectives of the project were:
▶ To cut routing and processing times for interbank operations.
▶ To permit and facilitate "continuous" exchanges.
▶ To reduce the cost of exchanges.

---

[19]The ninth cheque record exchange center is to be installed in Lyons by the end of 1988.

The work on designing the system is being carried out within the Interbank Teleclearing System Group, which was set up in June 1983.[20]

The Interbank Teleclearing System (Système Interbancaire de Télécompensation —SIT) is a general purpose exchange system designed to carry most bulk automated operations, i.e., those that can be channeled via the computer clearing centers, which it will eventually replace, and cheque records. It was originally intended that the system should carry 3.6 billion transactions per year once it was fully operational, but this figure is likely to be raised to take account of the inclusion of cheque records, which are expected to increase substantially in number.[21]

Its overall architecture and mode of operation are based mainly on:

▶ Direct and continuous exchanges of single messages each covering a whole series of transactions between members.

▶ Automatic transmission of a payment message to the accounting center by the issuer after the authentication of each exchange; the accounting center is responsible for recording the messages exchanged and calculates each SIT working day the balance on each member's account, which it transmits to the Bank of France for entry in its books.

▶ Access to the system via terminals that support members' issuing and/or receiving software.

▶ The use of joint centers: the accounting center managed by the Bank of France (described above), the backup center and the management center (the role of the last being to supervise the working of the system).

▶ The use of the TRANSPAC network for communications between terminals and with the joint centers.

▶ The obligation on each member to accept traffic addressed to it.

▶ Operation 22 hours a day (from 8 A.M. one day to 6 A.M. the next), six days a week (from 8 A.M. on Monday until 6 A.M. on Sunday).

Participation in SIT is open only to credit institutions within the meaning of the law of January 24, 1984, on the activity and supervision of credit institutions, plus the Bank of France, the central banks of the overseas departments and territories, the Treasury regarding its banking activities, the financial services of the Postal Administration and the Deposit and Consignment Office, all of which are the paying agents for payment media passing through the exchange system.

Implementation will be in three phases, of which only the first has so far been commenced:

▶ The pre-network pilot scheme, which began operations on May 16, 1988; using a small number of terminals, it aims to test the working of the system unladen, in other words without operation accounting.

▶ The network pilot scheme, which should begin at year-end 1989; its purpose is to carry out trials in real time, including accounting but with a low throughput (up to about 5 percent of potential traffic).

▶ Full implementation, which should be under way by early 1990 and enable the SIT to carry 90% of its potential traffic by 1991.

*(vi) Securities clearing and settlement systems*

The need to assure domestic and foreign investors that their transactions are executed securely has led the Paris market to equip itself with systems guaranteeing simultaneous settlement and delivery after verification that the contracting institutions have sufficient cover on *securities* and *cash* accounts, respectively:

---

[20]The Bank of France is an ex officio member of the decision-making bodies as well as being a member of the Group.

[21]See Section IV for general remarks concerning the National Cheque Record Exchange System.

*The SATURNE system* (automated system for the standardised processing of settlements of negotiable claims), launched in September 1988 by the Bank of France, chiefly handles operations in Treasury bills (with some 400 participants and a volume of Fr.fr. 435 billion).

Current accounts in Treasury bills and cash accounts are opened in the books of the Bank of France, which verifies adequacy of cover during clearing (there are at least four clearing sessions a day), thereby enhancing the liquidity of the market (daily transaction volume of Fr.fr. 10 to 60 billion).

With SATURNE it is possible to register and monitor the execution of bilaterally agreed securities lending operations.

In due course this system, which already extends to bills issued by the specialised financial institutions (Crédit National, for example) and—since the beginning of 1989 — to finance companies, could handle operations in certificates of deposit and commercial paper, should the authorities decide, and the issuers agree, to de-materialise these instruments.

*The RELIT project* (securities settlement and delivery) will guarantee the secure execution of stock exchange transactions by bringing into operation a unique clear-ing system designed to carry out settlement and delivery of securities five days from the date of the trade, and which will replace the current bilateral arrangements.

This system, which is scheduled to come into operation in 1990, will be based on automated market procedures that will make it possible, in particular, to match trades between parties and to effect clearing of completed transactions before the balances are entered in the books of SICOVAM (securities accounts) and of the Bank of France (cash accounts).

Settlement of RELIT operations will be irrevocable to guarantee simultaneity with the delivery of securities. On the other hand, institutions may, if necessary, be required to deposit collateral with the central bank, whose role as the focal point for cash settlements serves to limit systemic risk.

In a second phase, transactions denominated in foreign currencies will be executed via the same system.

## IV   GENERAL REMARKS

Two major issues of current concern to the banking industry are being examined by the Working Party on Payment Media; they relate to:
▶ Generalisation of the procedure for the exchange of cheque records.
▶ The risks arising from the development of electronic funds transfer systems.

### 1. Generalisation of the Procedure for the Exchange of Cheque Records and the Pricing of Payment Instruments

The creation of an interbank system for the exchange of cheque records was one of the first issues to be examined by the Working Party on Payment Media. Until recently a number of institutions had opposed the adoption of such a procedure, and the scheme was eventually implemented only as part of local initiatives by regional banks; it therefore handles only a small fraction of interbank exchanges of cheques. However, in view of recent developments, and especially the creation of the SIT, the issue has been broached again and there now seems to be a consensus in favor of exchanging cheque records nationwide. The future system, which will be called the National Cheque Record Exchange System (Système National d'Echanges d'Images-Chèques — SNEIC), will use the SIT.

In some places, a residual volume of bilateral exchanges will probably continue to be justified. They will be organised within the regional exchange centers, which by definition will be few in number and are likely to remain of marginal importance.

Although the technical feasibility of the system poses no serious difficulty, its economic and financial aspects raise a number of problems:

▶ The dematerialisation of collections will necessarily be accompanied by a shortening of execution and settlement times, but this will affect institutions differently, according to whether they participate mainly as presenters or as payers; it is therefore to be feared that the balance of interbank exchanges will be upset.

▶ The terms applied to customers will inevitably tend to reflect the future characteristics of interbank collections. The accounts of drawers (mainly individuals) will certainly be debited earlier, but the period before crediting to beneficiaries will also be reduced; the impact of this change, which will primarily affect interest-bearing accounts and those subject to very tight cash management, will be considerable.

▶ It is feared that the status of the cheque may become perpetuated or consolidated due to the aforementioned improvements, which, together with exemption from charges, may give this instrument an optimal quality/price ratio to the detriment of entirely automated payment media that the banks are seeking to promote (direct debits, interbank payment orders, credit cards, and so forth).

In short, the establishment of the SNEIC cannot be divorced from the broader question of the charges for banking services, since it jeopardises the float stemming from cheque collection operations, an important element in bank liquidity and hence in banks' income.

This fundamental issue, which has been raised several times in the past but never resolved, will be the focal point of the political decisions to be made in the light of this document.

### 2.  Reliability of Electronic Funds Transfer Systems

The development of funds transfer systems based on computers and telecommunications is likely to produce a number of substantial advantages, but it also raises problems on account of the risks inherent in such systems.

The implementation of "continuous" systems will thus make it possible to lengthen the time-scale for exchanges, close accounts later than in conventional systems, and increase the number of direct participants; but on the other hand, there is a danger that the changes will delay realisation that a bank has a liquidity problem, given the differences in the size and quality of banks. Moreover, with a larger number of operations and more rapid exchanges, the principle of revocability that prevails in conventional exchanges becomes difficult to apply in a "continuous" system, where it appears to be out of the question to interrupt the flow of data and recalculate accounting days *a posteriori*.

The modernisation of operations also calls for a review of the rules on the date of crediting funds.

The Bank of France and the banking industry are examining these issues and giving thought to the measures to be taken so that this new technological advance can be exploited safely and reliably for the parties involved.

## V   CONCLUSIONS

The current trend reveals a number of significant traits:

▶ The banks' determination to reduce the cost of managing payment media, which still represents a substantial part of their overall costs despite their efforts to raise productivity over many years. This is reflected in their sustained campaign to encourage the use of the most economic payment instruments and circuits.

▶ The development of alternatives to the cheque, paperless as far as possible; these may be electronic payments by card for local transactions or formulas such as credit transfers, direct debits, and telematic home-banking operations for payments over distances.

▶ The rationalisation and modernisation of exchange circuits with the establishment of systems based exclusively on computers and telecommunications to handle the bulk of interbank exchanges; hence, the SIT (Interbank Teleclearing System) should carry not only all operations currently channeled via the computer clearing centers but also most cheques, which would have to be converted into electronic cheque records in the context of the SNEIC (National Cheque Record Exchange System).

▶ The security of payment systems, a fundamental objective present in all projects. This constant concern applies both at the level of payment instruments and at that of interbank exchange systems. In the first case, the most significant example relates to the National System for Payments by Card, entailing the creation of a network to route authorisation requests from retailers and the associated replies and above all the use of a microprocessor in the card. In the second case, it is the computerisation of networks that poses the problem of security in a new form, both technical (network penetration risks, breakdowns) and financial.

▶ Competition and cooperation between banks continue to overlap considerably; competition extends far beyond the technical sphere, as illustrated by the establishment of the National System for Payments by Card.

Competition is emerging in new forms; under the combined effect of deregulation and technological progress, which is tending to take away the local character of operations if effected by telecommunications means, many nonbanking enterprises are in a strong position in relation to banks and will tend to play a heightened role in the future development of payment systems.

Appendix

**The General Organisation of Funds Transfers**
**Present Circuits**

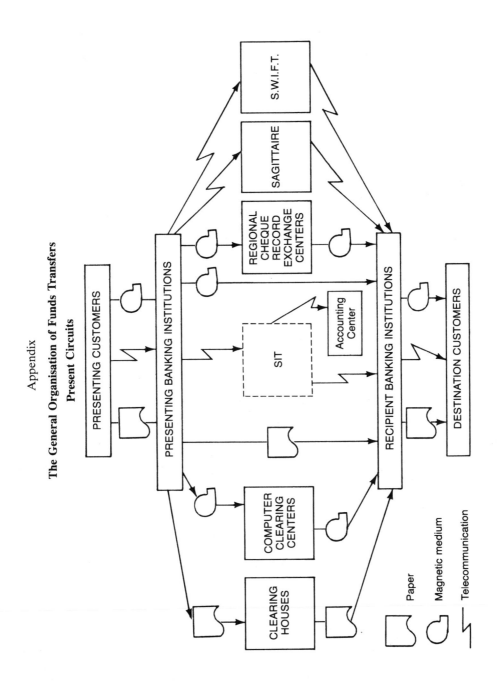

# 4 GERMANY

# Germany

## I  INTRODUCTION

In the Federal Republic of Germany—as in other western industrialised countries—enterprises and households hold most of their liquid assets in the form of sight deposits with credit institutions, i.e., in the form of deposit money, rather than as cash. At the end of 1987, domestic nonbanks' holdings of deposit money were more than twice the amount of bank notes and coin in circulation in the nonbank sector (DM 266 billion compared with DM 124 billion). Almost all large transactions are effected on a cashless basis by means of deposit money (approximately 6.3 billion cashless payments with a total value of DM 17,848 billion in 1987), whereas cash continues to predominate in small transactions effected by households (an estimated 40 billion cash payments with a total value of approximately DM 1,000 billion). The instrument that traditionally dominates cashless payments is the credit transfer, which accounts for about 55 percent of the total number of transactions, followed by the direct debit (36 percent), whereas the cheque, with a share of approximately 9 percent, is relatively unimportant. Other payment media, including credit cards and debit cards, play a comparatively minor role.

The number of cashless payments has increased steadily in recent years (by almost half since 1977; see Appendix). However, the amount of cash in circulation and hence the number and value of cash transactions have also increased steadily over the same period. As the annual growth rates of cashless payments have slowed in the last few years to slightly over 2 percent, their impact on cash transactions has become negligible. This will only change if, in addition to the small number of current POS applications, electronic checkouts accepting multiple payment cards (e.g., the Eurocheque card) in the future replace cash transactions to a greater degree. However, with ever-higher fees for cashless payments and the increasing installation of ATMs, the use of cash for small transactions has tended to become more attractive in the last few years. In view of the fees envisaged by the banking industry for a future bank POS system, traders have for years openly declared their lack of interest in replacing cash. The low number of cheque transactions relative to other countries is not by itself a sufficient incentive for retailers to introduce POS systems.

The high cost of processing payment transactions is prompting the banking industry to automate to a constantly increasing extent. In the case of cashless payments, this is reflected in the growing proportion of transactions that are processed electronically rather than using paper media. Almost two-thirds of all payments initiated by nonbanks are now exchanged electronically between banks, either on data media (magnetic tape, diskette, or cassette) or by means of data telecommunication and, upon receipt, are automatically booked through to the customer's account and printed out in the customer's statement of account. Most of these payments are already submitted in electronic form for collection or for transfer by the initiators themselves, particularly when regular payments are involved (e.g., standing orders, salary transfers, payments to utilities by means of direct debits). The banks are also making it possible for their corporate customers to submit single payments to them in a paperless form, e.g., on diskette. Private customers can use either a videotex machine (home banking) or, and this is more common, a multipur-pose bank teller machine for the paperless initiation of credit transfers. For other payments that continue to be submitted by customers in paper form, there are agreed procedures in the banking industry for integrating them into electronic interbank payments (e.g., the so-called electronic payment transfer (EPT) procedure for transfers; cheque truncation). The paperless procedure enables payments to be processed far more cheaply and rapidly than does the paper-based alternative, which involves the processing of vouchers by machine-reading the code lines (OCR-A characters). Wherever the speed of a payment is a factor, as is the case with account management and transfers in general, the banks are using data telecommunication rather than physical media both within their respective networks and also in-creasingly in dealings with their customers.

# II   INSTITUTIONAL FRAMEWORK

### 1. Institutions Handling Payments

In Germany, the responsibility for providing the economy and the population with cash and for handling cashless payments lies with the credit institutions, the post office, and the central bank.

Under the Banking Law, the execution of cashless payments and their settlement (giro business) is a banking activity. This requires a license from the Federal Banking Supervisory Office except in cases where special laws (i.e., the Bundesbank Law, the Post Office Law) authorise individual institutions to execute payment transactions. The problem of the handling of cashless transactions by nonbanks hence does not arise at all. At the end of 1987, a total of approximately 58 million giro accounts were held with banks and postal giro offices, via which some 6.3 billion cashless transac-tions were executed in 1987; 92 percent of giro accounts were held with banks, the remaining 8 percent being postal accounts.

Most of the 4,543 credit institutions (with just under 40,000 branches—excluding post offices and sub-post offices) are actively involved in handling payments. They belong, with few exceptions, to one of the following three banking categories, which form separate giro networks based on internally agreed handling and clearing procedures (see Section III.2.*(b)*):

▶ Commercial banks, the three largest of which (the "Grossbanken," i.e., Deutsche, Dresdner, and Commerzbank) have each set up an extensive giro network linking their branches.

▶ Savings banks (the overwhelming majority of them public-law institutions), whose operations are restricted to a particular locality or region. Together with their 12 central institutions, the 586 savings banks form a uniform giro organisation,within which most transactions between savings banks are processed.

▶ Cooperative banks, whose operations are also restricted to a particular locality or region. Like the savings banks, the 3,476 cooperative banks, together with their six central institutions, form a uniform giro organisation.

The postal giro offices form a further giro network for handling the cashless transactions of their account holders. Since the credit institutions also hold postal giro accounts, the postal giro offices to a certain extent constitute interfaces for payments to and from the bank networks. However, the most important link for transactions between the bank and post office giro networks is the Bundesbank's giro network (see Sections II.2.*(b)* and III.2.*(c)*).

### 2. The Role of the Central Bank in Payment Transactions

*(a) The role of the central bank in cash payments*

Under the Deutsche Bundesbank Law, the Bundesbank (the central bank) is required to regulate the volume of money in circulation, and accordingly to provide the economy with bank notes and coin in the denominations required. For this purpose the note-issuing prerogative was conferred on the Bundesbank, under which it is responsible for producing, supplying, and regularly renewing bank notes, replacing damaged notes, calling in notes, and checking the circulation of payment media for counterfeit money. The Bundesbank does not, however, operate its own note-printing works. The production of coins (minting prerogative) is, on the other hand, the responsibility of the federal government (Ministry of Finance); the Bundesbank acquires the coin needed for circulation from the federal government at its nominal value.

In 1987, the Bundesbank dispensed DM 277 billion to the credit institutions and the post office via its branch network to provide the economy with cash and took back from them DM 264 billion. With currency in circulation totaling approximately DM 136 billion at the end of 1987, this means that money returns to the central bank roughly twice a year.

The bank notes that return to the central bank are checked; counterfeit, damaged, and dirty bank notes are rejected and—with the exception of counterfeit notes—destroyed. Likewise, counterfeit coins and coins called in or those no longer fit for circulation are withdrawn. Machines are increasingly being used by the central bank to check the completeness, genuineness, and fitness for circulation of notes and to sort them accordingly. For this purpose bank notes have been designed to be machine-compatible.

*(b) The role of the central bank in cashless payments*

The central bank is required by law to ensure that banking arrangements are made to handle domestic payments. The central bank fulfills its statutory responsibility by providing the banks and the post office with a giro network, in the form of its clearing facilities, which has a neutral impact on competition (see Section III.2.*(b)* for details). The central bank's giro network, which is composed of just under 200 branch offices and 11 computer centers, constitutes the link between the giro centers of the banking industry and the post office. The central bank also exerts a certain influence on the banks' terms for handling payments by means of its business conditions, its handling procedures, its debit and credit conditions, and its scale of charges. Through its participation in payments the Bundesbank aims, moreover, to encourage moves towards shorter processing times and to promote the further transition to rational, paperless handling procedures. It therefore seeks to ensure that its payment facilities remain attractive from a technical and organisational point of view and that they take account of recent developments.

The German credit institutions make extensive use of the central bank giro system, in particular for internetwork payments. In 1987, a total of 2,238 million credit transfers, cheques, and direct debits were transmitted via the Bundesbank's payment facilities, representing more than one-third of the payment orders received by the banks from customers. It is left to the credit institutions to decide whether and to what extent they route payments via the Bundesbank instead of within their own networks, and whether they use the central bank's local clearing or its intercity system. For its part, the central bank can regulate the extent of its participation via its fees and conditions, although traditionally it charges only for special services. For the smaller private commercial banks the central bank's giro network is virtually the only means available for executing certain payments to other credit institutions on behalf of their customers without having to depend on their competitors. As a rule, the total amounts or balances of bank customers' payments exchanged directly between credit institutions and the claims and liabilities arising from interbank payments are also settled (immediately and finally) in the books of the central bank, with which all the banks and the post office must hold part of their liquid reserves (minimum reserves).

In addition to the clearing and settlement function it performs for the banking industry, the central bank acts as the fiscal agent of the federal government and—to a limited extent—of the Länder, and handles their payments. In 1987, approximately 108 million credit transfers (in particular salaries, pensions, and social security payments) were executed and 48 million cheques and direct debits were collected on behalf of the federal government.

### 3. National Payment System Bodies

Subject to the provisions of Germany's antitrust legislation, the banking industry has for the past 30 years used the Management Working Party of the Central Credit Committee (ZKA) as a forum for coordinating organisational and technical procedures to ensure a cost-effective, rapid, and secure payment system. More recently, the post office also joined the committee. As a result of this coordinating activity, the handling of interbank payments, as well as of payments involving bank customers, has been standardised in a whole series of agreements. Without itself being a member of the Central Credit Committee, the Bundesbank plays an advisory, and at times also a guiding, role in its discussions. For instance, it chairs the Management Working Party's two sub-committees on "Automation" and "Security Procedures for Data Transmission." In addition, the Bundesbank has acceded to most of the agreements to ensure, in the interests of a rational payment system, that procedures are standardised and that vouchers and data records can be transmitted without difficulty from one network to another.

At the beginning of 1982, a national body called the Payment System Information Group (IZV) was set up on the initiative of the Bundesbank. The function of this body, which consists of high-ranking representatives from the central associations of the banking industry and the post office under the chairmanship of the Bundesbank, is to discuss fundamental and current issues concerning the development of cash and cashless payments and communications technology, and to exchange information on plans and intentions. Any suggestions made by the Payment System Information Group are then followed up by the Management Working Party.

In addition to the payment system bodies already mentioned, a private-sector institution called the Payment Systems Company (GZS) was set up by the banking industry in 1982; this company concerns itself primarily with the Eurocard and Eurocheque card systems and their further development (e.g., for POS payments at electronic check-outs in the retail trade; see Section III.1.*(c)*).

### 4. Legal Foundation for the Execution of Payments

The Banking Law specifies that the execution of cashless payments requires an appropriate license from the Federal Banking Supervisory Office. The central bank and the post office derive the authority to carry out payment transactions from the Bundesbank Law, and the Postal Administration and the Post Office Laws, respectively.

There are no specific laws governing the organisational and technical aspects of handling payments; these aspects are covered in general by the provisions of the Civil Code, in particular those concerning the law of agency. In addition, the provisions of the Cheques Law that relate to cheque collection must be complied with. To manage the high volume of payments efficiently, the agencies handling payments have formulated certain rules, within the framework laid down by law, on the execution of payments.

In particular:

▶ The relationship between the banks and the post office is regulated by agreements between the central associations of the banking industry, the Federal Ministry of Post and Telecommunications, and the central bank (see Section III).

▶ The relationship with bank customers is regulated by the general business conditions of the banks and the central bank, the user conditions of the post office, special regulations and notices, and standardised forms.

Any contractual or recommended uniform payment system arrangement must be reported to the Federal Cartels Office via the Federal Banking Supervisory Office and accompanied by an explanatory statement. These agencies have in each case to make sure that the contractual or recommended arrangements are not likely to result in undesirable developments from the banking supervisory point of view or in the excessive restriction of competition, and in particular that they will not place other participants in the payment system (especially bank customers) at an unfair disadvantage. If contractual agreements and recommendations are not reported, they remain inadmissible or without effect.

## III  PAYMENT SYSTEMS

### 1. Payment Media Available to Bank Customers

*(a) Cash payments*

In Germany, households make most of their payments for their daily needs in cash. The number of cash payments is estimated at 40 billion and their value at just under DM 1,000 billion, corresponding to 86 percent of all payment transactions in terms of number, but only 5 percent in terms of value.

Currency in circulation consists of bank notes in seven denominations (DM 5, 10, 20, 50, 100, 500, and 1,000) and federal coin in eight denominations (1, 2, 5, 10, and 50 Pfennig and DM 1, 2, and 5). There are, in addition, a small number of DM 10 coins, but since these are principally collectors' items, they only rarely turn up in payment transactions. Bank notes and coins are legal tender, although coins have to be accepted by the public only up to a certain amount. At the end of 1987, total currency in circulation—including cash on hand at banks—amounted to DM 136 billion, with bank notes accounting for DM 126 billion (92 percent and federal coin for DM 10 billion (8 percent). Cash on hand at banks amounted to DM 12 billion.

Cash payments are increasingly being automated in Germany. Vending machines for the sale of goods (e.g., cigarettes, provisions for journeys) outside shop opening hours and services (e.g., tickets for travellers, parking facilities) have been in operation for many years. Quite early on, the banking associations and the post office reached agreement on a uniform system of cash dispensers for the whole of the Federal Republic with a view to improving the service offered to customers and reducing the cost of cash withdrawals. By the end of 1987, the banks had installed a total of approximately 5,000 cash dispensers nationwide, which can be used to obtain cash by any of their own or their competitors' customers who are in possession of a magnetic-stripe Eurocheque card and a personal identification number (PIN). The number of these predominantly multipurpose cash dispensers is still rising steadily. To minimise losses in case dispensers are misused, Eurocheque cardholders may draw no more than DM 400 per day from dispensers installed at banks other than their own. All withdrawals are verified on-line against a register of cancelled cards and a register of transactions at the authentication centers of the central associations of the banking industry and the post office to prevent fraudulent withdrawals or other unacceptable transactions. These authentication centers are due to be interconnected by telecommunication means before the end of 1988. As an alternative, it will also be possible for authorisation to be granted by the bank with which cardholders have their account ("on the customer's account") instead of centrally. Withdrawals from cash dispensers are cleared under the normal direct debit procedure via the magnetic tape clearing (see Section III.1.*(b)*). The procedure is also gradually being extended to withdrawals made by German Eurocheque cardholders in other European countries and vice versa. In the future, the technical infrastructure is due to be expanded to include the authorisation of transactions using Eurocheque cards at electronic check-outs (POS procedure). (See Section III.1.*(c)*.)

*(b) Cashless payments*

In Germany, cashless payments are effected by means of credit transfers (55 percent of the total number of transactions in 1987), cheques (9 percent), and direct debits (36 percent). Other payment media, such as money orders and receipts, and also payments with credit and debit cards are relatively unimportant (accounting for less than 1 percent of transactions).

The *credit transfer* traditionally predominates in Germany, although the percentage of total payments for which it accounts is lower than it once was (in the savings bank sector it fell from 72 percent of customers' cashless payments in 1966 to 67 percent in 1972 and 53 percent in 1987). In the past few years, the credit transfer has reasserted itself; since 1983, it has accounted for an average of 55 percent of the total number of transactions effected by the banking industry as a whole. The earlier decline was attributable less to the banks, which essentially prefer the credit transfer as a means of maintaining liquidity, than to the economy's need to use other more appropriate payment methods, such as direct debits, for specific purposes.

A credit transfer is an order given by a customer to his bank to arrange for the sum of money indicated therein to be debited from his giro account and credited to the payee's bank account. Customers can also issue standing orders to their banks for regular payments to specific payees (e.g., rent to the landlord). The bank then undertakes to execute the credit transfer on the date specified. Frequently the payee sends the payer not only a request for payment (e.g., a premium invoice in the case of an insurance company and one of its policy holders) but also preprinted, precoded credit transfer forms indicating the payee bank's details, to which the payer simply has to add details of his account number and bank and his signature. If the payer does not have a giro account, he can pay in the requisite amount in cash at a bank or post office for transfer to the payee. An important factor for the recipient of a credit transfer is that—barring a few exceptions—the funds transferred are definitively and unconditionally available to him as soon as his account has been credited, and also that the transfer can no longer be reversed. With a cheque, on the other hand, this is only the case once the collection process initiated by the recipient of the cheque has been concluded, i.e., once a cheque has finally been debited from the account of the person who issued it.

Payers with EDP equipment may use only electronic data media (magnetic tape, or also diskettes or cassettes for smaller quantities) to submit regular bulk payments (e.g., wages, salaries, state social insurance payments) to the banks for execution via the paperless exchange of data media (magnetic tape clearing). The proportion of paperless credit transfers has continued to increase appreciably in the past few years. In 1987, approximately 1.7 billion credit transfers, or just under half of the total, were made in a paperless form. The remaining 1.8 billion transfers, in particular single transfer orders from corporate customers without appropriate EDP equipment and from banks' private customers, were issued in paper form and were then largely processed in that form by means of the optical reading of their OCR-A codelines. However, the banks have for years been trying to incorporate these orders into the electronic payment system at the earliest possible point by inputting the necessary details manually via a VDU or automatically via optical character readers. To this end the banking associations and the post office, with the participation of the central bank, reached an agreement as long ago as 1984 on the conversion of paper-based credit transfers into data records and their transmission within the electronic payment system (EPT procedure; see also Section IV). Certain reservations regarding this conversion still exist within the banking industry, because for individual credit institutions the effort required to record the data will not necessarily be offset by the benefits of electronic data processing. For this reason, it is not yet compulsory for institutions to convert paper-based credit transfers into data records; however, the number of transfers converted has increased considerably in the past few years. The savings banks, for instance, are already transforming all credit transfers for DM 500 and above transmitted within their own network, and some branches of the three major banks are even converting internetwork payments. Future developments will depend, in particular, on the availability of reasonably priced optical character readers and on whether there is a further move to credit transfer forms which, by their structure, facilitate the optical reading of handwritten numbers and letters.

In parallel with their efforts to convert paper media, the banks are trying to persuade corporate customers to submit not just their instructions for bulk payments but also those for other credit transfers on diskette or by telecommunication means so as to avoid paper from the outset. For this purpose, they are making an increasing number of electronic banking products available to their customers (for example, the recording of credit transfer data on diskette as an integral part of the customer's accounting system; cash management via videotex; the direct transmission of credit transfer orders from customers' PCs to the banks' computers). The products offered by the different credit institutions have been partly standardised through agreements between the banking associations. In addition, the banks have set their charges in such a way as to encourage private customers to make greater use of self-service facilities such as multipurpose ATMs and videotex equipment to issue instructions for credit transfers (see Section III.1.*(e)* on home banking).

Incoming electronic credit transfers can be booked automatically through to a customer's account and the important data printed out in his statement of account. Paper-based credit transfers, on the other hand, are delivered to the payee.

The *cheque* has never been as popular in Germany as in most other western countries; in 1987, it accounted for only 9 percent of the total number of cashless transactions (14 percent in value terms). This phenomenon is attributable partly to the preference given to credit transfers early on, in particular by the savings bank organisation and the post office, and partly to the fact that the central bank did not introduce a multilateral collection and clearing system for cheques until 1950. Since that date, the number of payments made by cheque has increased, but the proportion of cashless payments for which the cheque accounts has declined steadily (in the savings bank sector, for instance, this percentage fell from 21 percent in 1966 to 9 percent in 1987). Two contrary trends have been apparent here: As automation progressed, corporate customers switched on a large scale from cheques to credit transfers and on an even larger scale to direct debits, because these two types of payment orders could be generated directly from automated data bases onto magnetic tapes and submitted in this form to the banks for execution. Moreover, the accrual of interest in the interval before the debiting of cheques was in part offset by the rise in the cost of mailing them. On the other hand, individuals' use of cheques to pay for consumer goods and services increased once the banks started to guarantee the payment of Eurocheques for up to DM 400 backed by a cheque card. At the end of 1987, there were over 20 million Eurocheque cards in circulation.

When payments first began to be automated, the banks considered the cheque more machine-compatible than the credit transfer because only its amount had to be additionally encoded for OCR processing, whereas the credit transfer also required the encoding of the payee's bank account details unless forms provided by the payee were used. Today, however, the fact that the cheque in principle has to be collected and presented in paper form represents a significant disadvantage. The cheque is consequently more expensive to process than an electronic payment involving the dispatch of data media as well as slower than the transmission of electronic data records by telecommunication means. In 1985, the banking industry, the post office, and the central bank therefore decided to dispense with the physical presentation of cheques for up to DM 1,000. Under the truncation procedure on which they agreed, cheques are retained by the first bank concerned, wherever this is possible, and then, using the data contained in the code lines, are collected together with direct debits via the paperless exchange of data media (magnetic tape clearing). The original cheques are usually recorded on microfilm and destroyed after two months. As a result, more than half of all cheques are now truncated, with the banks and the post office carrying just over two-thirds of the conversions and the Bundesbank's computer centers the remainder. The central bank regulates the degree of its involvement by means of a conversion fee or preferential terms for cheques already converted by the banks. Like direct debits, truncated cheques can be charged automatically to the issuer's account and the details printed out in his statement of account. It was already customary not to return cashed cheques to their issuers.

Under the German Cheques Law, cheques may not be certified in such a way that the drawee bank is obliged to pay. The purpose of this prohibition is to prevent cheques acquiring a function similar to that of bank notes. An exception is made for the central bank, which, when cover is available, may confirm the payment of cheques drawn on it.

The *direct debit,* which was introduced by the banking associations in 1963, has greatly simplified the collection of regular payments (e.g., subscriptions, insurance premiums, rent, public utility bills, and taxes). Nowadays more than one-third of all cashless payments effected in Germany take the form of direct debits, and their importance relative to other payment media is continuing to increase.

The direct debit is made out by the creditor (payee) and presented to his bank for the collection of the equivalent amount from the debtor's (payer's) bank. In contrast to the credit transfer, the payment operation is initiated by the payee, who is thus himself responsible for ensuring that his claim on the payer is settled on time. However, this presupposes that the payer either authorises the payee to collect the amount (authorisation of collection) or authorises his bank—by agreement with the payee—to pay direct debits from that payee by drawing on his account (authorisation of debit).

Customers with EDP equipment are in principle obliged to use magnetic tape to submit direct debits to banks and postal giro offices for collection. As with credit transfers, small quantities of direct debits are also accepted on diskette or cassette. In 1987, approximately 2.2 billion direct debits were processed using the magnetic tape procedure, i.e., almost 90 percent of the total. The banks accept the remaining paper-based direct debits for collection together with cheques, and use OCR voucher-reading to process them. In parallel with the procedure for credit transfers, the banks have now reached an agreement (the Electronic Direct Debits [EDD] Agreement) whereby paper-based direct debits will be converted into data records, for example by means of data entry via a VDU or OCR system, at the first bank involved and will be collected electronically, together with the direct debits already submitted by customers on a paperless basis, via the magnetic tape clearing procedure.

In principle the banks, the post office, and the central bank would like all cashless payments to take the form of the three standardised payment media: credit transfer, cheque, or direct debit. However, the banks and the post office have also developed payment instruments of their own for specific purposes, of which only the crossed money order and the receipt are of some significance.

The post office's *crossed money order* is a paper instrument akin to a cheque. It is intended for the use of firms and public authorities (as payers) that have large numbers of payments to make to customers who do not have a giro account or whose bank is not known (e.g., disbursement of lottery winnings). Instead of sending his payment instructions directly to the payee, as occurs in the case of a cheque, the payer submits the relevant data to his postal giro office on magnetic tape. The post office debits the total value of the money orders and handling charges from the payer's account, prints the money orders, and adds an authentication stamp (the equivalent of a payment guarantee) before sending them to the respective payees. Payees can either cash their order at any post office or present it to their bank for collection in the same way as a cheque.

*Receipts* can be used in the banking industry to collect amounts that have been paid out in cash. For instance, if one bank pays cash to a person on presentation of a savings book issued by a second bank, the value of the payment can be reclaimed from that second bank on presentation of the voucher receipted by the customer. However, since it is not legally possible for receipts to be collected in the central bank clearing network, they have in recent years increasingly been supplanted by direct debits.

### (c) Payments by card (credit and debit cards)

#### Payments by card in the retail trade (types of payment cards)

*Credit cards* do not yet play a major role in Germany, but their use has increased significantly in the last two years. Currently (as of the middle of 1988) over 2 million credit cards issued by the main credit card organisations (Amexco, Diners, VISA, the Payment System Company's Eurocard in association with MasterCard/Access) are in circulation; they are accepted by a large number of German enterprises (e.g., 85,000 in the case of Eurocard), including retailers, hotels, restaurants, and airlines. In 1987, sales to domestic credit cardholders amounted to about DM 11 billion, or approximately 2 percent of turnover in the retail trade. As a rule, credit card transactions do not generate any immediate payments via the banking system. The credit card transactions reported by retailers are aggregated by the credit card companies and the total amounts due are credited to retailers by means of credit transfers, while cardholders receive a consolidated monthly statement, which they settle by means of a direct debit, cheque, or credit transfer. Only VISA cards, which are at present issued by only three credit institutions (bank credit cards), also offer genuine consumer credit facilities. In the case of VISA cards, the amounts due are cleared centrally by one of the issuing banks.

In view of the level of commission charged—in some cases as high as 7 percent—and the considerable effort associated with the authorisation and processing of payments, retailers were previously reluctant to accept credit cards, and their use was to a large extent restricted to shops selling luxury goods or catering to a high proportion of foreign clients. Only recently have retailers come to see the credit card as a competitive device, and have either negotiated more favorable group contracts with the credit card companies (e.g., petrol station chains), or have instead issued their own *retailer credit cards* (e.g., the Hertie Golden Customer Card). These cards are designed to promote customer loyalty and boost customer-targeted sales promotion, and at the same time to put pressure on the unduly high commission charged by the traditional credit card companies. To extend the range of outlets where retailer credit cards are accepted and thereby make them more attractive to cardholders, an increasing number of joint products are being issued (using banks as clearing agencies), which can be used at several, and in some cases even at competing, outlets (e.g., the airlines' Air-Plus card and the "DKK" card planned by the retail trade and the hotel and catering association).

*Debit cards* are payment cards issued by the credit institutions that enable customers to effect transactions on their account at banks' self-service facilities—e.g., at cash dispensers or machines that print statements of account—by using a personal identification number (PIN). In the future, customers will also be able to use such cards to make cashless payments at retailers' POS terminals. Such transactions will not be aggregated, as occurs with credit card payments; instead, they will either be debited on-line from the customer's bank account as soon as they have been authorised, or, on the basis of data media provided by the retailer (or the data transmitted each day by the retailer via a telecommunication network), they will be directly debited by the retailer's bank using the magnetic tape procedure.

The most widely distributed debit card in Germany is the Eurocheque card. It still performs its traditional function as a cheque guarantee card, but thanks to the addition of a magnetic stripe it can now also be used as a debit card without a cheque. Special features have been incorporated to protect Eurocheque cards against duplication. Through various agreements and POS trials that have been conducted in Berlin and Munich since 1983, the credit institutions have laid the foundations for extending the already versatile role the Eurocheque card plays in self-service banking (see Section III.1.*(c)* and in the future using it as a means of accessing a nationwide uniform POS system (probably as from 1989, see Section III.1.*(c)*). The system will also include the experimental introduction of a Eurocheque card incorporating a microchip to permit off-line authorisation. Plans to develop the Eurocheque card into a new multipurpose card which, through cooperation with the credit card companies, could also have been used as a credit card, foundered only recently as a result, in particular, of antitrust considerations.

As an alternative to the Eurocheque card, the credit institutions have also created special debit cards for use at a given bank or at banks belonging to a given association, so that a customer who, for example, is not sufficiently creditworthy to be issued a Eurocheque card may also have a means of access to electronic self-service banking.

*Stored value cards (prepaid cards)* can store a certain purchasing power and then be used in the place of small amounts of cash to pay anonymously for services. Microchips are preferred to magnetic stripes in the design of stored value cards because they offer greater storage capacity and are more difficult to forge. Stored value cards are distributed on a large scale by the post office in the form of phone cards. The possibility of using stored value cards as a genuine substitute for cash in a wide range of circumstances (the electronic wallet) is also being discussed.

### Payments by card via ATMs, self-service banking

In addition to straightforward cash dispensers, the banks are also installing an increasing number of multipurpose ATMs or are supplementing cash dispensers with other customer-operated bank terminals with specific functions (such as VDUs to initiate credit transfers or machines which print out statements of account). These machines are designed to enable customers to carry out as many of their routine cash and cashless payment transactions as possible. Apart from account inquiries and the printing of statements of account, commonly used self-service facilities relating to cashless payments include ordering items ranging from printed forms to Eurocheques, presenting cheques for collection, and making entries in savings books. Banks are installing videotex machines as well as their own self-service terminals to permit the on-screen initiation of credit transfers (see Section III.1.*(e)*). At the branches of a few banks, payment instructions can now only be initiated using self-service machines.

Customers can access the banks' self-service facilities by using their own bank's card, the card issued by the association to which their bank belongs, or their Eurocheque card, in each case by keying in their PIN. Except when obtaining cash from cash dispensers (Eurocheque cash dispenser pool, see Section III.1.*(a)*), customers are still largely restricted to their own bank, although a few groups of credit institutions have already made their self-service facilities more widely accessible by means of their association's card (for example, using the savings banks' S card, customers can print out a statement of their account, even at a savings bank other than their own).

*Payments by card at electronic check-outs (POS procedure)*

Under the POS procedure, a cashless payment is triggered as soon as a card holder makes a purchase at an electronic check-out and—once the transaction has been authorised via a telecommunication link either to the card issuer or to an authentication center—the amount in question is debited from the customer's bank account and credited to that of the retailer (see also Section III.1.*(c)*). Thus, this replaces payment by cash or cheque.

Until now, the POS activities of the German credit institutions have not gone beyond regional tests in Berlin and Munich, which have been based on the use of the Eurocheque card and the customer's secret code (PIN). The reason for this lies in the lack of unity within the banking industry regarding the cards to be included (whether the banks' own cards, and even the competing credit cards, should have access), authorisation issues (whether the registers of cancelled cards and of transactions should be centralised, or whether authorisation should be "on the customer's account" at his credit institution), considerations regarding the separation of authorisation from clearing, as well as the retail trade's unwillingness to accept the charges demanded by the credit institutions (0.7 Pfenning per transaction and 0.2 percent of turnover) in addition to the cost of the necessary equipment and telephone charges. However, as a result of the very favorable outcome of the Berlin and Munich trials, the banks' POS system is scheduled for extension to all parts of the Federal Republic by 1989 at the latest, initially on the basis of the Eurocheque card only. The system will retain identification by PIN code and all transactions will be authorised on-line, although—as in the case of transactions at cash dispensers—authorisation will be given at a regional authentication center of the banking industry or the post office, or even decentrally "on the customer's account" at the card-issuing bank, rather than centrally by the Payment Systems Company (GZS). Clearing of the transactions between the participant credit institutions will also no longer be effected centrally by the GZS, but instead will be carried out cost-effectively by the banks concerned—separately from authorisation—via the normal direct debit collection procedure (magnetic tape clearing). This system would be able to accommodate a partially off-line authorisation procedure using smart cards. In 1988-89, a supplementary trial based on Eurocheque cards incorporating microchips that can carry out a PIN check, store transactions, and recalculate limits as well as magnetic stripes for other purposes (so-called hybrid cards) is due to be held in the Regensburg area.

As far as processing is concerned, there is now very little difference between the banks' POS system, which uses debit cards, and electronically connected credit card terminals, which give authorisation and carry out paperless clearing using file transfers. By early 1988, the post office had installed over 1,000 MAKATEL EFT POS terminals throughout the Federal Republic to handle transactions using any of the four international credit cards. It is envisaged that, in the future, these terminals will also handle transactions using a Eurocheque card and a PIN. Meanwhile, the flexibility offered by the inclusion of the Eurocheque card in a POS system has already been attained to a large extent by the private supplier of one POS system, which was originally based exclusively on credit cards. In other cases, existing terminal networks of nonbanks have been connected to a credit card company to create a POS system. This approach, admittedly, has increased the number of EFT POS applications overnight, but it does not display the desired flexibility. There will be a further increase in POS applications in the retail trade that uses retailers' own credit cards; there are already full-service packages on the market covering everything from the issue of cards right through to the processing of payments. Finally, the post office issues telephone credit cards, with the number of units used being included in the cardholder's monthly telephone bill.

*(d) Bank payment networks to which customers have access*

In both the paper-based and paperless payment systems, customer payments can be transmitted smoothly into and out of the banks' networks, since uniform standards have been adopted for printed forms and for the format of data records in both interbank and customer transactions. Before the printed forms submitted by customers are routed into the interbank payment system, the banks add codes to them, group them together with others, sort them, and forward them together with new aggregated data media and instructions. Data records presented by customers are subject to a similar process. In this case, the bank constructs new data files from the customers' data records and creates its own header and trailer records for the data media before routing them into the interbank payment system. It is even possible for a customer, in consultation with his bank, to structure his magnetic tapes or diskettes containing credit transfer or direct debit instructions in such a way that the magnetic tape can be routed directly into the interbank system (e.g., to the central bank) without needing to be processed by the customer's bank.

A standard data record has also been adopted by the credit institutions for their customers' S.W.I.F.T. instructions on magnetic tape. This means that customers, whatever their bank, use a standard data record for electronic foreign payment instructions and that the credit institutions can route such payment instructions into the S.W.I.F.T. network without difficulty.

*(e) Transmission of customers' payment instructions to their bank by means of telecommunication*

The post office's *videotex service* (BTX), which has been available in the whole of the Federal Republic since 1984, has enabled the banks to provide home-banking services. Using either their home facilities (a television set suitably converted for use as a terminal or a videotex-compatible PC) or one of the publicly installed videotex terminals, customers can communicate in conversational mode with their bank's computer center via the telephone network and use various banking services. For competitive reasons, the banks invested heavily in their videotex service in the early years. However, their investment has not yet paid off because, in comparison with other European countries, private customers in Germany have been slow to accept the videotex service: By the middle of 1988, the banks had only 120,000 videotex subscribers with 135,000 videotex accounts (so-called Telekontos). The banks make no special charge for holding videotex accounts, unlike other suppliers of data and computer services, which normally have such charges credited to their accounts via videotex.

The banks' security arrangements for videotex provide that payment orders and other transactions can only be executed if the PIN and an allocated transaction number (TAN) are keyed in along with the account number. To avoid fraud, access to an account is automatically blocked if a PIN is wrongly keyed in three times in a row, and the supply of new TANs is also automatically blocked the third time a TAN is incorrectly entered. The Payment Systems Company is currently investigating the extent to which the security of videotex can be improved further by the introduction of smart cards.

Banks' corporate customers — unlike their private customers — have greeted videotex enthusiastically as an inexpensive way of transmitting data by telecommunication. It was thus a natural progression for the banks to develop videotex cash management systems (i.e., self-service facilities offering, in particular, access to account data and the possibility to carry out transactions) for their corporate customers. These systems use both security software (e.g., codes, varying levels of authorisation) and security hardware to guarantee the maximum possible security, particularly in payment instructions.

The credit institutions and the post office are currently working on an additional joint product designed to permit the secure and protected transmission of data files that contain too large a volume of payment transactions data to be handled quickly by videotex or a cash management system. This product, which will be installed initially on customers' PCs and subsequently as part of any other computing system they might have, will enable data to be transmitted by telecommunication rather than on physical media.

## 2. Handling of Payments Within the Banking System

*(a) Handling of payments within the giro networks of the credit institutions and their associations*

In Germany, the savings banks' and credit cooperatives' associations each have their own giro network with which to carry out intercity payments to virtually any location. In addition, the large banks and the post office can carry out cashless payments between large towns and cities via their internal networks (see Section II.1). All the giro networks make the greatest possible use of electronic data processing. A total of some 80 computer centers (excluding the Bundesbank's) are involved in the processing of payments, as well as in other tasks.

The computer centers process the payment vouchers forwarded to them using optical character recognition, while payments on magnetic tape (or on diskette or cassette) are processed in accordance with the agreements on the exchange of paperless data media. Only credit transfers and items for collection are processed separately for technical reasons. The standardised layout of the code lines and the uniformity of the data records mean that direct debits, debits from the clearing of cash dispenser withdrawals, and debits relating to truncated cheques can all be processed together and be forwarded, likewise together, to the recipient institution, where they can be recorded automatically and itemized in the customer's statement of account.

The computer centers of the first bank to receive payment instructions forward them—if necessary via other computer centers—to the bank of the recipient of the credit transfer or the issuer of the cheque/payer of the direct debit or their accounting center. In the exchange of paperless data media within networks, telecommunication is increasingly being used instead of sending magnetic tapes. The computer centers of the associations' giro networks are interconnected by telecommunication systems that can be used for the same-day transmission of urgent payments (e.g., salary transfers sent in by the payer on magnetic tape). In addition, bank computer centers and their affiliated banks are now internally linked by telecommunication networks in their respective areas, so that payments can be transmitted throughout in paperless form and with no need for the participating credit institutions to exchange data media.

Customers' paper-based credit transfers and other paper items sent for collection are sorted by the banks according to whether their destination is an account held at the bank itself (internal transfer), at another bank within the same giro network (intranetwork payments for other savings banks or credit cooperatives), or at an unrelated bank (internetwork payments). Internetwork payments are further sorted into those destined for a recipient in the same location (local payments) and those destined for a recipient in another town or city (intercity payments).

In the case of *internal transfers* the transaction is generally executed with 24 hours, and does not affect the bank's liquidity. The larger the institution and the greater its regional coverage, the higher the proportion of transactions accounted for by internal transfers will be.

*Intranetwork payments,* both paper-based and paperless, destined for other credit institutions within the same giro network are forwarded and settled within the network itself, unless a credit institution prefers to transmit all noninternal instructions unsorted via the central bank in order, for example, to take advantage of the comparatively favorable account-crediting terms offered by the central bank's collection procedure.

*Internetwork payments* must be transmitted at some stage in the payment process—at least by the time they reach the place in which the recipient institution is located—into a clearing system to which that institution belongs. How they are handled depends on the routes and clearing facilities available in each case. The following two possibilities exist for *local payments:*

▶ Direct interbank exchange of the payment instrument and settlement of the countervalues in the accounts that the banks maintain in each other's books, at central clearing institutions, or at the central bank.

▶ Transmission of the payment instrument or data media to the central bank, provided it has a branch in the same location or nearby, for forwarding to the recipient's credit institution and settlement in the giro accounts held at the central bank by the two banks concerned (see Section III.2.*(b)*).

*Intercity payments* to unrelated credit institutions can be introduced by the first institution to receive the instructions into either:

▶ The institution's or association's giro network.

▶ The central bank giro network (see Section III.2.*(b)*) for forwarding to the bank of the payee/payer.

To take advantage of the float, the credit institutions usually keep high-value paper-based credit transfers and all credit transfers transmitted via the magnetic tape clearing within their own giro networks for as long as possible and only transmit them to the recipient institution or its accounting center at the last possible stage (in the local clearing). By contrast, any other credit transfers and items sent for collection (cheques, debits relating to truncated cheques, and direct debits) are transmitted at the earliest possible stage either directly into the giro network of the recipient institution or to the central bank. The use of different routes for different instruments explains why the central bank's involvement is far less in the case of credit transfers than in that of the collection of payment instruments (21 percent of nonbank credit transfers are routed via the central bank, compared with 55 percent of nonbank collection instructions).

In the case of paper-based payment instructions, the institution that first receives them must decide not only which route to use but also whether, in view of the customer's instructions or internal bank standards, they need to be handled by means of an accelerated procedure (e.g., telegram or urgent transfer in the case of credit transfers), or whether they should be transformed into data records and transmitted via the procedure for paperless payment instruments (EPT procedure for credit transfers or cheque truncation — see Section III.1.*(b)*).

## *(b) Central bank clearing facilities for interbank payments*

The Bundesbank's clearing facilities are available on the same terms to all banks involved in payments. The Bundesbank offers the following clearing procedures for the processing of interbank payments:

### *Local clearing*

Banks in the approximately 200 locations in which the Bundesbank has a branch are able to exchange cheques, direct debits, and other claims as well as credit transfers with one another in the *daily local clearing procedure*. In 1987, 269 million payments (mainly credit transfers) for a total value of some DM 65,287 billion were exchanged at the clearing offices of the central bank. The high value of payments principally reflects credit transfers resulting from money market and foreign exchange dealing, particularly in the major international banking center of Frankfurt (95 percent of the overall total cleared). At the close of settlement (e.g., 2:00 P.M.) each Bundesbank branch determines the clearing balance for each bank participating in its clearing and debits or credits its central bank account with the clearing balance. To cover debit balances, the Bundesbank's branches may take account of the giro account balance, the proceeds of cheques and direct debits presented for collection the day before, as well as securities eligible as collateral for credit. (They also have the authorisation of the credit institutions automatically to cover any debit balance that might still be outstanding at the end of the day by an advance). Until all debit balances have been covered, the participants in clearing are merely custodians of the clearing instruments delivered to them, and may not finally dispose of the funds received. By the early crediting of the proceeds of credit transfers to their customers' accounts, the participants in clearing hence expose themselves to the risk of default by the payer bank. It is up to each participant in clearing to see that this risk is limited.

The central bank plans to introduce an electronic clearing system modelled on that of other countries (e.g., CHIPS in the United States) as an alternative to the conventional paper-based clearing in operation hitherto. Via the computers at the 11 computer centers (regional computer centers) operated by the central bank, which will remain the agency responsible for electronic clearing, the banks will be provided with the facility to transmit urgent or high-value credit transfers (e.g., incoming S.W.I.F.T. payments) to one another in electronic form and by telecommunication means. They will thus no longer have to print vouchers and, because of the better information, will have earlier access to inpayments, although, even with electronic clearing, they will not be able to dispose finally of the funds before the settlement date and until all debit balances have been covered. Unlike the present paper-based local clearing, electronic clearing will not be performed independently by the central bank branches in the various locations, but instead all the banks in a federal Land that possess the appropriate EDP equipment will be directly connected with their regional Bundesbank computing center, thereby extending the circle of credit institutions among which clearing is performed electronically (regional clearing). However, the banks' settlement balances will continue to be recorded decentrally in their giro accounts with the central bank branches.

There is a legal assumption of payment for items sent for collection that are presented for clearing in the daily local clearing procedure. Cheques and direct debits that are unacceptable owing to lack of cover or for any other reason must therefore be returned within one or two days; otherwise, they will be considered as irrevocably cashed.

In the case of paper-based *local credit transfers* (outside the daily clearing procedure), the central bank branches execute credit transfer instructions from all giro account holders to the giro account of a beneficiary at the same branch, but only if the initiator's account contains sufficient cover (the giro account balance plus the proceeds of instruments to be credited on the same day plus, if necessary, an advance to cover any overdraft). The amounts due are credited directly to the giro account of the beneficiary credit institution, which then (by contrast with credit transfers settled in the daily local clearing) has immediate, full, and final title to them. The giro account holders initiating the instructions are, however, at liberty to decide whether they wish to make use of this option, or whether, to avoid sorting, they prefer local credit transfers to be executed within the automated intercity payment system. Under the second option, the countervalue of the credit transfers is not credited on the same day, however.

In 1987, the central bank clearing facility was used for 65 million local credit transfers with a total value of DM 6,306 billion.

### Intercity clearing

The central bank giro network can be used to reach any bank in the Federal Republic. The intercity payment system can handle paper-based, paperless (recorded on magnetic tape or diskette), and telegraphic payments. The banks can use the Bundesbank's simplified cheque and direct debit collection procedure to collect cheques as well as paper-based and paperless direct debits.

In 1987, the Bundesbank's intercity payment system was used for 1.9 billion payments, of which 0.4 billion were credit transfers with a total value of DM 6,841 billion, and 1.5 billion were cheques and direct debits with a total value of DM 2,685 billion (of which approximately 0.6 billion transactions and DM 2,074 billion were accounted for by cheques).

The intensive use made of the Bundesbank's giro network prompted it to automate the handling of payments early on. Its first clearing computer center came on stream in 1971. The Bundesbank now has a computer center in each of the 11 federal Länder, where 99 percent of intercity payments are processed automatically. The number of paperless payment items processed via the magnetic tape clearing is already more than twice that of payment vouchers processed using optical character recognition of their code lines, whereas in 1983, the proportions were more or less equal. This evolution can be attributed, in particular, to the further increase in paperless direct debit transactions and to the shift towards cheque truncation. To speed up intercity payments routed via the central bank computer centers, the Bundesbank has in the last few years set up a telecommunication network between its 11 computer centers, via which all paperless credit transfers, provided they do not have a specified date, and some direct debits are transmitted. The time taken for paperless intercity payments to be effected via the Bundesbank's network has thereby been reduced by one day to a maximum of 24 hours.

The remaining 1 percent of intercity payments that are not processed by machine at the Bundesbank's computer centers consist of high-value credit transfers that, principally because of their urgency, are transmitted via the shortest route (hitherto by post, telex, or telephone), i.e., without going through the computer centers, to the branch at which the payee has his account. With a view toward speeding up and automating these high-value payments further, a telecommunication network has been set up between the Bundesbank's branches (Urgent Payments Procedure), which is used to execute not only high-value credit transfers (i.e., currently DM 100,000 or more) but also credit transfers that were hitherto transmitted telegraphically, for which a charge is made, and which are always credited on the same day. Payment orders from account holders are still paper-based, so that the central bank branch that receives them converts them into electronic data records using a VDU. Since it is already possible to submit diskettes instead of magnetic tapes in the exchange of paperless data media via the computer centers, it is envisaged that diskettes will in the future also be accepted for payments submitted via the Urgent Payments Procedure and that diskettes will likewise be supplied to payees. The next step will then be to enable giro account holders to initiate payments or obtain data via telecommunication networks (electronic counter). Furthermore, the Bundesbank intends that the remaining low-value, paper-based credit transfers, which are neither processed by machine at the computer centers, nor covered by the Urgent Payments Procedure between central bank branches, should in the future be converted into data records so that they can be enchanged in paperless form via the computer centers (active central bank participation in the EPT procedure — see Section III.1.*(b)*).

Just as in the case of local payments, the Bundesbank does not take any risks regarding intercity payments but executes them only once it has ascertained that the requisite cover exists. Once the incoming funds have been credited to the account of the payee, he has final and unreserved title to them.

Only 0.4 percent of all items sent for collection are not processed by machine in the central bank payments network, the majority of them being foreign cheques that do not conform to German guidelines on format and coding. As a consequence of the ever-greater use of direct debits and the truncation of cheques for amounts up to and including DM 1,000 (see Section III.1.*(b)*), the ratio of machine-processed paper-based payments to paperless payments, expressed in terms of the number of payments collected rather than their value, has gone from more or less 1:1 in 1980 to 4:11. In 1987, 45 percent of the cheques presented to the Bundesbank were already truncated; of the remaining paper-based cheques, the Bundesbank itself converted just under 40 percent. To take advantage of the especially favorable account-crediting conditions that, so as to promote paperless payment transactions, have been introduced for truncated cheques submitted separately for processing under the exchange of paperless data media (i.e., payee's account is credited on the day of presentation instead of the customary one day later), and to avoid the Bundesbank's charge for truncating cheques, the banks have increasingly switched to truncating cheques themselves since the procedure was introduced in 1985.

*(c) Securities clearing*

Securities transactions in which no instruments change hands are carried out by the credit institutions' jointly operated facilities known as collective securities deposit banks or security-clearing associations. Transactions between participant dealing banks are settled and delivered two days after the conclusion of a deal under a standardised, centralised procedure that involves the processing of EDP listings at the computer center of the competent security-clearing association. Outside the field of stock exchange dealings, individual instructions concerning nonphysical securities held on deposit at security-clearing associations can be issued by the account-holding credit institutions, just as in the payment system, by means of security transfer cheques, the form of which varies according to the type and purpose of the instruction. The security-clearing associations maintain clearing accounts to determine the cash balances of the credit institutions linked with them. The settlement of balances (funds clearing) is effected under an agreement with the local central bank branch, whereby the competent Land central bank, on behalf of the security-clearing associations, enters the balances arising from funds clearings on the giro accounts held with it by the clearing members (i.e., the credit institutions). Settlement (i.e., final crediting of the amounts) occurs only once all debit balances from clearing have been covered, which must take place everywhere no later than 12 noon. Only then are the transfers made between the security deposits of the dealing banks.

## IV   FUTURE DEVELOPMENTS IN CASHLESS PAYMENTS

The foreseeable medium and longer-term developments in cashless payments include:

*(a) Further decline in paper-based payments in favor of paperless payments*

The present high proportion of paperless payments (already over 60 percent) will continue to rise as a consequence of the following developments, the greatest potential for rationalisation lying with credit transfers:

▶ Greater use of the banks' self-service facilities by private customers and of electronic banking products by corporate customers to initiate paperless credit transfers (via diskette or telecommunication networks).

▶ Increasing conversion into data records of the remaining paper-based credit transfer instructions by the first credit institution to which they are submitted, under the EPT procedure and with the active participation of the central bank.

▶ A decline in the use of cheques, owing to the further expansion of POS systems based on the Eurocheque card, which is the most widely distributed card, but also on credit cards.

▶ Increasing conversion of cheques into data records as a result of a higher ceiling for cheque truncation.

*(b) Further replacement of physical data media by telecommunication in cashless payment transactions*

Two separate trends can be distinguished here:

▶ Closer contacts between customers and their banks by means of cash management systems, PCs with videotex and computer links for the secure transmission of data files.

▶ More widespread use of telecommunication in the linking of the banks' various payment networks, in which process the central bank will play an important role as an intermediary (electronic clearing, electronic counter).

In the course of these developments, questions relating to the ways in which telecommunication networks can be protected against unauthorised access (e.g., encryption, authorisation) will become increasingly important.

*(c) Partial replacement of cash transactions by POS procedures and stored value cards*

*(d) Harmonisation of electronic payment procedures*

As part of the process of European integration and as a result of international standardisation, the future European internal market will require a standardised electronic payment system going beyond S.W.I.F.T., which may involve, for example, modification of the data record format for the domestic exchange of paperless data media and of the related telecommunication protocols. Other developments designed to integrate payment system messages with firms' (i.e., bank customers') electronic messages (e.g., EDIFACT) will presumably also require adjustments to the payment system.

Appendix

## Development of Cash, Sight Deposits, and Cashless Payments in Germany

| Year | Bank Notes[1] | | Coin[1] | | Sight Deposits of Domestic Nonbanks[1] (DEM million) | Number of Giro Accounts[1,3] (millions) | Cashless Payments[2] | |
|---|---|---|---|---|---|---|---|---|
| | Number (millions) | Value (DEM million) | Number (millions) | Value (DEM million) | | | Number of Transactions[3] (millions) | Value (DEM billion) |
| 1975 | 912 | 55,143 | 16,746 | 5,406 | 132,214 | 43 | 4,000 | 7,261 |
| 1976 | 947 | 59,038 | 17,918 | 5,700 | 129,738 | 44 | 4,100 | 8,023 |
| 1977 | 1,018 | 65,567 | 19,237 | 6,098 | 143,177 | 45 | 4,250 | 8,897 |
| 1978 | 1,108 | 74,799 | 20,779 | 6,578 | 166,908 | 47 | 4,350 | 9,503 |
| 1979 | 1,150 | 79,386 | 22,381 | 6,989 | 171,581 | 49 | 4,500 | 10,352 |
| 1980 | 1,196 | 83,730 | 24,074 | 7,461 | 174,388 | 51 | 4,750 | 11,685 |
| 1981 | 1,200 | 83,790 | 25,590 | 7,817 | 171,850 | 52 | 5,000 | 12,766 |
| 1982 | 1,221 | 88,575 | 26,859 | 8,120 | 185,664 | 53 | 5,150 | 13,074 |
| 1983 | 1,277 | 96,073 | 28,431 | 8,619 | 201,527 | 54 | 5,300 | 13,852 |
| 1984 | 1,318 | 100,636 | 29,545 | 8,956 | 215,413 | 55 | 5,600 | 14,800 |
| 1985 | 1,354 | 105,416 | 30,847 | 9,303 | 232,476 | 56 | 5,930 | 16,114 |
| 1986 | 1,424 | 113,983 | 32,198 | 9,750 | 247,737 | 57 | 6,165 | 16,840 |
| 1987 | 1,501 | 125,608 | 33,531 | 10,293 | 265,742 | 58 | 6,338 | 17,848 |

[1] As of the end of the year.
[2] Debits to nonbanks' giro accounts in the year in question.
[3] Partially estimated.

# 5 ITALY

# Italy

## I   INTRODUCTION

Various types of payment instruments are used by households, businesses, and government.

A number of structural and institutional factors contribute to the still extensive use of cash. Among the former are the fragmentation of the distribution network and the structure of the labor market, in particular the low ratio (compared with other major countries) of the labor force to the total population; the latter include the methods of wage/salary payment and the size of the central bank's branch network.

The cheque is the most widespread bank instrument; payment orders are of less importance, above all for low-value transactions, although in value terms they account for a high proportion of total bank payments.

Bank payment orders and giro transfers are little used for retail operations, since the Postal Administration, owing partly to its extensive network of offices, is able to offer a range of more convenient alternative services to broad groups of users.

Credit cards and ATMs have become more widespread in the last few years. More recently, systems for electronic funds transfer at the point-of-sale (EFT POS systems) and home/corporate banking systems have been introduced.

Within the interbank circuits the exchange of paper instruments by mail still plays an important role and electronic procedures are little used.

The Bank of Italy provides clearing and interbank transfer and settlement services in each of the 95 provincial capitals. Its electronic data transmission network enables interbank transactions, including intercity payments, to be transferred and settled the same day.

A further structural characteristic of the Italian payment system is the low degree of integration between the two major circuits, that of the banks and that of the Postal Administration. Not all of the instruments used in either of the two circuits are also acceptable in the other; the telecommunication networks are not interconnected; the Postal Administration, until recently, was not a member of the clearing system.

Regarding securities transactions, two systems have been in operation since the beginning of the 1980s for the centralised management of government securities and other securities, respectively, enabling operations to be effected by means of simple book entries.

The payment system in Italy has recently undergone important changes, with innovative products and services becoming more and more widespread. Moreover, telematic infrastructures shared by the entire banking system have been developed.

The main factors stimulating change are technological innovation and the need for the banks to counter the decline in their intermediation activity and the growth in processing costs associated with increasing volumes of paper-based instruments.

The authorities, and the central bank in particular, have actively promoted a more efficient system. In addition to intervention in a regulatory context, action has recently been taken to revise and strengthen the powers granted in payment systems and securities transactions to interbank bodies such as the CIPA (Interbank Convention on Problems of Automation), the SIA (Interbank Society for Automation), and the Società Monte Titoli.

The work of the central bank has also taken the form of an in-depth analysis of the state of the payment system presented in its "White Paper on the Payment System in Italy," published in 1987. On the basis of the courses of action sketched out, the Bank of Italy and the CIPA have put forward an integrated plan of projects directed at speeding up the process of transformation in the payment system.[1] The projects, which also involve a change in the services directly offered by the Bank of Italy, will be implemented mainly in 1989.

## II    INSTITUTIONAL FRAMEWORK

### 1. Regulatory Framework

The main providers of payment system services are the Postal Administration, the banking system, and the Bank of Italy.

In the absence of specific regulations governing the provision of payment services, an important supervisory and regulatory role is played by the central bank by virtue of its powers of supervision of the credit system, which is the chief private sector provider of payment media.

The existing regulatory framework still relates almost exclusively to credit instruments and paper-based securities.

### 2. The Role of the Individual Operators in the System

The *Bank of Italy* participates in the system in a variety of ways: directly offering instruments and services, regulating the activity of the banking system, coordinating and promoting interbank initiatives, and acting as agent of the Treasury for incoming and outgoing payments.

As the issuing authority, the Bank of Italy has the exclusive right to issue bank notes. In particular, it has the sole right to issue notes in denominations of Lit. 1,000 and above. The denominations of bank notes are fixed by law passed by Parliament, while their characteristics, the quantity to be issued, and the date on which they are to be put into circulation are determined by decree of the Minister for the Treasury. The Treasury may issue directly currency in denominations of Lit. 1,000 or less in the form of coins or, when required, in the form of state notes.

Another payment instrument issued by the Bank of Italy is the cashier's cheque (vaglia cambiario), which is a credit instrument with guaranteed cover used chiefly for payments on behalf of the Treasury, for example, for tax refunds.

The Bank of Italy also offers banks a funds transfer service for the settlement of interbank transactions through "centralised accounts for advances and deposits."

The central bank operates a clearing service for both funds and securities transactions.

Finally, since 1980, the Bank of Italy has provided a system of centralised management of government securities, which can be used by all economic agents who habitually engage in securities transactions: banks, special credit institutions, stockbrokers, and finance companies.

The Banking Law promulgated in 1936 invests the Bank of Italy with the power to supervise the banking system with a view toward protecting savings and regulating lending activity. Its supervisory powers also enable the central bank to exercise a controlling and regulatory influence over banks' activities in payment services. One

---

[1] *Il sistema dei pagamenti in Italia: progetti di intervento (The Payment System in Italy: Plans for Action)*, published in April 1988.

area of supervisory control that is of particular importance for the provision of such services is that concerning the establishment of new branches and ATMs. The Bank of Italy has, in fact, been given special responsibilities in setting technical security requirements for ATM networks.

The services provided by the *postal system* at its 13,958 offices are postal current accounts and a cash transfer facility (money orders).

At the end of 1987, the *banking system* comprised 1,109 banks with 15,365 bank branches. All the categories of bank (commercial banks, savings banks, cooperatives, and rural banks) operate in the area of payment services. The main payment instruments offered to customers are the cheque, the banker's draft, and the payment order. Additional services offered are arrangements for paying utility bills, taxes, and rent and for collecting bills of exchange.

In the last few years, a number of cooperative ventures have been undertaken in new types of "point of contact" with customers: A national ATM network has been established, and there have been local trials with POS systems; plans have been drawn up for a national POS network.

In addition, the degree of integration within the banking system has been increased by the creation of infrastructures and procedures for automatic data transmission such as the interbank network, set up in 1986, and the SETIF (Interbank Electronic Funds Transfer Service), which has been in operation since 1980 using magnetic data carriers as the transmission medium.

The banking system has established a number of bodies for developing joint projects and managing services of common interest:

▶ *The CIPA (Interbank Convention on Problems of Automation)*, which is an association of approximately 90 banks, whose main object is to develop joint projects especially in payment services. Within it the Bank of Italy is vested with powers of guidance and coordination and is responsible for issuing directives to ensure the proper operation of the projects launched under the auspices of the CIPA. The Management Committee and the General Meeting of the CIPA are chaired by a representative of the Bank of Italy, which also provides the secretariat.

▶ *The SIA (Interbank Society for Automation)*, which provides services and infrastructures of common interest to the banking system and, if necessary, operational support for the activities of the central bank in the payments field. The Bank of Italy holds 40 percent of its capital. Another 40 percent is owned by the Italian Bankers' Association.

▶ *The Società Monte Titoli* is a company providing services aimed at rationalising the custody and administration of transferable securities. In particular, it offers centralised management services for all securities, with the exception of government securities, which, as mentioned earlier, are centralised at the Bank of Italy. Its shareholders comprise the Bank of Italy, the banks, and the stockbrokers. The Bank of Italy has the right to appoint a director to the board. The law also allows shareholders to transfer shares only to the Bank of Italy, which is the only shareholder entitled to hold more than 7 percent of the share capital.

## III  PAYMENT SYSTEMS

### 1. Payment Instruments

#### (a) Cash

The legal tender in circulation consists of six denominations of bank note (Lit. 1,000, 2,000, 5,000, 10,000, 50,000, and 100,000) issued by the Bank of Italy and eight denominations of coin issued by the Treasury (Lit. 5, 10, 20, 50, 100, 200, 500, and

1,000); Lit. 1,000 coins, which are made of silver, do not normally circulate. At the end of 1987, 97.9 percent of the stock of currency in circulation, which amounted to Lit. 51, 125 billion, was accounted for by bank notes and the remainder by coins. The large denominations (Lit. 50,000 and 100,000) represented 34 percent of the total number of notes in circulation, while in 1980 they covered only 21.5 percent of the total.

In recent years, the unit of account has come to appear inadequate owing to the lira's considerable loss of purchasing power. In this connection a bill currently before Parliament proposes the adoption of a new monetary unit, called the "new lira," with a value corresponding to the current Lit. 1,000. This would make for a simplification of statistical and accounting data and bring the value of the lira more into line with that of the currencies of the major industrial countries. The bill provides for eight denominations between one and one thousand "new lira" and would thereby establish the legal basis for extending the scale towards the top of the current range of denominations.

Cash is the predominant form of payment for the purchase of consumer goods by households and is also frequently used for the payment of wages and salaries.

At the end of 1987, the ratio of the stock of currency in circulation to GDP was equal to 5.2 percent and that of currency in circulation to domestic household consumption 8.6 percent. The downward trend in these ratios, which in 1980 had stood at 6.3 percent and 10.1 percent, respectively, is attributable both to more careful management of cash holdings by the public and to a wider utilisation of bank instruments. The high inflation in the first half of the 1980s and the growth in opportunities for investment in alternative liquid assets increased the opportunity cost of holding cash. Other factors in this process are the increasing number of bank current accounts and the spread of direct crediting of such accounts for the payment of wages/salaries and state pensions. The spread of ATMs has also contributed to more careful management of cash holdings, Finally, the growth in the banks' "point of contact" has increased the convenience of using bank instruments.

*(b) Instruments, other than cash, issued by the Bank of Italy*

The Bank of Italy issues cashier's cheques for amounts of not less than Lit. 50,000 and not more than Lit. 500 million against cash payment of the corresponding amount. They are cashable at any bank office, including those of the central bank, and may be used for payments to the state and for payments at post offices. Although individuals may request the issue of cashier's cheques, the use of this instrument is limited in practice to certain special nonrecurring payments carried out by the central bank on behalf of public entities (tax refunds and the payment of severance awards to state employees). In 1987, the Bank of Italy issued a total of 4.6 million cashier's cheques for a total amount of Lit. 21, 360 billion.

*(c) Payments in deposit money (excluding cards)*

*Postal instruments*

Postal current accounts are an efficient channel for making and receiving payments. Payment operations associated with these accounts are increasingly processed on an automated basis through networks of terminals which enable postal current-account holders to effect payment and encashment operations automatically in real time.

The Postal Administration provides three payment services in connection with postal current accounts: current-account cheques, inpayments to current accounts, and postal giro transfers; in addition, it operates a cash transfer service (money order service).

*Postal current accounts* enable holders to make and receive payments via the network of post offices. At the end of 1987, the number of accounts stood at 475,000, having registered no significant change over the preceding years. The volume of inpayments to these accounts in 1987 was 492 million, for a total value of Lit. 240,414 billion. These payments are made by presenting printed forms prepared for optical reading at post offices and are generally recurrent and fairly small, for example, utility bills. The amount may be paid in cash, cashier's cheques, banker's drafts, or credit notes; bank cheques, on the other hand, are not accepted. On the whole, transmission times for funds and accounting data are short: Funds deposited in another town become available after three days. The cost to the user varies between Lit. 700 and 900. Inpayment forms may also be used to have funds transferred between postal current accounts. In 1987, 13.3 million postal giro operations were effected for a total of Lit. 118,755 billion. There were 10.6 million cheque withdrawals in the same year for a total of Lit. 218,615 billion. In addition, 17 million special cheques, for a value of Lit. 12,223 billion, were issued for the payment of state pensions.

In the last few years, there have been a number of important projects for the automation of the postal current-account system. More than 2,000 post offices have been equipped with machines able to enter information on paying-in forms in machine-readable characters so as to facilitate subsequent processing. In addition, new services have been made available to users: postal cheques drawn by account holders with the requisite personal code can be cashed in real time at main area post offices; account holders who receive mass payments can receive data on payments made to their order on electronic media; large users may have cheques issued by automated means; postal giro transfers may be effected in real time.

In 1987, 21 million *money orders* were issued for a total value of Lit. 43, 831 billion. Money orders are generally used to remit sums to persons who are not holders of a postal current account. They are issued against payment of the amount in cash and are sent to the post office nearest the home of the beneficiary, who may either collect the sum in cash or have it credited to his postal current account. The money order service is subject to a maximum value limit of Lit. 1 million. When the order is issued, the sender pays a charge according to its value, ranging for ordinary money orders from a minimum of Lit. 700 for amounts of less than Lit. 20,000 to a maximum of Lit. 5,300 for an amount of Lit. 1 million.

The lack of integration between the banking and postal circuits encourages the use of cash. As a first step towards closer links between the two circuits, a plan has been drawn up for *Postal Administration membership of the clearing system* for bank items. In a first stage, the Postal Administration would submit for clearing all bank items it received in payment; the banks, on the other hand, would only be able to present some post office items (special-series cheques and ordinary cheques cashable in real time). In the medium term, Postal Administration membership would be extended to cover all items.

### Bank instruments[2]

*Current-account deposits with banks,* in addition to being used for transactions purposes, traditionally in Italy have been a form of financial investment given that they bear rates of interest that are competitive with other financial assets. At the end of 1987, such deposits totaled Lit. 302,063 billion; in the same year, current-account

---

[2]The data relating to bank payment operations are taken from an annual survey of a sample of 75 CIPA member banks that together account for approximately 80 percent of transferable deposits held with the Italian banking system.

deposits accounted for 21 percent of private-sector financial assets, excluding share-holdings. The average amount on a current account was Lit. 15.611 million. In the last few years, however, these deposits have increasingly taken on the function of liquid funds: In 1980, for example, the average amount held on current account was Lit. 22.3 million at 1987 prices. In addition, there has been a considerable increase in the number of current accounts, from 28.2 per hundred inhabitants in 1984 to 34.2 in 1987.

*Cheques.* The cheque is the most widely used bank instrument: In 1987, customers drew 452 million cheques on their current accounts for a total of Lit. 994,000 billion. Households issued 15 cheques per account for an average amount of Lit. 1.3 million, in addition to approximately four cheques for an average amount of Lit. 0.5 million used to withdraw cash. Nonfinancial firms made greater use of this instrument, issuing 40 cheques per account for an average value of Lit. 3.7 million. Factors of cost and limited acceptability stand in the way of a more widespread use of the cheque. The cost to the user, comprising stamp duty of Lit. 300 plus a bank charge of between Lit. 500 and 800, makes the cheque an expensive instrument to use for low-value transactions. Its limited acceptability results both from the difficulty of cashing cheques except at the branch where the drawer's account is held and from the length of time taken by the collecting bank to make available to the customer the amounts of the cheques paid in to his account. With a view to achieving wider acceptability of the instrument a number of banks some time ago introduced *cheque cards,* personal cards by which the issuing bank guarantees to honor cheques below a certain limit (Lit. 200,000). At the end of 1987, over 1.3 million cheque cards were in circulation. Moreover, in November 1988, an interbank agreement on cheque cards came into force; it provides for the issue in Italy of the uniform cheque card, which will guarantee both ordinary cheques drawn on Italian banks and circulating in Italy, and uniform Eurocheques drawn abroad on Italian banks.

In order to realise cost and time savings, some years ago each bank office was allotted a special identity code (CAB—codice di avviamento bancario). Printed in magnetic characters on cheques (and on any other document to be transmitted from one point in the banking system to another), the CAB facilitates automatic processing.

There are currently two different interbank cheque processing procedures. *Local cheques* drawn on other banks in centers where the Bank of Italy has a branch are exchanged at the bank item clearing with same-day settlement on the accounts held with the central bank; *out-of-town cheques,* on the other hand, are sent by mail to the drawee bank and the corresponding amounts are entered on reciprocal correspondent current accounts maintained by the banks. The time required for funds to be made available is on average three to four days for local cheques; for out-of-town cheques it is longer, reaching a maximum of 29 days. This divergence is due to the fact that, in the case of cheques presented, at the clearing, the collecting bank is informed of the status within a predetermined and short period of time, given that by convention cheques are returned within a maximum time-limit of two days. On the other hand, in the case of items sent by mail, there are no established procedures for notification of status, and the banks therefore make the funds available to customers only after an estimated period beyond which the cheque can be presumed to have been honored.

With a view toward increasing the efficiency of the cheque circuit, in particular regarding out-of-town cheques, two projects have recently been drawn up by the Bank of Italy and the CIPA. Under the first, implemented at the end of 1988, the banks exchange out-of-town cheques on a bilateral basis at clearing houses or departments. The stipulation of a maximum period for returning cheques (six to seven days) reduces the time taken to make funds available to customers. The implementation of an interbank cheque truncation project scheduled for the medium term, on the other hand, depends partially on the current regulatory framework, which stipulates, in particular, that an instrument must be physically available at the place of payment to enable it to be protested.

*Banker's drafts.* The banker's draft (assegno circolare) is similar in its characteristics to the cashier's cheque and the traveller's cheque. It is issued solely by specially authorised banks and central credit institutions (52 at the end of 1987) against cash or debit to the applicant's account. This issue procedure tends to increase the acceptability of banker's drafts and facilitates their collection within the banking system. Moreover, by virtue of their particular characteristics, banker's drafts are extensively used for automated mass payment, chiefly for the payment of wages and salaries.

In 1987, 208 million banker's drafts were issued for a total value of Lit. 395,000 billion and an average value of Lit. 1.9 million. Approximately 70 million banker's drafts were issued for payments of wages and salaries; their average value is fairly low (approximately Lit. 0.7 million), since for a single salary payment the banks generally issue several smaller drafts of equal value to increase their usability and avoid the whole sum being cashed at once.

Banker's drafts are issued by the banks free of charge, since it is to their advantage to have the funds at their disposal between the time of issue and the time of encashment. However, the banks must pay stamp duty on drafts issued at a rate of 6 percent per annum and must also hold on deposit with the Bank of Italy 40 percent of the value of the drafts in circulation, either in cash or in negotiable securities, by way of guarantee for the holders of such paper.

The procedures for interbank processing of banker's drafts are similar to those for cheques: Local items are presented for clearing, while out-of-town items are sent for collection by mail. For the banker's drafts, however, there is no problem of ascertaining their status. Therefore, the release of funds to the customers regarding the drafts exchanged by mail can take place quickly.

*Payment orders and direct credits.* Payment orders and direct credits are less widely used but generally involve larger values than cheques and banker's drafts. In 1987, 104 million operations of this kind were carried out, accounting for a total value of Lit. 2,350,000 billion.

During the 1980s, the banking system has developed automated management techniques with a view toward reducing the volume of paper media generated by the conventional processing of credit transfers. The automated techniques are applied, in particular, for payment orders in favor of a large number of beneficiaries (e.g., salaries, pensions) and involve the transmission, by the customers to the banks, of magnetic tapes containing the information necessary to effect the credit transfers. In 1987, banks executed 53.5 million payment orders submitted by customers on magnetic media, 80 percent of which represented wage and salary payments. An increasing share of these payments takes the form of direct credit transfers to bank current accounts (approximately 50 percent in 1987) owing to, *inter alia,* an agreement concluded in 1984 between the state and the banking system providing for the direct crediting of the wages/salaries of some categories of public employees. In 1987, direct crediting was also extended to public employees' pensions. Nevertheless, a relevant share of the payment orders initiated by magnetic media is still executed by the issuing banker's drafts (45 percent in 1987).

In recent years, the volume of credit transfers exchanged among banks via electronic means has increased considerably. In 1987, about 4.5 million credit transfers were handled via SETIF, which is an interbank system for automated sorting of payment orders using magnetic tapes as the transmission medium; in addition, 10 million payment orders were exchanged among the banks via the interbank network (SITRAD — Interbank Data Transmission System).

The terms applied to the execution of payment orders generally comprise a commission of between Lit. 500 and 3,000 in addition to the debiting of the originator's account, with value date up to two days previously. The average time taken for the funds to be made available to customers amounts to seven days for credit transfers transmitted by mail and five days for operations processed by electronic means.

Payment orders and direct credits are usually settled by entries on accounts that the banks hold with other banks on a reciprocal basis. Only large-value transfers, for Lit. 500 million or more, are settled on the accounts held with the Bank of Italy via the clearing houses and departments.

*Direct debits.* In 1987, some 27 million direct debits were executed by banks, representing a total of Lit. 21,700 billion, chiefly regarding recurrent payments, such as the payment of public utility bills.

This instrument is largely managed by automated techniques. The creditor sends the tape of preauthorized debits to the bank providing the service or, in the case of telephone bills, to the SIA. The items are then sorted and forwarded to the recipient banks via SETIF. The settlement is effected by entries on banks' reciprocal accounts.

### (d) Card-based transactions

*ATMs.* At the end of 1987, 4,367 ATMs were in operation in Italy. On the same date, 505 banks with a network of 3,050 machines belonged to the Italian Bancomat network, and more than 3.9 million Bancomat cards were in circulation. In 1987, CIPA banks' customers (see footnote 2) effected approximately 45 million operations via ATMs, of which 44.5 million were cash withdrawals, 0.1 million credit transfers and payments of public utility bills, and 0.1 million inpayments.

The number of ATMs in service has grown appreciably in the last few years. The objective of the banks in installing these machines has been to achieve cost savings and improve service quality in the provision of cash. This factor, together with the spread of current accounts among lower-income households, has led to an increase in the proportion of cash withdrawals in the total payment services provided by the banking system.

In 1986, the existing regulations, which viewed the installation of ATMs in locations away from bank premises as a form of network expansion that required express authorisation from the Bank of Italy, were greatly simplified. Banks are now required to inform the Bank of Italy if they intend to install machines at remote sites; the Bank of Italy may prohibit installation within 30 days of receipt of the notification. The ATMs may be brought into service provided they satisfy certain conditions, in particular, provided they meet the technical security requirements laid down by the Bank of Italy.

The Bancomat system came into operation in 1983, and enables the holder of a (magnetic stripe) Bancomat card to withdraw cash from any machine in the network. The system may be joined by any bank operating in Italy provided it is able to comply with the system's rules. Since July 1988, some 200 Bancomat machines have also offered nonresident Eurocheque cardholders the possibility of making cash withdrawals in Italy. The only service the Bancomat machines currently offer on a shared basis is cash dispensing, from 6 A.M. to 10 P.M. seven days a week, with daily and monthly drawing limits that vary according to bank and customer, but are of the order of Lit. 500,000 and Lit. 2-3 million, respectively. To raise the level of security of the system the banks belonging to the Bancomat system were recently linked on-line. The coordinator of the system, the SIA, checks withdrawals from the banks linked on-line against the centralised card files. The interbank exchange of data relating to shared-system operations is effected via the SETIF system, which is also managed by the SIA (see below).

In addition to the fixed costs incurred in installing ATMs, issuing cards, and generating personal identification numbers, the card-issuing bank pays the disbursing bank and the SIA commissions of Lit. 1,500 (plus VAT) and Lit. 150 (plus VAT), respectively, on each withdrawal by its customers from an office of another bank. The commission charged to customers on each operation varies appreciably depending on the bank's particular policy.

*POS systems.* POS systems have only recently made their appearance. The first experiments were launched in 1985 by local banks in connection with sporting and cultural events. In the absence of accumulated experience with such systems, no regulatory framework has yet been created for the establishment of POS networks. However, the granting of authorisations for such schemes has been made subject to the adoption of appropriate security standards.

A number of projects undertaken on the initiative of individual banks or groups of banks are in the course of completion. These schemes, most of which are based on the Bancomat card, provide for POS terminals to be connected in real time to the SIA, which can immediately carry out the necessary checks. The debiting and crediting of the customer's and retailer's accounts, respectively, are carried out subsequently. At the end of 1987, 355 terminals were in operation in the experimental schemes mentioned; approximately 2.2 million Bancomat cards were authorised for use on POS systems. The number of transactions carried out in 1987, although modest in absolute terms at 197,000, showed a rapid rate of growth: While in the first half of the year the average monthly transaction volume was 8,300, in the second half it stood at 24,500.

Among the other projects, mention should be made, in particular, of the scheme promoted by 14 banks in certain provinces in Lombardy for an off-line POS system based on the use of a "memory card" (OSCAR card); 335 terminals are scheduled for installation under this scheme.

POS systems appear likely to spread at a significant rate; in this connection it may be noted that between June 1987 and March 1988, authorisation was given for the installation of 3,300 terminals. The interest of the banks in establishing POS networks is partly motivated by the need to compete against the expansion in payment services (essentially credit cards) offered by major retailers.

*Credit cards.* Although on the whole limited, the use of credit cards has grown appreciably in recent years. There are currently two *bank cards* on the Italian market: BankAmericard and CartaSì. At the end of 1987, there were 1.7 million cards in circulation that had been used during the year in 4.9 million transactions (0.9 million of them abroad) for a total value of Lit. 750 billion (Lit. 136 billion representing payments made abroad). The CartaSì card, which was introduced in 1986, is distributed by Servizi Interbancari, a company set up for the purpose with about 40 of the biggest Italian banks as shareholders. The member banks refinance any credits extended by Servizi Interbancari in connection with the use of the card. Abroad CartaSì cardholders have access to networks linked to Eurocard and MasterCard; in addition, Servizi Interbancari has entered into an agreement with the VISA organisation.

Carta Sì and BankAmericard are multifunction cards and can be used to make cash withdrawals at ATMs. CartaSì can also be used as a debit card at POS terminals.

At the end of 1987, 0.6 million *travel and entertainment* cards (American Express and Diners Club) had been issued. During the year they were used in 7.5 million transactions (1.9 million of them abroad) for a total value of Lit. 1,605 billion (Lit. 499 billion abroad).

*Credit cards issued by large retailers and other firms* have recently acquired some importance. The spread of these cards, which according to some estimates numbered approximately 0.1 million at the end of 1987, is encouraged by the fact that generally no subscription fee is charged.

### (e)  Other payment instruments
#### Home and corporate banking

Home-banking and corporate-banking services are not yet well developed, although the latest data available suggest that the banks are showing more interest in providing their customers with this type of service.

According to a CIPA survey on the state of automation in the banking system, in 1987, approximately 14 percent of the respondent banks (representing over 90 percent of the entire banking system, excluding the rural and artisans' banks) provided home-banking and cash-management services. In 1985, the figure had been 7.3 percent.

The growth of home-banking services was encouraged by the decision of the CICR (International Committee for Credit and Savings) in September 1986, that home-banking facilities could be freely provided as long as the banks had means of ensuring the security of the systems adopted, in particular, the protection of data passing between the user's terminal and the bank's data-processing systems.

The provision of home-banking services by the banking industry is conditioned by the fact that users are accustomed to maintaining multiple banking relationships. A study has therefore been launched by the CIPA to define common operational standards for home banking and to plan joint initiatives.

*Commercial bills and bank receipts.* Bills of exchange and bank receipts still represent an important instrument of payment, especially for firms. In 1987, the volume of these instruments handled by the banking system amounted to 159 million, for a total value of Lit. 297,099 billion.

Bank receipts have now gradually supplanted bills of exchange for reasons relating both to stamp duty and to company organisation. Regarding the latter, in 1985, the banking system introduced a procedure for electronic bank receipts (Ri.Ba.), managed by the SIA. This procedure provides for the collection of trade debts in the form of electronic bank receipts. Its main characteristic is that it eliminates physical bank receipts in dealings between the creditor and his bank and between the latter and the recipient bank. Furthermore, the procedure allows the creditor to get quick information about the status of receipts in electronic form. Ri.Ba. has proved highly successful: in 1987 the SIA handled some 15 million electronic bank receipts.

## 2.  Exchange and Settlement Circuits

### (a)  Bank networks
#### Interbank circuits

Two logically distinct phases can be identified within the interbank payment system, relating, respectively, to the exchange of payment data and documents and to the settlement of the debtor and creditor positions arising from the transactions effected.

There are three types of channel for the transmission of data and accounting documents: mail, clearing, and electronic systems. According to a sample survey, in 1986, approximately 50.6 percent of the most common payment operations (cheques and payment orders) were exchanged by mail, 45.4 percent via the clearing houses, and 4 percent by electronic means.

The settlement of transactions takes place either through the accounts that the banks hold at the Bank of Italy or through bilateral correspondent accounts. Approximately 46 percent of interbank payment operations are settled through the centralised accounts for advances and deposits, either directly or via the clearing, and 54 percent through correspondent accounts, with procedures for the settlement of balances at the clearing houses in this case varying widely. Items exchanged electronically are also settled via these accounts.

### Daily clearing of bank items

Bank items are cleared by the Bank of Italy via the clearing houses and clearing departments. The former are located at 11 branches in the main cities and the latter at all the other 84 provincial capitals without a clearing house.

Banks with a large turnover of items are entitled to participate in the daily clearing of bank items at the clearing houses or clearing departments. At the end of April 1988, there were 260 participants in the clearing system, plus the branches of the Bank of Italy and the provincial Treasury offices. The value of items presented for clearing in 1987 amounted to approximately Lit. 4,500,000 billion.

The clearing system accepts paper-based transactions (cheques and banker's drafts, cashier's cheques, credit notes, bills of exchange, and invoices) and, provided prior agreement has been reached among the members, collection operations of any kind (interbank deposits, payment orders for customer account, liquid balances on correspondent accounts, securities, and foreign exchange transactions). The latter operations are exchanged on presentation at the clearing of a form known as a "memorandum" indicating the amount, the reason for the operation, and the counterparty. Operations exchanged in this way may also involve members operating in different centers. Data must be presented at the clearing house or department in paper form in a "session" and not later than 1:30 P.M.

An automated procedure enables a single net position to be determined at the national level for each bank and debited or credited to the "centralised account" of the bank concerned.

Settlement of operations takes place on the same day they are cleared by means of crediting (or debiting) the final clearing balances to the accounts with the Bank of Italy. Banks clearing at several houses or departments may opt for centralised settlement of balances at a single branch of the Bank of Italy, which usually also holds the centralised account for advances and deposits.

A reform of the clearing system is under way. With the new procedure documentary operations will be exchanged at the local clearing, including out-of-town cheques, which, as mentioned earlier, are currently exchanged by mail and settled on correspondent accounts. Wholesale operations will be handled completely electronically from initiation by the originator to notification of the recipient. They will utilise either the "electronic memorandum" system (which is the logical development of the "memorandum" procedure) managed by the Bank of Italy, or the SIPS system (Interbank Payment System via the SIA), which will be managed by the SIA on behalf of the Bank of Italy and will initially cover only nonresident lira operations. Finally, the retail operations processed via SETIF (which is described in more detail below) will gradually be admitted to the clearing system. Under the new system, data will be exchanged electronically, the clearing session will be extended into the afternoon (4 P.M.), and the range of information available to the Bank of Italy and the clearing members will be expanded. The separation of notification and exchange, with the latter also possible outside the clearing house, will prepare the way for the implementation of cheque truncation. A diagram showing the medium-term outlook is appended to this chapter.

### Electronic funds transfer systems

*SITRAD* (Interbank Data Transmission System) started operating in June 1986. It consists of a series of sectorial networks (STACRI, SECETI, COOPELD) interconnected by a network managed by the SIA to which the major banks and the Bank of Italy belong directly. The network carries payment orders, interbank giro transfers between correspondent accounts and free-format messages, i.e., those relating to nonaccounting information. In 1987, the system handled some 10 million payment operations, for a total value of Lit. 53,500 billion and 3.9 million free-format messages. Transactions exchanged via SITRAD are settled at present through correspondent accounts.

*STACRI* (Automated Telecommunications System Between Italian Savings Banks) was established in 1980, and is managed by the ICCRI (Central Institute for Italian Savings Banks). It enables members to execute certain funds transfer operations electronically (e.g., payment orders, giro transfers, Bancomat operations) and to debit or credit correspondent accounts with other savings banks; these accounts are centralised at the ICCRI. Thus STACRI permits multilateral clearing, which has made it possible to reduce the liquid balances held on correspondent accounts by the savings banks; these balances fell from Lit. 165 billion in 1978 to Lit. 8 billion in 1986.

*SETIF* (Interbank Electronic Funds Transfer Service), managed by the SIA, started operating in 1981. SETIF permits the automated execution of interbank payment operations such as payment orders, banker's receipts, public utility bills, and withdrawals from the shared Bancomat network (from Bancomat machines of banks other than the customer's own). At present, the system is based on the exchange of magnetic tapes, but it will soon use the SITRAD network for the transfer of messages. In 1987, SETIF handled 54 million payment operations for a total value of approximately Lit. 54,000 billion. SETIF is centrally managed by the SIA for the collection, processing, and sorting of data. Participation in the system is open to all banks as either direct or indirect members.

### Direct debiting/crediting of centralised accounts

The centralised accounts for advances and deposits permit banks to manage their liquidity in a single account for each institution. Operations on centralised accounts can be grouped under three headings: the debiting of cheques, cash withdrawals and inpayments, and debit/credit transfers in respect of various operations.

At the end of April 1988, centralised accounts were held by 356 banks, of which 285 were also making use of the Bank of Italy credit lines. The accounts can be debited or credited by any of the Bank of Italy's branches. Since the second half of 1986, however, it has been possible for banks to request transmission of the information relating to the debit/credit entries ("daily statement") via the interbank network rather than obtaining it in the traditional manner from the branches of the Bank of Italy.

The project for "direct debiting/crediting of centralised accounts" currently being implemented will enable participants to effect operations directly via SITRAD and to receive information on account entries effected and the new account balance in real time.

### Securities clearing and settlement systems

The clearing and settlement of securities transactions are executed through the clearing houses and the centralised deposit systems at the Bank of Italy and the Società Monte Titoli.

The securities settlement system makes it possible to execute securities contracts between clearing house members in line with stock exchange practices (daily settlement) or at the intervals indicated in the stock exchange calendar, approved annually by Treasury Ministry decree (monthly settlement).

The clearing houses located in the cities with stock exchanges that have a large volume of business, *viz.,* Florence, Genoa, Milan, Naples, Rome, and Turin, effect end-of-month settlements regarding forward contracts, options, and contangos, chiefly in shares. Daily settlements are effected at the Milan, Rome, and Turin clearing houses regarding spot contracts concluded three days previously, chiefly in government securities and bonds. The monthly settlement procedure, which also accommodates transactions between members of different clearing houses, can also be used to settle contracts regarding pre-emption rights.

In addition to the banks, stockbrokers, stock exchange dealers, and financial companies, provided they have been admitted to the stock exchange, may take part in the securities contract settlements upon request. The numbers currently participating are 215 banks, 216 stockbrokers, and 107 stock exchange dealers. The total value of the securities handled in the daily and monthly settlements amounted in 1987 to Lit. 872,229 billion.

The settlement procedures provide for presentation at the clearing of the debit and credit items for each security by each participant in paper form, calculation of the balances for each security, and settlement of cash balances via the daily clearing of bank items and of the balances in securities via the system of centralised management of securities or by physical delivery at the clearing house of securities not available in the centralised deposit system.

There are plans to make it possible for data to be transmitted electronically, to increase the number of certificates deposited with the centralised management systems, and to admit new types of contract to the settlement procedures. Moreover, additional services will be offered, including extending the settlement between different clearing houses to spot contracts.

The system for the "centralised management of government securities" was launched in January 1980, and is based on the principle of fungibility within each type of security deposited. Centralised securities accounts are currently held by 285 banks, 71 stock-dealing and financial houses, and 220 stockbrokers. On December 31, 1987, the Bank of Italy's vaults contained securities to the value of Lit. 580,000 billion, or 86.7 percent of the nominal value of government securities in circulation. Other types of securities, mainly shares, are centralised with the Monte Titoli. On December 31, 1987, the Monte Titoli held 50 percent of the securities eligible for centralised management.

The "centralised securities accounts" system currently being set up will allow subscribers to manage deposited securities in a single account held with any Bank of Italy branch. The exchange of data between operators will be handled by SITRAD, which in the future may also be used for direct debiting and crediting of accounts.

## IV    GENERAL REMARKS

The developments that have taken place in the Italian payment system in the last few years and its foreseeable future evolution raise a number of questions that are currently the subject of wide debate among the participants in the system. The issues include the choice between cooperation and competition; the new kinds of risk connected with the use of electronic payment systems; the adaptation of the regulatory framework to the requirements imposed by technological advance; the entry of nonbank intermediaries into the market for payment services; and the integration of different national systems.

Forms of cooperation underlie all payment systems. In the past, these have centered on the use of common infrastructures, such as clearing houses, and the definition of uniform rules of conduct for the banks.

With the introduction of electronic technology in the payment system, the scope of cooperation is being extended to new areas such as that of ATMs. However, excessive cooperation may lead to a weakening of competition and a loss of market efficiency. Achieving the optimum balance between cooperation and competition is therefore essential if new technologies are to be harnessed in the payment system to maximum advantage.

The decision to opt for cooperation in the field of ATMs has not been extended to include POS systems, for which it was considered useful to allow an initial experimental phase. Given the availability of alternative, rapidly evolving technologies, the introduction of a number of different pilot schemes will enable the market to decide which system is to be preferred from the standpoints of cost-effectiveness and use acceptance. Were, on the other hand, a wide-ranging agreement on cooperation to be sought too early, the system might as a result converge on a level of technology that would risk quickly becoming obsolete.

Moreover, in contrast to ATMs, POS systems can be efficient even if their geographic base is limited, since retail payments, the typical transactions for which POS systems are used, are in fact chiefly local.

In any case, to rule out the possibility of interconnecting the different networks at a future date, it was decided that the systems should adopt common operating standards. In addition, the Bank of Italy decided that pilot schemes would be authorised subject to the adoption of appropriate security standards.

One step towards limiting the scope of cooperation was taken with the revision of the CIPA undertaken in 1986. The new Convention states that joint interbank initiatives may focus most usefully on the establishment of infrastructures and the adoption of standards.

With the widening application of electronic technology certain payment-related risks will assume a growing importance: systemic risks due to the inability of one bank to meet its obligations regarding the rest of the system at the time of final settlement; technical risks arising from network malfunctions and risks connected with "computer crime." The whole set of problems relating to risk is being analysed and investigated and was taken into account in designing the new clearing and settlement system for interbank transactions.

Systemic risks can be reduced by the use of regulatory instruments, by promoting the use of particular settlement channels, or by introducing appropriate market rules.[3] The courses of action hitherto adopted in Italy fall into the last two categories.

In particular, it was decided to promote the direct debiting/crediting of accounts with the central bank which, as real-time settlement systems, do not present the risks inherent in clearing systems owing to the existence of a time lag between exchange and settlement. However, daylight overdrafts on the accounts with the Bank of Italy will not be permitted.

Further appropriate action to counter systemic risks consists of measures to limit individual banks' exposure within the clearing system. To this end, the forms of contract adopted in the SIPS project are based on the novation of liabilities, with the

---

[3] See T. Padoa-Schioppa. "Credit Risks in Payment Systems: The Role of Central Banks," a paper delivered at the Tenth International Conference on Payment Systems, Rome, March 15-17, 1988.

result that only the bilateral balances between participants, and not the individual items channeled into the process managed by the SIA, enter the national clearing system operated by the Bank of Italy.

Finally, adequate information systems and links with the SIA will be established to monitor clearing system participants' exposure during the day.

Once electronic clearing and settlement systems have been introduced and more is known about the scale of credit risk, it will be possible to define measures aimed at reducing such risk further.

To counter the technical risks connected with network malfunctions and the spread of computer crime, action has been taken both in the field of ATMs and in that of electronic clearing and settlement systems.

The ATMs of the Bancomat system are now linked on-line at the national level, thus enablling wthdrawals to be checked in real time. Since the adoption of the on-line link, the number of frauds on the Bancomat network have dropped substantially. In addition, the Bank of Italy has been given special responsibilities in setting the technical security requirements for ATM networks.

With a view toward limiting the risk of malfunctions in the electronic clearing and settlement systems it manages directly, the Bank of Italy is taking steps to ensure a high degree of operational continuity in its own internal data-processing environment. Moreover, as the majority shareholder, the central bank is in a position to exercise control over the management policies and organisational structure of the SIA, which, as has already been mentioned, manages the interbank network.

The development of the payment system will necessitate changes to the current *regulatory framework,* which relates mainly to paper-based payment and debt instruments.

A number of legal problems arise above all in connection with the personal cheque, in particular as regards "protesting"; these problems must be resolved before an efficient interbank cheque truncation system can be put in place.

The use of electronic systems for the clearing and settlement of interbank transactions will make it necessary to draw up suitable regulations to deal with the risks arising from technical malfunctions and the spread of computer crime.

Moreover, rules will have to be introduced concerning the nature and revocability of payment operations effected via POS systems and other electronic devices.

Finally, the process of decertification designed to increase the security and speed of securities transactions will require regulatory changes in order to update the principle of paper-based negotiable securities, whereby title is embodied in the paper instrument.

The presence of nonbank operators in the market for payment services in Italy is not significant at the moment, being limited to a few major retailers that have issued their own credit cards. However, given the continuing development in technology and the growing diversification of the financial markets, it seems likely that new intermediaries will enter the market.

This will pose further problems in adapting the existing regulatory framework, which, as already pointed out, only gives the Bank of Italy regulatory powers over the activity of the banks. What will be required is a framework that would enable the whole payment system to be regulated on an integrated and systematic basis.

Finally, an issue that is now the subject of discussion is the *integration* of the Italian system with those of other countries. While in the past such integration was largely based on connections between private institutions, the need for growing cooperation among national authorities is now widely felt. For instance, the settlement of cross-border securities transactions will involve some form of integration among national and international centralised securities deposit systems.

# V  CONCLUSIONS

Over the next few years competition between the different suppliers of payment services will most likely accelerate the evolution of the payment system.

The awareness that the existence of forces for change does not automatically bring benefits for users, suppliers, and society at large has led the central bank to step up its own activity in this particular area. The projects that have been described here constitute an important stage in the work undertaken by the central bank. They are as yet only partly implemented, completion being scheduled for 1989-90.

Their objectives are various: some are aimed at making the exchange of cheques faster and more efficient within the banking system; another group of projects is designed to create a telematics-based clearing and settlement system; other plans aim to foster the elimination of physical transfer of certificates in the settlement of securities transactions; finally, one project is aimed at linking the bank and postal circuits via the clearing houses.

These projects, together with the initiatives taken by the CIPA and within individual or small groups of banks, are likely to produce several results in the foreseeable future, such as greater and more uniform speed in funds transfers, lower costs for the suppliers of payment services, better quality of information on collections and payments, reduction of the credit risks due to the time lags between the exchange and settlement of transactions, and greater control over the technical risks associated with the use of electronic systems.

Appendix

**Clearing and Settlement Procedures**
(The system described in this chart will start operating in 1989)

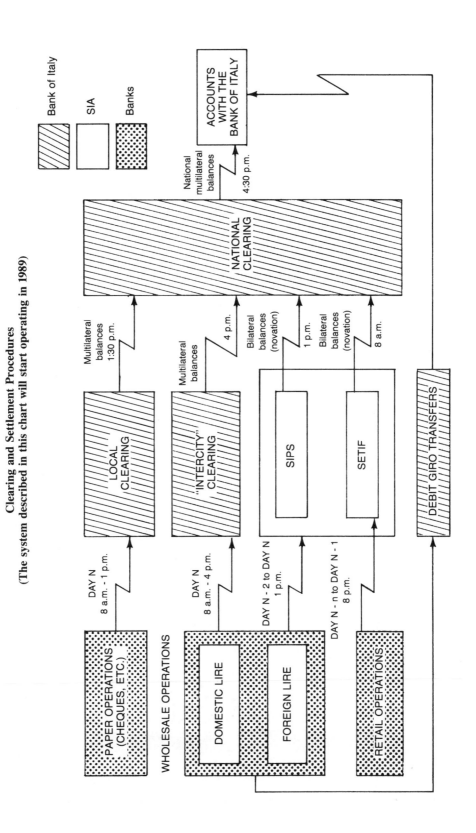

# 6 JAPAN

# Japan

## I INTRODUCTION

In Japan, individuals, firms, and government use a variety of payment instruments.

Individuals traditionally use cash for purchasing goods and services from retailers. Cheques have not gained in popularity despite the efforts made by banks in the 1960s to encourage their use by individuals. Since the late 1950s the banks have been promoting credit cards and preauthorised direct debit and credit systems, which have become widespread. And recently certain firms have begun issuing prepaid cards, a practice that is increasing rapidly. It could be said that, in the personal sector, payment methods have evolved from using cash to electronic media, bypassing personal cheques. Because cash is still widely used for retail transactions, financial institutions have installed a large number of cash dispensers and ATMs so that personal customers can easily withdraw cash.

Firms make extensive use of cheques, bills, and promissory notes. These instruments are collected and settled through the financial institutions' branch networks and local clearing houses. Recently, the volume of electronic funds transfers— including prearranged direct credits — using the interbank network has grown rapidly. Wages and salaries were formerly paid monthly in cash, but nowadays most companies use the prearranged direct credit system. Firms with a large staff send magnetic tapes instead of paper orders to the banks for payroll processing. The direct credit system is also becoming more popular for the payment of pensions and dividends.

Payments by the government are commonly made by government cheques.

## II  INSTITUTIONAL FRAMEWORK

### 1. Institutional Structure

Most payment services are offered by private financial institutions. These include the ordinary banks, which comprise city banks and regional banks, the trust banks, sogo or mutual banks,[1] credit associations, credit cooperatives, and agricultural cooperatives. The separate institutional groups are governed by separate laws. Those other than the ordinary banks are specialised institutions engaging in specific areas of business activity, such as lending to small businesses or the agricultural sector and long-term credit business. During periods of fast economic growth the specialised financial institutions and the ordinary banks have successfully shared functions and complemented one another. However, following a decline in the demand for funds after the Japanese economy entered the current period of stable growth, they have become competitors and their business activities have increasingly converged, so that now practically all institutions offer virtually the same payment facilities.

At the same time, however, the private financial institutions have cooperated in establishing interbank networks such as clearing houses and the Zengin System (see below) to increase the efficiency of the payment systems.

---

[1]The institutional status of sogo or mutual banks will become identical to that of ordinary banks during 1989.

The postal savings administration, a government financial institution, has the largest deposit share, consisting mostly of term deposits. It also operates payment services utilising its transferable deposit accounts, such as the postal transfer system, cash dispensers, ATMs, prearranged crediting of salaries and debiting of public utility charges, all of which compete with those operated by private financial institutions.

Recently nonbanks, namely, finance companies, retailers, securities companies, and insurance companies, have begun to enter the hitherto traditional business domain of the banks, offering payment services via credit cards or providing close substitutes for deposits. Technological advances, in the telecommunication field in particular, have given impetus to this development.

## 2. The Role of the Central Bank

The Bank of Japan, the central bank and issuer of the currency, aims through its operations to stabilise the value of the currency and thereby contribute to the stable growth of the Japanese economy. Another objective is to support and develop a sound financial system, with emphasis on the payment system. To achieve these aims the bank regulates the money supply, on the one hand, and devotes itself to maintaining a sound payment system, on the other. It also provides various payment services for client financial institutions and carries out payment operations on behalf of the Treasury by cashless means. The payment services enable financial institutions that keep chequing accounts with the head office or branches of the bank (34 offices in all) to make payments or settlements by drawing cheques on the bank. In addition, the bank executes funds transfers between client financial institutions using the accounts held at the bank. The net credit or debit balance resulting from the clearance of cheques and bills is also settled by means of transfers of funds between chequing accounts held at the bank's head office or branches. Similarly, the net balance arising from domestic exchanges in the Zengin System is settled through a "settlement account" with the bank. The bank is developing an electronic payments network, namely, "BOJ-Net" (see below), which started its funds transfer operations in the autumn of 1988. Thus, the bank acts as the pivot of the Japanese payment systems.

To maintain the stability of these systems, the bank supervises private payment systems by approving the establishment of and changes to charters regulating private payment systems, and conducting on-site examinations of their member financial institutions.

The government holds an account with the bank on which it draws by cheque. Orders for Treasury payments from the government's account, including social security benefits, may also be sent on magnetic tape to the various financial institutions, which credit the appropriate amount to the beneficiaries' accounts by batch processing.

# III   THE PAYMENT SYSTEM

## 1. Payment Media Available to Customers

### (a)  Cash payments

#### Legal framework

The present currency system in Japan was established in 1882 with the founding of the Bank of Japan. Bank notes issued by the bank are legal tender without limit in all public and private sector transactions (Article 29 of the Bank of Japan Law). The maximum value of the bank note issue is fixed by the Minister of Finance with the approval of the cabinet (Article 30), and the bank is required to maintain collateral equivalent to the value of bank notes issued (Article 32). This collateral comprises gold and silver bullion, foreign exchange, SDRs, bills, government bonds, advances to the government, and secured loans.

Coin is issued by the government, which supplies the Bank of Japan with the quantities required for payments over its counters. The individual coins now in circulation are issued under the Unit of Currency and Issue of Coins Law introduced in 1988, which stipulates that they must be accepted in settlement in amounts of up to 20 times a given denomination (Article 7, e.g., up to Yen 2,000 in 100-yen coins). In the case of payments made to the government, such as taxes, there is no limit to the acceptability of coins utilised (according to the directives of the Ministry of Finance).

### Demand for cash

Bank notes and coin in circulation in Japan at the end of 1987 totaled Yen 31,927 billion, of which the portion held by private financial institutions to meet cash withdrawals from accounts amounted to Yen 3,344 billion, or 10.5 percent of the total. The bulk of the funds withdrawn from financial institutions is used for the payment of wages and salaries, for personal consumption, and for the settlement of small business transactions. In recent years, cashless payment media, such as cards and funds transfers, have become common, but in the household and retail sectors a large proportion of payments is still made in cash.

Cash in circulation is influenced by consumers' propensity to hold cash and by payment practices, neither of which is considered likely to change radically in the short term. Although an increase in personal income and consumption will boost the demand for cash, it is cyclically absorbed in accordance with financial conditions and the phase of the business cycle. Hence, the outstanding cash in circulation during the last 10 years has remained broadly stable at approximately 7 percent of nominal GNP.

## (b) Cashless payments

### Paper-based payments

Cheques, bills, and promissory notes are used as paper-based cashless instruments of payment. Cheques include government cheques, bank cheques, and postal cheques. The cheque is the principal instrument of paper-based payments but, for the most part, cheques are used by public authorities and firms and are not widely employed by the general public. It is rare for individuals to receive salaries or purchase goods and services by means of cheques. Bills and promissory notes are used for payments in the business sector and are also eligible for discounting by private financial institutions. The average value of cheques, bills, and promissory notes cleared during 1987 at the clearing houses in Japan was Yen 15,009 billion per day, of which cheques cleared accounted for some 90 percent. It may be noted, however, that recently the volume of transactions using paper-based payment instruments has been stagnating.

### Paperless payments

#### (i) Preauthorised direct debit

The preauthorised direct debit system was first introduced in 1955 for the settlement of telephone bills. The system expanded rapidly from the early 1960s and is now used extensively for the payment of taxes, school tuition fees, insurance premiums, credit card bills, loan repayments, and public utility charges. The payee delivers a magnetic tape or a bill recording direct debit information to the financial institution in question, which debits the appropriate amount from the payer's account. The transaction is conducted on the basis of a three-party agreement between the payer, the payee, and the financial institution. A handling charge is paid by the payee to the financial institution for each transaction, but this is fairly low compared with the actual handling cost.

To enhance the efficiency of the direct debit system the so-called integrated account was introduced in 1972. While time deposits are the most common form of savings in Japan and ordinary deposit accounts are utilised mainly for personal settlement purposes, the integrated account combines these two types of account in a single passbook and, in addition, offers an overdraft facility. Direct debits are deducted from the ordinary account and, if it is short of funds, the shortfall is automatically made up with an overdraft against the collateral of the time deposit. Thus, the integrated account offers both savings and overdraft facilities and has become widely accepted.

### (ii) Prearranged direct credit

The prearranged direct credit system was initially used for the payment of wages and salaries, dividends, and pensions. The direct crediting of wages and salaries, for example, was begun in 1969 on the basis of agreements between employers and several banks and has evolved to the point where it is used by most leading Japanese firms. Initially, transfer orders were paper-based, but with the spread of office automation, most firms today deliver their transfer orders on magnetic tape.

In the light of this, the Tokyo Clearing House and the Osaka Clearing House have operated a magnetic tape exchange system since 1975 in which 104 financial institutions currently participate. For example, a firm sends its transacting bank a magnetic tape containing instructions for the crediting of wages and salaries, with details of the bank branch code, account number of each employee, and the amount to be credited. The bank sends the tape to the clearing house. The clearing house then consolidates all such tapes and sorts the entries by payee banks, producing new tapes for these banks, which then credit the employees' accounts. The funds are settled through the clearing house. Magnetic-tape-based direct crediting has significantly reduced payment transaction costs for both the employers and the banks. The system also has the advantage of relieving employees of the risks involved in carrying large sums of cash. Recently, many banks have begun offering a cash management service in which each firm is able to send the information required for the direct credit transaction via a wire service to the designated payee banks.

### (c) Card-based payments

#### At retail outlets

Credit cards are gaining in popularity as a payment instrument at retail outlets. Although exact figures are not available, by 1987 some 120 million cards had been issued by banks, bank-affiliated credit card companies, finance companies, department stores, and others. Settlement of credits is effected once a month by means of prearranged direct debits. Those who wish to use credit cards are required first to conclude prearranged direct debit contracts with banks and credit card companies. After a purchase has been made, transaction slips are mailed to the card issuers and then card users are notified of the accumulated amount to be debited from their bank accounts and settle either in full or on an instalment basis. However, banks and bank-affiliated credit card companies are not at present allowed to offer their card users instalment payment facilities in accordance with an administrative regulation.

#### Cash dispensers and ATMs

##### (i) Automated handling of cash

Cash dispenser services using cash cards began with the introduction of off-line computer systems at some city banks in 1969, and spread rapidly following the adoption of on-line computer systems by many financial institutions after 1970.

Automated deposit machines and ATMs were first installed in 1973 and 1977, respectively. The latest ATMs are capable of many functions in addition to the withdrawing and receiving of deposits. These include providing remittances and issuing card loans, together with facilities for accepting coins. ATMs with these multiple functions are spreading rapidly.

From a regulatory point of view, cash dispensers and ATMs installed outside the premises of financial institutions and their branches are treated as separate branches by the Ministry of Finance (MOF), therefore requiring separate authorisation from the MOF in the same way as actual branches. However, since 1987 this authorisation has been replaced by simple notification of the MOF. As a result, many financial institutions have installed cash dispensers and ATMs not only inside almost all of their offices and branches, but also outside their premises, at locations such as department stores and company offices. These cash dispensers and ATMs are generally in operation from 8:45 A.M. to 7 P.M. on weekdays and from 9 A.M. to 2 P.M. on Saturdays, which is longer than normal bank opening hours.

### (ii) Interbank cash dispenser networks

There are two types of interbank on-line cash dispenser networks. One features the reciprocal use of cash dispensers on the basis of a cooperative agreement among financial institutions. This type of on-line network was launched in 1980, and at present nine are in operation, run exclusively by different categories of financial institution, namely, city banks, regional banks, trust banks, sogo or mutual banks, credit associations, labour credit associations, agricultural cooperatives, and the postal savings administration, plus 51 local networks run jointly by financial institutions from different categories. There is no charge for cardholders' withdrawals of cash from their card-issuing bank's cash dispensers, but there is a small fee for using them after 6 P.M. or using another institution's cash dispensers.

The second type of network is the NCS or Nippon Cash Service, established jointly by 36 banks in 1974, and numbering to date 53 participating banks. The NCS has installed 360 cash dispensers mainly in railway stations, hotels, department stores, and large supermarkets in the three largest metropolitan areas. Cards issued by NCS-participating banks can be used at these outlets on payment of a small charge for the service.

### At POS terminals

There are two methods of payment at POS terminals, namely, a deposit-based method and a prepaid method. The real-time deposit-based method, called bank POS, uses cash cards issued by financial institutions for the payment of goods and services. The bank POS was introduced at the end of 1984, and 21 financial institutions are currently operating bank POS machines at supermarkets, filling stations, and other retail outlets. When a customer purchases goods and services using a cash card at a POS terminal during the operating hours of computers at financial institutions, these institutions make real-time payments by transferring a sum equivalent to the amount of the purchase from the customer's deposit account to that of the retail outlet after verifying that the customer's deposit balance is sufficient. In the off-line operations, which apply for example when a customer purchases goods and services during the hours when the computers of the financial institutions are not operating, the parties involved make a short-term credit to the customer within prearranged limits that is recorded and settled electronically on the following business day.

In the prepaid method, customers purchase prepaid cards in advance and use them to make multiple payments up to the value stored. The issuers of the prepaid cards are at present limited to the suppliers of the goods and services and prepaid card companies. Financial institutions are not allowed to issue such cards. Prepaid cards arc suitable for payments of small amounts and are widely used for purchases of many kinds of goods and services, including payment for calls from public telephones and fares on public transport. To date, the goods and services that can be purchased by a single prepaid card are restricted. The legal problems arising from the multipurpose use of prepaid cards are currently being discussed.

### Experiments with chip cards

The cards used in the above-mentioned methods of payment are all magnetic-stripe or embossed cards. Recently, various experiments have been initiated, mainly among banks, using chip cards for payments. In comparison with a magnetic-stripe card, a chip card has a much larger memory capacity and is able to delete and rewrite data.

With these characteristics, chip cards are able to combine the functions of credit cards, cash cards, and prepaid cards. Moreover, owing to their security advantage, they are also suitable for off-line applications at POS terminals. Thus chip cards are expected to reduce banks' computer workload. It is believed, however, that it will be some timc before chip cards are widely used because of the high issuing costs.

### (d) Firm banking and home banking

In response to deregulation in telecommunications, banks are trying to expand their services to include firm banking and home banking.

Firm banking, or cash management services for firms, is offered by many banks. The types of services provided are (1) financial and accounting services, such as keeping track of each transaction and informing firms of the outstanding deposit balance; (2) funds transfer services, such as transferring funds to other accounts and providing a prearranged direct credit system for the payment of wages and salaries; and (3) current financial and economic information services. The telecommunication devices used between firms and banks include telephones, telefaxes, and on-line computer connections.

Cash management services are provided not only by individual banks, but also by the cash management network systems, in which many banks participate. There are four such systems now in operation. The types of services they provide are basically the same as those provided by individual banks. There is the advantage, however, of firms being provided with services by different banks simultaneously when connected to one of the network systems.

A number of banks are conducting home-banking trials using a "CAPTAIN," or videotex network, system operated by Nippon Telegraph and Telephone Corporation. This system enables the customer to be informed of his outstanding deposit balance and to initiate funds transfers at home. In the future, other financial operations, and shopping and reservation services are expected to be added. However, at present, home-banking services are not widely utilised. This is because prearranged direct credit and debit systems offering wages and salaries and public utility payment services are still predominant, and in addition, terminals for use at home are still very expensive. It is believed that it will be some time before home-banking services gain in popularity and become widely used.

## 2. Exchange Circuits Within the Banking System

### (a) Intrabank networks

The most important feature of existing intrabank networks is an integrated on-line, real-time processing system connecting branch terminals to the computer center via telecommunication lines. Today all city banks and many regional banks use such a system. Moreover, large banks are at present introducing highly sophisticated network systems connecting their overseas branches. The on-line systems, which have existed in their present form since about 1970, have not only reduced operating loads and shortened customer waiting time but have also enabled banks to develop new services in the payment field.

In addition to the private banks' on-line systems, the postal savings administration established a computerised on-line system in 1984, covering 23,000 post offices throughout Japan, and providing payment services equivalent to those of private banks.

### (b) Interbank networks

#### The bill-clearing system

Clearing houses are operated by bankers' associations in each district. Under the bill-clearing system, there are currently 185 clearing houses throughout Japan. City banks, regional banks, trust banks, long-term credit banks, sogo or mutual banks, credit associations, credit cooperatives, and branches of foreign banks participate in the system, either directly or indirectly. Items cleared, by value during 1987, amounted to approximately Yen 4,173 trillion, of which more than four-fifths were cleared in Tokyo. Data for the last five years show that the total value of clearings has risen about 2.6 times, while the number of items cleared (approximately 396,000 in 1987) has tended to decrease slightly.

The daily clearing house procedure for bill clearing is as follows (see also Appendix 1). First, the net balances are calculated on an institution-by-institution basis at 10 A.M. on the working day following bill collection, and second, settlement is carried out by transfers between the banks' current deposits at the Bank of Japan at 1 P.M. on the same day.

To maintain the soundness of the bill-clearing operations, two safety measures can be implemented if need be. These are the suspension of transactions and the submission of a small amount of collateral. First, the suspension of transactions is a measure that prevents any firm found issuing dishonored bills twice within six months from effecting transactions with a member financial institution of the clearing house for two years. Second, if a member financial institution cannot settle a debtor balance that is within the value of the collateral deposited with the clearing house, then the collateral is sold and used to offset the amount outstanding.

From the point of view of efficiency, the use of MICR-printed bills and cheques has facilitated the computerisation of clearing operations.

#### The Zengin System

Domestic exchange transactions between private financial institutions are effected through the nationwide Zengin System, an on-line telecommunication network linking financial institutions and the Zengin computer center, which was completed in 1973 and is operated by the Tokyo Bankers' Association. This system comprises direct participants, including city banks, regional banks, trust banks, long-term credit banks, foreign banks, and indirect participants, including credit cooperatives, labor credit associations, and agricultural cooperatives that consign settlement to their agency banks. The participating financial institutions numbered 5,298 at the end of 1987. The volume of transactions handled by the Zengin System during 1987 totaled 454 million and was valued at Yen 1,024 trillion. Transactions mostly consisted of credit transfers, which accounted for approximately 80 percent by volume and 95 percent by value.

The system operates as follows (see also Appendix 2). When a payer requests a remittance, the payer's bank instructs the payee's bank via the Zengin computer center. The payee's bank then credits the payee's account. The funds are available to the payee simultaneously, because the settlement of interbank funds transfers is guaranteed and finalised by the Bank of Japan. Transactions involving receipts and payments via the Zengin System are calculated in the net balance of each participant and are settled by means of transfers between the banks' current deposits at the Bank of Japan at 1 P.M. on the next working day.

If a debtor bank fails to settle, the Bank of Japan finalises the settlement by extending credit on behalf of the debtor bank. Then, the Bank of Japan covers its credit by liquidating the collateral of the debtor bank, which amounts to the average value of the previous year's daily transfers. However, if the collateral is not enough, the participating banks bear joint responsibility for settlement. To prevent the banks' debit values growing excessively large, the net credit limit management system has been implemented since June 1987. The aim of this system is to maintain the banks' net balances between the total amount remitted and total amount received at a fixed multiple level of each bank's average remitted amount during the previous year. In addition, to ensure the security of the computer hardware, separate centers have been set up in Tokyo and Osaka.

### The yen-based settlement system for foreign exchange

Yen-based settlements of foreign exchange transactions are concentrated in this system, which was introduced in 1980 and is operated by the Tokyo Bankers' Association. To date, 83 banks, including 45 foreign banks, participate in the system.

Under this system (see also Appendix 3), the member banks exchange payment instructions on the floor of the Tokyo Bankers' Association at 1.30 P.M. and also tabulate funds received and paid and the net payments; they make settlements through their current deposit accounts at the Bank of Japan at 3 P.M. on the same day.

The system is to be operated through the BOJ-Net (see Appendix 5), and with its implementation, the number of participants is expected to increase from the present 83 to 146. Once this system is operational, payment instructions will be carried through the on-line network of the BOJ-Net, and the net balances of the participating banks will be automatically calculated in the computer center of the Bank of Japan. The final settlement will then be conducted according to the results of this calculation.

### The Tokyo Dollar-Clearing System

Settlements (see also Appendix 4) of dollar and dollar-call transactions in Tokyo usually proceed in the following manner. First, settlements are made by transferring funds between the dollar deposit accounts that participants hold with the same Tokyo branch of U.S. banks, for example, that of the Chase Manhattan Bank. Second, the net settlement balances in the Tokyo branch are transferred to the New York head office and settled through CHIPS. This process is called the Tokyo Dollar-Clearing System. The U.S. banks that provide these settlement services, such as the Tokyo branch of the Chase Manhattan Bank, extend overdrafts to participants with net debit positions. Thus, the banks are exposed to credit risks because of the time difference between Tokyo and New York. These credit risks become larger as the amount settled in dollars increases. Therefore, at the Tokyo branch of the Chase Manhattan Bank, a limit to the overdraft facility for the end of the day has been set for participants to reduce exposure to this risk.

Moreover, the Bank of Japan is encouraging banks to study "netting by novation" as a method of reducing risks with foreign exchange transactions. The idea of netting by novation is that whenever a foreign exchange transaction is entered into by two parties, the obligation regarding that transaction is automatically netted with the previous obligation in the same currency and with the same future settlement date, so that both obligations are novated into a single new obligation. This enables the outstanding gross obligations to be reduced.

*The BOJ Financial Network System*

The Bank of Japan has been developing the BOJ Financial Network System (BOJ-Net for short), which consists of two major parts, namely, the funds transfer system and the securities transfer system. The Bank of Japan started its funds transfer system operations in mid-October 1988, connecting the customer financial institutions directly with the computer center at the Bank of Japan through an on-line network. The paper-based transactions between the Bank of Japan and its customer financial institutions can now be processed through this electronic network.

Of the 640 institutions holding accounts at the Bank of Japan, roughly 330 participate in this system, including city banks, regional banks, long-term credit banks, trust banks, sogo or mutual banks, foreign banks, and securities houses.

The present BOJ-Net performs the following functions: (1) interbank funds transfers through the accounts of the financial institutions at the Bank of Japan; (2) interbank funds transfers with payment instructions for third parties; and (3) the real-time monitoring of participants' reserve positions. The system focuses mainly on the settlements of large-scale transactions and provides a same-day settlement service.

The BOJ-Net is to be extended to cover the yen-based settlement system for foreign exchange. Government bond transfers will also be processed via the BOJ-Net in the future.

Because the BOJ-Net plays an important part in the Japanese payment system, it stresses system reliability and safety, and thus comprehensive security measures have been adopted, including backup facilities. All data in the circuit are encrypted to prevent tapping and modification.

The introduction of the BOJ-Net is expected to provide the appropriate infrastructure for the payment system and thereby contribute to improving the stability and efficiency of the Japanese payment system as a whole.

# IV   GENERAL REMARKS

In line with the rapid development of electronic payment systems the volume of transactions has increased tremendously. In addition, because of the increasing number of participating institutions, owing largely to the internationalisation of the payment network, the existence of systemic risk has been gradually recognised by those concerned. In other words, the risk of default by a participating institution, or of failure by the computer of one participant, might result in the successive default by or failure of other institutions.

Recently, among participating institutions in the payment systems, various measures have been introduced to avert such systemic risks. For example, in the Zengin System the net debit limit system was implemented on a trial basis in 1987. Moreover, in the yen-based settlement system for foreign exchange transactions, a net credit limit will be imposed once on-line processing via the BOJ-Net is complete. Although these attempts are being carried out only tentatively, it is expected that more and more measures to avert risk will be implemented eventually.

As the volume of electronic funds transfers increases, so the problem of ensuring the legal soundness of such transactions has come to light. On this subject, there have been discussions among the parties concerned, including the Bank of Japan, on whether or not the current statutes in force to regulate paper-based funds transfers are sufficient for electronic funds transfers.

# V   CONCLUSION

Payment systems in Japan are evolving towards a paperless and cashless future, both in the corporate and the household sector. However, it is believed that the importance of cash payments will not decrease in the near future, providing the share of demand for cash regarding nominal GNP remains stable. It is certain that the share of cash will decline in comparison with that of electronic funds transfers. Nevertheless, the cash transaction—it is still believed—will continue to play an important role as one of the principal payment instruments, its advantages being its very anonymity and universality.

The extent to which electronic payment systems can evolve largely depends on the security and convenience they can provide. In this sense, it is important, first, that the soundness of private financial institutions—which are, after all, the most important members of the payment systems—be maintained, second, that risks arising from payment systems as a whole be managed adequately, third, that each transaction be safeguarded legally, and, finally, that payment instruments be standardised technically.

Appendix 1

**Mechanism of the Bill-Clearing System
(Tokyo Clearing House)**

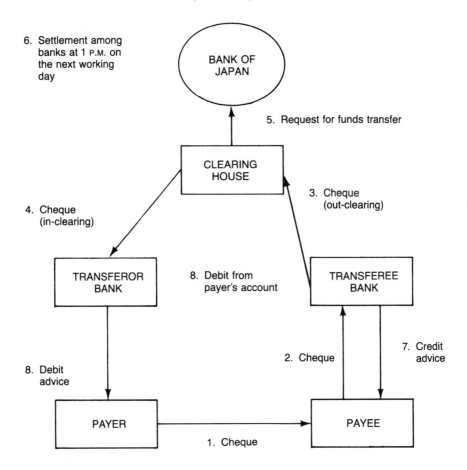

6. Settlement among banks at 1 P.M. on the next working day

BANK OF JAPAN

5. Request for funds transfer

CLEARING HOUSE

4. Cheque (in-clearing)

3. Cheque (out-clearing)

TRANSFEROR BANK

8. Debit from payer's account

TRANSFEREE BANK

2. Cheque

7. Credit advice

8. Debit advice

PAYER

PAYEE

1. Cheque

Appendix 2

**Mechanism of the Zengin System**

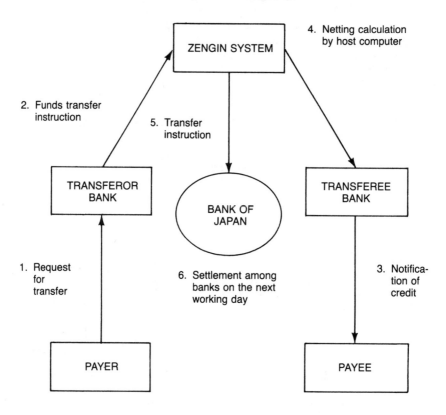

Appendix 3

**Mechanism of the Yen-Based Settlement System for Foreign Exchange**

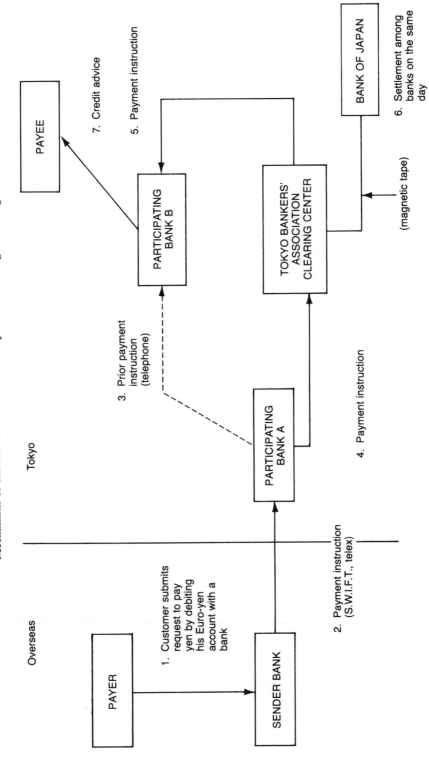

Appendix 4

## Mechanism of the Tokyo Dollar-Clearing System

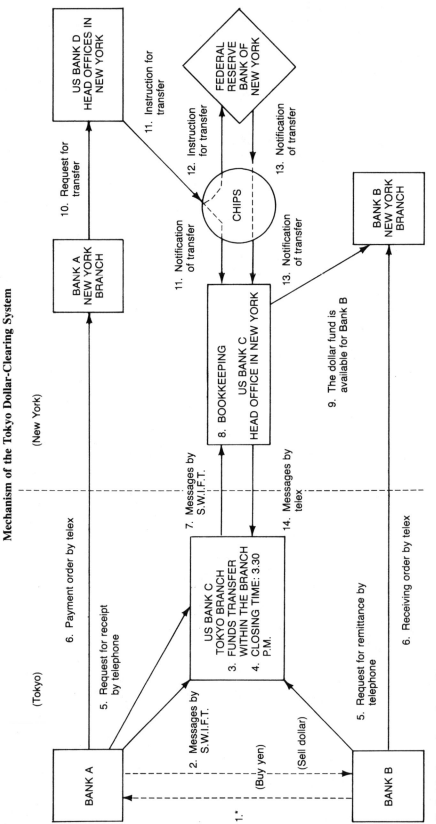

*1. Spot foreign exchange transactions.

Appendix 5

**Mechanism of the BOJ-Net**

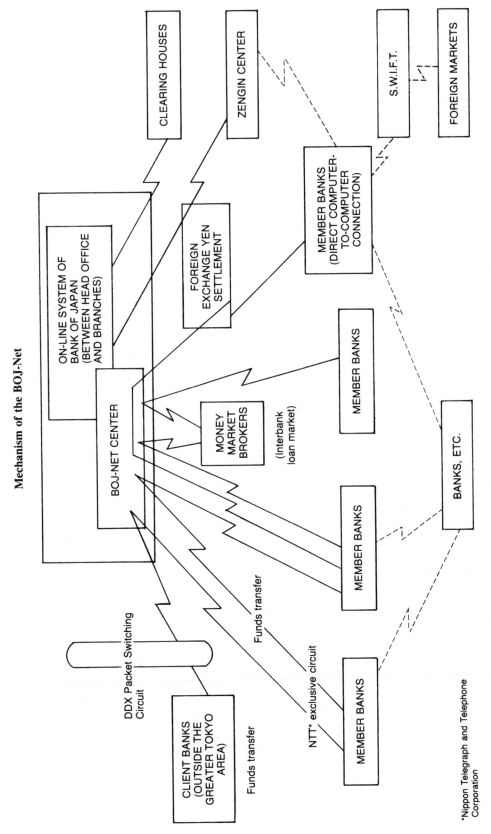

# 7 THE NETHERLANDS

# The Netherlands

## I  INTRODUCTION

The Netherlands is a densely populated country, with a great many banks, including the Postbank (the former Postal Cheque and Giro Services) that offers, as far as payment and savings facilities are concerned, the same services as the other banks.

In the Netherlands, payment services are offered by the banks; there are no nonbank institutions offering payment transfer services.

The Netherlands is very much a giro country. Of total cashless payments, 80 percent are made by means of some form of giro transfer and 20 percent are made by (guaranteed) cheque. Cashless payments are processed in three (interconnected) transfer circuits: the circuit of the Nederlandsche Bank (the central bank), that of the banks, and that of the Postbank. While the share of the central bank in the processing of payments is small (less than 1 percent of transactions), the banks' circuit and that of the Postbank are about equal in size. These two systems offer a wide variety of services to the customer (see Section III). There is close cooperation in transfer services, especially between the banks, and this has led to a highly efficient payment system. At the level of the banks' circuit, interbank cooperation is reflected in the Bank Giro Center, an automated clearing house, in which practically all the banks (though not the Postbank) participate.

Because of this highly efficient payment system and the wide use of guaranteed cheques, there was for a long period of time little interest in electronic payment services compared with other developed countries. In recent years, however, the banks have been installing more and more ATMs. POS systems have also come into operation. Credit card payments do not play a significant role in the Dutch payment system. Until a year ago, payment services were free for private customers. At present, the services of the Postbank are still free, although no interest is paid on credit balances, while the banks make charges but offer interest on credit balances. Most Dutch households possess one or more payment accounts. At the end of 1987, there were 15.16 million accounts, or 1.04 per head of the population.

## II  INSTITUTIONAL FRAMEWORK

### 1. Institutions

Payment services are provided by the Nederlandsche Bank and the deposit-taking institutions, including the Postbank.

#### (a)  The Nederlandsche Bank

The Nederlandsche Bank is the central bank of the Netherlands. It is a state-owned limited liability company. The Bank Act of 1948 ensures that it has a large degree of independence of the government. The central bank has the sole right to issue bank notes.

Moreover, the Bank Act of 1948 contains a section that in general terms provides that the Nederlandsche Bank must facilitate domestic money transfers. The Nederlandsche Bank acts as the settlement institution for the banks and also as the cashier to the central government. The bank monitors developments in the banking sector closely. A special Payment Systems Policy Planning Department, which monitors both national and international developments, was set up in 1982. On the basis of the Bank Act of 1948, the bank claims an active role in the development of the payment system. Consequently it is closely involved in establishing the National Payment Circuit, an infrastructure that will integrate the existing payment circuits.

### (b)  Deposit-taking institutions

The banking sector in the Netherlands is made up of commercial banks, banks organised on a cooperative basis, savings banks, the Postbank, mortgage banks, and securities credit institutions. The last two types of institution, which have access to the payment system only through an account at a deposit-taking institution, do not offer payment services and will not be dealt with here. As is the case in many other countries, the different deposit-taking institutions offer the same range of services. As a result, and given the rise in costs and the decline in economic growth, competition has grown.

Until the 1960s, the banks did not play a significant role in payment transactions involving small amounts, but dealt primarily with corporate and institutional payments, while the former Postal Cheque and Giro Services handled virtually all the payment transactions of private individuals. This division of the market changed when the banks, prompted by their need for additional deposits that would enable them to expand their lending operations and improve their liquidity, began promoting the use of personal accounts by the public at large. Automation had advanced sufficiently to permit the processing of the large numbers of payment orders resulting from such accounts.

#### Commercial banks

There are 83 commercial (universal) banks with 2,338 branch offices. This figure includes establishments of foreign banks dealing mainly with payments on behalf of business customers. The banks offer a wide range of services to their customers; these include insurance, payment facilities, loans and mortgages, foreign exchange, stockbroking services, and in some cases even travel services. They operate on both the retail and the wholesale market. The largest are represented throughout the country and have a network of foreign offices.

#### Banks organised on a cooperative basis

The 926 banks in this category are organised under Rabobank Nederland and operate as a single institution. The Rabobanks maintain a total of 2,345 branches and are strongly represented in country areas. Originally, they were agricultural credit institutions, but they have developed a full range of banking activities and are now also represented in the cities. Although the individual banks are independent in many ways, the products that they offer are completely standardised. Rabobanks are primarily retail banks, but they have now entered the wholesale market, and Rabobank Nederland is opening foreign branches.

#### Savings banks

The 58 savings banks are nonprofit-making institutions, one of their objectives being to promote thrift. The need to remain competitive has encouraged concentration. Most savings banks cooperate in De Nederlandse Spaarbankbond, which owns a commercial bank, but the savings banks have remained independent and operate under their own names. Although they are still geared to collecting savings and deposits, they have gradually introduced a full range of banking facilities and stockbroking services. Some of them have expressed the wish to become commercial banks in a few years' time.

*Postbank*

The Postbank became a state-owned bank in 1986. It is the successor to the former Postal Cheque and Giro Services (PCGD), which provided payment facilities for almost 70 years. The Postbank has its own closed circuit for payments. It already offers many banking services and is putting pressure on the government to widen its range of services. For many years, the Postal Cheque and Giro Services were virtually the only institution offering payment services to private individuals. At the end of the 1960s, however, when the banks entered retail banking on a much larger scale, it faced competition and is now losing ground to the banks. Although the Postbank is fully state-owned, privatisation is under consideration.

*(c) Bodies responsible for monitoring and promoting developments in the payment system*

The Steering Committee on the National Payment Circuit is the only national body with responsibilities in this field. It is composed of representatives of the commercial banks, the cooperative banks, the savings banks, the Postbank, and the Nederlandsche Bank. The Ministry of Finance participates as an observer. Its aim is the technical integration of the three domestic transfer systems, ultimately on the basis of ISO standards for Open Systems Interconnection, so as to obtain an improved service at lower operational cost. The reason for developing the National Payment Circuit is that the Postbank, the legal successor of the Postal Cheque and Giro Services, holds no accounts with the banks, so that transfers between the banks' and the Postbank circuits tend to be relatively slow, while the execution and clearing of payments within each circuit are normally effected one day after receipt. In 1975, the Minister of Finance, pursuant to Article 9 of the 1948 Bank Act, invited the president of the central bank to chair a steering committee to study the integration of the three domestic transfer circuits; the committee's investigations were oriented toward a national transfer system possibly comprising decentralised processing of payment orders and large-scale use of electronic data communication. Work on the establishment of this system is still in progress.

The banks and the Postbank, under the chairmanship of the Nederlandsche Bank, are also discussing the implementation of a national POS system. They also cooperate, with regards to payment services, on Eurocard and on inpayments.

# III  PAYMENT SYSTEMS

## 1. Payment Media Available to Customers

*(a) Cash*

Bank notes and coin are the media used for cash payments. Both are legal tender, although the acceptance of coin by the public is compulsory only up to certain maximum amounts. All coins are produced by the Mint, an institution supervised by the Ministry of Finance, under the terms of the 1948 Coinage Act. The 1948 Bank Act stipulates that the Nederlandsche Bank has the sole right to issue bank notes.

At the end of 1987, the currency in circulation consisted of seven denominations of bank note (Fl. 1,000, 250, 100, 50, 25, 10, and 5) and seven denominations of coin (Fl. 50, 10, 2.5, and 1, and 25, 10, and 5 cents). The currency in circulation at year-end 1987 amounted to Fl. 33.3 billion, of which Fl. 31.8 billion was accounted for by bank notes. These figures exclude the notes and coins held at banks, which totaled Fl. 2.1 billion.

Over the year the volume of currency in circulation shows a distinct wave pattern, with peaks in the summer months and in December. Within each month, there is generally a low in the third week. In 1987, the bank note circulation fluctuated between Fl. 29.2 billion and Fl. 34.0 billion.

### Bodies managing the currency

Coins in denominations of less than 1 guilder are brought into circulation by the post office and bank notes and coins in denominations of 1 guilder or more are distributed by the central bank, through its head office and its 12 branches throughout the country, to banks, post offices, and some large enterprises. The often substantial amounts taken up by these institutions are debited to their current accounts with the central bank. The public in turn obtains from the bank branch offices and post offices all over the country the notes and coin necessary to meet normal household expenditure, withdrawals being debited to their accounts. Cash in excess of the public's needs is returned to the central bank, which is responsible for checking and replacing used notes and detecting counterfeits.

The stock of notes and coin held at the banks and the Postbank fluctuates between 4 and 6 percent of the currency circulation.

The Bank Act of 1948 gives the Nederlandsche Bank responsibility for the currency circulation in the Netherlands. Bank notes are put into circulation by meeting the demand from banks and the Postbank. As they will, on the other hand, tend to keep any debit balance at the Nederlandsche Bank (on which they must pay interest) as small as possible and, on the other, seek to invest cash not needed so as to earn maximum interest (the central bank does not pay any interest), they will hold their stock of bank notes at a minimum. Cash no longer needed by the banks and post offices is returned to the central bank and the remitter's current account is credited accordingly. In 1987, a total of 794.2 million bank notes (with a value of Fl. 56.3 billion) was taken up by the banks and a total of 782.2 million (with a value of Fl. 52.9 billion) was returned. The bank notes returned from circulation are handed in at the Netherlands Bank's head office or its branches in the country. The returned notes are processed centrally at the bank's head office. Bank note sorting at the Nederlandsche Bank is fully automated. In one integrated process, soiled notes and counterfeits (rare) are removed, the notes are counted, and their numbers registered. The machines used in this process are each equipped with a device to produce magnetic tapes for the large file registration system that is kept on the bank's central computer.

### Users

In the Netherlands, the average household makes most of its payments in cash. However, the larger the amount involved, the greater the tendency to use transfers or guaranteed cheques.

While no precise figures are available, the use of cash to pay wages, salaries, pensions, and social security benefits has become rare, with virtually all such payments now being effected by transfer. Apart from everyday expenses, cash is still used in cattle trading and in the used-car market, as well as when tax evasion plays a role.

No exact figure is available for the number of cash payments. As a rough estimate, 90 percent of all transactions are effected in cash. Their total value in 1987 has been estimated at about Fl. 530 billion.

### (b) Cashless payments

#### Deposit money

Approximately two-thirds of the money available to the economy for payment transactions at the end of 1987 was held in the form of sight deposits with banks and the Postbank, while the remaining one-third was held in the form of bank notes and coin. There were 15.16 million sight accounts (5.3 million administered by the

Postbank and 9.8 million by the banks) for a population of 14.6 million. Some 1.5 billion cashless payments using deposit money, for a total value of Fl. 2,480 billion, were made by bank and Postbank customers in 1987; transfers in the Netherlands Bank's books, mainly by banks, totaled approximately 0.8 million for a total value of Fl. 8,772 billion.

The commercial, cooperative, and savings banks operate 5,718 branch offices, all offering sight account facilities and the related payment services via the Bank Giro Center. The Postbank, which has its own circuit for payments, offers its payment services through the 2,705 post offices.

There is no general legislation governing transfer payments in the Netherlands; the normal civil and commercial laws apply. This means that no one is under an obligation to accept cashless payment in settlement of debts, because only coin and bank notes are legal tender. However, the legal view that has evolved over the years is that anyone who makes public (or causes to be made public) the fact that he holds an account is regarded as having given prior consent to payment into and/or transfers to that account, which he cannot therefore reasonably refuse. Planning is underway to include a provision in the new Civil Code to the effect that a transfer payment is equivalent in law to payment in coin or bank notes. Under the present legislation, the Financial Transactions Emergency Powers Act of 1978, these types of payment can only be equated in times of war or other exceptional circumstances. The Bank Act of 1948 contains a section that in general terms provides that the Nederlandsche Bank must facilitate domestic money transfers.

It is estimated that in 1987 approximately 1.5 billion cashless payments were effected through the banks and the Postbank. The banks handled 54 percent of transfers by volume and 55 percent by value, while the Postbank effected 46 percent of transfers by volume and 45 percent by value, primarily on behalf of private individuals.

*Payment instruments*

The banks and the Postbank offer the same payment services. The following payment instruments may be distinguished:

▶ Ordinary credit transfers.
▶ Preprepared transfers.
▶ Direct debits.
▶ Cheques.
▶ Cards.

Essentially three instruments are used: transfers, direct debits, and guaranteed cheques; others, such as the ordinary cheque and the credit card, play an insignificant role. Cash payments are used mainly in the personal sector for small day-to-day household purchases; as the value of the payment increases, and for all transactions in trade and industry, cashless instruments are preferred. Transfers are the most frequent medium used for the payment of rent, insurance premiums, gas, water and electricity bills, subscriptions, and so forth.

Wages and salaries are paid mainly by transfers into the earners' accounts. Transfers are also used on a large scale by public administrations. Of every 100 giro payments dealt with by banks and post offices in 1987, 81 were transfers (98.6 percent of the total value) and 19 were cheques (1.4 percent of the total value); the proportion accounted for by payments by holders of credit cards and other minor instruments is insignificant. In 1987, approximately 290 million guaranteed cheques were used for payments.

When making an *ordinary credit transfer,* the account holder instructs his bank to debit his account with the amount indicated in his transfer order, and to credit that amount to another account, likewise indicated by him, at a bank. Practically all nonrecurrent payments in trade and industry, as well as some household payments, are effected by means of ordinary credit transfers. This payment instrument is also used on a large scale by the central government and local authorities.

When used by households, the ordinary credit transfer is always in paper form; for corporate customers and government institutions it is in a nonpaper-based, machine-readable form.

*Preprepared transfers* fall into two categories; the regular transfer and the inpayment transfer. In the regular transfer, the account holder gives his bank a standing order to transfer, on fixed dates, fixed amounts to an account indicated by him. This (nonpaper-based) form of payment is frequently used for rent, subscriptions, insurance premiums, and so forth. On the fixed date the bank effects the transfer, and no further action by the account holder or the creditor is required. The second form of preprepared transfer, the inpayment transfer, is initiated by the creditor. Together with his bill, he sends the debtor a fully prepared transfer form, in most cases complete with the debtor's account number, which he knows from previous payments. All the debtor has to do is to sign the form and send it to his bank. This payment medium is used for both regular and nonrecurrent payments of either fixed or varying amounts, e.g., for telephone bills, insurance premiums, and subscriptions, as well as for bills for deliveries to regular customers. Unlike the regular transfer, this preprepared transfer is a paper-based instrument.

For inpayment transfers, the banks and the Postbank have developed a joint procedure.

*Direct debits* constitute a separate category, although they have much in common with inpayment transfers. The transfer is again initiated by the creditor, who has been authorised beforehand by the debtor to charge his account for goods delivered or services rendered, and no further action on the debtor's part is required. This procedure is frequently used, for example, by public utilities.

Direct debits can be made only within the individual transfer circuits.

Because a satisfactory transfer system was available to the public from an early date, the *cheque* never played a major role as a domestic payment instrument in the Netherlands. In the second half of the 1960s, however, the guaranteed cheque was introduced. The first (1967) was the guaranteed bank cheque issued by the banks for domestic use, and the second (1969) the guaranteed giro cheque of the Postal Cheque and Giro Services; the Eurocheque was introduced in 1973. The guaranteed bank cheque and the guaranteed giro cheque are guaranteed by the issuing institutions for amounts not exceeding Fl. 100 and Fl. 200, respectively; they are made available to account holders on request. The Eurocheque is guaranteed up to an amount of Fl. 300.

These three payment instruments can be used only in conjunction with a cheque guarantee card carrying the cardholder's account number and signature. The cheques can be used in the Netherlands for practically all purchases. In addition, the guaranteed giro cheque and the Eurocheque can be used in a number of other countries for cash withdrawals (both) or purchases (Eurocheques only).

In 1979, the banks introduced a new form of bank cheque that can only be used for the payment of taxes.

The use of *credit cards* is not significant, although it has increased somewhat. The credit card that is most used for payments within the Netherlands is the Eurocard, in which both the banks and the Postbank participate.

Retail chains are actively promoting their own *customer cards*. The volume and value of transactions are not known. Compared with the use of the payment instruments offered by the banks (and cash), however, their role does not appear to be significant.

The use of *ATMs* is growing. The banks began installing ATMs, with only a cash dispensing facility, in 1985. The customer uses the same card as for guaranteed cheques.

The use of *POS* terminals seems to be on the increase in the Netherlands. Following the launch of a joint pilot project of the banks and the Postbank in 1985, which was made permanent in 1987, the Postbank has begun to install POS terminals at petrol stations. Mainly on the strength of the response from both consumer and retail organisations, the banks and the Postbank, under the chairmanship of the Nederlandsche Bank, are now discussing the implementation of a national POS system. The customer uses the same card as for guaranteed cheques.

### Interbank networks accessible to customers

Any ATM installed by a savings bank can be used by all savings banks' customers. The ATM installed by a bank participating in the Bank Giro Center (with the exception of the savings banks) can be used by all the customers of the other participating banks.

It is expected that these banks and the savings banks will provide access to the other group's ATM networks in due course.

The POS terminals in the former pilot project are accessible to customers of both the banks and the Postbank.

There are no other intrabank or interbank networks that are accessible to customers.

### Others

The Postbank and the other banks have separate systems for urgent payments. The Postbank has a home-banking trial system with approximately 1,000 participants. It is to be continued after the trial period has ended in 1988. Several banks, notably also the Netherlands branches of large foreign banks, offer corporate cash management systems.

The form in which transfer instructions are given is gradually changing. The share of ordinary credit transfers submitted to the banks on transfer order forms which have to be converted manually into machine-readable transfer instructions decreased from 21 percent of the total of bank transfer items in 1977 to 16 percent in 1987. This is partly due to the fact that business customers are using more transfer orders that are machine-readable. Within the category of machine-readable transfer instructions there are also changes. The punched card has disappeared, while the diskette is making rapid headway. The volume of transfer instructions transmitted over data communication links is growing.

### Pricing policy

Until mid-1987, payment services were, for the most part, free of charge for the private customer, although there was an implicit cost-related charge to the virtual value date. On the other hand, the banks paid a very low rate of interest (¾ percent) on credit balances. Business customers were mainly charged commissions.

In mid-1987, the situation changed. At present the Postbank still makes no charges, but has dropped the payment of interest on credit balances. The banks make charges, but pay higher interest rates depending on the size of the credit balance. The nature of the charges differs per bank. The largest savings bank offers the VISA card and payment of interest on credit balances above a certain amount, and makes no other charges.

As a general rule, the central bank has stated that each institution's payment services have to cover the costs, thereby counteracting cross-subsidisation.

## 2. Exchange Circuits Within the Banking System

*(a) Transfer circuits*

Cashless payments are processed in three (interconnected) transfer circuits:
▶ The banks' circuit, in which the commercial, cooperative, and savings banks participate.
▶ The circuit of the Postbank.
▶ The circuit of the Nederlandsche Bank.

### *The banks' circuit*

The banks' circuit is basically a decentralised system. It is characterised by greatly varying levels of automation between banks. In 1967, the banks formed the Bank Giro Center to facilitate the collection and processing of transfer orders among themselves and between their own and the other transfer circuits. The system of the Bank Giro Center is fully computerised and is operated in two centers. The transfer orders received by the banks' branch offices, insofar as they are paper-based, are converted to machine-readable data carriers, nowadays practically all in the form of magnetic tapes. The data carriers are sent to the Bank Giro Center, where the information is processed in such a manner that for each individual bank a machine-readable data carrier is obtained, containing all the credits to accounts of that particular bank's customers.

The Bank Giro Center is merely an intermediary between the participating banks. It receives debit items and converts them into credit items, for individual banks and account numbers, by means of an automated system. The center does not know the balances on accounts, makes no entries in accounts and, consequently, does not itself produce statements of account. It is the individual banks themselves which, using automated processes, make the actual debit and credit entries in the accounts and produce the statements of account, which they send to their customers.

Although each bank has its own internal processing system for in-house payments, the Bank Giro Center is not only used for exchanging payments with other banks, the Postbank circuit, and the Nederlandsche Bank, but also for processing in-house payments for banks that choose to do so. Most savings banks are connected to the Bank Giro Center through De Bank der Bondsspaarbanken, a commercial bank owned by the savings banks. Many savings banks have only a regional base, but by operating their own data communication network they are able to offer services all over the country through each other's offices.

It is clear that these purely technical operations of the Bank Giro Center must be followed by financial settlement. For this purpose the participating banks have authorised the center to effect a daily clearing through the Nederlandsche Bank; the account of each bank is debited or credited with the difference between its total debit and credit items.

With the exception of the Postbank, all Dutch deposit-taking institutions participate in the Bank Giro Center. The way in which the Bank Giro Center functions leads the public to view the banks' transfer system as an integrated entity.

The Bank Giro Center also plays a role in the processing of guilder payments originating in foreign transfers. It operates a special system in which the guilder payments from the (Dutch) correspondent bank to the bank of the payee are processed (and cleared). The result is added to the clearing result of domestic payments.

At present some banks participate actively (i.e., make payments through the system), but most banks participate "passively" (i.e., only receive payments). It is expected that all banks will participate actively within a few years. The participants in this system also include the Postbank. Data from the system are also incorporated in the balance-of-payments returns to the central bank.

### The circuit of the Postbank

Processing at the Postbank is characterised by a high degree of centralisation, all payment items being processed in three central offices, and by a high level of automation. The booking process in these centers is divided into two parts: one in which the accounts are debited and one in which they are credited.

Prior to this process, the paper-based payment orders are converted and put onto machine-readable data carriers. But more and more users now present their orders for credit transfers or direct debits in the form of magnetic tapes.

Most of the booking procedure in the three centers is computerised, but verification of the debtor's signature, and checking that the name and number on the voucher belong to the correct account, is carried out manually. In the case of ordinary credit transfers the original voucher is attached manually to the daily statement and sent to the creditor. The circuit of the Postbank has greatly contributed to the success of the Dutch cashless payment system.

### The circuit of the Nederlandsche Bank

The circuit of the Nederlandsche Bank embraces only a limited group of account holders, mainly banks, money and capital market institutions, and public authorities. It operates through a centralised on-line/real-time system, which completes all transfer orders on the day of receipt. Statements of account are in the possession of the participants on the following day. The Netherlands Bank's circuit serves as the final settlement system for the other two systems. In addition to its role as a settlement institution, the central bank acts as cashier to the central government; transfers effected in that capacity in 1987 amounted to approximately Fl. 284 billion.

### (b) Exchange circuits, clearing, and settlement of transfers

To exchange items the banks, as already noted, use their Bank Giro Center. After processing, the resulting payment obligations are netted out so that an institution will either owe or receive an amount. Clearing figures are presented each working day to the Nederlandsche Bank via its on-line system at about 1 P.M. Until about 2.30 P.M. other items, for instance, payments stemming from money market transactions, can also be presented to the Nederlandsche Bank via the on-line system. The Nederlandsche Bank determines the banks' positions for that day. Items from the banks' circuit for the Postbank circuit are also passed through the Bank Giro Center. Settlement of these items is effected through an account held by the Bank Giro Center with the Postbank. This account is replenished regularly through a payment in the books of the Nederlandsche Bank.

The banks hold accounts with the Postbank for payments to be made from a postal giro account holder to a bank account holder. Ultimately, the amounts are withdrawn from the Postbank circuit through the account held at the Nederlandsche Bank.

### (c) Exchange circuit for securities

The system for exchanging securities is largely a giro system. The securities themselves are kept in safe custody by banks or by Negicef, the central safekeeping and administration institution, owned by the Stock Exchange Association, the banks, and the central bank (each with a one-third holding). The depositary records the right of a person to a specific number of securities. After (home) trading has taken place, the change of ownership is recorded by the depositary. In principle, this is done by communicating the trade data to the Securities Clearing Corporation. The selling party instructs Negicef to debit its account in a certain security and to credit the account of the Securities Clearing Corporation with Negicef to settle the transaction. The financial settlement is effected via the Kas-Associatie, a specialised banking institution which is a 60 percent subsidiary of the Stock Exchange Association. The banks, however, also use another settlement procedure, whereby the contracting parties themselves inform Negicef. The payments are also effected separately via the central bank on the initiative of the parties. In this way same-day settlement is possible. The point is that in the Netherlands there are no fixed rules on settlement dates in relation to trade dates.

A special place is occupied by the money market instruments CP (commercial paper) and CDs (certificates of deposit). At the request of the banks, the central bank acts as clearing institute and as depositary. Thus the administrative system of securities ownership is not only fully giro-based, but clearing and settlement can also take place on a same-day basis and the trade date can be the same as the settlement date. This point is of particular importance because of the money market aspect of CDs and CP.

## IV   GENERAL REMARKS

In the autumn of 1987, the central bank, pursuant to the Bank Act, issued a memorandum describing four aspects that in its view form the basic principles in the development of the payment system. They are:

▶ Uniformity of the infrastructure: There should be no competition in the provision of infrastructures, and there should also be an incentive to make the infrastructure transparent for the customer.

▶ Cost coverage: Payment services as a product should be cost-effective for every bank. Moreover, the pricing of services should foster the use of the more efficient among them.

▶ Product conditions: Everyone should be able to have access to the payment system, and the services should be transparent for the customer.

▶ Fraud and security: Special attention should be devoted to fraud and the security of the payment system.

The Minister of Finance has stated in Parliament that because of the private nature of the banking business, he sees no fundamental role for the government, but that he agrees with the view of the central bank mentioned above. In principle, the banks are in agreement with the memorandum. The central bank is currently examining its possible expansion.

A major topic of discussion, apart from the memorandum, is the cost-effectiveness of the payment services. Here the banks and the Postbank are in opposition. The banks state that their payment system is very costly as a result of the payment services provided for private customers. The Postbank, however, claims that its payment system is cost-effective and, besides, that the private customer is more lucrative than the corporate customer. This is also more or less the view of the largest savings bank.

A common problem for all banks, including the Postbank, concerns interbank charges. The situation in the Netherlands reveals a distinct pattern whereby some banks process more credit transactions and other banks more debit transactions, so that the one side does not offset the other in the "ordinary" way. Because the transactions costs for the debiting bank are much higher than the costs of the crediting bank, the "debit" banks are interested in introducing interbank charges.

## V   CONCLUSION

The Dutch payment system is efficient and well-organised. The payment services are characterised by gradual progress, with broad cooperation among the suppliers.

On the other hand, viewing the development of the payment system more generally, the issue of cost-effectiveness is a major obstacle.

Appendix

## Overview of (Domestic) Giro Transfer Flows in the Netherlands

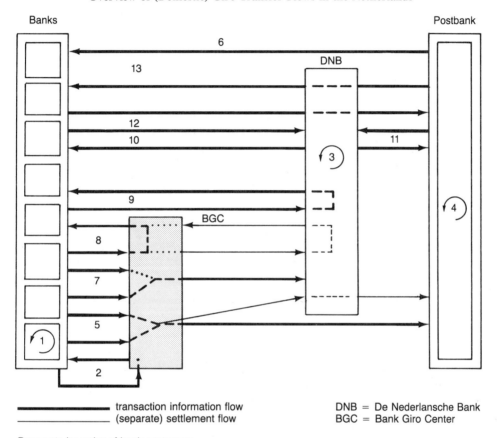

| transaction information flow | DNB = De Nederlansche Bank |
| (separate) settlement flow | BGC = Bank Giro Center |

Payments by order of bank customers

(1)  Payments between customers of the same bank.
(2)  Payments between customers of the same bank, processed through the Bank Giro Center.
(3)  Payments between customers of the Nederlandsche Bank.
(4)  Payments between customers of the Postbank.
(5)  Payments from customers of banks to customers of the Postbank.
(6)  Payments from customers of the Postbank to customers of banks.
(7)  Payments from customers of banks to account holders of the Nederlandsche Bank and vice versa.
(8)  Payments between customers of different banks.

Payments between banks

(9)  Payments between banks.
(10) Payments between banks and the Nederlandsche Bank and vice versa.
(11) Payments between Postbank and the Nederlandsche Bank and vice versa (and between customers of the Postbank and account holders of the Nederlandsche Bank).
(12) Payments between banks and Postbank.
(13) Payments between Postbank and banks.

# 8 SWEDEN

# Sweden

## I   INTRODUCTION

The development of payment systems in Sweden during the last decade has been characterised by an increasing volume of transactions and a process of continuing computerisation. The banks' data-clearing systems have been transformed into a channel for the exchange of information and interbank data. The volume of paper documents handled in daily banking business has been reduced. Today cheque clearing between banks is carried out entirely by electronic means. New, more advanced control systems have been introduced in the various fields of banking. The need for more timely and accurate information and faster payment transfer times is continually growing. A new network for data communication between banks will be introduced this year for the exchange of information and data via high-speed transmission lines.

An important feature of the 1980s has been that the banks have developed separate credit card systems. Deregulation of the credit market and intensified competition have encouraged the banks in this field, where they are able to use their technical know-how and financial resources, for example, to set up pilot EFT POS projects.

As more and more ways of using cards have been introduced, the number of cards issued has also increased. Today some 5 million cards are in use; the value of transactions using cards is estimated at S.kr. 40 billion a year and the number of transactions at about 50 million a year.

Despite the rapid expansion of credit card systems, only 2 percent of the total volume of payments is made with cards. They are most frequently used at retail outlets, where they account for 10 percent of the transaction volume.

The increased use of cards for payments at retail outlets has meant rising costs in this sector, and discussions are in progress on how to distribute these costs.

The most important payment systems in Sweden remain the giro systems, owing to their proven efficiency. About 90 percent of all payments by value are channelled through the giro systems, although the number of transactions represents only 10-15 percent of the total. Cash payments at retail outlets account for the bulk of the transaction volume.

During the last two years trials with electronic funds transfer systems have increased steadily. Since 1987, shopkeepers have been able to test terminals for the automatic verification of authorisation.

## II   INSTITUTIONAL FRAMEWORK

### 1. Bank of Sweden

A new Bank of Sweden Act will go into effect on January 1, 1989. It defines more explicitly than did the former legislation the status and responsibilities of the central bank regarding the payment system. Formerly it was only prescribed that the Bank of Sweden had the exclusive right to issue notes and coin and that these were legal tender. The new law also authorises the bank to decide on the design and denomination of notes and coin. The bank is responsible for ensuring that sufficient means of payment are issued; further responsibilities include replacing worn and damaged notes and circulating information on forgeries.

The Swedish banks perform various services for each other, and an efficient clearing system is therefore necessary. The final settling of accounts for these clearing transactions has always been extended through special cheque accounts at the Bank of Sweden. Since mid-1986, the settlements have been made at special clearing terminals set up by the bank; the banks' claims on each other are reported before noon every day and are automatically settled against the respective cheque accounts.

The Bank of Sweden does not cooperate in the development of payment systems. The bank does, however, observe developments in this field closely and takes account of their consequences, for example, for monetary policy. The bank's task of promoting a secure and efficient payment system is specifically mentioned in the new Bank of Sweden Act, as well as in the Instrument of Government.* This task implies, *inter alia,* that the central bank must also study the development of means of payment other than notes and coin, such as the Postal Giro, the Bank Giro, cheques, and credit cards.

### 2. Postal Giro

The Postal Giro is a separate department within the post office organisation. It used to cooperate with the government-owned commercial bank, "PK-Bank," for the purpose of investing its surplus funds, but since 1986 it has been free to invest its cash on the market.

The great bulk of payment transactions by the corporate and household sectors are made via the Postal Giro or the Bank Giro. The Postal Giro is the larger system, handling all kinds of transactions, from small payments by households to large government payments. Today the number of Postal Giro accounts stands at 1.5 million, with a daily average of 1.5 million transactions for approximately S.kr. 23 billion. The total value of transactions in 1987 was S.kr. 6,740 billion. The combined value of transactions handled by the Postal Giro and the Bank Giro accounts for 90 percent of all payments. By number, however, these transactions represent only 10-15 percent of all payments, the bulk being accounted for by cash payments at retail outlets.

The Postal Giro system is being used more and more by private individuals. This is because PK-Bank, which handles the large government salary payments, and the savings banks have their salary payment accounts linked to the giro system and because at the same time 600,000 individuals have their own Postal Giro accounts. The increase is also due to the fact that the Postal Giro can be used at post offices throughout the country with their long business hours.

During the last few years the Postal Giro has introduced new financial services for its business customers. A terminal information system provides customers with advice on better cash management, and on-line transmissions can be made by the customer to the Postal Giro computer system. Small and medium-sized companies can use the system to integrate their cash management programs with the payment system of the Postal Giro.

Together with the large credit card companies, the Postal Giro has constructed a system for verifying and authorising credit card purchases—the KC-System. The system requires special shop terminals connected to the computers of the Postal Giro, which in turn are linked to the computers of the credit card companies.

---

*The first of the four fundamental laws comprising the Swedish Constitution.

Since September 1986, the Postal Giro, through its S.W.I.F.T. membership, has had access to S.W.I.F.T's international computer network for bank transactions. This has meant an increase in payments from foreign banks in particular.

The increased use of the Postal Giro system has made it practical for customers to coordinate all their systems; efforts have therefore been made in this direction. One procedure that has been developed, for example, involves the paying company sending its payment orders on magnetic tape or via telecommunication to the Postal Giro, which automatically distributes the payment to the accounts of the payees. The payees are at the same time notified of the transfers. This kind of electronic procedure has made it possible to reduce the volume of written information.

Various transactions are constantly being made more efficient. The Postal Giro's pricing policy aims at reducing the current dependence on interest revenues and increasing fee income instead. In February 1988, for example, several fees were raised, including those for payments from Postal Giro accounts made at post offices. Customers also have the option of posting their payment orders free of charge.

### 3. Bank Giro

The Bank Giro is a company owned by commercial banks, savings banks, and cooperative banks. In 1986, all foreign banks that were in the process of establishing themselves in Sweden also became joint shareholders in the Bank Giro. The Bank Giro is used to make large-scale payment transfers between bank accounts. There are no separate bank giro accounts, but ordinary bank accounts are given a separate Bank Giro number. The giro system is administered by the Bank Giro Center.

The activities of the Bank Giro are divided into two categories: the giro system with 700,000 interconnected bank accounts and the contracts division. The activities of the latter consist in servicing ATMs and credit cards and, since 1987, the computer switch for on-line transactions between banks.

A giro procedure that has seen more frequent use during the last few years is payments to accounts with notification of the payee. Using the giro system for payment transactions reduces the number of cash and cheque transactions. An example of this is payments of those share dividends that can now be made through the Bank Giro.

Since 1986, the Bank Giro Center has participated in the Bank of Sweden clearing system; it is connected with the central bank via a terminal. Interbank transactions are netted at the Bank Giro Center, and then the net positions between banks are settled through their cheque accounts at the Bank of Sweden. The number of transactions cleared amounted to 152 million in 1987, for a total value of S.kr. 7,515 billion; by comparison, the value of interbank transactions cleared via the Bank Giro system in 1985 totaled S.kr. 2,888 million.

In 1987, the Bank Giro system handled 174 million giro transactions for a total value of S.kr. 1,290 billion, corresponding to a daily value of S.kr. 4 billion.

The more extensive use of computerised procedures in the business sector has also resulted in computerised payment transactions overtaking paper-based transactions. In volume terms the ratio is now 60:40.

The Bank Giro Center finances its expenditures through a membership fee based on the transaction volume and through transaction fees. The membership fee covers about 50 percent of the costs.

### 4. Banks

The Swedish banking system has a long tradition of extensive cooperation. Banks have usually agreed on the use of standardised procedures and systems rather than establishing their own particular systems.

The extent of this cooperation is evident from the range of banking services the banks perform for each other and for the benefit of all customers. This is aided by the fact that most transaction procedures are computerised and that computerisation has today reached an advanced stage in Sweden.

There are many reasons why the banks have been able to carry out extensive automation fairly easily. The structure of the banking system was well adapted to computerisation to begin with. Furthermore, the Swedish banks had also been cooperating in other fields for many years. It was therefore natural for the banks to coordinate their systems among themselves and with those of their customers.

Although Swedish banks today are highly automated, staff numbers have remained unchanged since the beginning of the 1980s. The adoption of computerised systems during the 1980s has aimed more at widening the base for decision-making and improving the service for customers than reducing personnel.

The introduction of more advanced verification systems has led to the fact that tellers' terminals and VDUs have been replaced by screen terminals that have both a data-capture system and a control system. These terminals can be used for booking transactions with customers, calling up customers' balances, providing tellers with information, and updating account records. In the future, the terminals will probably be supplemented by credit card readers and keyboards for identification by PIN codes.

By using computerised verification systems, bank branches can provide a fast and efficient service to their customers. As a first step, transaction services have been automated. Self-service terminals have been installed in many bank branches, enabling the customer to carry out certain routine operations such as withdrawals from accounts, requests for statements of account, and transfers between different personal accounts. The aim has been to relieve personnel of routine work and instead make them qualified advisers in economic and legal matters. The banks are today following up this development by expanding their computerised information systems. The transaction offices of today will be replaced tomorrow by banking information centers. The large-scale use of data communication will provide the capacity for a substantially larger transaction volume in the future.

In the last few years service fees have been widely used by the banks. Self-service transactions are in principle free of charge or subject to only a small fee. There are fees penalising small transactions, such as cheque payments, credit card payments, and withdrawals of small amounts of cash, to limit the number of such transactions. High fees are charged for manual and advisory services to offset the costs involved. This will probably mean that, in the future, services at the counter will be subject to high fees, while terminal and ATM services will be free of charge.

The quality of a bank's advisory services is an important competitive ingredient that has given the banks an incentive to invest in the education and training of their employees.

### 5. Finance Houses

The market for credit cards has expanded rapidly in the last few years. Many of the large credit card systems have been introduced by finance houses, because their activities have hitherto not been regulated to the same extent as those of the banks. The Banking Inspection Board is the supervisory authority for the finance houses, and since July 1988, its authorisation has been required for setting up a finance house. The finance houses and their management now have to satisfy qualitative criteria, and there is also a minimum capital requirement.

The greater part of the credit card market is in the hands of the finance houses:

Two-thirds of all outstanding credit card debt is with the finance houses. Of the total of 278, 14, of which six are owned by banks, dominate the market. These 14 were administering 3.5 million accounts at the end of 1987.

Bank-owned finance houses have undergone a thorough restructuring during the last few years. Up to 1986, the management of credit cards business was coordinated by a jointly owned company. After the deregulation of the credit market and after having introduced a combined debit and credit card of their own, called the "bank card," the banks started to act independently on the credit card market. The parent banks decided in 1986 to manage the marketing and financing of the "Köpkort" card and MasterCard themselves. The outstanding stock of credit has gradually been transferred to the banks' own finance houses. This task was completed toward the end of 1987. The banks in question then introduced their own names on their credit cards. Two of the largest commercial banks named their credit cards "On-line" and "Svenska Pengar."

The credit card business of the savings banks is managed by their jointly owned company Sparbankskort. PK-Bank has for many years had its own credit card system, "PK-kort," which is managed by the post office.

## III   PAYMENT SYSTEMS

An overwhelming proportion (95 percent) of the transactions in retail trade is effected in cash, despite the introduction of new card systems. Of the rest, 4 percent are credit card payments and 1 percent cheques. Payments in cash are still simpler and cheaper for both retail traders and their customers. A restraining factor is that a small fee is charged for buying below a certain amount of money both on cards and on cheques.

### 1. Payment Media Available to Customers

*(a) Cash payments*

Pursuant to the new Bank of Sweden Act, which will come into effect on January 1, 1989, the unit of currency is called the Krona and is subdivided into 100 öre. Notes may be issued in the following denominations: 10, 20, 50, 100, 500, 1,000, and 10,000 kronor. For coins the denominations are 10 and 50 öre and 1, 5, and 10 kronor.

The Bank of Sweden distributes notes and coin free of charge up to a certain amount, above which a fee is charged, on a commercial basis.

The importance of notes as a means of payment cannot be easily estimated, because it is impossible to measure transaction velocity. However, their importance has diminished, in particular since the expansion of the giro systems. In value terms, notes account at most for 10 percent of all payment transactions, but they are predominant in terms of the number of transactions, with 95 percent of transactions at retail outlets being effected in cash.

*(b) Cheques*

In Sweden the banks agreed to redeem each other's cheques many years ago. A precondition for this was that all information on the cheques was standardised regarding account number, identification, size, and so forth. About one-third of all cheques are passed through the clearing system, which operates in the following way: the cashing bank keeps the cheque, while the issuing bank receives information via its terminal as to which account to debit and which bank has cashed the cheque; information about the cheque itself can be requested afterwards, but it is seldom needed.

The settlement of payments by cheque is now a completely electronic process. The last step in this direction was taken in 1986, when the Bank of Sweden started to collect daily clearing data via terminals.

Today the growth in cheque payments is slow. The market has been taken over by credit cards and ATMs. On average, each individual writes only 10 cheques annually. The number of cheques written has increased only moderately lately, and the turnover is 140 million cheques a year.

### (c) Card payments

The use of credit cards has expanded during the last five years. The market is constantly changing, with new ownership structures, new contract conditions, and new fields of application. Cards that can be used internationally are on the increase, as is the practice of charging fees for more and more services. A special fee, for example, is charged for cash withdrawals abroad.

As mentioned, most credit cards are managed by finance houses. The number of credit card systems is now about 200, but only 10 of these can be used all over the country and are not restricted to one branch or chain of stores. At the end of 1987, there were 4 million credit cards on the market.

Some cards have a very short credit term, with payment being made on a specified date in the month following the transaction. Most of these cards are issued by petrol companies and car-hire firms. In addition to these cards, whose use is restricted to a single firm's services, there are three all-round credit cards: Eurocard, American Express, and Diners Club. These are primarily used as travel and entertainment cards. They are financed through fees charged to retailers and a yearly fee payable by the cardholder. By 1986, these three card companies had issued about 400,000 cards.

### (d) Cards at retail outlets

For a number of years the banks have been offering bank cards that can be used as credit cards and in cash dispensers. The card is linked to the card holder's bank account, which in turn can be connected to a credit facility. If credit has been given by a credit card company, the cardholder, when paying with his card, indicates on the bill concerned whether his credit card account or his bank account is to be charged. At present this bank card cannot be used at POS terminals, but is accepted by ATMs.

A new system of authorisation is being developed for use at retail outlets, hotels, and restaurants. An authorisation and credit limit verification system developed by the Kontocentralen, described below, is now being implemented. Through the authorisation terminals shop assistants can easily verify the authorisation and cover for each transaction.

### (e) Cards at POS terminals

The terminals connected on-line to the authorisation system can be used today to charge customers' accounts directly. Such terminals are undergoing trials in several cities. As it is expected that this system will be expensive, discussions are taking place on how the costs for the electronic transmission of payments should be distributed among banks, retailers, and customers. Retailers would like it to be possible to use all cards at any one terminal. POS pilot projects are now being carried out in shops by commercial banks and savings banks through two special companies, SERVO AB and Babs. The latter leases terminals and electronic writers to the shops; electronic card readers, a device that retailers have long been asking for, are also used. The tests will serve as the basis for a decision at the beginning of 1989. The test being performed by the savings banks is interesting in that holders of their cards are using them in an environment other than a bank branch.

Since the summer of 1988, cooperation with a petrol company has enabled holders of savings bank cards to use them to buy petrol at 500 filling stations by keying in the same PIN code as for cash withdrawals. This has focused attention on the problem of security at filling stations. The solution has been to use special security boxes owned by the Babs Company and rented by the filling stations.

Since 1986, one of the large commercial banks has also been testing POS terminals in some store chains.

### (f) Bank cards at ATMs

The first step in the development of electronic payments was cards for cash withdrawals at ATMs. Today these cards can also be used in shops, hotels, and restaurants. In Sweden there are two competing ATM systems: Bankomat, owned by the commercial banks,and Minuten, managed by the savings banks.

Now a third generation of ATMs is being installed. They are on-line, which means that the cardholders can ask for a list of their latest withdrawals or an up-to-date statement of account. Transfers to other bank accounts, however, are not possible.

The on-line connection with the bank's data center has enabled customers to monitor their balance more efficiently. This check is automatically performed with every transaction.

Thus far, 1,600 ATMs have been installed; only about 100 of them are inside bank branches. About 140 million transactions are performed at ATMs yearly—approximately the same as the number of cheque transactions. The average amount withdrawn is S.kr. 550. About one-third of all withdrawals are for amounts of between S.kr. 100 and 200.

New services have been added lately; for example, the cards can be used for cash withdrawals abroad. The opposite, i.e., foreign visitors to Sweden using their cards in Swedish ATMs, will certainly be possible at a later date. Most ATMs are connected to the data center of the respective banks through leased telecommunication lines. The bank computers are in turn connected with each other through an electronic switchboard at the Bank Giro.

### (g) Giro systems for individuals

Competition has been heightened during the last few years, especially when the deregulation of the Swedish credit market started at the beginning of the 1980s and the struggle to attract depositors became more intense. The savings banks have introduced a system linking salary accounts to the Bank and Postal Giros. Before that the giro systems could only be used by firms. Today one million of the savings banks' salary accounts are linked to the giro systems. This has led other banks to introduce similar systems.

Furthermore, the Postal Giro and the Bank Giro have recently introduced an invoice payment system called "autogiro," which allows an account holder, for example, to authorise a firm to debit his account automatically on a specific date. This kind of giro is especially suitable for anyone who has regular payments to make, such as rent, hire purchase instalments, credit card payments, and telephone bills.

### (h) New methods of payment

Some time ago, trials with home banking were started on a small scale. How many people will be prepared to use this system in the future is uncertain. Existing giro systems in practice offer an equivalent service, i.e., customers can make their payment transactions at home but without an expensive terminal. This procedure can be further automated through the autogiro for automatic transfers of recurrent payments.

In Sweden, as in other countries, "smart cards" with built-in microprocessors are being developed. This kind of card will function as an electronic wallet and cheque. Tests in other countries have shown that this electronic cheque is far more simple to use than a written cheque, and it is proof against fraudulent use. Currently these cards are still too expensive to be introduced on the market.

# IV   EXCHANGE CIRCUITS WITHIN THE BANKING SYSTEM

## 1.  Interbank Clearing

The Swedish banks perform a variety of services for each other, and an efficient clearing system is therefore essential. The need to obtain value from other banks for their cheques was the basis for the first manual clearing system, which was superseded in the mid-1970s by electronic clearing. Under the new arrangements the cheque itself is retained by the cashing bank while the relevant data on the cheque are transmitted electronically to the drawee bank via the Bank Giro. There the amount of the cheque is debited to the customer's account. All the banks participate in the cheque clearing system, as does the post office. The clearing system has now been enlarged so that it functions as an interbank circuit. Other transactions that have been computerised within the clearing system include salary payments, bank money orders, withdrawals from accounts, and deposits. Data are transmitted on magnetic tape or on-line via the Bank Giro. The electronic clearing system is a perfect example of how the banks have reduced the volume of paper handled simply by coordinating their systems.

The preceding description refers only to clearing transactions between banks. Settlement is effected at the central bank, where every bank has a cheque account. Each day at noon every bank reports its balances *vis-à-vis* the other banks, whereupon claims and liabilities are matched and settled between the accounts of the respective banks. If a debit balance occurs in this process, the bank in question can cover it by borrowing from the Bank of Sweden.

In short, the Swedish bank clearing system is now entirely computerised. It consists of two stages: a clearing system, with transactions transmitted electronically between the banks, and the settlement at the Bank of Sweden, which is also effected electronically.

## 2.  Kontocentralen

In 1983, eight credit card companies and retailers' associations set up a joint company, Kontocentralen (KC), to conduct a market test of an electronic verification and authorisation system. The test was undertaken in conjunction with the Swedish Telecommunication Authority and proved successful. In January 1987, the tested system was put into permanent operation. Initially it encompassed nine card systems, and three more have now joined the system. Currently some 3,300 terminals are linked to the KC system.

Originally it was intended that the verification system should also include the data-capture process. A growing interest by the large banks in retail payment systems has led to this part of the test being given priority and conducted separately by a special syndicate of banks that has the task of developing an electronic system for this purpose. This system will, however, also be under the control of Kontocentralen.

## 3.  The Money Market Clearing Center

In the autumn of 1987, a proposal was put forward concerning a Money Market Clearing Center that would operate a centralised management system for securities traded on the Swedish money market and bond market. It is intended to create an electronic system for the management of securities brought together in one institution with a register of the holders to dispense with the physical transfer of securities and funds between buyers and sellers on the market. To guarantee the liquidity of the system, the Bank of Sweden acts as lender of last resort. In practice this means that the Bank will intervene during temporary disturbances so that the system will not be brought to a halt. At present the system is operated manually, but the electronic system will be introduced in 1989.

### 4. The Independent Credit Information Agency

A credit intelligence agency, the Independent Credit Information Agency, will compile a register of credit cardholders who are in serious breach of their obligations, for example, by failing to make payments when due, exceeding credit limits, or gaining access to credit under false pretenses. All credit cardholders will be notified of the existence of the register.

### 5. Standard Security System

Corporate payments, as well as private payments and securities transactions, must be safeguarded at both the transmission and the accounting stage. To facilitate communication with the banks, it is essential that a standard security system be adopted by all the parties concerned, and this is now in the process of being established in Sweden.

## V   GENERAL REMARKS

The issues currently under discussion include the progressive computerisation of more and more bank services owing to the high costs of services performed manually and increased competition to attract customers. Typically, banks are currently installing terminals at their branches for customers to carry out their transactions themselves. These self-service transactions are free of charge, while services such as information and advice involving bank staff carry a small fee. This trend will continue and in turn raise questions concerning the public's willingness to accept and adapt to technical innovation.

# 9 SWITZERLAND

# Switzerland

## I   INTRODUCTION

It is a characteristic feature of the development of the Swiss payment system that more abstract payment instruments take longer to gain acceptance than they do elsewhere. This can be said both of the replacement of coins by paper money and of the replacement of paper money by deposit money.[1] The 1980s have seen an acceleration in these processes. While sight deposits increased by 47.7 percent from Sw.fr. 36.9 billion at year-end 1980 to Sw.fr. 54.5 billion at year-end 1987, the currency in circulation (notes and coin) rose over the same period by 12.3 percent from Sw.fr. 22.0 billion to Sw.fr. 24.7 billion (see Table 1 of Appendix 1). The cash ratio[2] declined accordingly from 37.3 percent (1980) to 31.2 percent (1987).

In the area of cashless payments Switzerland belongs to the group of so-called giro countries, i.e., those in which the giro transfer predominates. The cheque, by contrast, never achieved widespread popularity, although it has more recently come to be used more widely.

Cashless payment facilities are offered by the banks and the Postal Administration. Whereas the Postal Administration, with its postal giro system, has played a major role in the field of bulk payments since 1906, it was only in the 1960s, with the advent of the salary account, that the banks developed the bank giro transfer system to cater to the general public.

Alongside paper-based payment instruments such as the bank or postal giro transfer, paperless payment services employing data carriers have been used increasingly since the mid-1970s. The main users of these facilities are commercial customers of the banks and the Postal Administration.

A further step was taken in 1987 with the introduction of the SIC (Swiss Interbank Clearing) electronic system, which has now replaced the paper-based interbank payment system and a large part of that using data carriers.

## II   INSTITUTIONAL FRAMEWORK

### 1. The Swiss Confederation

In 1848, all coinage rights were transferred from the cantons to the federal government. Swiss coins are struck at the federal mint in Berne. The Swiss National Bank merely places its services at the disposal of the federal government for the distribution and withdrawal of coins.

In 1891, Article 39 of the Federal Constitution conferred on the federal government the exclusive right to issue bank notes (bank note monopoly). Exercising its currency prerogative, the federal government transferred this right to the Swiss National Bank in 1907. The note-issuing privilege is granted only for 20 years at a time.

---

[1]See Schweizerische Nationalbank (1982), pp. 287-299.
[2]The cash ratio is defined as the share of notes and coin in $M_1$. $M_1$ is defined as currency and private households' and firms' sight deposits with banks and the Postal Administration.

## 2. The Swiss National Bank

The Swiss National Bank was created by the National Bank Law on October 6, 1905, and commenced operations on June 20, 1907. The Swiss National Bank's chief function is to regulate the country's currency circulation, to facilitate payment transactions, and to pursue a credit and monetary policy serving the interests of the country as a whole.[3]

The National Bank Law gave the Swiss National Bank the right to develop its own cashless payment system and to open a giro account for every economic agent. The bank has made only limited use of this right. Since 1986, it has operated giro accounts exclusively for banks, public entities, foreign central and commercial banks, and international organisations.[4]

## 3. The Banking Sector

The Swiss Banking Act groups banks into banks in the strict sense and banks in the broadest sense. Banks in the broadest sense include, along with banks in the strict sense, finance companies and sole traders that publicly solicit deposits.[5]

Banks in the strict sense are themselves sub-divided into cantonal banks, large banks, regional and savings banks, loan associations and agricultural credit cooperatives, other banks, foreigh-controlled banks, branches of foreign banks, and private banks. At year-end 1987, there were 622 banks and finance companies with 4,202 offices operating in Switzerland.

As a rule, Swiss banks undertake all types of banking business, although there are a number of specialised groups of bank. The private banks, for example, focus on investment management, and the regional and savings banks on mortgage business.

Within the payment system the banks are both the retail distributors of cash and suppliers of cashless payment services to their customers.

Since 1935, the banks have been subject to supervision by the Federal Banking Commission. A number of banking associations exist to protect the common interests and rights of the banks, with the Swiss Bankers' Association in Basle as their umbrella organisation.

In 1981, the banks assigned responsibility for the administrative and technical operation of the bank clearing system, which handles both paper-based and paperless payments, to Telekurs AG, a joint venture of the Swiss banks. At year-end 1987, the system comprised 342 participating banks with a total of 2,894 offices. The remaining banks pass their payments through the Swiss National Bank's paper-based giro system, through the postal giro system or through correspondent banks. In addition to its responsibilities in the bank clearing system, Telekurs AG operates the SIC electronic payment system (see Section III 2.*(a)*) and the Swiss Cheque Center (see Section III 1.*(b)*) on behalf of the Swiss National Bank and processes securities transactions on behalf of the Swiss Securities Clearing Company (Schweizerische Effekten-Giro AG, or SEGA) (see Section III 2.*(b)*). In addition, it provides a financial and stock exchange information service and is the parent company of the Eurocard (Switzerland) SA credit card organisation.

## 4. The Postal Administration

The postal giro system was introduced in 1906, with the aim of making payment transactions easier, simpler, and cheaper. Thus, a year even before the Swiss National Bank was founded, the Postal Administration received authorisation to open a

---

[3]Federal Constitution, Article 39, paragraph 3.
[4]See Schweizerische Nationalbank (1982), pp. 287-299.
[5]See Schweizerische Nationalbank (1982), pp. 18-32.

sight account for every economic agent and developed a payment system to serve the public, corporate, and private household sectors.

Postal giro payments are handled at a nationwide network of 25 postal cheque offices and 3,858 post offices (1987). With over 1.17 million postal cheque account holders and approximately 500 million transactions per year. the postal giro system plays a major role in bulk payments.

# III  PAYMENT SYSTEMS

## 1. Payment Media Available to Customers

### (a) Cash payments

#### Legal basis

The Coinage Act of December 18, 1970, regulates the Swiss monetary and coinage system. The unit of currency is the Swiss franc, which is legal tender in Switzerland and in the principality of Liechtenstein. One Swiss franc is divided into 100 centimes. Coins exist in eight denominations (Sw.fr. 0.01, 0.05, 0.10, 0.20, 0.50, 1, 2, and 5) and notes are issued in six denominations (Sw.fr. 10, 20, 50, 100, 500, and 1,000).

#### The role of the Swiss National Bank

Under the terms of the National Bank Law the exclusive right to issue bank notes was vested in the Swiss National Bank, which is responsible for the design, production, issue, withdrawal, and destruction of bank notes. The Swiss National Bank distributes the bank notes required by the banks and the Postal Administration through its two head offices (in Berne and Zurich), eight branches, one agency of its own, and 20 external agencies run by cantonal banks.

#### Importance of cash payments

The currency (notes and coin) in circulation increased by 12.3 percent from Sw.fr. 22.0 billion at year-end 1980 to Sw.fr. 24.7 billion at year-end 1987. Over the same period sight deposits with banks and post offices rose by 47.7 percent from Sw.fr. 36.9 to 54.5 billion (see Table 1 of Appendix 1).

The value of bank notes in circulation rose by 14.3 percent from Sw.fr. 21.7 billion in 1980 to Sw.fr. 24.8 billion in 1987 (see Table 2 of Appendix 1). At an annual average of Sw.fr. 24.8 billion in 1987, it exceeded its corresponding year-earlier level by Sw.fr. 0.8 billion, or 3.3 percent; this was an appreciably larger increase than in the previous three years.

The shift in the demand for bank notes toward the Sw.fr. 1,000 denomination, which has been observed for a number of years, became more pronounced in 1987. While the total stock of notes in circulation exceeded the previous year's level by 3.3 percent, the stock of Sw.fr. 1,000 notes increased by 5 percent. The share of Sw.fr. 1,000 notes in the total value of notes issued rose from 40.9 percent in 1980 to 44.2 percent in 1987.

### (b) Cashless payments (excluding cards)

#### The postal giro system[6]

The basis of the postal giro system is the postal cheque account. Postal cheque accounts are subject to the confidentiality of the post. The names of account holders are, however, published in a register, unless they expressly object to being included.

---

[6]On the postal giro system, see J. Marbacher (1976), pp. 137-214; on the development of the postal giro system, see P. Portmann (1987).

The main characteristics of the postal cheque account can be summarised as follows:
▶ No payment of interest.[7]
▶ No initial deposit.
▶ All giro transfers executed free of charge.
▶ Twice a month a statement of account free of charge.
▶ No overdraft facilities.
▶ No third-party cheques may be presented (guaranteed Eurocheques in Swiss francs are accepted).

At year-end 1987, 1.18 million private households and firms held postal cheque accounts.[8] Compared with 1980 (0.94 million accounts), this represented a 25 percent increase (see Table 3 of Appendix 1). Balances on postal cheque accounts remained unchanged at around Sw.fr. 12.5 billion between 1980 and 1983, rose in 1984 to Sw.fr. 15 billion, and have since fallen again to Sw.fr. 13.7 billion.[9] The share of postal cheque account balances in total balances on sight accounts fell from 29 percent in 1980 to 21 percent in 1987.

The postal giro service offers paying-in, giro transfer, and paying-out facilities.[10] Private households' over-the-counter cash inpayments at post offices and giro transfers credited to postal cheque accounts dominate the bulk payment system.

Inpayments and giro transfers are paper-based. As of January 1, 1989, the Postal Administration's green inpayment forms have been replaced by OCR-readable forms with code lines. With these forms it will be possible to make payments from one postal cheque account to another, from a postal cheque account to a bank account, from a bank account to a postal cheque account, and from one bank account to another.

The postal cheque account also offers a direct debit facility for the automatic payment of regular bills. For cash withdrawal from a postal cheque account there is the postal cheque, the payment order, and the outpayment form. In addition, any postal cheque account holder can obtain guaranteed postcheques, which can be used within Switzerland and abroad for withdrawing cash or as a payment medium. Within Switzerland, cheques are guaranteed for up to Sw.fr. 300. As in the case of the Eurocheque, the guarantee is evidenced by means of a personal guarantee card.

A further service offered by the postal payment system is the "collective order facility," which enables a participant to submit credit instructions on a data carrier for settlement. The number of transactions handled by the collective order facility grew between 1980 and 1987 from 1.8 million to 72.8 million.

In addition, there is the so-called inpayment form with reference number facility. The user to whom payment is due makes out his bills and payment forms and sends them to the payers. At the Postal Administration's computer center the payment forms presented are recorded by OCR and the total amounts are credited to the user's postal cheque account. Each user is sent details of the payments made on his chosen data carrier.

---

[7]As of May 1, 1989, credit balances on postal cheque accounts will bear interest at a rate of 2 percent, but only up to an amount of Sw.fr. 10,000. Under the Postal Services Law the rate of interest must be at least 1 percent below the Swiss National Bank's discount rate (currently 3.5 percent). Accounts may be overdrawn by a maximum of Sw.fr. 1,000 up to 28 days only.

[8]For the statistical data relating to the postal giro system, see Schweizerische PTT-Betriebe (1988), pp. 14-18.

[9]The balances on postal cheque accounts shown in Table 3 are not comparable with the sight deposits with nonbanks in Table 1, which represent postal sight balances excluding the postal cheque account balances of banks and the federal government.

[10]The following postal payment facilities are under development: telegiro; data transmission for users of the collective order facility and the inpayment form with reference number facility; standing order facilities; and direct debit facilities.

*Bank systems*

*(i) The bank giro system*

Until June 30, 1988, the means of effecting payments between banks was the bank giro form introduced in 1971. Bank giro transfers were processed by Telekurs AG, where they were recorded by OCR, sorted by bank, and transmitted to the payee bank. The credit and debit totals were then cleared through the banks' giro accounts with the Swiss National Bank.

The number of bank giro transfers processed shrank from 10.2 million in 1980 to 4.6 million in 1987 (see Table 4 of Appendix 1) as the banks increasingly utilised the paperless data carrier clearing (see (iv) below). In mid-1988, the paper-based system was entirely replaced by the SIC electronic system (see Section III 2.*(b)*). Since July 1, 1988, bank customers have been able to use the new, standardised bank and postal inpayment forms with code lines for their payment orders. These inpayment forms enable the banks largely to automate the processing of payment orders.

*(ii) Bank cheques*

Standard cheques drawn on a Swiss bank and Eurocheques are processed centrally by the Cheque Center at Telekurs AG, which is subject to supervision by the Swiss National Bank.[11]

Any bank that holds a giro account at the Swiss National Bank, has signed the corresponding agreements and has lodged a deposit as security may participate in the cheque processing system.

Eurocheques and standard Swiss cheques are presented to the Cheque Center each day for collection. On the basis of the cheques presented, the Cheque Center compiles lists or magnetic tapes of credit items for the presenting banks and debit items for the drawee banks. The total credits and debits for each bank are then posted to the banks' giro accounts at the Swiss National Bank.

In 1980, the Cheque Center processed 7.6 million Eurocheques and standard Swiss cheques. In 1987, over 17.5 million cheques were presented to the Cheque Center (see Table 4 of Appendix 1). The number of cheques processed rose by an average of 18.3 percent per annum between 1980 and 1984; between 1985 and 1987, however, the annual rate of increase fell to 5.5 percent.

*(iii) Swiss Bankers' Travellers' Cheques*

Swiss Bankers' Travellers' Cheques, which have been issued jointly by the Swiss banks since 1975, are available in denominations of Sw.fr. 50, 100, 200, and 500. In 1987, 7.7 million cheques were sold for a total value of Sw.fr. 954 million, compared with a total value of Sw.fr. 896 million in 1986.

*(iv) Payments using data carriers*

Paperless transfers using data carriers, so-called data carrier applications, include the "data carrier clearing," which is restricted to payments originated by banks, and those services also available to bank customers, *viz.*, the "paperless wage and salary payment" and "data carrier exchange" facilities and the "direct debit procedure."[12]

The service most frequently used by bank customers is the data carrier exchange facility. The user delivers a data carrier containing the payments to be effected to Telekurs AG and at the same time sends his bank a payment order for the total

---

[11]The Swiss National Bank must exercise its supervisory powers regarding the Cheque Center so that the center can qualify as a clearing house managed by the central bank under the terms of Article 1,118 of the Law of Contract.

[12]While payments from one bank account to another and from a bank account to a postal cheque account can be executed using data carrier exchange, data carrier clearing can handle payments from a postal cheque account to a bank account as well.

amount to be debited. The total credits and debits for each bank are then posted to the banks' giro accounts at thc Swiss National Bank. The data carrier exchange service was introduced in 1977 to supplement the older paperless wage and salary payment facility. Regularly recurring claims can be collected via the direct debit procedure; the payment in this case is initiated by the payee.

The volume of transactions using data carrier applications quadrupled from 13.1 million in 1980 to 53.8 million in 1987 (see Table 4 of Appendix 1). In 1987, 19.6 million of these payments were executed by data carrier exchange, 2.6 million by paperless wage and salary payment, 3.9 million by the direct debit procedure, and 27.7 million by the data carrier clearing system. The SIC electronic payment system replaced the data carrier clearing system at the end of 1988, but the customer-oriented data carrier applications—the data carrier exchange, paperless wage and salary payment, and direct debit facilities—have been retained.

### (c) Cards in use

One in three of the Swiss population (i.e., some 2.2 million persons in 1987) now possesses a card which can be used either as a cashless payment instrument (Eurocheque, credit, and EFT POS cards) or to make cash withdrawals at cash dispensers (Bancomat and Postomat cards).

The cards have magnetic stripes and, in some cases, multiple functions. For instance, the Eurocheque card issued by the banks can be used as an identification card for Eurocheques, as a cash card for making withdrawals at bank cash dispensers and as an EFT POS card (ec-DIRECT service). The Postal Administration and one of the credit card organisations offer their customers a combined credit-cum-Postomat card with credit card and cash dispenser functions.

#### At retail outlets

##### (i) Credit cards

Credit cards and travel and entertainment cards have gained ground in Switzerland in the 1980s. Between 1981 and 1987, the number of cards issued increased by 170 percent, although the rate of increase has been tending to slow down (see Table 5 of Appendix 1). The credit card organisations predict that the market will reach saturation point with around 1 million credit cards at the beginning of the 1990s.

The credit card organisations represented in Switzerland are American Express Corporation, VISA, Diners Club, and Eurocard. In 1987, there were 700,000 cards in circulation, i.e., one in 10 Swiss inhabitants held a credit card, although an individual may have more than one card.

##### In-house

In addition to the usual international credit cards, there are a large number of credit cards issued by large retailers and petrol companies. These enable the cardholder to make cashless purchases of goods or services from the company concerned.

##### Prepaid cards

Calls can be made from a number of public telephones using a stored value card (Taxcard) issued by the Postal Administration and obtainable from post offices. Taxcards have a magnetic stripe and the stored value is used up as and when calls are made.

#### At ATMs

Switzerland has two independently operated, noncompatible cash dispenser networks, the Postal Administration's Postomat network and the banks' Bancomat network. While in 1984 only 424 machines were in operation, by the end of 1987, there were 1,239. The value of withdrawals made at cash dispensers doubled over the same period, from Sw.fr. 3.5 billion to Sw.fr. 7.23 billion (see Tables 6 and 7 of Appendix 1).

### (i) Bancomat

The first Bancomat was installed in 1968. By the end of 1980, the number of cards issued had risen to 126,000 and the number of machines to 211.

In 1985, development of a new Bancomat system was begun, using the converted old machines together with machines that had previously been operated on a regional basis by the various groups of banks. The new system is known as ec-Bancomat, since the Eurocheque card gives access to the Bancomats.

Bank customers have access to Bancomat machines 24 hours a day, seven days a week. A maximum amount of Sw.fr. 1,000 can be withdrawn on any one day.

In 1987, there were 1.1 million Eurocheque cards with a Bancomat function in circulation (see Table 6 of Appendix 1); 17.2 million withdrawals, for a total value of Sw.fr. 5.98 billion, were made from 1,045 machines. The value of withdrawals increased by 27 percent compared with the 1986 total, and was eight times that of 1980. From January 1, 1989, the Eurocard credit card will also have access to the Bancomat system.

### (ii) Postomat

The Postal Administration began installing cash dispensers in 1978. Between 1980 and 1987, the number of machines rose from 59 to 194 (see Table 7 of Appendix 1). In 1987, 210,848 postal cheque account holders owned Postomat cards, with which they made 4.2 million withdrawals for a total of Sw.fr. 1.2 billion. It is planned to further extend the Postomat network to approximately 300 machines by the end of 1988.

### (iii) Indoor ATMs

A number of banks have their own indoor ATM networks. These systems permit electronic handling of a wide range of banking operations, such as outpayments, account balance queries, and voucher print-outs.

A few banks operate automated self-service bank offices that cater, *inter alia,* for inpayments and purchases of foreign exchange or gold in addition to the usual ATM services.

### At POS terminals

At present there is no nationwide EFT POS system.

In 1985, Telekurs AG began with the pilot installation of an EFT POS system (ec-DIRECT). While in 1985, with 16 terminals in operation, 24,000 transactions were registered for a total value of Sw.fr. 1.1 million, in 1987, over 1 million transactions were carried out at 551 terminals for a total of roughly Sw.fr. 36 million. The system initially extended only to cashless payment at filling stations, but since mid-1988 it has also been possible to use the Eurocheque card as an EFT POS card for purchases at a number of shopping centers.

In April 1987, a large retailer started a pilot EFT POS system. Today approximately 6,000 customers make use of this service. Since 1988, the Postal Administration has been conducting trials with a pilot EFT POS scheme in association with this major retailer. In contrast to the card used by the latter, the Postal Administration uses a card containing a microchip, which records all payments effected.

### (d) Intrabank and interbank networks accessible to customers

The home-banking facilities available in Switzerland are discussed in *(e)* below.

### (e) Others

Users of home-banking facilities can communicate with the bank's computer either directly via a terminal or indirectly via the Videotex system.

Videotex is an interactive system for the transmission and retrieval of stored text or graphics over the Postal Administration's telephone and data transmission networks.[13] The system commenced operations in early 1987, and by year-end 1987 numbered approximately 7,500 participants.

A number of banks offer home-banking or cash and portfolio management services.[14] Bank customers can use these systems to obtain, at any time, information about the current status of their accounts or deposits, to execute payment orders, and to issue instructions to buy or sell securities. In addition, they may consult various other information services, such as the latest stock exchange prices, exchange rates, and interest rates.

## 2. Exchange Circuits Within the Banking System

### (a) The Swiss National Bank giro system

The paper-based giro system, which has been in existence since 1907, is open to banks, public entities, foreign central and commercial banks, and international organisations. The bank and postal giro systems are connected via accounts held by the Swiss National Bank with the postal giro system.

Giro accounts are operated free of all charges. Services include inpayments and outpayments, transfers, and the cheque. The Swiss National Bank's own giro forms must be used for transfers. At the end of 1987, there were 990 giro customers (960 in 1986), 142 of which were foreign institutions (133 in 1986). The giro system is used above all by institutions that are not participants in SIC.

### (b) The Swiss Interbank Clearing (SIC) system[15]

SIC is an electronic payment system developed by Telekurs AG in collaboration with the Swiss banks and the Swiss National Bank during the period 1981-86.

Participants are connected via a transmission network to the computer system (see Figure 1 of Appendix 2). The computer center facilities are provided by Telekurs AG on behalf of the Swiss National Bank. The Swiss National Bank undertakes the administration of the accounts. Participants' accounts are administered centrally on the system. The participating banks' balances on their SIC accounts (SIC clearing accounts) and on their giro accounts (master accounts) are giro balances *vis-à-vis* the Swiss National Bank and thus central bank money.[16] Legally, the two accounts form a single entity, although physically they are managed separately.[17]

SIC operates 24 hours a day every bank business day. Payment instructions can be submitted around the clock for settlement on the same day or on one of the following 10 bank business days. Settlement of a payment is irrevocable and final. Accounts may not be overdrawn.

The SIC clearing day begins with the transfer of balances from the participants' master accounts to their SIC clearing accounts. Before a payment instruction is carried out, a check is made to ensure that there are sufficient covering funds on the initiator's SIC clearing account. If this is not the case the payment is held pending in a queue file until sufficient cover has accumulated from incoming funds.

At the end of each SIC day the total credit and debit items booked over the SIC clearing account are transferred to the master account so that it again shows the participant's overall position.

---

[13]On Videotex and home banking, see G.D. Lehmann (1986), pp. 131-133.
[14]On cash and portfolio management systems, see A. Spahni-Klass (1988), pp. 211-243.
[15]On SIC, see Ch. Vital and D.L. Mengle in *Economic Review*, Federal Reserve Bank of Richmond, Richmond, November/December 1988.
[16]On the significance of SIC for central bank policy, see M.J. Granziol (1987).
[17]For a discussion of SIC's legal basis, see M. Hess (1988).

Payments from SIC participants to a postal cheque account are effected via the Swiss National Bank's postal cheque account with SIC.

SIC was brought into operation in stages between mid-1987 and the end of June 1988. In December 1988, SIC handled some 210,000 payments a day (monthly average of daily figures). The average daily value of transfers was approximately Sw. fr. 100 billion (see Table 8 of Appendix 1).

### (c)  Securities clearing (SEGA)

The Swiss Securities Clearing Company (Schweizerische Effekten-Giro AG, or SEGA) was established in 1970 to facilitate and rationalise the collective custody of securities and the execution of securities transactions. Shareholders are Swiss banks, the shares having been allotted taking into account the different categories of bank, stock exchange centers, and regions.

Through the central collective custody of freely negotiable securities SEGA contributes to an efficient national securities transfer system.[18] To use SEGA's services a bank must hold a giro account at the Swiss National Bank, sign the corresponding agreements, and lodge a deposit as security.

In 1982, SEGA supplemented its "delivery without payment" service with the "delivery against payment" system, under which a transaction is considered final when the securities have been transferred and payment effected. In 1984, a "delivery of new issues against payment" service was also introduced owing to the sharp growth in issuing activity in Switzerland since the beginning of the 1980s.

Telekurs AG performs the technical processing on behalf of SEGA. Settlement is through the participants' giro accounts at the Swiss National Bank in the form of credit and debit totals. Payments effected in the context of SEGA processing are provisional until their settlement on the giro accounts at the central bank. In the event of a participant being unable to meet his obligations, the system provides for the SEGA processing to be cancelled and repeated excluding the transactions of the participant concerned.

In 1987, 455 banks used SEGA's services (see Table 9 of Appendix 1); 4.4 million securities transfers were recorded, 80 percent of which were effected under the "delivery against payment" facility. The value of transactions rose from Sw. fr. 91 billion in 1984 to Sw. fr. 322 billion in 1987.

With its "SECOM" (SEGA Communications) project SEGA aims to link together the securities transfer and payment components of each securities transaction so as to create a truly integrated procedure.[19] There are two ways in which this might be achieved: Either the participants keep cash accounts with SEGA, or the payment component is handled through SIC. These solutions are still under study.

### (d)  Options and financial futures clearing (SOFFEX)

Since May 1988, SOFFEX, the Swiss Options and Financial Futures Exchange, has been operating an electronic exchange for options and financial futures.[20] The new exchange ensures transparent trading. The computer system is operated by Telekurs AG on behalf on SOFFEX. Initially, options are being offered on Swiss bearer shares and participation certificates.

With the SOFFEX computer system, trading and clearing are fully electronic. In the clearing system all transactions, premiums, and exchange charges are booked to the appropriate accounts of the participants. In addition, positions are evaluated and margins calculated.

---

[18]See Albisetti (1987), pp. 594-595.
[19]See H. Haeberli (1988).
[20]See SOFFEX (1987).

Settlement of credit and debit items arising out of SOFFEX processing is through the giro accounts at the Swiss National Bank.

## IV   GENERAL REMARKS

In recent years, the credit risks arising in connection with interbank payments have increased sharply with the surge in the volume of funds. The size and source of these risks are influenced to a large degree by the way in which the payment system is organised. The optimum system for Switzerland was held to be one in which each payment executed would be irrevocable as long as the paying bank had sufficient funds on giro account with the Swiss National Bank.

With the coming on stream of SIC in 1987, this concept was implemented for the major part of Swiss interbank payment transactions and has worked well.

In the service applications sector (data carrier exchange, paperless wage and salary payment, direct debit procedure, cheque clearing, ec-Bancomat, ec-DIRECT), through which a part of the bulk payments traffic is channeled, and in the securities clearing system all payments are subject to each participant's ability to meet its net obligations. This procedure does not satisfy the criteria mentioned above. The objective of future efforts will be to find ways of implementing irrevocability of payments in these areas, too.

## V   CONCLUSION

The role of cashless payment facilities, such as the bank or postal transfer, transfers using electronic data carriers, and payment by credit cards, has grown in Switzerland in recent years.

Although private households and firms are making increasing use of the various cashless payment instruments, payment in cash still occupies an important place.

The use of cash has been made more flexible in terms of both time and place through the expansion of the cash dispenser networks operated by the banks and the Postal Administration. The perception that only a nationwide network of compatible machines would promote their use among consumers led the banks and the Postal Administration to expand their systems. The breakthrough came in 1985, when the banks redesigned their Bancomat system at both the technical and organisational levels.

Pilot EFT POS trials have been conducted in Switzerland only since 1985. They have not yet provided conclusive evidence regarding customer acceptance or the cost/benefit ratio.

In the area of interbank payments, a new infrastructure was put in place in 1987 with the SIC system, which, for the foreseeable future, will be at the center of further developments in this field.

Appendix 1

### Table 1
### Development of Cash and Sight Deposits, 1980-87[1]

| | 1980 | 1981 | 1982 | 1983 | 1984[4] | 1985 | 1986 | 1987 |
|---|---|---|---|---|---|---|---|---|
| GNP | 177.3 | 193.9 | 205.1 | 213.9 | 226.0 | 241.3 | 254.5 | 266.3[5] |
| Currency[2] | 22.0 | 21.3 | 22.5 | 22.6 | 23.7 | 23.3 | 24.4 | 24.7 |
| Percentage of GNP | 12.4 | 10.9 | 10.9 | 10.5 | 10.5 | 9.6 | 9.5 | 9.2 |
| Transferable deposits at deposit-taking institutions | 26.2 | 23.2 | 28.4 | 28.6 | 31.4 | 33.9 | 36.2 | 43.1 |
| Percentage of GNP | 14.7 | 11.9 | 13.8 | 13.3 | 13.9 | 14.0 | 14.2 | 16.2 |
| Transferable deposits at nonbank institutions | 10.7 | 10.7 | 10.5 | 10.8 | 12.9 | 12.2 | 11.1 | 11.4 |
| Percentage of GNP | 6.0 | 5.5 | 5.1 | 5.0 | 5.7 | 5.0 | 4.3 | 4.2 |
| Total transferable deposits | 36.9 | 33.9 | 38.9 | 39.4 | 44.3 | 46.1 | 47.3 | 54.5 |
| Percentage of GNP | 20.8 | 17.5 | 18.9 | 18.4 | 19.6 | 19.1 | 18.6 | 20.4 |
| $M_1$[3] | 58.9 | 55.2 | 61.4 | 62.0 | 68.0 | 69.4 | 71.7 | 79.2 |
| Currency as a percentage of $M_1$ | 37.3 | 38.5 | 36.6 | 36.4 | 34.8 | 33.5 | 34.0 | 31.2 |

[1]Values at year-end, in billions of Swiss francs.
[2]Bank notes and coins.
[3]$M_1$ is defined as currency plus total transferable deposits.
[4]The definition of the monetary aggregates was revised in 1984.
[5]Estimate.

### Table 2
### Development of the Note Structure[1]

| Denominations | 1980 | 1981 | 1982 | 1983 | 1984 | 1985 | 1986 | 1987 |
|---|---|---|---|---|---|---|---|---|
| 1,000 | 40.9 | 40.4 | 40.4 | 41.7 | 42.5 | 43.1 | 43.5 | 44.2 |
| 500 | 19.8 | 19.3 | 18.7 | 17.9 | 17.3 | 16.8 | 16.3 | 15.8 |
| 100 | 29.4 | 30.2 | 30.6 | 30.2 | 29.9 | 29.8 | 29.8 | 29.7 |
| 50 | 4.5 | 4.6 | 4.7 | 4.7 | 4.7 | 4.7 | 4.7 | 4.7 |
| 20 | 3.3 | 3.4 | 3.4 | 3.4 | 3.4 | 3.4 | 3.4 | 3.5 |
| 10 | 1.8 | 1.9 | 1.9 | 1.9 | 1.9 | 1.9 | 2.0 | 1.9 |
| Total[2] | 21.7 | 21.9 | 22.0 | 22.7 | 23.3 | 23.6 | 24.0 | 24.8 |
| Increase[3] | +2.8 | +0.9 | +0.5 | +3.1 | +2.6 | +1.3 | +1.7 | +3.3 |

[1]Percentage share of each denomination in the total value of notes (annual average).
[2]Total value of notes in billions of Swiss francs (annual average).
[3]In percentages.

### Table 3
### Postal Giro Accounts, 1980-87[1]

| | 1980 | 1981 | 1982 | 1983 | 1984 | 1985 | 1986 | 1987 |
|---|---|---|---|---|---|---|---|---|
| Account holders[2] | 0.94 | 0.99 | 1.03 | 1.06 | 1.10 | 1.13 | 1.15 | 1.18 |
| Value of accounts[3] | 12.4 | 12.7 | 12.4 | 12.6 | 15.0 | 14.5 | 13.5 | 13.7 |
| Transactions[4] | 560 | 437 | 454 | 461 | 471 | 485 | 500 | 512 |
| Transactions via SAD[5] | 1.8 | 5.4 | 9.6 | 16.9 | 23.0 | 33.9 | 52.8 | 72.8 |

[1]Year-end figures.
[2]Number of account holders in millions.
[3]Values in billions of Swiss francs.
[4]Number of transactions in millions (inpayment and outpayment orders and remittances).
[5]Number of transactions in millions. SAD (collective order facility) is a cashless payment application on data carriers.

Appendix 1

### Table 4
### Cashless Payments Applications by the Banks 1980-87[1]

| Application | 1980 | 1981 | 1982 | 1983 | 1984 | 1985 | 1986 | 1987 |
|---|---|---|---|---|---|---|---|---|
| Bank giro | 10.2 | 10.0 | 8.6 | 8.0 | 7.6 | 7.3 | 6.2 | 4.6 |
| Payments on data carriers[2] | 13.1 | 17.0 | 24.1 | 30.2 | 37.1 | 41.3 | 47.0 | 53.8 |
| Cheques | 7.6 | 10.0 | 11.1 | 13.2 | 14.9 | 16.1 | 16.8 | 17.5 |
| SIC[3] | n.a. | n.a. | n.a. | n.a. | n.a. | n.a. | n.a. | 4.7 |
| Total | 30.9 | 37.0 | 43.8 | 51.4 | 59.6 | 64.7 | 70.0 | 80.6 |
| Increase[4] | | 19.7 | 18.4 | 17.3 | 15.9 | 8.5 | 8.2 | 15.1 |

[1]Number of transactions in millions.
[2]Payments on data carriers are DTA (data carrier exchange facility), BLG (paperless wage and salary payment facility), LSV (direct debit procedure), and DTC (data carrier clearing system).
[3]SIC was introduced in June 1987 and replaced the bank giro system in June 1988 and the data carrier clearing system in December 1988.
[4]In percentages.

### Table 5
### Credit Card Market, 1981-87[1]

| | 1981 | 1982 | 1983 | 1984 | 1985 | 1986 | 1987 |
|---|---|---|---|---|---|---|---|
| Cards issued, in thousands | 260 | 325 | 376 | 452 | 540 | 630 | 700 |
| Percentage increase | | 25 | 16 | 20 | 21 | 17 | 11 |
| Retailers, in thousands (contracts) | 32 | 38 | 46 | 55 | 70 | 82 | 89 |
| Value of transactions, in billions of Swiss francs[2] | | | | | | 2.4 | 2.7 |

[1]All figures are rough estimates.
[2]Purchases by Swiss inhabitants and nonresidents in Switzerland.

### Table 6
### Bancomat Cash Dispenser System, 1980-87

| | 1980 | 1981 | 1982 | 1983 | 1984 | 1985 | 1986 | 1987 |
|---|---|---|---|---|---|---|---|---|
| Number of machines installed | 211 | 237 | 254 | 273 | 281 | 494 | 819 | 1,045 |
| Number of cards issued[1] | 126 | 159 | 208 | 250 | 294 | 852 | 934 | 1,103 |
| Number of transactions[2] | 2.2 | 3.4 | 4.7 | 6.2 | 7.8 | 8.8 | 12.8 | 17.2 |
| Value of transactions[3] | 0.7 | 1.2 | 1.6 | 2.1 | 2.6 | 3.0 | 4.5 | 6.0 |

[1]In thousands.
[2]In millions.
[3]In billions of Swiss francs.

Appendix 1

### Table 7
### Postomat Cash Dispenser System, 1980-87

|  | 1980 | 1981 | 1982 | 1983 | 1984 | 1985 | 1986 | 1987 |
|---|---|---|---|---|---|---|---|---|
| Number of machines installed | 59 | 72 | 101 | 104 | 143 | 150 | 167 | 194 |
| Number of cards issued[1] | 84 | 117 | 138 | 156 | 171 | 185 | 196 | 210 |
| Number of transactions[2] | 0.9 | 1.6 | 2.1 | 2.7 | 3.2 | 3.6 | 3.9 | 4.2 |
| Value of transactions[3] | 0.2 | 0.5 | 0.6 | 0.8 | 0.9 | 1.0 | 1.1 | 1.2 |

[1]In thousands.
[2]In millions.
[3]In billions of Swiss francs.

### Table 8
### Development of SIC Transactions

| Year/month | Number of Transactions | | | Value of Transactions* | | |
|---|---|---|---|---|---|---|
|  | Monthly Total | Daily Figures | | Monthly Total | Daily Figures | |
|  |  | Average | Peak Day |  | Average | Peak Day |
| **1987** |  |  |  |  |  |  |
| July | 391,169 | 17,007 | 22,797 | 1,870 | 81 | 99 |
| August | 522,863 | 24,898 | 40,278 | 1,722 | 82 | 103 |
| September | 615,255 | 27,966 | 43,276 | 1,773 | 81 | 123 |
| October | 822,221 | 37,374 | 50,624 | 1,917 | 87 | 132 |
| November | 918,249 | 43,726 | 62,358 | 1,824 | 87 | 139 |
| December | 1,247,903 | 56,723 | 72,029 | 1,603 | 73 | 97 |
| **1988** |  |  |  |  |  |  |
| January | 1,118,389 | 55,919 | 76,839 | 1,774 | 89 | 130 |
| February | 1,279,421 | 60,925 | 88,258 | 1,953 | 93 | 136 |
| March | 1,645,989 | 71,565 | 106,255 | 2,187 | 95 | 120 |
| April | 1,568,299 | 82,542 | 122,442 | 1,862 | 98 | 115 |
| May | 1,930,068 | 96,503 | 144,945 | 1,843 | 92 | 154 |
| June | 2,885,069 | 131,140 | 281,352 | 2,328 | 106 | 147 |
| July | 3,423,815 | 163,039 | 267,350 | 2,213 | 105 | 140 |
| August | 3,398,110 | 154,460 | 279,369 | 2,322 | 105 | 136 |
| September | 3,428,466 | 155,839 | 274,943 | 2,205 | 100 | 143 |
| October | 3,475,424 | 165,496 | 288,955 | 2,207 | 105 | 154 |
| November | 3,729,613 | 169,528 | 318,816 | 2,345 | 107 | 203 |
| December | 4,450,540 | 211,930 | 299,373 | 2,000 | 95 | 127 |

*Values in billions of Swiss francs.

Appendix 1

**Table 9**
**Development of the Securities Clearing System (SEGA)**

|  | 1980 | 1981 | 1982 | 1983 | 1984 | 1985 | 1986 | 1987 |
|---|---|---|---|---|---|---|---|---|
| Participants | 300 | 309 | 319 | 405 | 410 | 422 | 430 | 455 |
| Number of transactions in millions | 1.53 | 1.64 | 1.74 | 2.30 | 2.36 | 3.15 | 3.69 | 4.39 |
| Percentage increase |  | 7.2 | 6.1 | 32.2 | 2.6 | 33.4 | 17.1 | 18.9 |
| Value of transactions in billions of Swiss francs |  |  |  |  | 91.0 | 177.0 | 266.4 | 322.3 |
| Percentage increase |  |  |  |  |  | 94.5 | 50.5 | 21.0 |

Appendix 2

**SIC Components**

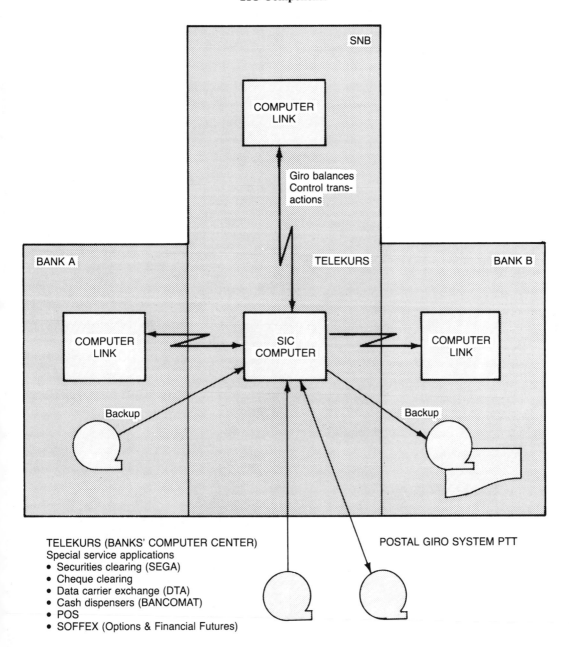

TELEKURS (BANKS' COMPUTER CENTER)
Special service applications
- Securities clearing (SEGA)
- Cheque clearing
- Data carrier exchange (DTA)
- Cash dispensers (BANCOMAT)
- POS
- SOFFEX (Options & Financial Futures)

POSTAL GIRO SYSTEM PTT

# 10 UNITED KINGDOM

# United Kingdom

## I  INTRODUCTION

The payment system in the United Kingdom has experienced significant changes in recent years. The changes have had an impact on both the structure of the system, which has been totally reorganised, and its day-to-day operations, where consumers now enjoy greater competition for their business together with the benefits of a wider range of available electronic services allied with the continued efficient operation of the established paper-based systems.

The background to the formation of the Association for Payment Clearing Services (APACS) in 1985, and the resultant reorganisation of the structure of the payment system, is described in Section II, "Institutional Framework."

### 1. Banks

Two recent events have imposed a higher level of competitive pressure on the banks — particularly in the area of the provision of money transmission facilities: first, the reorganisation of the payment clearing systems in 1985, resulting from the formation of APACS, which allowed for membership to be opened up to any appropriately regulated financial institution meeting explicit and objective criteria for entry, and, second, the enactment of the Building Societies Act, 1986, which gave societies the freedom to provide a wider range of money transmission and financial services. However, for several years the major banks had already been concentrating their efforts on the retail side of their businesses and using a variety of techniques to attract new customers. Many aspects of information technology have been utilised to this end, and all the large banks are making substantial investments in updating computer systems, networking branches, providing cash-management systems for business customers, and experimenting with home banking for personal customers. While most bank ATM networks are now mature, EFT POS is on the threshold of major growth, and consideration of the card products to be offered has been a factor in the banks' reassessment of their credit card affiliations.

### 2. Building Societies

As noted, a major deregulation of the building societies movement was set in motion on January 1, 1987, when the Building Societies Act, 1986 came into effect. The new legislation gave societies the freedom to adopt a range of new powers (after obtaining consent from their members) to expand the provision of financial services. The larger societies are now able to offer a wide range of services: money transmission, cheque guarantee cards, credit cards, unsecured lending, stockbroking facilities, unit trusts, estate agency, property development and conveyancing, and so forth. The new legislation also allows a society to change its mutual status, by incorporation as a public limited company.

At present the signs are that the major societies are seeking to take full advantage of the benefits available to them after deregulation. In the field of money transmission and the provision of personal banking services generally, where economies of scale can secure greater profitability, the societies are competing aggressively, particularly in the provision of card-based products and interest-bearing current accounts.

### 3. Credit Cards

A wide and ever-increasing range of credit cards is available to customers in the United Kingdom, and transaction volumes are increasing by approximately 20 percent per annum. Holders of ordinary bank credit cards are able to pay a range of regular bills, including public utility bills, by automatic charging to a credit card account. A number of factors, described in Section 11.5, have introduced a significantly higher level of competition in the credit card market during 1988.

### 4. Automated Clearings

The reduction of the minimum value of a CHAPS payment, from £10,000 to £7,000, in July 1988, is expected to encourage the greater utilisation of the Clearing House Automated Payment System (CHAPS) and increase the values and volumes of traffic channeled through this EFT mechanism. A further reduction to £5,000 may take place in 1989. Average daily values passing through CHAPS have since late 1987 exceeded those of the Town Clearing, and a daily turnover of £50 billion is not exceptional.

The use of BACS Ltd., the automated clearing house for the bulk exchange of automated debits and credits, continues to grow. BACS actively markets the use of its system as a payment medium and has launched a variety of advertising campaigns, including TV commercials, to increase customer awareness. A number of public utilities and other companies also promote to their customers the use of direct debiting via BACS as an easy and convenient method of payment. As may be seen from the statistical tables, BACS plays a very important role in the UK payment system.

### 5. Electronic Funds Transfer at the Point-of-Sale

In recent years, a number of EFT POS experiments have been conducted by banks and building societies, but their impact in transaction terms has been limited, particularly in the case of systems accepting debit cards. Over the past two years credit card data-capture systems have seen significant growth, as have on-line authorisation systems developed by the major bank credit card companies.

The major banks and building societies, after a number of false starts, are now developing a single national EFT POS scheme with an open and competitive membership and a single terminal at each point of sale that will accept a number of different cards. This venture is being accomplished through the medium of EftPos UK Ltd., a company set up under APACS, which will provide a central processing and settlement function. Particular features of the EftPos UK scheme are the achievement of a higher degree of security in the system by the use of public key cryptography techniques and the achievement of agreed standards for settlement and other aspects of management and control. An inaugural scheme is scheduled to begin live operation in autumn 1989, in three locations (Edinburgh, Leeds, and Southampton) with up to 2,000 terminals. Institutions are continuing with their individual projects, and indeed several new projects have been introduced since EftPos UK was set up. It is expected that institutions will uncouple their processing services from the central EftPos UK system once the inaugural scheme is running smoothly, and that the individual projects will be modified and brought into the national scheme. By the mid-1990s, it is conceivable that up to 200,000 terminals will be connected in some way with EftPos UK.

### 6. Corporate Cash Management

The services offered by the banks to meet the requirements of their corporate customers continue to expand. These customers are able, through their banks, to utilise the facilities offered by BACS and by CHAPS, and the S.W.I.F.T. message switching network to transmit international payment instructions.

### 7. Future Developments

As previously noted, considerable advancement in the use of technology, both in new developments and in existing systems, will be seen over the next decade. The impetus is currently directed towards the development and implementation of on-line real-time systems, which will enable institutions actively to monitor movements and exposures on major customers' accounts.

The establishment of the EC internal market by 1992 has implications for membership and access to the payment clearing systems. However, the open nature of the current structure and the fact that some 300 non-UK banks already have offices in London and the provinces will, to some extent, reduce the effect that this development will have on the money transmission mechanisms.

In the area of electronic data interchange (EDI) the banks will wish to ensure that developments do not occur that allow payment instructions, possibly netted out, to pass through networks out of their overall control so that, as a result, they lose the initiative for a vital part of their corporate payments business. The UK banks are conscious of this possible threat and are closely involved in EDI developments, both in the United Kingdom and internationally.

## II  INSTITUTIONAL FRAMEWORK

### 1. The Clearing Structure

A payment clearing system has existed in London for some 200 years, and for much of that time was operated through the medium of the Bankers' Clearing House. The Clearing House was for many years owned and controlled by the major retail banks through the Committee of London Clearing Bankers (CLCB), although participation in the clearings was also granted to other banks including, *inter alia,* the Bank of England in 1864, the Co-operative Bank and the Central Trustee Savings Bank (now the TSB) in 1975, and National Girobank (now Girobank) in 1983. However, none of these banks shared in the ownership of the Clearing House, nor did they have any direct role in the control of the clearings. In March 1984, all 10 participating banks in the Bankers' Clearing House set up a working party of senior bankers, known as the Child Committee, to review the organisation, membership, and control of the payment clearing systems in the United Kingdom. During the review extensive consultations were held with a range of interested parties. In conducting the review, the working party sought the development of a structure that would retain the essential integrity and effectiveness of the clearings, while meeting criticisms of the arrangements in existence at that time. It sought, at the same time, to create a robust and flexible structure that would accommodate possible future changes in membership, in the clearing systems, in banking technology, and in the payment industry as a whole. In December 1984, the report "Payment Clearing Systems: Review of Organisation, Membership and Control" was published. It recommended bold and far-reaching changes to the organisation of the payment clearing systems, principally consisting of the creation of a new structure and new rules for obtaining membership of the operational clearings, with an umbrella organisation at the pinnacle of the proposed structure to oversee the development of the operational clearings and of the payment industry as a whole. Individual clearing companies were to be set up beneath the umbrella organisation as companies limited by shares, with control and ownership of the organisation and the individual companies in the hands of participating member institutions.

The 10 banks accepted in full the recommendations contained in the report, and the task of implementation was spread over the following year. The umbrella body, which was named the Association for Payment Clearing Services (APACS), was established in December 1985, and three operational clearing companies were set up as follows:

▶ Cheque and Credit Clearing Company Ltd. — responsible for the bulk paper clearings of cheques and credits in England and Wales (the paper clearings in Scotland and Northern Ireland were not included in the new structure).

▶ CHAPS and Town Clearing Company Ltd. — responsible for the high-value (currently £7,000 and over for CHAPS and £10,000 and over for Town), same-day settlement clearings. CHAPS provides an electronic guaranteed sterling credit transfer service to its members and is available throughout the United Kingdom. The Town Clearing covers only high-value cheques drawn on and paid into members' branches within the designated Town Clearing area of the City of London.

▶ BACS Ltd. provides an electronic bulk clearing for direct debits, standing orders, and other automated credit transfers.

A fourth company, EftPos UK Ltd., was established in December 1986, to develop, implement, and manage a national EFT POS system in the United Kingdom and to handle the reconciliation and settlement of the transactions to be cleared through the scheme following its inauguration.

The individual clearing companies are responsible for the day-to-day operation of their clearings and enjoy a high degree of autonomy. All settlements are carried out over accounts maintained at the Bank of England. The settlement institutions are required to maintain balances sufficient to meet their obligations in each clearing. Settlement membership of each company is open to all institutions that meet explicit and objective criteria. These criteria, which are designed to preserve the integrity and efficiency of the clearings, require a prospective member to be engaged in the provision of payment and transmission services in the United Kingdom, to be appropriately supervised (by the Bank of England or the Building Societies Commission), to hold settlement account facilities at the Bank of England, to comply with the technical and operational requirements of the clearings, to pay an entry fee and a fair share of the operating costs, and to meet a minimum volume requirement of 0.5 percent of traffic through the clearing(s) in question. (In BACS a relaxation of the volume criterion was allowed as from June 1988 for institutions handling volumes of 5 million items or more in the year preceding application.) Another feature of the new structure is that it is possible for an institution to join a single clearing company, whereas in the past membership of the Bankers' Clearing House required settlement membership of all the clearings. All settlement members of the individual clearings have automatic membership of APACS.

In addition to the clearing companies, two other operational groupings have been brought under the APACS umbrella to manage certain functions that do not require the same structural approach. These are the Currency Clearings Committee, which operates the London U.S. dollar (retail) clearing and the London Currency Settlement Scheme; and the Cheque Card Policy Committee, which is responsible for the operation of the domestic cheque guarantee card scheme and the participation of UK institutions in the Uniform Eurocheque Community.

APACS also provides a forum for a wide range of committees and working groups both to enable its members to examine and consider new developments in money transmission matters and to ensure the continued day-to-day smooth running of the existing systems and the maintenance of their financial integrity and operational efficiency. In addition, APACS, together with its members, is closely involved in considering ways to meet the rapidly developing requirements of participants in the various financial markets and is helping its members in preparing evidence for the Review Committee on Banking Services Law (the Jack Committee) regarding the legal aspects of the payment systems.

In December 1985, upon the formation of APACS, the first institutions to benefit from the more open and objective membership criteria were Citibank NA and Standard Chartered Bank plc. Both joined the two high-value same-day settlement clearings operated by CHAPS and Town Clearing Company Ltd.

A full list of members of APACS and the operational clearings appears in Appendix 1.

## 2. Role of the Central Bank

The Bank of England does not have any statutory powers regarding payment clearing systems, nor does it supervise their operations. The bank was, however, closely involved in the work of the Child Committee and fully supported its recommendations. Under the rules of APACS, the bank, as central bank, has membership as of right on the boards of the individual clearing companies and is represented on all the various policy-making committees that operate under the APACS umbrella. However, the legal powers the bank enjoys from this representation do not exceed those of any other member. The bank's special role is recognised in discussions on public policy issues.

The APACS rules also ascribe to the bank a special position with regard to applications for settlement membership of any of the clearing companies: eligibility for membership is determined by a set of objective criteria (described above), one of which is that the applicant must have obtained the agreement of the Bank of England to provide settlement account facilities in the relevant clearings (settlement of all the APACS operational clearings takes place over accounts held by the participants with the bank).

The only payment medium for which the Bank of England has a statutory role is the bank note: The bank has gradually assumed the sole right of note issue in England and Wales, under the Bank Charter Act, 1844. This act also separated the note-issuing function of the bank from its other activities by dividing the bank into two departments for accounting purposes. The accounts of the Issue Department relate solely to the production, issue, and payment of bank notes and to the portfolio of securities by which the note issue is backed. The Banking Department, which under the terms of the 1844 Act embraces the rest of the bank's activities, issues bank notes to, and receives them from, its customers, including in particular the major retail banks.

## 3. Supervisory and Regulatory Authorities

There is no statutory supervision or regulation of the payment systems operating in the United Kingdom.

Supervision of banks is vested in the Bank of England by the Banking Act, 1987, which replaced the Banking Act, 1979. The act has a broadly similar structure to the earlier legislation, but one major difference is that the former two-tier system of authorisation (recognised banks and licensed institutions) has been replaced by a unified system with a single category of authorised institution. The act requires an institution to have prior authorisation before a "deposit," as defined, may be accepted. Certain institutions have been exempted from the provisions of the act because their activities are regulated by other legislation: For example, building societies are supervised by the Building Societies Commission (under the Building Societies Act, 1986), responsible both to the Treasury and to Parliament. As of the end of February 1988, 313 institutions incorporated in the United Kingdom and 254 institutions incorporated outside the United Kingdom were authorised under the

Banking Act, and at the end of 1987, 137 building societies were supervised by the Building Societies Commission.

### 4. Other Authorised Institutions

Those banks in the United Kingdom that are not members of APACS but are authorised (whether incorporated inside or outside the United Kingdom) under the Banking Act, 1987 to accept deposits, play a fairly limited role in the payment system. Although some provide a range of money transmission services through the medium of agency arrangements, most concentrate on the provision of wholesale banking facilities. In the building society movement only the relatively larger societies (currently those with assets in excess of £100 million) are permitted to offer money transmission and other services as noted in Section I.2 above.

### 5. Other Institutions

Certain other institutions are involved in the payment system. The state-owned National Savings Bank operates through post offices. Many deposits with the National Savings Bank tend to be longer-term savings and therefore play only a minor part in the money transmission system. However, depositors of the National Savings Bank Ordinary Account, as well as being able to draw cash at post offices, can arrange to make payments by standing orders, by warrants (similar to cheques) payable to third parties, or by transfers initiated at post office counters.

The post office is itself only involved in the provision of payment services through its responsibilities for issuing and redeeming postal orders and for handling the cash payment of various state benefits to the public. It also operates Girobank under a service contract, although plans have been announced for the sale of Girobank as part of the government's privatisation program.

Government departments make many of their payments by means of payable orders drawn on the Paymaster General's Office or, in a few cases, on themselves. The banks collect these through the General Cheque Clearing system.

### 6. Credit Card Issuers

Bank credit cards continue to play an increasing role in the UK payment system. There are two main card-issuing groups, VISA and Access. At the time of this writing, 28 institutions in the United Kingdom were affiliated to VISA, of which 16 issue their own cards. Barclaycard originally processed all VISA card transactions, but the Co-operative Bank, TSB, the Bank of Scotland, and Girobank now carry out their own card processing. Access is affiliated to MasterCard and Eurocard and is operated by the Joint Credit Card Company, which was formed in 1972 by Lloyds Bank, Midland Bank, National Westminster Bank, and Williams and Glyn's Bank (now The Royal Bank of Scotland) and has since been joined by Clydesdale Bank, Coutts & Co., the Bank of Ireland, Northern Bank, and Ulster Bank. Each member bank issues an Access card under its own name. Many building societies now offer their customers VISA or Access credit cards.

During 1988, the four major banks (Barclays, Lloyds, Midland, and National Westminster) all took up direct membership of both VISA and MasterCard.

American Express and Diners Club both issue travel and entertainment cards which are in widespread use.

Save and Prosper and Chase Manhattan Bank in London both launched VISA credit cards during 1988, offering lower annual percentage interest rates than those charged by the major VISA and Access credit card issuers.

In addition, as noted in Section III.1(c) below, many retailers offer card-based credit facilities to their customers.

# III   PAYMENT SYSTEMS

## 1. Payment Media Available to Customers

### (a)  Cash payments

The Bank of England has the sole right of note issue in England and Wales, under the Bank Charter Act, 1844. The bank currently prints and issues notes in four denominations—£5, £10, £20, and £50—and these notes circulate freely throughout the United Kingdom. Three banks in Scotland and four banks in Northern Ireland retain the right to issue their own sterling notes, but, apart from a small fiduciary issue, these must be fully covered by holdings of Bank of England notes, or of coin. The banks draw the notes they require from the head office and five branches of the Bank of England and distribute them through their own cash centers. Soiled notes and those surplus to requirements are returned to the bank and removed from circulation; alternatively, surplus notes can be held at the banks' cash centers for reissue. To counteract the tendency for the lives of notes to shorten, which together with inflation had led to an excessive and expensive issue of new notes, the Bank of England encourages the use of higher denomination notes and restricts the issue of new notes to the banking system by negotiating quotas with the major banks and by reissuing used notes. A factor of growing importance for the production and supply of bank notes is the increasing number of ATMs installed by banks and building societies; the consequent demand for clean, machine-usable notes is being met partly from the output of note-sorting machines installed by the Bank of England and the major retail banks.

The amount of cash drawn from ATMs continues to grow, increasing by 16 percent between 1986 and 1987 to stand at some £23 billion. The spread of ATMs (there are now over 12,000 in the United Kingdom) has changed the behavior patterns of bank and building society customers and has brought an increase in the frequency, but a reduction in the average amount, of cash withdrawals from ATMs as opposed to withdrawals made over counters.

The Royal Mint is responsible for the production and issue of coin throughout the United Kingdom. Coins are currently in general issue in seven denominations: 1 penny, 2, 5, 10, 20, and 50 pence and £1 (some £2 coins have also been issued but are rarely seen). Coins equivalent to 5 (one shilling) and 10 pence (two shillings) issued prior to decimalisation in 1971 are still in circulation. New, smaller 5 and 10 pence coins will be issued in June 1990 and June 1992, respectively. The Royal Mint delivers coin to bank cash centers or direct to their branches, against payment by the banks. However, coin surplus to the banks' requirements normally cannot be returned to the Mint, and banks occasionally have to store considerable quantities of surplus coin. At year-end 1987, the value of notes and coin in circulation with the public totaled £14.5 billion. It has been estimated that some 12 billion payments of £1 or more and some 50 billion payments of less than £1 are made each year in cash, and that cash accounts for some 90 percent of all payments made in the United Kingdom. However, in real terms there has been a decline in the use of cash in recent years because of the growth in the use of bank media for the payment of wages and salaries and for the consumers' expenditures.

The move away from the payment of wages in cash has not, however, been as pronounced as expected over the last few years, and approximately one-third of all employees continue to be paid in cash. The Wages Act, 1986, which came into force on January 1, 1987, removed the statutory entitlement of workers to receive their wages in cash. However, despite efforts by many employers to convert their staff to cashless pay, the attraction of cash remains, particularly among the large numbers of part-time workers.

*(b) Cashless payments*

An estimated 52 percent by volume of all cashless payments in 1987 were made by cheque, amounting to almost 11.7 million items per day, excluding cheques drawn for cash. Payment by cheque, however, is generally acceptable at the point-of-sale only if the drawer presents a cheque guarantee card issued by the bank on which the cheque is drawn. The major retail banks, with the exception of Barclays, have since 1969 participated in a joint Cheque Card Scheme, under which some 21.5 million cheque guarantee cards had been issued to their customer at year-end 1987. Cheques drawn under the terms of the scheme, and supported by these cards, are guaranteed up to an amount of £50. In addition, some 12 million (1987) VISA credit cards issued by Barclays, TSB, and other banks also double as guarantee cards for cheques drawn on the issuing bank. To guarantee the encashment of cheques in continental Europe, most banks issue Eurocheques and guarantee cards to their customers under the Uniform Eurocheque Scheme. Because of the existence of the domestic cheque guarantee arrangements, Eurocheques are rarely used by UK holders within the United Kingdom.

At the time of this writing, some 17 building societies offer cheque-book facilities to their customers, combining interest-bearing transaction accounts with automatic transfer facilities and additional features, including direct debits, standing orders, ATM access, and automatic overdrafts. These societies offer chequing accounts through an agency clearing facility negotiated with a settlement member of the Cheque and Credit Clearing Company, with the exception of Abbey National, which is itself a full settlement member of that clearing. Many banks and other financial institutions also offer high-interest and money market chequing accounts, but a restriction on the minimum amount of withdrawal per cheque (typically £50-£300) is usually applied.

The paper-based bank giro credit clearing accounted for 8.5 percent (including interbranch credits) of cashless payments by volume in 1987. This system is used for making consumer payments to large organisations, such as public utilities and mail-order companies.

Electronic direct debits, standing orders, and other credits are processed by BACS Ltd. Direct debits allow recipients of large numbers of payments, such as insurance companies and public utilities, to collect those payments automatically from bank or building society accounts after the account holder has signed a mandate authorising his bank to pay specified direct debits for either a regular fixed sum or a variable amount. In 1987, 8.5 percent of the volume of cashless payments was made by direct debit.

Standing orders and electronic credits, which together accounted for 13 percent of all cashless payments by volume in 1987, are both initiated by the payer. Standing orders are used largely by individuals for the payment of regular fixed sums; while in the past electronic credits tended to be used mainly for the disbursement of bulk payments such as salaries and wages, they are now increasingly being used for other transactions, such as corporations' purchase ledger payments.

Some 36,000 companies in the United Kingdom can originate payments through BACS, but these have to be addressed to an account with one of the 16 settlement members of that clearing. Each originator has to be sponsored by its bank.

Cashless payments can be made through the post office either by postal order or by Girobank transfer. Postal orders are a convenient way of making low-value payments, particularly for those not having a bank account. They are available in various fixed denominations up to £20. Their use has been declining sharply in recent years, and in 1987, only some 54 million were issued, compared with 70 million in 1983 and 170 million in 1978. The average value of postal orders issued in 1987 was £5.

Girobank operates a full banking service. Paper transfers can be made between account holders, or, by use of the Transcash service, a transfer can be made from a nonaccount holder to an account holder. Some state benefits are paid by means of cheques drawn on Girobank, and these can be cashed at post offices.

The Department of Social Security issues order books containing a number of vouchers, which may be used on specific dates to draw cash from post offices regarding various state benefits such as old-age pensions. In 1987, some 870 million of these vouchers were issued. Although these payments are paper-based, they are not usually counted as cashless payments because they can only be exchanged for cash and cannot be credited to an account.

Payable orders, another form of debit instrument, are issued by the Paymaster General's Office and by some other government departments; these are treated in the same manner as cheques and are collected through the interbank cheque clearing system.

Travellers' cheques, issued by banks, building societies, and other bodies, are widely used as a safe and convenient method of taking currency abroad but are seldom used by UK residents within the United Kingdom.

*(c) Bank cards*

*At retail outlets*

Card-based payments can be effected at many retail outlets in the United Kingdom by means of a credit card or a charge card. At the end of 1987, 24 million bank credit cards had been issued. In 1987, some 500 million payments were made using these cards for a total value of some £16.7 billion. At the end of 1987, 45 percent of all bank credit cards were Access cards, affiliated to MasterCard and Eurocard, issued by nine banks (the Bank of Scotland, Clydesdale Bank, Lloyds Bank, Midland Bank, National Westminster Bank, The Royal Bank of Scotland, Northern Bank, the Bank of Ireland, and Ulster Bank). The remainder were issued by institutions affiliated to VISA: 40 percent by Barclays Bank (Barclaycard), 11 percent by TSB (Trustcard), and 4 percent by others. As noted in Section II.5 above, a number of major banks have recently taken up direct membership of both VISA and MasterCard.

Bank credit cards have a credit facility with a preset limit ranging from £200 upwards. Cardholders are normally required to make monthly repayments of 5 percent of the outstanding balance or £5, whichever is the greater, although in 1987, approximately 40 percent of bank cardholders settled their monthly accounts in full, without incurring interest. The average balance outstanding on bank credit cards in 1987 was £236, and the average value of each transaction was £32. Banks do not usually charge a joining fee or an annual subscription fee to the cardholder. In addition to bank-issued credit cards, there are 1.5 million travel and entertainment charge cards in issue to UK residents: 1 million of these are issued by American Express and 0.5 million by Diners Club.

Retailers have issued some 9 million "in-store" cards. These usually only serve one store group and many operate on a "budget" basis, with a monthly subscription and a revolving credit facility of 20 or 30 times this amount. Other retailer cards operate in the same way as travel and entertainment charge cards or bank credit cards.

Since 1982, many banks have issued "gold" or premium cards. A subscription is payable on these cards, but they have no preset spending limits and are usually linked to a substantial unsecured overdraft facility with a bank.

The fraudulent use of cheque guarantee cards and credit cards continues to be of great concern to the issuing institutions in the United Kingdom (although some improvement was seen in 1987). A redesigned cheque guarantee card is to be issued by the institutions participating in the joint Cheque Card Scheme, starting in October 1988, and stretching over two years. This will replace the existing card, which was reformatted for security purposes in 1984. The new standard card will incorporate a logo and a hologram featuring the head of William Shakespeare and will also incorporate other security features. The card will continue to have a guarantee limit of £50. However, fewer than half the existing guarantee cards in issue will be replaced by the new standard card. Many issuing institutions will provide cards that, while remaining within the rules of the Cheque Card Scheme, will perform several additional functions: ATM withdrawal, EFT POS, and so forth. These multifunction debit cards will demonstrate their guarantee capability by featuring the Shakespeare logo on the reverse. (They are described in more detail below.)

At year-end 1987, Access, American Express, Diners Club, banks affiliated to VISA and various major retail stores have introduced card and credit verification schemes using automated authorisation telephones and terminals at the point-of-sale.

### At ATMs

At mid-1988, a total of 12,500 ATMs were in service in the United Kingdom. Of thcsc, 79 percent belonged to one of the four principal shared networks (the percentage will increase to over 90 percent by year-end 1988, when the TSB joins one of the networks). A table illustrating the networks and their respective ATM and customer base appears in Appendix 2.

Most bank ATMs are sited on bank premises. Of these, 67 percent are accessible from outside and are known as "through-the-wall" machines, 24 percent are sited in the customer areas of banks, 5 percent are sited in the lobby areas of banks, and 4 percent are at remote sites, e.g., at supermarkets. Almost all building society ATMs are "through-the-wall" machines. Some 27 million bank (debit) cards have been issued for carrying out cash withdrawals from ATMs against a charge to customers' accounts. In addition, most bank credit cards can also be used to obtain cash advances (charged to customers' credit card accounts). In many cases, the use of VISA credit cards in ATMs cuts across domestic card-sharing arrangements.

In 1987, some £18.5 billion was withdrawn by cardholders from bank ATMs and some £5 billion from building society ATMs. The average value of each bank machine withdrawal was £34, while that of each building society machine was £45. Each bank and building society machine was used an average of 1,000 times per week, but with considerable variation between networks and individual machines. Typically, cardholders can withdraw up to £100 daily from a machine, but several banks approve withdrawals up to a prearranged weekly amount. Most cardholders can order new cheque books and full or interim statements and make balance inquiries and deposits via ATMs, and at more advanced ATMs, now being installed by banks and building societies, customers can make bill payments, funds transfers, and standing order inquiries, and order Eurocheques. The hours during which ATMs are available for use varies, "through-the-wall" machines and some lobby machines being potentially available 24 hours a day. ATMs located in the customer areas are only available during normal banking/building society hours, and those sited remotely and the other lobby machines are available during shopping or office hours. In addition to domestic sharing arrangements, several international sharing arrangements exist. Approximately 1,700 UK VISA issuers' ATMs are included in the international arrangements that cover approximately 21,700 machines in 22 countries around the world. The ATMs of the Access banks are not yet connected to the International MasterCard network, but Access cardholders have access to 2,700 Spanish ATMs. Most banks in the United Kingdom issue international Eurocheque cheque cards, which can, if they are valid for use in ATMs, be used to withdraw cash from some 6,500 participating ATMs in the 20 countries issuing Eurocheque cheque cards. At the time of this writing, some 42 million cards have been issued by some 10,000 issuing banks and are accepted at over 5 million retail outlets. In the United Kingdom, only Midland Bank ATMs permit Eurocheque card withdrawals, but only for cards issued in Belgium, Germany, Ireland, Luxembourg, the Netherlands, Portugal, and by Midland Bank itself. In 1987, a reciprocal agreement was concluded between LINK and PLUS (the shared ATM network operating in North America) giving LINK cardholders access to some 11,000 ATMs sited on the mainland of North America, and giving some 67 million cardholders of the PLUS network access to LINK ATMs.

*At point-of-sale terminals*

The major UK retail banks first announced their intention to develop a national scheme for electronic funds transfer at the point-of-sale—EFT POS—in May 1983. The work continued under the umbrella of APACS, and in December 1986, a new clearing company, EftPos UK Ltd., was set up within the APACS structure to develop, implement, and manage a national system for EFT POS in the United Kingdom. A Business Service Specification has been drawn up as a consultative document, in which the commercial framework, the nature of the inaugural EftPos UK service, and subsequent future development are set forth. In accordance with principles established by APACS, membership of the company is open to appropriately regulated financial institutions which are able to meet specific entry criteria; access may also be gained (by a nonmember) on an agency basis as a sponsored service provider. However, for the Inaugural Service, which is scheduled to begin in autumn 1989, and will operate in Edinburgh, Leeds, and Southampton with up to 2,000 terminals, membership has had to be somewhat restricted for technical and operational reasons. The national service will establish rules, standards, settlement procedures, and rigorous levels of security. In addition, it will introduce a Card Scheme under which cards issued by institutions joining the scheme will eventually bear a common logo and be acceptable at every EftPos UK terminal. Terminals will be able to accept debit cards, credit cards, and charge cards. Once the scheme has proved itself in the Inaugural Service, individual members will have the option of uncoupling their processing services from the central EftPos UK system, but will remain members of EftPos UK Ltd. and be required to adhere to the rules, regulations, and standards of the national scheme. Members will thus be able to offer a range of simple or enhanced value added services of their own choice, in their own time, in locations and to retailers of their own choosing. Crucially, therefore, each member will be able to make its own investment decisions as to how far and how fast it wishes to develop its EFT POS services. Many of the bank and building society members of EftPos UK Ltd. are continuing to develop and extend their own schemes while remaining committed to the concepts of the national scheme.

There are now over 20 EFT POS schemes operating in the United Kingdom. Most are operated by banks in conjunction with credit card companies, with terminals located in petrol stations and High Street stores. Most existing schemes operate off-line, capturing data for later transmission to the processing center, and accept various credit cards, charge cards, and some debit cards. The largest service with on-line capability is the Barclaycard PDQ scheme, which is growing rapidly with 5,000 terminals in June 1988. The off-line PISCES data-capture scheme for petrol retailers, run by a National Westminster Bank subsidiary, had 3,800 terminals at mid-1988. The longest-established scheme remains Clydesdale Bank's Counterplus, which operates at some 30 petrol stations and two retailers in Scotland with approximately 70 terminals in place. Like Counterplus, most EFT POS schemes currently operating are aimed more at securing technical and operational experience than market share. However, the marketplace is developing rapidly, and there is a reasonable prospect that some 200,000 terminals may be in place in only a few years.

British Telecom has introduced telephones that accept payment for telephone calls (50p minimum) by credit and charge cards, which are passed through a reader on the call box.

British Telecom's Phonecard, a stored-value card for use in certain public telephone call boxes, and the installation of Phonecard call boxes continue their growth. The Phonecard is preloaded with a store of value that is consumed as calls are made but is not rechargeable. It is sold in several unit denominations at post offices and many retail outlets.

A number of multifunction debit cards have been introduced by the banks in the past year as initiatives for cashless shopping. In June 1987, Barclays Bank introduced Connect, a multifunction debit card, under the VISA label, incorporating three cards in one: a cash card, a cheque guarantee card with a £50 limit, and a card for use at the point-of-sale. Initially, most transactions are paper-based, because relatively few retailers have the appropriate terminals, but over time the paper debit vouchers will be replaced by electronic debit messages. The launch of Connect encountered strong opposition among retailers, because Barclays proposed to charge them the same transaction commission as that charged on VISA credit card transactions. The retailers' view was that the card was a cheque substitute and that transaction charges should therefore be levied on the same, flat rate, basis. In the event Barclays amended their pricing structure to allay the retailers' concerns, thereby establishing what the retailers considered to be a vital precedent for the pricing of all debit card transactions. In the spring of 1988, the launch of two additional multifunction debit cards was announced. The first was by Lloyds Bank, again under the VISA label (hitherto Lloyds had been solely an Access card issuer), to be introduced in the summer of 1988. This card incorporates the same three functions as the Connect card but, in addition, offers a personal overdraft facility and protection under the Consumer Credit Act. The second card, SWITCH, is to be introduced in October 1988, in a joint project undertaken by three banks—Midland Bank, National Westminster Bank, and The Royal Bank of Scotland. The project is also open to other banks and building societies. In addition to a common SWITCH symbol, each card will bear the name of the individual issuing bank. This card, again, will function as a cheque guarantee card with a £50 limit, as a cash withdrawal card, and as an initiator for "electronic cheque" transactions at EFT POS terminals where the SWITCH symbol is displayed, and, most importantly, as a debit card under the rules of EftPos UK, which means that the card may also be used at any terminal bearing the EftPos UK logo.

A recent innovation in technology in the United Kingdom has been the introduction of cheque-writing machines at the point-of-sale in the major branches of some of the larger High Street retailers. The customer is required only to confirm that the details printed on the cheque are correct before signing it.

Several major retailers have introduced substantial EFT POS networks for handling in-house cards. It has been reported that at year-end 1988, some 10,000 terminals had been installed.

*(d) Other media*
   *Home banking*

Both screen-based and telephone-based home-banking services are available in the United Kingdom.

Screen-based services include the Nottingham Building Society's and the Bank of

Scotland's joint service called Homelink, the Bank of Scotland's own HOBS service, Clydesdale Bank's service called Telebank, and The Royal Bank of Scotland's Royline. Subscribers to Homelink, which dates back to 1983, receive a terminal that plugs into their television set and connects by telephone to British Telecom's Prestel viewdata service. Funds can be transferred betweeen accounts with the society and with the bank, and arrangements can be made for payments to a limited number of third parties. It can also be used as a teleshopping and telemessaging system. Telebank operates under much the same principle as Homelink, and the equipment used is compatible with that used for Prestel's viewdata system, but it is connected to Midland Bank's Fastrak services. In addition to the services offered by Homelink, Telebank also offers a bill-payment service and a special interest-bearing account. The Bank of Scotland's HOBS service, which is reported to have approximately 4,000 subscribers, is also available through Prestel; it includes an electronic cash management package for small businesses and offers two higher interest rate bands. The Royal Bank of Scotland's Royline, the most recent screen-based service, provides an office banking service for small and medium-sized business customers.

Voice-response home-banking services are currently offered by two banks and two building societies, using the domestic telephone and an electronic keyboard called a tonepad. Other institutions are expected to offer similar services in the future. To gain access to the account, a PIN code and/or password must be keyed into the tonepad. A number of services are available to customers, including the transfer of funds between accounts, requests for statements, foreign currency or travellers' cheques, and payment of bills. The TSB's Speedlink service has some 50,000 subscribers, who together carry out over 12,000 transactions per week. One in 10 of Nationwide Anglia Building Society's FlexAccount customers use their FlexAccount home-banking service. No statistics on the other services are currently available. Voice recognition services (using the domestic telephone only) are offered by the Royal Bank of Scotland (Phoneline) and National Westminster Bank (Actionline). When customers dial up the service, the bank's central computer verifies their identity by their voice characteristics.

### Chip cards

The use of chip card technology in the United Kingdom has only recently commenced and is unlikely to have any great impact for several years, given that magnetic-stripe cards and terminals are widely established. Citibank and Midland Bank each have trials running: Citibank's Electronic Wallet card is charged with electronic credits and is redeemable at banks in London, Jersey, and Marbella in Spain. Midland's Meritcard (contactless chip card) is being tested by students and staff on the campus of Loughborough University. The card has three principal functions: First, as an electronic cheque (PIN entry) for higher value transactions up to a weekly limit; second, as an electronic wallet (PIN entry for recharging only) loaded at the Midland campus branch or at some retailers, with maximum capacity of £20; third, the card retains a record of the last 64 transactions, in either payment mode. A further trial has been launched by Thomas Cook, the travel subsidiary of Midland Bank, with Smart Card International. The card, which is aimed primarily at the business travel market, facilitates the issue of documentation required for travel purposes, including travellers' cheques, airline tickets, boarding cards, and travel itineraries. The cards incorporate a personal pocket computer with a small screen and keyboard and can be used, once the holder's security identity number is keyed in, to withdraw cash from Thomas Cook outlets or any other participating financial institutions. Barclays Bank has also launched a chip card trial at a country club sports complex. In this trial the card will also be used for a number of nonfinancial applications.

*Corporate cash management*

By mid-1988, all the major UK retail banks and several foreign banks in London were offering cash management systems for their corporate customers, and some provided systems for small business customers. The level of sophistication and range of services offered by the banks vary widely and include customer initiation of electronic funds transfers, foreign exchange transaction reporting, electronic balance and transaction reporting, cheque and cash remittance, retrieval of information from a number of banks with conversion into a spreadsheet and international cash management services, while more recent innovations include links, via banks, to S.W.I.F.T. and to CHAPS. The corporate treasurer accesses the services offered by his bank through a desk-top terminal linked to the bank's computer.

Another corporate service is the Bank of Scotland's Transcontinental Automated Payments Service (TAPS), which helps customers to make regular payments to be credited direct to beneficiaries' bank accounts overseas (e.g., pensioners living abroad) in the local currency of the country of residence, using the domestic electronic clearing system of the country in which the accounts are held, often through an ACH (automated clearing house). These payments can, at the time of this writing, be made to beneficiaries in Australia, Canada, Ireland, France, South Africa, the United States, and the Federal Republic of Germany; in addition, Belgium, Denmark, Finland, the Netherlands, Norway, Sweden, and Switzerland are scheduled to be brought into the system shortly.

*(e) Interbank and intrabank networks accessible to customers*

Bank customers in the United Kingdom may input payments direct to BACS but have only indirect access, through the agency of their bank, to CHAPS and S.W.I.F.T. However, before a customer can submit bulk payments (credits or debits) to BACS for processing, he must be sponsored by one of the sponsoring banks, with which he must hold an account. An account holder with a bank that is not eligible to sponsor customers for BACS can still submit data, provided the bank has itself been sponsored. Once sponsored, a customer can deliver data for processing to BACS on magnetic tape, cassette (although this medium is currently being phased out) or diskette, or by direct telecommunication link (Bacstel).

The Clearing House Automated Payment System (CHAPS), which has been in operation since February 1984, is a system for making guaranteed same-day sterling payments between the 14 settlement bank members. Customers of these banks, including nonsettlement banks (known as participants and which currently number some 190), can make use of CHAPS to send and receive eligible payments anywhere within the UK branch networks of the settlement members.

Customers of banks in the United Kingdom also benefit from S.W.I.F.T., the worldwide message-switching network, which until June 1987, was restricted to the banking community; since then, use of the network has been opened up to categories of participants that include securities brokers and dealers, recognised exchanges for securities, central depositories, and clearing institutions. Nonbank customers cannot make direct use of S.W.I.F.T.; their instructions must be submitted via their bank.

## 2. Exchange Circuits

*(a) Introduction*

There is no uniform pattern of exchange circuits within different banks in the United Kingdom. Some banks pass to their branches all the effects (cheques, paper credits, and other items) relating to customers of each branch, while other banks may choose to truncate some of those effects at, for example, one of their own regional clearing centers. Some banks truncate effects for personal customers but pass on to their branches all effects for corporate customers.

All the major banks in the United Kingdom are highly computerised: Data capture for the updating of accounts regarding debit and credit clearing items (both paper and electronic) generally takes place in a bank's regional or central clearing office, with the accounts themselves being maintained on computers in those regional or central offices. Transactions at an account holder's own branch—e.g., the encashment of cheques—are, however, generally captured for account-updating purposes at that branch: this process is assisted by the growing number of on-line counter and other terminals installed in banks' branches.

### (b) Intrabank or intragroup networks

Intrabank items in the paper debit clearings are transported from the bank branch where they are paid into each clearing bank's regional or head office clearing center; from there they may be passed on to the account-holding branch, or they may be truncated. Intrabank paper credit items follow the same route via the clearing center to the beneficiaries' branch.

Only a limited amount of intragroup processing occurs in the United Kingdom.

### (c) Interbank circuits and networks

#### Paper clearings

As described in the section "Institutional Framework," the day-to-day management and control of the London Clearing House and, therefore, responsibility for all the paper clearings operating in London are now in the hands of APACS. Separate clearings for local paper take place in Edinburgh, among the four retail banks in Scotland that form the Committee of Scottish Clearing Bankers (CSCB), and in Belfast, among the five retail banks operating in Northern Ireland that form the Northern Ireland Bankers' Association (NIBA).

The paper passing through the London Clearing House is divided into three categories: Town Clearing and General Clearing for debit items, largely cheques and bankers' payments, and Credit Clearing for credit transfers.

A same-day settlement service is provided by the Town Clearing, which is restricted to cheques, bankers' drafts, and certain other items of £10,000 or more that have been drawn on and paid into any of the 100 or so offices of the settlement members within the central area of the City of London. All items passing through the Town Clearing must be paid, or returned unpaid, on the same day. The Town Clearing remains a manual system. In 1987, the value and volume of items passing through the Town Clearing exceeded £8,300 billion and 4 million, respectively, giving an average value of some £2 million per item. In 1987, the total increase in value over the previous year was only 2 percent, while the total volume dropped by 8 percent. A factor contributing to this decline in Town Clearing volumes is that since the CHAPS system was implemented in February 1984, many of the payments that would previously have been made via the Town Clearing now pass through CHAPS, the electronic high-value same-day settlement clearing.

The Debit, or General Clearing as it is commonly known, operates under the Cheque and Credit Clearing Company Ltd. on a three-day cycle for the clearance of cheques and other debit items not eligible for the Town Clearing. Cheques paid into branches of the clearing settlement member institutions that are drawn on other banks/institutions are exchanged the following day in the Clearing House: settlement is effected on the third day. If a cheque is not acceptable to the paying bank for any reason, it is returned to the branch where it was originally paid in and the value of the cheque is reclaimed through BACS or the paper clearing. In 1987, the volume of items passing through the General Clearing totaled some 2 billion, for a total value of £860 billion (making an average value per transaction of £430). This was an increase of 5 percent in volume and 12 percent in value over the previous year. The processing of cheques exchanged in the General Clearing has been highly automated for several years, using magnetic ink character recognition techniques (MICR). Cheques drawn on a bank/institution in England or Wales and paid into a bank/institution in Scotland or Northern Ireland are passed, via a local agent, into the General Clearing. Cheques drawn on a bank/institution in Scotland or Northern Ireland and paid into a bank/institution in England or Wales are similarly dealt with by an agent and passed to the drawee banks/institutions: A four-day clearing cycle applies to such items drawn on Scottish banks and a five-day cycle to those drawn on banks in Northern Ireland. The interbank settlements in Scotland and Northern Ireland take place bilaterally.

The Credit Clearing (or bank giro) was largely a manual system until January 1984, when the addition of encoded information to all bank giro credit vouchers made this paper clearing capable of automated processing. The code is machine-read by MICR techniques, sometimes in combination with optical character recognition methods (OCR), whereas cheque processing only uses MICR. This clearing also operates on a three-day cycle, with items being exchanged in the clearing house on the second day and the credit to the beneficiary's account and the interbank settlement taking place on the third. In 1987, some 180 million items passed through the credit clearing for a total value of £92 billion.

Some 14 banks in the United Kingdom participate in the Uniform Eurocheque Scheme that operates throughout Europe and in certain non-European countries. Overseas banks collecting Eurocheques drawn on UK bank branches send items to the UK Eurocheque Clearing Center, where details are input on magnetic tapes, which are then delivered to each paying bank. Details of each cheque are subsequently forwarded to the paying branches while the Eurocheque remains at the Clearing Center. Eurocheques encashed or received by UK banks drawn on foreign banks are remitted to one of six out-clearing centers for onward transmission to the respective European counterparts' clearing center.

Two further paper clearings take place in London: the London U.S. Dollar Clearing and the London Currency Settlement Scheme (LCSS). The London U.S. Dollar Clearing enables dollar cheques and drafts, payable in London, to be cleared and subsequently settled via payments through CHIPS in New York, on the same day. "Wholesale" U.S. dollar transactions are not eligible for this clearing, which is confined to "retail" paper. In addition to the seven settlement members (Bank of Scotland, Barclays Bank, Coutts & Co., Lloyds Bank, Midland Bank, National Westminster Bank, and the The Royal Bank of Scotland), there are currently some 80 other banks participating in the scheme. The London Currency Settlement Scheme, formerly known as the Insurance Companies Currency Scheme, provides clearing facilities for cheques drawn in Australian dollars, Canadian dollars, Deutsche mark, Dutch guilders, French francs, Italian lire, and Japanese yen. In addition to the seven settlement members (the same as those in the U.S. Dollar Clearing), there are currently a total of 23 banks (in the United Kingdom) participating in the scheme.

*Automated clearings*

*(i) BACS*

BACS Ltd. (named Bankers' Automated Clearing Services Ltd. until 1986) has, as of December 1988, 16 (shareholding) members, comprising 14 banks and two building societies, with another building society accepted for membership in June 1989. All member banks and building societies participate in BACS by submitting data themselves and/or by sponsoring their customers for direct input to BACS. There are currently some 36,000 BACS users. The originators of payments submit data to BACS by means of magnetic tape, cassette (this method is currently being phased out), or diskette, or, since mid-1983, by direct telecommunication link (Bacstel). BACS is currently conducting trials with a new method of providing telecommunication links for its corporate users. The new service, called Bacsnet, uses electronic data interchange (EDI) services to transmit BACS payment instructions, allowing companies to combine documentation and funds transfer in a single automated operation.

Each submission to BACS consists of a number of credit items matched by one debit item for the total, or a number of debit items matched by one credit item. Submissions of standing orders are prepared by the banks/building societies holding the accounts from which the standing orders are to be paid; submissions of automated bank giro payments are prepared by customers initiating those payments, while submissions of direct debits are prepared by the customers who are to receive those payments. The BACS processing system sorts these items according to the bank branches to which they are addressed and prepares detailed tapes for those banks: The debits and credits are applied to the destination accounts on the third day of the cycle of operations, when the interbank settlement also takes place. In 1987, BACS processed some 1 billion items, of which 32 percent were bank giro credits, 23 percent standing orders, and 45 percent direct debits. These automated payments represented one-third of the total bank clearings. The value of items processed in 1987 totaled some £356 billion. The volume and value of items processed rose by 13.5 percent and 18.2 percent, respectively, between 1986 and 1987, demonstrating the continuing and substantial growth in activity in this longest-established electronic clearing.

### (ii) CHAPS

The Clearing House Automated Payment System (CHAPS) became operational on February 9, 1984, as an electronic interbank system for sending guaranteed unconditional sterling payments from one settlement bank, on behalf of itself or its customers, to another settlement bank for same-day settlement. Unlike the paper-based Town Clearing, it is available nationwide, but it is restricted to payments of £7,000 or more (this threshold was reduced from £10,000 on July 4, 1988, and may possibly be reduced further in 1989).

There are currently 14 CHAPS Settlement Members communicating directly via British Telecom's Packet SwitchStream Service (PSS) by means of standard computers and software, known as Gateways, which also provide an interface to each bank's own internal data base. There is thus no central installation. In addition to the Settlement Members, other users, categorised as participants, have access to the CHAPS system through an agreement with one of the Settlement Members and via a terminal operated through that member. There are currently some 190 participants using the system, comprising overseas and domestic banks, based in London and elsewhere in the United Kingdom, and subsidiaries and divisions of the Settlement Members.

The interbank settlement is effected electronically at the end of each day, across the Settlement Members' accounts held at the Bank of England. In 1987, some 4.3 million payments were made through CHAPS for a value of £7,332 billion, an increase of 39 percent and 77 percent, respectively, over 1986.

### Clearing settlement

The interbank settlement for the operational clearings takes place as follows. In the Cheque and Credit Clearings on the morning of settlement day, net positions are agreed at the clearing house and a series of debit or credit vouchers are delivered to the Bank of England for posting to the settlement accounts. The settlement figures for BACS are provided on magnetic tape on the day before settlement and are posted to the settlement accounts during the morning of settlement day. As noted above, CHAPS settlement figures are produced electronically on the system shortly after 3.00 P.M. each working day. The tape is subsequently transferred from the Bank of England's CHAPS computer, and the resultant obligations are posted to the accounts of the settlement banks shortly afterwards. Settlement of the Town Clearing takes place at around 4.45 P.M. each afternoon in the clearing house, where net debit or credit positions are agreed and vouchers are delivered to the Bank of England for posting to the accounts of the relative Settlement Members.

*Securities transaction systems*

The Central Gilts Office service (CGO) began live operations on January 2, 1986, and is operated by the Bank of England. The system was developed jointly by the Bank of England and the Stock Exchange to provide a computerised book-entry transfer system for the settlement of Stock Exchange transactions in gilt-edged (British Government) securities. A feature of the service is that the payment for each purchase within the system is guaranteed by the settlement bank of the buying member under an Assured Payment System, so that stock can be transferred electronically against certainty of payment.

In 1987, a group of 36 institutions, comprising major banks, discount houses, merchant banks, money brokers, and the Bank of England, set up LondonClear Ltd. to establish an automated trading and settlement system for money market instruments lodged in a central depository at the Bank of England. This project had to be abandoned in the summer of 1988, because of doubts about its costs, which meant it could not achieve the critical mass of committed support necessary to ensure its financing. However, the Bank of England considers a centralised transfer system for money maket instruments to be a desirable addition to the facilities offered by London. As a result, the bank is itself developing an alternative system to that proposed by LondonClear, which will fulfill similar objectives. This service will be named the Central Moneymarkets Office (CMO).

Three depositaries for money market instruments are already operating in London. Principally these act as depositories for U.S. dollar certificates of deposit, but they also handle other paper; they are operated by First National Bank of Chicago, Citibank, and Manufacturers Hanover Trust. Each provides clearing facilities for instruments denominated in various currencies and units of account—U.S. dollars, sterling, yen, Australian dollars, Deutsche mark, ECUs, and SDRs. Payments are settled through the normal clearing mechanisms.

Talisman, the International Stock Exchange's settlement system, enables member firms to settle transactions automatically in over 7,500 securities. All stock in Talisman is transferred into the heart of the settlement system, SEPON (Stock Exchange Pool Nominees). The details of each security deposited in SEPON are captured in electronic form by Talisman, and stock settlement is achieved by book-entry transfer with payment made generally via the Town Clearing. While the stock is being processed in the system it becomes dematerialised, but once it is released from SEPON, certificates are reconstituted for delivery to the purchaser.

The Institutional Net Settlement service (INS) was introduced in the summer of 1988 by the International Stock Exchange. It provides a centralised settlement system for institutional investors, allowing them to settle all their transactions on a net basis directly with the Stock Exchange.

A new service called TAURUS (Transfer and Automated Registration of Uncertified Stock) is currently being developed by the Stock Exchange for member firms and investors. The service, which is expected to commence live operations during 1989, will dispense with the need for physical holding of share certificates. On settlement, stock will move between TALISMAN and TAURUS by computerised book-entry transfer, and the movements will be confirmed to the TAURUS member (the direct account holder). A member may act for one of its customers through subaccounts within its main TAURUS account. All transfer movements will be reported automatically and agreed with the company registrar of the stock involved. Settlement of moneys will be effected via INS where the direct account holder is not a member of the International Stock Exchange.

*Other circuits and networks*

In April 1988, some 48 banks, including the Bank of England, were members of S.W.I.F.T., the worldwide message-switching system, and 200 banks in total (in the United Kingdom) were connected to the network. UK has two regional processor sites situated in a secure environment on BACS premises.

An increasing number of banks and institutions also make use of private teleprocessing networks for the provision of their corporate cash management systems and to facilitate other financial transactions.

## IV  GENERAL REMARKS

At present, the structure of the payment clearing system in the United Kingdom is being subjected to a number of conflicting pressures. These pressures, which span institutional, technological, legislative, and other aspects of the payment system, can be summarised as follows:

▶ The retail banks are competing increasingly vigorously to retain or extend their personal customer base: Money transmission facilities are often being used to attract customers, but as account charges are not levied on personal customers who remain in credit, it is necessary for the banks to cross-subsidise these costs from other profitable services sold to those customers.

▶ At the same time those personal customers are becoming more willing to open additional accounts with rival institutions or shift their banking business in pursuit of more attractive card-based or paper-based services.

▶ Furthermore, many building societies are using the opportunity of recent changes in their legislation to compete heavily in the personal sector by offering transaction accounts and other "banking" services.

▶ The dividing line between a payment service and other forms of value-added services is becoming harder to distinguish, so enabling computer bureaus to seek to supply an increasingly wide range of services both to banks and directly to their customers.

▶ Banks' corporate customers are becoming increasingly demanding in their requirements for services and facilities, while at the same time their direct borrowing needs have not grown, so reducing the scope for cross-subsidisation between the charges for different banking services.

▶ The use of cheques as a payment medium continues to grow (partly, at least, because customers are not charged the full cost of handling paper payments); but at the same time Britain remains a heavily cash-dependent economy, with only 72 percent of the adult population having some form of transaction account.

▶ The growth in direct membership of the UK payment clearings, which has occurred since APACS was formed in 1985, may not yet be complete. There is a possibility that further institutions, in particular UK building societies, and perhaps also financial institutions from other EC member states (or elsewhere in the world), will seek settlement membership as they put in place new business strategies to take advantage of the formation of the single market after 1992.

▶ The UK legislation relating to banking services, including the payment clearing system, is currently being examined: It is possible that the Review Committee will recommend changes in the legislative arrangements for the payment systems.

▶ Finally, banks are becoming increasingly aware of the nature, and extent, of the exposures they incur to other banks, and to customers, through the payment clearing systems and through other mechanisms, such as securities settlement systems, and are seeking ways to control and reduce those exposures.

These pressures are not, of course, all unique to the United Kingdom; what they do exemplify, in the particular mix in which they are being experienced in the United Kingdom, is that the forces for change that were widely foreseen a few years ago have by no means run their course and will continue to have an impact on all participants in the payment clearing systems.

## V    CONCLUSIONS

While significant changes are undoubtedly taking place in the transaction profiles of the UK economy, and in the structures and day-to-day operations of the UK payment systems, and will continue to take place under the pressures outlined in Section IV of this study, these changes are evolutionary rather than revolutionary and must be kept in perspective.

There can be no doubt that over the next few years electronic funds transfer systems and associated services will be more widely used by both corporate and personal customers. Transaction growth in the CHAPS and BACS clearings will continue at a high rate, while, as the national EFT POS service develops, debit cards will be used for an increasing number of "electronic cheque" transactions. However, despite these undisputed trends, current forecasts suggest that paper clearing volumes are unlikely to decrease in the short term and, indeed, may continue to grow until the early 1990s.

Furthermore, in volume terms cash remains the most important means of payment in the United Kingdom and its pre-eminence is bolstered by the continuing growth in the number of ATMs in commission and the amounts of cash withdrawn from them. Although there is some evidence that a growing proportion of large purchases is made by noncash means, cash remains a highly efficient medium for smaller transactions. Moreover, one-quarter of the adult population still does not have access to current-account facilities and therefore has no option but to make everyday payments in cash. Indeed, it seems unlikely that there will be any rapid decline in the size of the unbanked sector, especially since this group of potential customers is of little interest to the banks or building societies.

A brief forecast might be that by the mid-1990s, while there may be a modest fall in the volume of cash transactions and a fairly significant rise in electronic payments, cheques will remain an important medium of payment and the prospect of a truly cashless society will remain generations away.

**Membership of APACS and the Operational Clearing Companies**

| APACS | CHAPS and Town Clearing | Cheque and Credit Clearing | BACS | EftPos UK |
|---|---|---|---|---|
| Bank of England | Bank of England | Bank of England | Bank of England | Bank of England |
| Bank of Scotland | Bank of Scotland | Bank of Scotland | Bank of Scotland | Bank of Scotland |
| Barclays Bank | Barclays Bank | Barclays Bank | Barclays Bank | Barclays Bank |
| Citibank | Citibank | | | |
| Clydesdale Bank | Clydesdale Bank | | Clydesdale Bank | Clydesdale Bank |
| Co-operative Bank | Co-operative Bank | Co-operative Bank | Co-operative Bank | Co-operative Bank |
| Coutts & Co. | Coutts & Co. | | Coutts & Co. | |
| Girobank | Girobank | Girobank | Girobank | |
| Lloyds Bank | Lloyds Bank | Lloyds Bank | Lloyds Bank | Lloyds Bank |
| Midland Bank | Midland Bank | Midland Bank | Midland Bank | Midland Bank |
| National Westminster Bank | National Westminster Bank | National Westminster Bank | National Westminster Bank | National Westminster Bank |
| The Royal Bank of Scotland | The Royal Bank of Scotland | The Royal Bank of Scotland | The Royal Bank of Scotland | The Royal Bank of Scotland |
| Standard Chartered Bank | Standard Chartered Bank | | | |
| TSB England & Wales | TSB England & Wales | TSB England & Wales | TSB England & Wales | TSB Group |
| Yorkshire Bank | | | Yorkshire Bank | Yorkshire Bank |
| Abbey National Building Society | | Abbey National Building Society | Abbey National Building Society | Abbey National Building Society |
| Halifax Building Society | | | Halifax Building Society | Halifax Building Society |
| Nationwide Anglia Building Society | | Nationwide Anglia Building Society (accepted for membership as from June 1990) | Northern Bank (accepted for membership as from December 1988) Nationwide Anglia Building Society (accepted for membership as from June 1989) | Nationwide Anglia Building Society |
| 18 | 14 | 11 | 15 | 14 |

Appendix 2

**The Networks and Their Respective ATM and Custom Base**

| Principal Networks | Number of ATMs | Estimated Number of Cards (in millions) |
|---|---|---|
| (a) Lloyds Bank<br>Barclays Bank<br>The Royal Bank of Scotland<br>Bank of Scotland | 4,179 | 10.4 |
| (b) National Westminster Bank<br>Midland Bank<br>Clydesdale Bank<br>Northern Bank | 4,019 | 9.7 |
| TSB will link their ATMs to this network in 1988 | 1,672 | 5.5 |
| (c) LINK:<br>Abbey National Building Society<br>Nationwide Anglia Building Society<br>Girobank<br>Co-operative Bank<br>Funds Transfer Sharing<br>(a group of building societies and authorised institutions) | 1,000 | 4.0 |
| (d) MATRIX:<br>a group of seven large building societies | 650 | 2.5 |
| Other networks:<br>Halifax Building Society<br>Yorkshire Bank | 800<br>187 | 2.6<br>0.7 |
| Total | 12,507 | 35.4 |

In addition to these networks there is a shared ATM network operating in Northern Ireland.

The LINK and MATRIX networks will merge in 1989, and Halifax Building Society has announced that it will be joining LINK.

# 11 UNITED STATES

# United States

## I  INTRODUCTION

Demand and other chequable deposits maintained by consumers, businesses, and state and local governments have an aggregate value of about $550 billion and support daily payments amounting to more than $1.6 trillion. As a result, these deposits turn over an average of three times per day. The remaining payments are made with cash and amount to about $6 billion a day.

The bulk of payment activity is concentrated in New York City and is associated with securities trading, including transactions in commercial paper, and foreign exchange trading. Demand deposits in New York City banks turn over approximately 11 times per day, compared with 1.4 times at all other banks.

The volume of payments and the rapid turnover of funds in the United States demand efficient and highly reliable payment systems. In addition, the geographic size of the country and the large number of depository institutions complicate the interbank payment systems. Largely because of these factors, more than 80 percent of the dollars transferred in the United States are sent over large-dollar electronic funds transfer networks. At the same time, commerce is highly dependent upon cheques, and 16 percent of all dollar payments are made with them. The use of electronic payments—the automated clearing house (ACH), point-of-sale (POS), and automated teller machines (ATMs)—is growing, but these payment systems account for only about 2 percent of the value of all payments.

## II  INSTITUTIONAL FRAMEWORK

The payment systems in the United States are directly influenced by the large number of depository institutions and the resulting complex interbank payment networks. To ensure that payment systems function smoothly and that all depository institutions have access to them, the Federal Reserve System plays an important role in regulating the payment mechanism and provides a number of payment services to depository institutions. In addition, the payment practices of the government directly affect the payment practices of individuals and businesses.

### 1.  The Banking Industry

The banking industry in the United States has total assets of $1.7 trillion and 36,163 institutions. Of these institutions, 14,376 are commercial banks and 21,787 are thrift institutions (17,919 credit unions, 2,892 savings and loan associations, 501 federal savings banks, 367 mutual savings banks, and 108 cooperative banks).[1,2]

While the banking system in the United States is composed of a large number of institutions, it is more concentrated than the preceding statistics suggest. First, 128 multibank, multistate holding companies control 1,361 commercial banks, which

---

[1]See Appendix A for definitions of each type of institution.
[2]Federal Deposit Insurance Corporation, *Assets and Liabilities: Report of Income for Commercial and Mutual Savings Banks,* December 31, 1987.

account for 46 percent of the total bank assets and 47 percent of total deposits.[3] Second, the 348 banks with assets in excess of $1 billion account for 53 percent of the total assets, while the 8,043 banks with assets of less than $50 million account for only 7 percent of total assets.[4]

In the United States a so-called dual banking system allows for the chartering, supervision, and regulation of commercial banking organisations at both the federal and state levels. The differences between national and state charters, however, are relatively insignificant. Federally chartered banks must belong to the Federal Reserve System and be insured by the Federal Deposit Insurance Corporation (FDIC).[5] One-third of commercial banks have national charters. State-chartered banks are not required to join the Federal Reserve System or obtain federal deposit insurance. However, 95 percent of commercial banks (13,607) are members of the FDIC. Furthermore, all depository institutions are subject to reserve requirements imposed by the Federal Reserve.

All banks must conform to state laws that dictate their operating boundaries. Most states permit banks to operate branch offices throughout the state. About 30 percent of the states limit the location of bank offices. In addition, the Bank Holding Company Act of 1956 prohibits a bank holding company from acquiring banks outside its home state, unless the states specifically authorise entry through acquisition by out-of-state banking organisations.

Nearly all states have now adopted laws that permit bank holding companies in other states to acquire banks within their boundaries. In most instances, the laws permit entry only if the state in which the bank holding company has its head office has a reciprocal agreement. By the end of 1987, 44 states and the District of Columbia had enacted laws that permitted some type of entry by out-of-state bank holding companies. In 29 cases, the laws provide for the eventual entry by banks located in all states.

The expansion of interstate banking is expected to have a significant effect on the nation's payment mechanism during the next decade. The formation of large, multistate bank holding companies will increase the number of payments processed within one organisation, which should contribute to economies of scale. Furthermore, these organisations have the financial ability to take advantage of the efficiencies of electronic technology to increase the speed of processing payments and to reduce costs. Thus the emergence of interstate banking is seen as a major factor that will lead to an increased use of electronic payments in the United States.

## 2. The Role of the Banking Industry

Depository institutions play a major role in providing payment services in the United States. Most payments, in terms of dollar value, are made from demand or other chequable deposits held with depository institutions. In 1987, demand deposits held by commercial banks totaled $293 billion, and other chequable accounts totaled $254 billion.[6]

Since the early 1980s, all depository institutions have been permitted to offer money transfer services. Most depository institutions offer their customers a wide

---

[3]Board of Governors of the Federal Reserve System, *Annual Statistical Digest, 1987.*
[4]Federal Deposit Insurance Corporation, *Assets and Liabilities: Report of Income for Commercial and Mutual Savings Banks,* December 31, 1987.
[5]Institutions that are insured by the FDIC pay for the insurance based on their deposit size. If an insured institution is closed, all deposits up to and including $100,000 are covered.
[6]Board of Governors of the Federal Reserve System, *Federal Reserve Statistics Release H.6,* "Table 5. Components of Money Stock, Liquid Assets, and Debt," September 1, 1988, p. 6.

range of payment services, including the use of cheques or cheque-like instruments, namely, negotiable orders of withdrawal and share drafts, wire transfers of funds, the automated clearing house services, and money orders and travellers' cheques. In addition, many depository institutions permit their customers to access their deposit accounts via automated teller machines.

Large depository institutions process and account for all types of deposit transfers initiated by their customers. Smaller institutions rely on the services of larger institutions, called correspondent banks, or third-party service bureaus that specialise in processing payments and providing deposit-accounting services. Both paper and electronic interbank payments are cleared and settled through local clearing houses, large correspondent banks, and the Federal Reserve System.

### 3. The Role of the Government

The Department of the Treasury is responsible for printing currency and minting coin. The 12 Federal Reserve Banks and their 25 branches, the operating arms of the nation's central bank, provide a variety of services to depository institutions and to the United States Government and its agencies. Included among those services are the distribution of currency and coin, the collection of interbank cheques, and the clearing of wire transfers of funds and automated clearing house payments. The Federal Reserve also acts as the fiscal agent for the federal government. In this capacity the Federal Reserve Banks hold U.S. Treasury deposits, pay Treasury cheques, process government automated clearing house payments and funds transfers, and issue, service, and redeem U.S. Government obligations. The U.S. Postal Service, unlike its European counterparts, plays a very small role in providing payment services. Its sole function is to sell postal money orders, which in 1987 amounted to $12.5 billion.

### 4. Regulation of the Payment System

A patchwork of federal and state laws, Federal Reserve regulations, and case law developed over the years governs the payment system in the United States. The most important statute addressing paper-based payments is the Uniform Commercial Code (UCC). The UCC was drafted in 1953 and sets forth the rights and liabilities of all parties who deal with cheques, drafts, notes, and certificates of deposit. It has been adopted in part or in its entirety by all states and is amended periodically to incorporate changes in laws, regulations, and customs. It is currently being expanded to address the rights and liabilities of parties to large-dollar electronic funds transfers.

Small-dollar electronic funds transfers, principally consumer-oriented automated clearing house payments, ATM transactions, and POS transactions are governed by Regulation E. This regulation was issued by the Federal Reserve in response to the Electronic Funds Transfer Act of 1978. It applies to all financial institutions and takes precedence over state law to the extent that it provides greater consumer protection than state law. Regulation E sets forth standards for financial disclosure, card issuance, access, and error resolution procedures. It also addresses the rights and liabilities of both consumers and financial institutions.

## III  PAYMENT SYSTEMS

### 1. Payment Media

*(a)  Cash*

Cash is popular for many types of payments in the United States because it is readily accepted, convenient, and anonymous. Because most of these transactions have a low value, cash transactions account for only 0.4 percent of the total value of all payments.[7]

At the end of 1987, the value of currency in circulation was $179.8 billion and the value of coin in circulation was $16.7 billion. Currency and coin in circulation has remained at approximately 4 percent of GNP during the 1980s. A recent survey indicated, however, that aggregate U.S. household expenditures made with cash (currency and coin) grew from 30 percent in 1980 to 34 percent in 1986.[8]

The official media for cash payments are Federal Reserve notes and coins, both of which are legal tender for all public and private debt. The federal government is, by law, the sole issuer of notes and coin, and it is entrusted with the responsibility and authority to regulate the quantity and character of all money.

Notes are printed by the Bureau of Engraving and Printing, and coins are produced by the United States Mint. Both are a part of the Treasury Department. Currently, Federal Reserve notes in the following denominations are issued: $1, $2, $5, $10, $50, and $100. Coins are issued in six denominations: 1, 5, 10, 25, and 50 cents and $1.

The Federal Reserve purchases currency from the Treasury Department at its production cost. In 1987, currency with a face value of $81.2 billion was purchased at a cost of $156.3 million.[9] Before currency is issued to the public, the notes must be secured by legally authorised collateral, principally U.S. Government and agency securities held by the Federal Reserve Banks.

While notes are a liability of the Federal Reserve System when they are issued, coin is transferred to the Federal Reserve at its face value by the Bureau of the Mint and remains a liability of the Treasury Department. In the fiscal year ending September 30, 1987, the Mint produced 12.6 billion coins with a face value of $458 million, at a cost of $120.6 million.[9]

The Federal Reserve System ensures that the economy has enough currency and coin to meet the public's demand. Currency and coin are put into circulation by the Federal Reserve Banks and branches, which use depository institutions for distribution to the public. When depository institutions need to replenish their supply of currency and coin, they order cash from their local Federal Reserve Bank or branch. When the public's need for cash declines or when depository institutions have cash that is unfit for further circulation, the excess or unfit cash is returned to a Federal Reserve office.

### (b) Cheques

Other than cash, the paper cheque is the most frequently used means of payment in the United States. In 1987, approximately 47 billion cheques were written, and volume is growing at an annual rate of about 4 percent. Of these cheques, approximately 55 percent, or 26 billion, were written by individuals; 40 percent or 19 billion, by businesses; and 5 percent, or 2 billion, by federal, state, and local governments.

Individuals write 87 percent of their cheques to businesses, 11 percent to other individuals, and 2 percent to governments. Businesses write 57 percent of their cheques to other businesses, 41 percent to individuals, and 2 percent to governments. Governments write 78 percent of their cheques to individuals, 16 percent to businesses, and 6 percent to other government entities.[10]

---

[7]David B. Humphrey and Allen N. Berger, *Market Failure and Resource Use: Economic Incentives to Use Different Payment Instruments,* May 1988.

[8]Robert B. Avery and others, "The Use of Cash and Transaction Accounts by American Families," *Federal Reserve Bulletin,* February 1986.

[9]The difference between the face value of currency and coin and the cost of production is called seignorage.

[10]Federal Reserve Bank of Atlanta, "Displacing the Check," *Economic Review* (special issue), August 1983.

Depository institutions' charges to consumers and businesses for the use of cheques vary widely and depend on the types of accounts maintained and the range of services provided. Monthly account-maintenance fees may be assessed as well as charges for payment services. The charges may be paid explicitly or implicitly through minimum balance requirements.

Because cheques are paper instruments, they must be transported physically between payers and payees and between the payer's (collecting) and the payee's (paying) banks. Inherent in this process are delays, which contribute to float or uncollected funds. The factors contributing to float include delays in postal delivery, delays by recipients in depositing cheques, and delays in the clearing process. Clearing delays average 1.6 days.[11]

In 1987, total cheque float in the United States amounted to approximately $677 billion. Using the 1987 average short-term Treasury bill rate of 5.8 percent, the "value" or "cost" of total float was approximately $39 billion. Of this amount, $14.4 billion was due to delays in mail delivery, $9.4 billion to delays before cheques were deposited, and $15.8 billion to the collection process.[12]

In 1987, the United States Congress adopted the Expedited Funds Availability Act, which regulates when funds from cheque deposits must be made available for withdrawal by depository institutions. As of September 1, 1988, in most cases, depository institutions must make funds available for local cheques no later than the third business day after deposit and for nonlocal cheques no later than the seventh business day after deposit. On September 1, 1990, the availability schedule will be shortened and will require that funds be made available for local cheques by the second business day following deposit and for nonlocal cheques by the fifth business day following deposit.

In response to the act, the Federal Reserve implemented rules to speed the collection and the return of cheques in 1988. These rules cover endorsement standards to be used by depository institutions when processing cheques, shorter schedules for notification of nonpayment for large-dollar dishonored cheques, and requirements for institutions to expedite the return of dishonored cheques to the depository institutions with which they were first deposited.

In addition, all Federal Reserve Banks were authorised to offer optional cheque truncation services—that is, the capture of cheque payment information in electronic form—to eliminate some of the handling of paper cheques. Depository institutions may also receive cheque payment information in electronic form to expedite processing.

Image processing and bar-code technology are two of the longer-term initiatives currently being studied as potential means of improving the cheque collection system. Image processing involves capturing the image of a cheque and storing the digital information on a magnetic disk or other storage device. The image may then be used to transmit the cheque information to the paying institution and thus eliminate the delays inherent in transporting paper cheques. Bar-code technology has the potential to enable paying institutions to employ automated systems to bar-code endorsements on the back of dishonored cheques. Such machine-readable endorsements would enable banks to process dishonored cheques more efficiently and return them faster.

*(c) Large-dollar funds transfers*

Funds transfer services are used primarily by depository institutions and their

---

[11]Bank Administration Institute, *BAI Return Item Study,* 1985.

[12]Based on William C. Dudley, "Tug-of-War Over Float," Morgan Guaranty Survey, (New York, December 1983), and David B. Humphrey and Allen H. Berger, *Market Failure and Resource Use: Economic Incentives to Use Different Payment Instruments,* May 1988.

corporate customers to make very large time-critical dollar payments. In 1987, 84 million payments with a value of $281 trillion were made via the two large-dollar funds transfer networks in the United States—the Fedwire service provided by the Federal Reserve Banks and the Clearing House Interbank Payments System (CHIPS) operated by the New York Clearing House Association. In addition to these two funds transfer networks, depository institutions transfer funds between their customers' accounts on their own books and use Telex and the Society for Worldwide Interbank Financial Telecommunication (S.W.I.F.T.) to send transfer instructions to other institutions.

Fedwire is used principally for domestic payments, while over 70 percent of CHIPS payments are dollar-denominated international payments. For example, Fedwire is used for interbank overnight loans, interbank settlement transactions, corporate-to-corporate payments, and settlement of security transactions. In contrast, CHIPS is used to settle foreign exchange transactions and Eurodollar placements.

Depository institutions' typical charges for sending a funds transfer range from $2.00 to $10.00

*(d)  Automated clearing house*

The ACH mechanism has grown rapidly since its inception in the early 1970s. During 1987, approximately 850 million payments were processed over the ACH, with a value of nearly $3 trillion. Total ACH transaction volume, however, represents less than 2 percent of all cashless payments made in the United States.

The Treasury Department or other federal government agencies, which use the ACH primarily to make Social Security, salary, and pension payments originated 44 percent of ACH payments. The private sector's use of the ACH is also dominated by salary and pension payments, which account for approximately 40 percent of commerical ACH payments. In addition, the ACH is used actively for insurance premium payments (35 percent of commercial ACH payments) and cash concentration transactions (11 percent of commercial ACH payments). Over the last several years emphasis has been placed on expanding the uses of the ACH. In particular, significant effort has been devoted to encouraging its use for corporate-to-corporate payments and for clearing off-line point-of-sale payments. Despite these efforts these types of payments account for little more than 1 percent of ACH transactions.

A number of factors have contributed to the slower-than-expected growth in the use of the automated clearing house in the United States. Many users of cheques benefit from the float created during the collection process. Because float costs are not explicitly passed on to cheque writers, an incentive exists for those making payments to pay by cheque and thus delay debits to their accounts. The benefits of also using the ACH have not been marketed effectively to consumers. Where they have, the use of the ACH has been very successful. For example, the Treasury Department has aggressively advertised the advantages of direct deposit to Social Security recipients and has encouraged its use for salary and retirement payments to government employees. Due to these efforts 46 percent of Social Security recipients receive their benefits through direct deposit and 67 percent of government employees receive their salary payments electronically. In addition, Social Security recipients residing in the United Kingdom have been able to receive their benefits through direct deposit via the British ACH, BACS, since 1987. About 80 percent of these recipients have chosen to take advantage of direct deposit. Conversely, less than 10 percent of U.S. employees in the private sector receive salary payments through the ACH.

*(e)  Automated teller machines*

The use of ATMs has grown rapidly since their introduction in 1969. They are now widespread in the United States, and most of the nation's banks and thrifts, and to a lesser extent credit unions, provide ATM access to consumers. In 1987, about 151 million ATM cards were outstanding in the United States. About 67 million were used at least once a month,[13] and approximately 30 million were used seven times a month.

ATMs are typically installed at depository institutions, supermarkets, convenience stores, shopping centers, airports, and office buildings. In 1987, a total of 76,000 ATMs[14] were in use, and 70 percent, or 53,200, were part of one or more of the 125 shared networks.[15] Most installed machines are multipurpose machines, offering several of the following services: cash withdrawal, deposit, transfers between accounts, cash advance, direct access to a credit card account, bill payment, and balance inquiry.

Approximately 4.7 billion transactions, excluding balance inquiries, were processed in 1987, and one-third of these transactions were executed at ATMs owned by institutions other than the card-issuing institution, i.e., at foreign machines. Transaction volume per machine averaged 5,000 transactions.

About 85 percent of all ATM transactions were cash withdrawals, and they had an aggregate value of $95 billion. More than 10 percent were deposits, with an aggregate value of nearly $200 billion, and less than 1 percent was initiated to make bill payments, with an aggregate value of $2 billion.

Only 20 percent of card issuers charge their customers for use of their ATMs. Most card issuers, however, charge cardholders fees ranging from $0.25 to $0.75[15] for using other depository institutions' terminals.

*(f)  Point-of-sale*

POS systems result in a direct debit to a consumer's account for purchases of goods or services and a credit to the merchant's account. POS services vary widely in the United States, and transaction volume is low. In 1987, about 60 million[16] transactions were processed.

In June 1988, there were 43,500 POS terminals in the United States—17,300 at gasoline stations, 14,600 at specialty stores, 9,900 at supermarkets, and 1,700 at convenience stores.[17] The largest POS network in the United States is Interlink, which is operated by five California banks.

In general, retailers have been slow to adopt POS because they disagree with suppliers over pricing and security issues and do not see significant benefits to be drawn from offering this payment option. Nevertheless, oil companies, supermarkets, convenience stores, and fast food restaurants, where purchases are typically made with cash or cheques, are beginning to adopt POS systems. To promote POS, a number of oil companies are offering their customers cash discounts when payments are made via POS, and supermarkets and convenience stores are permitting customers to make payments that exceed the purchase price of goods and to receive the difference in cash. Department stores with long-established proprietary credit card systems are the least likely to offer POS because there is no consumer benefit, and

[13]*The Nilson Report,* HSN Consultants, Inc. (Los Angeles, California), No. 422, February 10, 1988.

[14]Linda Fenner Zimmer, "ATMs 1988: The Light at the End of the Tunnel," *Bank Administration,* vol. 64 (May 1988), p. 23.

[15]Trans Data Corporation, 1987 ATMs and Debit Cards, (Salisbury, Maryland), 1987.

[16]*POS News,* Barlo Communications (Chicago, Illinois), June 1988, p. 1.

[17]*Ibid.,* p. 1.

some of these retailers realise considerable income from their credit card operations.

It is rare for card issuers to charge for the use of debit cards. When a fee is charged, it is typically $0.10 per transaction.

### (g)  Credit cards

Credit cards are not true payment instruments because they do not result in a direct transfer of funds from the payer to the payee. In the case of bank cards, the cardholder is granted a loan by the card-issuing bank. The merchant's bank pays the merchant, usually at a discount, and subsequently settles with the cardholder's bank. Credit cards do, however, displace payment transactions by aggregating them into single daily or weekly payments to merchants and monthly payments for consumers. For example, in 1987, consumers made 5.4 billion payments for the 9.1 billion transactions completed with credit cards.

Credit cards issued by financial institutions, travel and entertainment companies, and retailers are a safe and convenient substitute for cash and cheques. Over 71 percent of the families in the United States have some type of credit card and 82 percent of these families used their cards to make one purchase or more a month.[18]

In 1987, there were 841 million credit cards in circulation, or 7.8 cards per person between the ages of 17 and 65.[19] The largest issuers of credit cards are retailers, accounting for 45 percent of all credit cards in circulation. Cards issued by financial institutions, primarily VISA and MasterCard, account for 24 percent; cards issued by oil companies account for 14 percent; cards issued by telephone companies account for 9 percent; cards issued by travel and entertainment companies account for approximately 3 percent; Sears Discover Card accounts for 3 percent; and all others (airlines, auto, hotels, and so on), account for 2 percent.

In 1987, credit card billings amounted to $374.8 billion. Of this total, $97.7 billion was accounted for by VISA and $68 billion by MasterCard. At the end of 1987, total credit card debt outstanding equalled $156.9 billion,[20] with bank card debt accounting for $91.4 billion, or nearly 60 percent of the total.

Consumers typically pay bank card issuers an annual fee of $15 to $20. Finance charges are generally assessed after a 15- to 30-day grace period at rates of 15 to 21 percent.

### (h)  Other payment media

Two other payment media are available in the United States — telephone bill-paying and home-banking services. In 1987, about 280 financial institutions offered telephone bill-paying services, a decrease of 30 percent since 1981. Volume amounted to less than 30 million transactions.

When telephone bill-paying services were introduced in the early 1970s, they were introduced by thrift institutions interested in offering payment services. Since that time, thrifts have gained the right to offer transaction accounts and their original motivation no longer exists. Furthermore, these services have not always proven to be profitable.

Telephone bill-paying enables consumers to instruct their financial institution to make payments on their behalf over the telephone. Some systems rely on the financial institutions' employees to record payment information. Other systems use voice-activated recorders or permit consumers to enter data via TouchTone telephones. The financial institution, in turn, makes payments to payees in one of two ways: by issuing a composite cheque covering all of its customers' payments and

---

[18]On average, each family makes eight purchases a month with a credit card.
[19]*The Nilson Report,* HSN Consultants, Inc. (Los Angeles, California), May 1988.
[20]*Ibid.*

preparing a listing identifying each individual payment, or by transmitting the individual payments to the payee's financial institution via the ACH. Customers may be charged transaction fees, which range from $0.10 to $0.20 per transaction, or they may be charged a monthly fee, which ranges from less than $2.00 to $6.50 per month.

Home-banking services were offered by about 40 financial institutions to approximately 90,000 households and small businesses in 1987. Three banks accounted for three-quarters of the total subscribers. Transaction volume is estimated at 2.4 million transactions a year.

Home-banking services are accessed over telephone lines via proprietary terminals, personal computers, and adapted television sets. They are typically offered as part of a package of videotex services, which may include stock quotations, news, reservation, and banking services. Customers subscribing to banking services are allowed to make balance inquiries, to initiate payments to participating payees, and to transfer funds between accounts. Payments are made to payees by means of cheques or the ACH. The average charge for home-banking services is $8 to $15 per month for individuals and $20 to $50 per month for small businesses, plus telephone line charges of about $3 to $4.50 per hour.

## 2. Exchange Circuits Within the Banking System

### (a) Cheques

Approximately 30 percent of the cheques written in the United States are deposited with the depository institutions on which they are drawn. This percentage has risen in recent years as a result of bank mergers and acquisitions. The remaining 70 percent of cheques are deposited with another depository institution and must be collected from the institution on which they are drawn.

Interbank cheques are collected through local clearing house associations, correspondent bank arrangements, and the Federal Reserve. Interbank cheques are handled by an average of three banks and may involve as many as five.[21] Depository institutions located in the same geographic area may exchange cheques directly or may exchange them with participants in local clearing house associations. Clearing house transactions are usually settled through net debit and credit entries to accounts maintained with other clearing house members or through the institutions' accounts at the Federal Reserve.

Interbank cheques drawn on institutions outside the geographic area in which a depository institution is located may be deposited with correspondent banks or with the Federal Reserve. Correspondent banks that have established relationships with other correspondent banks present cheques drawn on each other directly. Smaller depository institutions often rely on a correspondent bank, which may collect the cheques through local clearing houses, other correspondent banks, or the Federal Reserve. Correspondent banks settle with these smaller institutions through accounts they maintain on their books for them. The Federal Reserve settles for the cheques it collects through the reseve or clearing accounts it maintains for depository institutions.

Cheques cleared by the Federal Reserve and correspondent banks are processed on high-speed equipment that itemises, records, endorses, and sorts cheques based on information contained in the magnetic ink character recognition (MICR) line printed along the bottom of cheques. On average, this equipment processes 100,000 items per hour.

Cheques are transported between collecting and paying institutions in a variety of ways. Cheques cleared locally are usually transported by ground couriers, while

[21]Federal Reserve Bank of Atlanta, *A Quantitative Description of the Check Collection System,* 1981.

cheques drawn on institutions in regions distant from the collecting depository institutions are usually delivered via air transportation. The Federal Reserve has an extensive air transportation network to exchange cheques among Federal Reserve offices for ultimate delivery to paying institutions.

Federal Reserve fees for cheque collection services vary based on the time of deposit and the amount of sorting performed by the depositing institution. On a volume-weighted basis, Federal Reserve fees amount to approximately $0.026 per cheque.

### (b)  Large-dollar funds transfer networks

Fedwire is a sophisticated electronic payment network. It consists of large, multi-purpose computers that operate funds transfer application software at each of the 12 Federal Reserve Banks, a packet-switching data-communications network that links the Federal Reserve Banks, and 12 local data-communications networks that link depository institutions to the Federal Reserve Banks.

Over 11,000 depository institutions use Fedwire. Approximately 7,000 of these institutions are connected to the Federal Reserve via local data communications networks. These institutions originate nearly 99 percent of all transfers. The remaining depository institutions request the Federal Reserve to send transfers over the telephone.

There are three types of electronic connections used by depository institutions—dedicated leased lines, shared leased lines, and dial-up or switched circuits. High-volume institutions typically have dedicated leased lines linking their computers to the Federal Reserve's computers (about 200 institutions). Medium-volume institutions use shared circuits to link their terminals or personal computers to the Federal Reserve (about 1,500 institutions). Low-volume institutions use switched connections to link their terminals or personal computers to the Federal Reserve (about 5,300 institutions).

Fedwire transfers are actually accounting entries effected on the books of the Federal Reserve. The sending depository institution authorises the Federal Reserve to debit its account and credit the account of the depository institution that is to receive the transfer. Each funds transfer is settled individually as it is processed.

The Federal Reserve assesses depository institutions $0.47 to send or receive a Fedwire. In addition, it charges a monthly fee of $400 to institutions with dedicated leased line connections, $250 to institutions with shared circuits, and $60 to institutions with switched connections. These monthly fees cover the use of the connections for all priced electronic services, not just the funds transfer service.

The CHIPS network has 137 participants. CHIPS participants exchange messages over dedicated leased lines that link their computers or minicomputers to the CHIPS central computer.

CHIPS participants send payment instructions to the central CHIPS computer, where the instructions are edited and recorded and then transmitted to the receiving institution. During the day the CHIPS computer maintains running balances of all payment instructions sent and received by each participant. At the close of business, the net value of each participant's transfers is computed, and each participant is advised of its balance. Participants in net debit positions send Fedwires to a special account at the Federal Reserve Bank of New York. When the account is fully funded, CHIPS sends Fedwires to each participant in a net credit position. All CHIPS transfers are considered final payments once all settlement transfers are completed.

CHIPS participants pay a one-time membership fee of $50,000 and a minimum monthly charge of $2,500. A fee of $0.29 is assessed to send or receive a transfer that passes all edits. In addition, each participant is responsible for the expense associated with the circuits required to connect with the CHIPS computer, which ranges from $700 to $1,000 per month.

Compared with other cashless payments, Fedwires are unique in that the Federal Reserve treats them as final and irrevocable payments. That is, once the Federal Reserve has delivered an advice of credit to the receiving depository institution, it will not reverse the credit. On the CHIPS network the sender of a CHIPS payment guarantees the payments to the receiving depository institutions. Nevertheless, CHIPS payments are provisional payments until final settlement is effected on the books of the Federal Reserve at the close of business.

The operation of large-dollar funds transfer networks results in credit exposure for the Federal Reserve and for the participants on CHIPS. In the case of Fedwire, when transfers are sent that exceed the reserve or clearing account balance of the sending institution, the Federal Reserve is exposed to the risk of loss should the sending institution suspend operations or be closed before it covered the payment. In the case of CHIPS, if a participant were unable to settle its position at the close of business, CHIPS rules currently permit the payments sent and received by that participant to be taken out of the settlement totals. This process, called unwinding, would create significant potential risk for all CHIPS participants.

During the early 1980s, daylight overdrafts associated with funds transfers averaged $80 billion a day across Fedwire and CHIPS. Because of the significant exposure associated with such sizable extensions of credit, the Federal Reserve implemented a program to reduce payment system risk in 1985. The program's objectives were to control daylight overdrafts incurred on the books of the Federal Reserve, to improve operational and credit controls at depository institutions, and to reduce risk on private networks. The program requires depository institutions that incur daylight overdrafts on Fedwire or that participate on private networks to evaluate their creditworthiness, their operational controls, and their credit policies. Based on the self-assessment, each institution selects a "cap," which is a multiple of its capital and serves as a limit on the amount of daylight overdrafts that the institution may incur across all large-dollar funds transfer networks. CHIPS participants are also required to establish bilateral net credit limits with each other participant as a means of controlling their credit exposure, and they are currently developing alternatives to achieve payment finality.

The Federal Reserve is studying other methods for reducing payments system risk further, including charging for daylight overdrafts, prohibiting daylight overdrafts, and requiring higher clearing account balances to eliminate or reduce daylight overdrafts. The continued focus on the risks associated with large-dollar funds transfer networks has resulted in improved credit and operational controls at depository institutions and a reduction in the ratio of daylight overdrafts to dollars transferred over large-dollar networks.

*(c) Securities clearing settlement*

Securities in the United States are cleared and settled through one of three mechanisms — (1) physical delivery against payment, (2) depository and clearing corporations, and (3) the Federal Reserve's national book-entry safekeeping and transfer system.

Many money market securities, such as certificates of deposit (CDs), bankers' acceptances (BAs), commercial paper, certain mortgage-backed securities, and some municipal government securities, are cleared and settled on the basis of physical delivery against payment. Broker-dealers instruct their respective clearing banks to deliver the appropriate securities physically and make payment, usually through Fedwire. Industry practice for wholesale trades (institution-to-institution) requires delivery of the securities in good form prior to payment. Retail trades normally require payment prior to delivery. Securities cleared on a physical delivery basis are heterogeneous and differ regarding face amounts, interest rates, issuers, issue dates, and maturity dates. Because of these differences, it is difficult to convert them to a book-entry or depository system.

Corporate securities (stocks and bonds) and eligible municipal government securities are handled through a national clearance and settlement system that comprises three depositories[22] and five clearing corporations.[23] Each depository is associated with national or regional stock exchanges, and provides custody (immobilisation) of physical securities combined with an electronic trade settlement service. The clearing corporations provide multi-issue trade comparisons and multilateral net settlement of payments. Payments are primarily made in next-day clearing house funds.

The depositories and the clearing corporations are linked nationally, allowing users of any depository to settle with users of another depository without the need for physical delivery of securities. These interfaces also include international linkages with the Canadian Depository for Securities, Ltd., and the International Securities Clearing Corporation (ISCC).[24] ISCC maintains a link with the International Stock Exchange in London for corporate stocks and plans to expand that link to include corporate bonds, British gilts, and U.S. Treasury bills. The possibility of linkages with Euroclear, Cedel, and the Japan Securities Clearing Corporation is also being explored.

Two new clearing corporations, the Mortgage-Backed Securities Clearing Corporation (MBSCC) and the Government Securities Clearing Corporation (GSCC), were established in 1987 to improve and facilitate the clearance and settlement practices for Ginnie Mae[25] mortgage-backed securities and federal government securities, respectively. Both clearing corporations plan to establish a multilateral, multi-issue net settlement mechanism for dealer-to-dealer trades.

Federal government securities (U.S. Treasuries and federal agencies) and some international organisation securities[26] are cleared and settled through the Federal Reserve's national electronic book-entry safekeeping and transfer system. Securities issued, maintained, and transferred on this system are in book-entry form only. The U.S. Treasury and most federal agencies no longer issue physical domestic securities. The Federal Reserve's System is unique and is an essential element of the country's $2 trillion government securities market. This system electronically links the 12 Federal Reserve Banks with depository institutions throughout the country via approximately 1,117 electronic connections. The book-entry system, like the funds transfer system, is a sophisticated electronic network that utilises the same data communications and hardware infrastructure that supports funds transfer operations. In 1987, depository institutions originated for themselves, their customers, and their correspondents over 9 million transfers valued at over $78 trillion. Most of these transfers were originated by five major clearing banks in New York City. Clearance and settlement is accomplished on a transfer-by-transfer basis. Each Federal Re-

---

[22]These depositories are the Depository Trust Company (DTC) in New York City, the Philadelphia Depository, and the Midwest Securities Trust Company (MSTC) in Chicago.

[23]The major clearing corporations are the National Securities Clearing Corporation (NSCC), the Midwest Securities Clearing Corporation, the Boston Stock Exchange Clearing Corporation, the Options Clearing Corporation, and the Pacific Clearing Corporation.

[24]The International Securities Clearing Corporation is a subsidiary of the National Securities Clearing Corporation (NSCC).

[25]Ginnie Mae refers to the Government National Mortgage Association.

[26]For example, those of the International Bank for Reconstruction and Development, the African Development Bank, and the Asian Development Bank.

serve Bank maintains securities and funds accounting records for local depository institutions. Transfers are originated by the sender of a security. The transfer message results in a securities debit to the sender and a securities credit to the receiver; simultaneously, the sender receives a funds credit and the receiver's account is debited. Payment is in immediately available, final funds.

*(d)  Automated clearing house*

ACH transactions are processed by the Federal Reserve, the Arizona Automated Clearing House Association, the Calwestern Automated Clearing House Association, the Hawaii Electronic Funds Transfer Association, and the New York Automated Clearing House Association. Currently, only the Federal Reserve provides both local and national services to its users. The private sector operators exchange transactions among their members and use Federal Reserve services to send payments to other regions of the country. VISA, the processor for the Calwestern Automated Clearing House Association, is planning to offer national ACH services in 1989.

Although the infrastructure of the ACH is comparable to large-dollar funds transfer networks, a large proportion of ACH participants deposit transactions on magnetic tapes and receive transactions on either magnetic tapes, diskettes, or paper listings. Of the 3,600 or so depository institutions that originate ACH transactions through the Federal Reserve, about 1,500 institutions transmit payment data electronically. These institutions originate 36 percent of the dollar value of all transactions. Of the 24,000 institutions that receive ACH transactions, only 5,300 receive them electronically, accounting for approximately 33 percent of total volume.

Because of the continued reliance on physical media for originating and receiving ACH payments, ACH operating hours continue to be tied to cheque courier schedules. To enhance the ACH mechanism, the Federal Reserve and private sector ACH operators are encouraging greater use of electronic transmission. The Calwestern Automated Clearing House Association provides services only to institutions that transmit and receive payment data electronically, and the New York Automated Clearing House Association will require all of its members to use electronic connections by January 1990.

ACH payments are processed in batches rather than as individual transactions. The originator's ACH processor edits and balances each batch of payment instructions and sorts them by local receiving institutions or the Federal Reserve office that serves the receiving institution. Once all payments have been sorted, private processors send payments destined for other parts of the country to the Federal Reserve. The Federal Reserve offices combine these payments with those they have processed and send them to other Federal Reserve offices over the Federal Reserve's interdistrict data communications network. Once the payment messages have been distributed to the proper Federal Reserve office, they are delivered to the receiving depository institutions.

The ACH is a value-dated mechanism, that is, transactions may be processed from one to four days before they are settled. The Federal Reserve accumulates accounting entries by settlement date and debits and credits the accounts of depository institutions on the settlement date specified by the originator of the payment. Private sector processors also accumulate accounting data as payments are processed. On the settlement day the processors calculate the net balance for each of their members and submit the balances to their local Federal Reserve office, where the entries are posted to the institutions' accounts.

Federal Reserve fees vary based on the location of the receiving institution and the time of processing. A fee of $0.01 per transaction is charged to the originator and receiver when both institutions are located in the same Federal Reserve zone; a fee of $0.017 per transaction is charged when the originator and receiver are located in different zones; and nighttime processing surcharges of $0.02 or $0.045 per transaction are levied for credit and debit transactions, respectively.

The finality of ACH payments differs according to the type of transaction. ACH credit transactions, where funds flow from the originator to the receiver, are treated by the Federal Reserve as final payments at the close of business on the settlement day after all accounting has been completed. ACH debit transactions, where funds flow to the originator of the payment from the receiver, are treated as provisional payments until the opening of business on the day following the settlement day. Thus, unlike Fedwire, the Federal Reserve has the right to reverse ACH transactions if an institution does not have sufficient funds in its account to cover its debit position.

The credit risk associated with the use of the automated clearing house mechanism is considerably less than the risk associated with large-dollar funds transfer systems, because of the relatively low value of payments flowing through the ACH. Several steps have been taken to control ACH risk. The operational and credit controls over ACH operations at depository institutions are now explicitly considered in each institution's self-assessment and therefore play a role in setting an institution's "cap." In addition, the Federal Reserve is monitoring the origination of ACH transactions and reserves the right to require prefunding or collateral if it appears that the institution will not be able to cover credit payments on the value date. Finally, to reduce the risks associated with the return of large-dollar debit transactions, the deadline for returning items was advanced, permitting them to be delivered to originating institutions earlier.

*(e)  Automated teller machines*

There are two types of ATM networks — shared and nonshared (proprietary). Transactions are authorised by verifying customers' account balances or by verifying transactions against parameters set by the card-issuing depository institutions. Transactions may update account balances at the time they are authorised, or a day's transactions may be accumulated and cleared at the end of the day, typically via the ACH.

Operators of shared networks permit customers of other institutions to access their terminals. A network switch facilitates the transfer of transaction messages between the ATM and the depository institution that issued the card and holds the customer's account. There are six national networks in the United States and about 125 regional, shared networks. The recent combination of the VISA and the Plus networks and the MasterTeller and the Cirrus networks created two of the largest shared, nationwide ATM networks in the United States, enabling consumers to access 20,000 and 21,000 ATMs, respectively. In addition, American Express and Sears Roebuck cardholders have access to over 13,000 ATMs each.[27]

ATM transactions are typically settled by posting net debit or credit balances to accounts maintained at a lead bank that serves as the settlement agent for the network. In a few cases, the Federal Reserve provides net settlement services for shared networks. The settlement entries are treated as provisional entries until the business day following the day on which the settlement data are received by the Reserve Banks. As with the ACH mechanism, depository institutions make funds available to customers before transactions are considered final. Again, because the dollar amounts are low, the risk of loss is minimal.

ATM processing costs vary considerably depending on the size of the network

---

[27]Trans Data Corporation, (Salisbury, Maryland), 1988.

operator, the size of each participating institution, and whether processing is done in-house or by a service bureau. In-house processing costs amount to about $0.15 per transaction. Service bureaus typically charge about $0.40 per transaction. In addition, interchange fees of about $0.05 per transaction are charged by network (switch) operators when cardholders use ATMs owned by other institutions.[28]

### (f) Point-of-sale

As in the case of ATM networks, a variety of approaches are used for processing POS transactions. The largest POS network in the United States, Interlink, is owned by a group of California banks that jointly developed the network. The network switch is currently operated by VISA. When POS transactions are processed, the switch transmits transaction information to the participating merchant's and consumer's bank(s). The merchant's account is credited immediately for the value of the transaction and the consumer's account is debited. Interbank settlement is generally effected through correspondent accounts on the business day following the transaction date.

Another approach to providing POS services is to piggyback them on ATM networks. Several oil companies, including Exxon and Mobil, accept debit cards issued by depository institutions that are members of one or more ATM networks. In some cases, the merchant acts as the switch and transmits transactions to the network, where the transactions are then transmitted to the consumer's bank and the merchant's bank. In other cases, the network provides all switching capabilities. Because institutions participating in ATM networks may post transactions at the time they occur or in a batch mode afterwards, POS transactions are handled in the same way. Interbank settlement is typically handled through correspondent balances.

Finally, some merchants, principally oil companies and grocery store chains, have implemented their own proprietary POS systems. In these instances, the merchant issues debit cards to his customers, which may be used to make purchases at the merchant's retail outlets. The merchant authorises all transactions, stores them during the day, and typically transmits them to his depository institution the next day for clearing through the ACH. This arrangement has the advantage of allowing a merchant to offer POS services to all of his customers, regardless of the depository institutions that maintain their accounts. At the same time, the merchant does not receive his funds until two days after the transaction date, and some items may be returned.

In 1987, 5 million on-line POS transactions were processed a month.[29] Interlink, the largest on-line debit network, processed 3.5 million transactions a month and Star, the second largest, processed 400,000 a month.[30] Conversely, 630,000 proprietary debit transactions a month were cleared off-line through the ACH, 550,000 of which were accounted for by the Arizona ACH POS project. Thus, 80,000 transactions a month were handled by the other five retail debit card networks. Because of the variety of processing options that are being tested and the differences in volumes, costs vary from $0.17 to $0.57 per transaction.

### (g) Credit cards

Credit card processing is becoming a fully electronic operation. Credit card transactions are authorised by a variety of means. They may be authorised by the

---

[28]Donald I. Baker and Roland E. Brandel. *The Law of Electronic Fund Transfer Systems: 1985 Cumulative Supplement,* (Boston, Massachusetts: Warren, Gorham & Lamont) 1985, pp. S6-2 to S6-5.

[29]*Bank Network News: EFT Data Book,* Bank Communications (Chicago, Illinois), November 25, 1987.

[30]*POS News,* Barlo Communications, (Chicago, Illinois), February 1988.

merchant, by the merchant's bank or its processor, by the network switch, or by the card-issuing bank or its processor. Furthermore, authorisations may be based on comparisons with negative files, activity, and dollar parameters, or a consumer's actual available credit balance.

About 25 percent of bank credit card transactions are authorised using automated systems that switch transactions to the card-issuing bank or a service bureau, where the consumer's account number is verified and the transaction amount is checked against available credit limits. After the transactions are authorised, they are typically stored by the merchant and transmitted electronically to the merchant's depository institution once a day. Smaller merchants authorise transactions based on their value or request authorisation via telephone. These merchants use paper drafts to request payment from their banks. The banks receiving the paper drafts convert them to machine-readable form.

The merchant's bank credits the merchant at a discount and then clears the transactions through one of the two national bank card networks—VISA or Master-Card. When the bank card networks receive the transactions, they are balanced and sorted by the card-issuing bank and settlement data for the merchants' banks and the card-issuing banks are calculated. The information is then transmitted to the merchants' banks and the card-issuing banks. Interbank settlement is effected through correspondent balances, in most cases. A few regional credit card processors use the Federal Reserve's net settlement services.

Typical merchant discounts range from 1 to 4 percent, depending on transaction and dollar volume. Processing fees assessed by the national card processors vary considerably depending on the services requested by their customers.

## IV   CONCLUSION

Large-dollar electronic funds transfers are used to transfer over 80 percent of the value of all payments in the United States. The two large-dollar funds transfer networks — Fedwire and CHIPS — are well established and relied upon for time-critical payments. As international payments grow and payment systems around the world become more interdependent, round-the-clock operations may become a reality. Such a development will heighten the need for effective policies to control the credit exposure faced by international payment system participants.

The securities clearance and settlement systems in the United States continue to move towards increased immobilisation of physical securities and the use of electronic trade comparison and multilateral, multi-issue net settlement. As settlement systems actively expand their international linkages further, clearing efficiencies are expected to occur. Such a trend will create new challenges for effective policies to deal with market risks and system contingencies.

The bulk of smaller dollar payments continues to be made using cash or cheques. ATMs have proliferated in the United States. Rather than being used for making payments, however, their primary use is to obtain cash. Automated clearing house transactions continue to grow at a rate of more than 20 percent a year. Effective marketing of the ACH among both consumers and businesses could contribute to significant changes in payment practices in the United States, as the Treasury Department's efforts have demonstrated. Furthermore, POS services are beginning to gain acceptance and are expected to continue to grow as merchants recognise their benefits and begin to promote their use among their customers.

The emergence of large, multistate bank holding companies should provide added impetus for increasing the use of electronic payments and book-entry securities services in the United States. These organisations have the financial capacity to develop the necessary operational capabilities. In addition, they have the ability to market the services effectively and the size to realise the cost efficiencies available through processing high volumes of electronic payments.

The forces for a major conversion to electronic payments are present in the United States. If such a conversion is to occur, it will be driven by users' demands for more efficient and cost-effective payment services, not by technological capabilities.

Appendix 1
# DEFINITIONS

**Commercial bank.** A financial intermediary that offers deposit (including chequing accounts), payment, and credit services to all types of customers. A commercial bank can be a national bank, meaning it received its charter from the federal government; or a state bank, meaning it received its charter from a state government. National banks are required to join the Federal Reserve System and state banks are allowed to join if they meet certain requirements and submit to regulation by the Federal Reserve.

**Cooperative bank.** A share-issuing institution that was a predecessor of building and loan associations. Until recently cooperative banks were not insured by the FDIC. All but five of the 108 institutions are located in Massachusetts, which required them to become insured by the FDIC by the end of 1985.

**Credit union.** A financial cooperative organisation of individuals with a common affiliation (e.g., employment, labor union membership, church membership, or residence in the same neighborhood). Credit unions accept deposits of members' savings in the form of share purchases, pay interest (dividends) on them out of earnings, and provide consumer credit to members. They also provide deposit accounts upon which share drafts can be drawn, much as chequing accounts.

**Depository institution.** Any of the following institutions that is empowered to perform banking business and does so as a substantial part of its operations: commercial banks, savings banks (mutual and stock), credit unions, building or savings and loan associations, cooperative banks, Edge Act and Agreement Corporations, foreign banks, New York State Investment Companies (most are owned by one or more non-U.S. banks), and industrial banks (including Morris Plan banks, thrift and loan companies, and industrial savings banks).

**Industrial bank.** A depository financial intermediary that functions much the same way as a commercial bank except that the industrial bank's loans are smaller, are made to individuals, and usually are repaid in installments.

**Mutual savings bank.** Accepts individuals' savings deposits and places most of their funds into mortgage loans. These institutions are prominent in many Northeastern states. A savings bank is between a commercial bank and savings and loan association in terms of the diversity of its assets and liabilities. Most savings banks are authorised to offer chequing type of accounts.

**Nonbank bank.** A financial institution that can make loans or accept deposits, but not both. Nonbank banks can engage in interstate banking by opening limited service banking facilities in states other than that of the parent company or bank. Also called "limited service banks."

**Savings and loan association.** A depository type of financial intermediary that accepts savings and time deposits and makes loans primarily for real estate and construction.

Most savings and loan associations are technically owned by the depositors who receive shares in the association for their deposits. Although they are not banks, they are generally considered to be part of the banking industry, and are often thought of as banks.

**Savings bank.** A mutual or stock bank that has the ability to accept all types of deposits, including demand deposits, to make consumer loans up to 30 percent of its assets, to make commercial loans up to 10 percent of its assets, and to make secured real estate loans without limitation.

**Thrift institution.** A mutual savings bank, savings and loan association, or credit union.

Appendix 2

### LEGAL AUTHORITY FOR THE FEDERAL RESERVE SYSTEM'S ROLE IN THE PAYMENT MECHANISM

The Federal Reserve Act ("the Act") became law in 1913 and established the Federal Reserve System as the cental bank of the United States.[1] By the terms of the Act, the System comprises a Board of Governors located in Washington, D.C. and 12 regional Federal Reserve Banks. The Act also provides that commercial banks may become members of the Federal Reserve ("member banks") and stipulates that all depository institutions must maintain reserves with the Federal Reserve. Each Federal Reserve Bank is given general authority under Section 4 of the Act (12 USC §341) to take such actions as are necessary to carry on the business of banking as set forth in other parts of the Act.[2]

At the direction of the Board of Governors, the 12 Federal Reserve Banks function as a nationwide collection system through which cheque and other commercial instruments may be collected. There are several specific provisions of law under which the Federal Reserve Banks exercise cheque collection functions. Paragraph 1 of Section 13 of the Act (12 USC §342) authorises each Federal Reserve Bank to receive cheques and other instruments for the purposes of collection and exchange.[3] Paragraph 13 of Section 16 of the Act (12 USC §360) requires every Federal Reserve Bank to receive on deposit at par cheques and drafts drawn on depository in-

---

[1]Federal Reserve Act, ch. 6, 38 Stat. 251 (1913) (codified at 12 USC §§221 *et seq.*).

[2]The Act does not give the Federal Reserve authority to provide commercial banking services to the public. The banking functions authorised in the Act are related to the Federal Reserve's responsibility to regulate the flow of bank credit and money, and to provide cash balance and payment services to all depository institutions and to the U.S. Government.

[3]The first paragraph of Section 13 of the Federal Reserve Act (12 USC §342) provides, *inter alia,* that:
    Any Federal Reserve Bank may receive from any of its member banks or other depository institutions, and from the U.S. Government, deposits of current funds in lawful money, national bank notes, Federal Reserve notes, or cheques and drafts, payable upon presentation, or other items, and also, for collection, maturing notes and bills; or, solely for purposes of exchange or of collection, may receive from other Federal Reserve Banks deposits of current funds in lawful money, national bank notes, or cheques upon other Federal Reserve Banks, and cheques and drafts payable upon presentation within its district, or other items, and maturing notes and bills payable within its district; or, solely for the purposes of exchange or of collection, may receive from any non-member bank or trust company or other depository institution deposits of current funds in lawful money, national bank notes, Federal Reserve notes, cheques and drafts payable upon presentation or other items, or maturing notes and bills, provided such non-member bank or trust company or other depository institution maintains with the Federal Reserve Bank of its district a balance in such amount as the Board determines taking into account items in transit, services provided by the Federal Reserve Bank and other factors as the Board may deem appropriate . . .

stitutions.[4] Paragraph 14 of Section 16 of the Act (12 USC §248(0)) provides that the Board of Governors may require each Federal Reserve Bank to exercise the functions of a clearing house for depository institutions.[5]

In addition, on August 10, 1987, Congress passed the Expedited Funds Availability Act,[6] which was designed to limit the amount of time depository institutions could hold funds deposited by customers. Section 609 of the Act gives the Board of Governors authority to issue regulations to carry out the provisions of the Act and facilitate compliance with its provisions. Specifically, the Board is required to consider several proposals to improve the cheque-processing system, including requiring wire notice of nonpayment, cheque truncation, direct return of cheques to institutions of first deposit, automating cheque returns, and endorsement standards.[7] Section 609 *(c)* of the Act gives the Board of Governors responsibility "to regulate any aspects of the payment system, including the receipt, payment, collection and clearing of cheques; and any related function of the payment system with respect to cheques."[8]

Pursuant to Sections 11, 13, and 16 of the Federal Reserve Act and the Expedited Funds Availability Act, the Board of Governors has promulgated Sub-part A of Regulation J (12 CFR §210.1), which is designed to afford the public and the banks of the country a direct, expeditious, and economical system for the collection of cheques. This regulation, issued by the Board of Governors under its statutory responsibilities, has the same force and effect as a statute passed by Congress. Sub-part A of Regulation J details the rights and liabilities of parties using Federal Reserve collection facilities and permits the Federal Reserve Banks to adopt "operating circulars" giving details of the time limits and other procedures established by the Federal Reserve Banks for collecting cheques. The operating circulars are viewed as contracts between the Federal Reserve and depository institutions.

---

[4]Paragraph 13 of Section 16 of the Act (12 USC §360) provides, *inter alia,* that:
   Every Federal Reserve Bank shall receive on deposit at par from depository institutions or from Federal Reserve Banks cheques and other items, including negotiable orders of withdrawal and drafts drawn upon any of its depositors and, when remitted by a Federal Reserve Bank, cheques and other items, including negotiable orders of withdrawal and share drafts and drafts drawn by any depositor in any Federal Reserve Bank or depository institution upon funds to the credit of said depositor in said Reserve Bank or depository institution . . .
To receive "at par" means the deposit must be accepted at the full face value of the cheque. Federal Reserve Banks are precluded from accepting cheques that are drawn on banks that do not pay their cheques at par.
[5]Paragraph 14 of Section 16 (12 USC §248(0)) provides, *inter alia,* that:
   the Board of Governors of the Federal Reserve System shall make and promulgate from time to time regulations governing the transfer of funds and charges therefor among Federal Reserve Banks and their branches, and may at its discretion exercise the functions of a clearing house for such Federal Reserve Banks, or may designate a Federal Reserve Bank to exercise such functions, and may also require each such Bank to exercise the functions of a clearing house for its member banks.
[6]Title VI of Pub. L.N. 100-86, 101 Stat. 552, 645 (codified at 12 USC §§4001 through 4010).
[7]Section 609(b) of the Expedited Funds Availability Act (12 USC §4008(*b*)).
[8]Section 609(c) of the Expedited Funds Availability Act (12 USC §4008(*c*)).

Moreover, under the Expedited Funds Availability Act, the Board of Governors, in May 1988, promulgated a new Regulation CC (12 CFR Part 229). This regulation implements the requirements of the Act by setting forth the requirements that depository institutions make funds deposited into accounts available according to specified time periods and disclose funds availability policies to their customers. Sub-part C of Regulation CC (12 CFR §§229.31 *et seq.*) includes rules to speed the collection and return of cheques. These rules cover the expeditious return responsibilities of paying and returning banks, authorise paying banks to return cheques directly to the bank that first handled the cheque for collection, provide that the paying bank must provide notice of nonpayment in the case of large-dollar returns, impose standard endorsement requirements on banks that handle cheques, and cover other, related matters. As with Regulation J, Regulation CC has the same effect as a statute passed by Congress.

The statutory basis for the Federal Reserve's involvement in the funds transfer and automated clearing house services is the same as that discussed above for paper cheques. In addition, paragraph 14 of Section 16 of the Act authorises the Board of Governors to regulate the transfer of funds among Federal Reserve Banks, and Section 13 authorises Federal Reserve Banks to receive deposits from their members and other depository institutions. In 1977, the Board of Governors issued Sub-part B of Regulation J (12 CFR §210.50) to govern the rights and responsibilities of depository institutions using the wire communications network. Sub-part B of Regulation J was issued pursuant to Sections 11, 13, 16, and 19 of the Act and has the same force and effect of law as does Sub-part A. It permits Federal Reserve Banks to adopt operating circulars that set forth the details of funds transfer operations.

In 1980, legislation was enacted requiring the Federal Reserve to establish schedules of fees for payment services.[9] Previously, the Federal Reserve Banks provided these services to members free of charge. One purpose of this provision was to enhance the efficiency of the payment system through increased competition. The Federal Reserve Act was also amended to provide all depository institutions with access to priced Federal Reserve services. All payment services provided by Federal Reserve Banks were explicitly priced by 1984.

The issuance and distribution of the nation's currency and coin is handled by the Federal Reserve Banks. New bills (i.e., Federal Reserve notes) are placed in circulation, fit currency is distributed as needed among depository institutions, and old, unfit currency is removed from circulation and destroyed. Paragraphs 1 and 3 of Section 16 of the Federal Reserve Act (12 USC §§411, 413) constitute the statutory authority for the issuance and redemption of Federal Reserve notes. Coin is distributed by the Federal Reserve Banks pursuant to the Sub-Treasury Act of May 1920 (31 USC §476) and Treasury Department Circular 55 (31 CFR §100).

---

[9]Monetary Control Act of 1980, §107, 94 Stat. 140 (codified at 12 USC §248a).

The 12 Federal Reserve Banks also serve as the federal government's principal fiscal agents. The activities performed as fiscal agent are under the general supervision of the U.S. Treasury Department, which reimburses the Federal Reserve Banks for most fiscal agency functions. The statutory basis for this role is Section 15 of the Act, which states that, when required by the Secretary of the Treasury, the Federal Reserve Banks "shall act as fiscal agents of the United States; and the revenues of the Government...may be deposited in such banks, and disbursements may be made by cheques drawn against such deposits."

# PART II

# STATISTICAL ADDENDUM

# NOTES ON COMPARATIVE AND COUNTRY TABLES

1 In the country tables percentages are calculated on the basis of amounts expressed in the domestic currency.

2 In the tables a dot instead of a figure means "data not available" or "data not reported," and "n.a." means "not applicable."

# Comparative Tables

**Comparative Table No. 1**
**Comparison of the Relative Importance of Points of Entry into the Payment System**
**at Year-End 1987**

| Countries | Number of Institutions* | Number of Branches | Number of Inhabitants per Branch |
|---|---|---|---|
| Belgium | 124 | 12,216 | 808 |
| Canada | 3,136 | 12,956 | 1,991 |
| France | 932 | 42,581 | 1,285 |
| Germany | 4,424 | 61,722 | 990 |
| Italy | 1,110 | 29,323 | 1,932 |
| Japan | 7,014 | 65,854 | 1,857 |
| The Netherlands | 1,068 | 8,423 | 1,733 |
| Sweden | 291 | 5,698 | 1,477 |
| Switzerland | 453 | 7,863 | 836 |
| United Kingdom | 705 | 43,172 | 1,315 |
| United States | 36,175 | 105,509 | 2,322 |

* Excluding the central bank.

**Comparative Table No. 2**
**Comparison of the Relative Importance of Transferable Deposits and Number of Accounts**
**at Year-End 1987**

| Countries | Value of Transferable Deposits (USD billions) | Number of Accounts (millions) | Number of Accounts per Inhabitant |
|---|---|---|---|
| Belgium | 21.40 | 9.49 | 0.96 |
| Canada | 64.00 | • | • |
| France | 586.20 | 150.10 | 2.70 |
| Germany | 168.00* | 57.70 | 0.95 |
| Italy | 267.30 | 19.90 | 0.35 |
| Japan | 993.50 | • | • |
| The Netherlands | 38.50 | 15.16 | 1.04 |
| Sweden | 70.73 | 28.54 | 3.40 |
| Switzerland | 41.00 | • | • |
| United Kingdom | 328.00 | 133.60 | 2.30 |
| United States | 547.00** | 124.00 | 0.50 |

* Sight deposits of domestic nonbanks (including deposits held at the central bank).
** This number represents chequeable deposits only. It excludes $414 billion in savings deposits and $913 billion in small time deposits.

**Comparative Table No. 3**
**Comparison of the Relative Importance of Cashless Payment Instruments**
**as a Percentage of Total Volume of Transactions in 1987**

| Countries | Cheques | Payments by Credit Card | Payments by Debit Card at POS | Paperless and Paper-Based Credit Transfers | Direct Debits |
|---|---|---|---|---|---|
| Belgium | 32.94[1] | <1.00[2] | 5.49[2] | 53.94 | 6.63 |
| Canada | 72.40 | 23.50 | 0.00 | 2.60[3] | 1.50 |
| France | 65.40[4] | • | 7.90 | 17.30 | 9.40 |
| Germany | 8.60 | 0.60[5] | 0.00 | 54.80[6] | 36.00[7] |
| Italy | 52.54[8] | 0.91[9] | 0.01 | 44.56 | 1.98 |
| Japan | 7.40 | 5.80 | . | 36.00 | 50.80 |
| The Netherlands | 19.00 | <0.50 | <0.50 | 64.50 | 16.50 |
| Sweden | 20.70 | 2.07 | negligible | 77.23 | • |
| Switzerland | 13.80[10] | 3.00 | 0.30 | 79.90 | 3.00 |
| United Kingdom | 57.00[11] | 11.00[12] | • | 22.00 | 9.00 |
| United States | 82.90[13] | 15.30 | 0.10 | 1.1[14] | 0.50 |

[1]  Including postal cheques and drafts.
[2]  Data of the Grand Duchy of Luxembourg partly included.
[3]  Paperless credit transfers only.
[4]  Including postal cheques.
[5]  Charge cards and bank cards, excluding retail cards.
[6]  Excluding interbank transfers.
[7]  Including cash-dispenser and ATM withdrawals made with ec-cards at banks other than that issuing the card.
[8]  Includes bank and postal cheques, banker's drafts, money orders, and cashier's cheques.
[9]  Includes payment transactions effected in Italy and abroad by resident holders of CartaSi, BankAmericard, American Express, and Diners Club cards.
[10]  Euro-, Bank-Swiss Bankers traveller and postal cheques.
[11]  Excluding an estimated 300 million cashed cheques.
[12]  Excluding transactions by holders of an estimated 9 million charge and budget cards, but including transactions by holders of over 1.5 million travel and entertainment cards.
[13]  Includes travellers' cheques and money orders.
[14]  Includes large-value transfers: FedWire and CHIPS and other credit transfers by ACH and ATMs.

**Comparative Table No. 4**
**Comparison of the Number of Cash Dispensers, ATMs, and EFT POS Terminals**
**at Year-End 1987**

| Countries | Cash Dispensers and ATMs | | EFT POS Terminals | |
|---|---|---|---|---|
| | Number of Machines Installed | Number of Inhabitants per Machine | Number of Terminals Installed | Number of Inhabitants per Terminal |
| Belgium | 802 | 12,315 | 15,388[1] | 642 |
| Canada | 5,400[1] | 4,777 | 79[2] | 326,532 |
| France | 11,500 | 4,760 | 70,000 | 781 |
| Germany | 7,500 | 8,147 | 6,663 | 9,170 |
| Italy | 4,367 | 12,975 | 774[3] | 76,161[3] |
| Japan | 62,181 | 1,967 | 564 | 216,844 |
| The Netherlands | 450 | 32,444 | 385 | 37,922 |
| Sweden | 1,650 | 5,091 | 520 | 16,180 |
| Switzerland | 1,239 | 5,303 | 572 | 11,486 |
| United Kingdom | 12,500[4] | 4,544 | 13,000[5] | 4,369 |
| United States | 76,031 | 3,222 | 43,439[5] | 5,640 |

[1]  Estimate.
[2]  Excluding some 100,000 POS terminals that are used for credit-card authorisation.
[3]  The figure comprises the POS terminals installed by a sample group of 71 banks that account for approximately 80% of current-account deposits of the entire banking system and those installed by the SIA.
[4]  ATMs only.
[5]  Does not include either dedicated credit authorisation terminals or retail electronic cash registration terminals.

**Comparative Table No. 5**
**Comparison of Share of Bank Notes in Currency in Circulation, in M$_1$ and in M$_3$ in Percentages**

| Countries | Percentage of Currency In Circulation | | Percentage of M$_1$ | | Percentage of M$_3$ | |
|---|---|---|---|---|---|---|
| | 1978 | 1987 | 1978 | 1987 | 1978 | 1987 |
| Belgium | 98.10 | 97.20 | 42.43[3] | 34.66[3] | • | • |
| Canada | 89.58[1] | 90.87[1] | 37.89[1] | 43.57[1] | 7.43[1] | 6.80[1] |
| France | 95.70 | 95.10 | 18.50[1] | 14.40[1] | 7.80[1] | 5.80[1] |
| Germany | 91.90 | 92.40 | 32.00[3] | 32.20[3] | 11.60[3] | 11.20[3] |
| Italy | 97.26[2] | 97.72[2] | 15.13 | 13.78 | 7.45 | 5.92 |
| Japan | 95.30 | 91.40 | 25.70 | 28.30 | 6.50 | 4.80 |
| The Netherlands | 95.30 | 95.40 | 30.90 | 32.40 | 9.90 | 10.50 |
| Sweden | 94.40 | 96.00 | • | • | 10.30 | 9.50 |
| Switzerland | 94.53 | 94.17 | 35.04 | 34.75 | 11.26 | 8.17 |
| United Kingdom | 91.80[1] | 84.50[1] | 30.00 | 14.50 | 16.00 | 7.10 |
| United States | 89.70 | 92.10 | 29.99 | 28.68 | 6.64 | 5.95 |

[1] Not including cash/bank notes held by financial institutions.
[2] Cash held by the nonstate sector.
[3] Including coin; not including cash held by financial institutions.

Note:  Year-end figures for: Belgium, Germany, Japan, The Netherlands, United Kingdom, and United States.
       End-of-month figures for France.
       Annual average for Canada, Italy, Sweden, and Switzerland.

# Country Tables

## Belgium
## A. Basic Statistical Data

Territorial area: 30,500 sq.kms.
Population: 9.88 million
Gross national product in 1987: (USD/BEF) 141.8/5,293 billion
Per capita GNP: (USD/BEF) 14,355/536,232

### A. 1 Monetary Aggregates
### 1987

| Items | Absolute USD/BEF (billions) | Per Capita USD/BEF | Percentage of GNP | Number of Accounts (millions) | Number of Accounts per Inhabitant |
|---|---|---|---|---|---|
| Total money supply[1] | 126.2 4,182.9 | 12.8 423.4 | 79.03 | | |
| Currency[2] | 12.4 411.6 | 1.3 41.7 | 7.78 | | |
| Transferable deposits[2] | 21.4 709.4 | 2,167 71,832 | 14.66 | 9.49 | 0.96 |

[1] Financial assets with a maximum maturity of one year held by nonfinancial companies and private individuals.
[2] Held by nonfinancial companies and private individuals at the end of 1987.

Note: The exchange rate used to convert BEF into USD for GNP was the average 1987 rate of 37.34; all other statistical data were converted at the end of 1987 at a rate of 33.15.

## Belgium
### A. 2 Transferable Deposits and Number of Accounts per Category of Institution
### at Year-End 1987

| Categories of Institution | Number of Accounts (millions) | Share of Market (%) | Value of Accounts[1] USD/BEF (billions) | Value of Accounts per Capita USD/BEF | Share of Market (%) |
|---|---|---|---|---|---|
| Commercial banks | 4.32[2] | 45.58 | 14.5 479.1 | 1,468 48,512 | 67.54 |
| Savings banks | 1.23 | 12.97 | 1.4 46.7 | 142 4,729 | 6.58 |
| Public credit institutions | 2.74 | 28.90 | 3.2 106.4 | 324 10,774 | 15.00 |
| Post office | 1.19 | 12.55 | 2.3 77.2 | 233 7,817 | 10.88 |
| TOTAL | 9.49 | 100.00 | 21.4 709.4 | 2,167 71,832 | 100.00 |

[1] Accounts held by governmental bodies not included.
[2] Estimate.

### Belgium
### B. Points of Entry into the Payment System

### B. 1 Institutional Framework
### at Year-End 1987

| Categories of Institution | Number of Institutions | Number of Branches | Number of Inhabitants per Branch |
|---|---|---|---|
| Commercial banks | 86 | 3,507[1] | 2,816 |
| Savings banks | 32 | 2,300[2] | 4,294 |
| Public credit institutions | 5[3] | 3,277[4] | 3,014 |
| Sub-total | 123 | 9,084 | 1,088 |
| Post office | 1 | 3,132 | 3,153 |
| TOTAL | 124 | 12,216 | 808 |
| Central bank | 1 | 23[5] | n.a. |

[1] 124 non full-size branches excluded.
[2] Estimate; 17,504 non full-size branches excluded.
[3] Two of these public credit institutions have affiliates (26 in total).
[4] 738 non full-size branches excluded.
[5] One of which is located in Luxembourg.

### Belgium
### B. 2 Cash Dispensers, ATMs, and EFT POS Terminals
### at Year-End 1987

| Cash Dispensers and ATMs | | | | | EFT POS | | |
|---|---|---|---|---|---|---|---|
| Number of Networks | Number of Cash Dispensers | Number of ATMs | Total Number of Cash Dispensers and ATMs | Number of Inhabitants per Cash Dispenser and ATM | Number of Networks | Number of EFT POS Terminals | Number of Inhabitants per EFT POS Terminal |
| 2 | | 732 | 732 | | 6[2] | 15,388[3] | 642 |
| 2[1] | 70 | | 70 | | | | |
| 4 | | | 802 | 12,315 | | | |

[1] Postal Cheque Office and American Express (whose cash dispensers also dispense traveller's cheques).
[2] Among which 4 nonbank networks (2 large retailers and 2 credit-card issuers).
[3] Estimate. Some double counting is inevitable.

**Belgium**
**C. Relative Importance of Cashless Payment Instruments**
**in the Payment System**
**1987[1]**

| Instruments | Volume of Transactions (millions) | Volume per Capita | Percentage of Total | Value of Transactions USD/BEF (billions) | Value per Capita USD/BEF | Percentage of Total |
|---|---|---|---|---|---|---|
| Cheques issued[2] | 243.8 | 24.7 | 32.94 | 400.2 13,266.2 | 40.5 1,342.7 | 5.95 |
| Payments by credit card[3] | 7.4 | 0.7 | < 1.00 | 1.0 32.7 | 0.1 3.3 | 0.01 |
| Payments by debit card at EFT POS | 40.6 | 4.1 | 5.49 | 1.5 48.6 | 0.2 4.9 | 0.02 |
| Paper-based credit transfers[4] | 311.9 | 31.6 | 42.14 | 6,252.8 207,280.2 | 632.9 20,979.8 | 92.90 |
| Paperless credit transfers | 87.3 | 8.8 | 11.80 | 66.8 2,215.6 | 6.8 224.3 | 0.99 |
| Direct debits | 49.1 | 5.0 | 6.63 | 8.4 279.1 | 0.9 28.3 | 0.13 |
| TOTAL | 740.1 | 74.9 | 100.00 | 6,730.7 223,122.4 | 681.2 22,583.2 | 100.00 |

[1] Some double counting is inevitable due to the settlement at regular intervals of credit card account balances through other payment media. Estimates for all statistics except for payments by debit cards at EFT POS and by credit cards. Interbank (as well as corporate) payments are included in the data for some instruments and therefore considerably inflate them when expressed in value.
[2] Postal cheques and drafts included.
[3] Including transactions by holders of travel and entertainment cards, and partly data of the Grand Duchy of Luxembourg.
[4] Inpayment transfers included.

## Canada
## A. Basic Statistical Data

Territorial area: 9.9 million sq.kms.
Population: 25.8 million
Gross national product in 1987: (USD/CAD) 405.1/537.2 billion
Per capita GNP: (USD/CAD) 15,704.1/20,824.9

### A. 1 Monetary Aggregates
### 1987

| Items | Absolute USD/CAD (billions) | Per Capita USD/CAD | Percentage of GNP | Number of Accounts (millions) | Number of Accounts per Inhabitant |
|---|---|---|---|---|---|
| Total money supply[1] | 245.9 | 9,532.0 | | | |
| | 321.5 | 12,461.8 | 59.8 | | |
| Currency[2] | 12.6 | 490.5 | | | |
| | 16.5 | 641.3 | 3.1 | n.a. | n.a. |
| Transferable | 64.0 | 2,483.6 | | | |
| deposits[3] | 83.2 | 3,227.2 | 15.5 | | |

[1] $M_2$ +, Table E1, *Bank of Canada Review*; average-of-Wednesday data for December 1987 (exchange rate used: 1.3074).

[2] Currency outside banks, Table E1, *Bank of Canada Review*; average-of-Wednesday data for December 1987 (exchange rate used: 1.3074).

[3] At year-end 1987.

Note: The exchange rate used to convert CAD into USD for GNP was the average 1987 rate of 1.3260; unless otherwise stated, other statistical data were converted at the year-end 1987 rate of 1.2993.

## Canada
## A. 2 Transferable Deposits and Number of Accounts per Category of Institution at Year-End 1987

| Categories of Institution | Number of Accounts (millions) | Share of Market (%) | Value of Accounts USD/CAD (billions) | Value of Accounts per Capita USD/CAD | Share of Market (%) |
|---|---|---|---|---|---|
| Chartered banks | • | • | 50.9 | 1,973.3 | |
| | | | 66.1 | 2,564.1 | 79.5 |
| Local credit unions and caisses populaires | • | • | 5.7 | 221.2 | |
| | | | 7.4 | 287.4 | 8.9 |
| Trust and mortgage loan companies | • | • | 6.8 | 264.0 | |
| | | | 8.8 | 343.0 | 10.6 |
| Governmental savings institutions[1,2] | • | • | 0.6 | 145.1[2] | |
| | | | 0.9 | 188.5 | 1.0 |
| Post office | n.a. | | n.a. | | |
| TOTAL | • | • | 64.0 | 2,483.6 | |
| | | | 83.2 | 3,227.2 | 100.00 |

[1] Province of Alberta Treasury Branches only, where end of period is March 31, 1988.

[2] Population of Alberta only.

**Canada**
**B. Points of Entry into the Payment System**

**B. 1 Institutional Framework**
**at Year-End 1987**

| Categories of Institution | Number of Institutions | Number of Branches | Number of Inhabitants per Branch |
|---|---|---|---|
| Chartered banks | 72[1] | 7,148 | 3,609 |
| Local credit unions and caisses populaires | 2,947 | 4,129 | 6,248 |
| Trust and mortgage loan companies | 115[2] | 1,523 | 16,938 |
| Governmental savings institutions | 2[3] | 156 | 88,788[4] |
| Sub-total | 3,136 | 12,956 | 1,991 |
| Post office | n.a. | | |
| TOTAL | 3,136 | 12,956 | 1,991 |
| Central bank | 1 | 9 | n.a. |

[1] Six operate nationwide.
[2] Only a few operate nationwide.
[3] Operate only in Alberta and Ontario.
[4] Population of Alberta and Ontario only.

**Canada**
**B. 2 Cash Dispensers, ATMs, and EFT POS Terminals**
**at Year-End 1987**

| Cash Dispensers and ATMs | | | | | EFT POS | | |
|---|---|---|---|---|---|---|---|
| Number of Networks | Number of Cash Dispensers | Number of ATMs | Total Number of Cash Dispensers and ATMs | Number of Inhabitants per Cash Dispenser and ATM | Number of Networks | Number of EFT POS Terminals | Number of Inhabitants per EFT POS Terminal |
| 40[1,2] | • | • | 5,400[1,3] | 4,777 | 4 | 79[4] | 326,532 |

[1] Estimate.
[2] Of which six are owned by nondeposit-taking institutions.
[3] Of which some 5,270 are owned by member institutions of the Canadian Payments Association.
[4] Excluding some 100,000 POS terminals that are used for credit-card authorisation.

**Canada**
**C. Relative Importance of Cashless Payment Instruments**
**in the Payment System**
**1987**

| Instruments | Volume of Transactions[1] (millions) | Volume per Capita | Percentage of Total | Value of Transactions[1] USD/CAD (billions) | Value per Capita USD/CAD | Percentage of Total |
|---|---|---|---|---|---|---|
| Cheques issued | 2,079.6 | 80.60 | 72.4 | 11,598.0 15,380.4 | 449,618.5 596.232.0 | 99.4 |
| Payments by credit card[2] | 676.0 | 26.20 | 23.5 | 29.0 38.5 | 1,126.4 1,493.7 | 0.2 |
| Payments by debit card at EFT POS | 0.1 | 0.01 | 0.0[3] | 0.0[3,4] 0.0 | 0.2 0.2 | 0.0[3] |
| Paper-based credit transfers | • | • | • | • | • | • |
| Paperless credit transfers, of which: | 72.6 | 2.75 | 2.6 | 38.4 50.9 | 1,479.4 1,961.8 | 0.3 |
| • transfers initiated at ATMs | 19.4 | 0.75 | 0.7 | 1.1 1.4 | 32.1 42.5 | 0.0[3] |
| • direct credits | 53.2 | 2.00 | 1.9 | 37.3 49.5 | 1,447.3 1,919.3 | 0.3 |
| Direct debits | 43.0 | 1.70 | 1.5 | 8.9 11.8 | 344.1 456.3 | 0.1 |
| TOTAL | 2,871.3 | 114.01 | 100.0 | 11,674.3 15,481.6 | 452,568.6 600,144.0 | 100.0 |

[1] All figures are estimates.
[2] Including transactions by holders of travel and entertainment cards.
[3] Insignificant.
[4] The value of payments by debit card at EFT POS during 1987 is estimated to have been USD 4.4 million or CAD 5.8 million.

**France**
**A. Basic Statistical Data**

Territorial area: 551.2 thousand sq.kms.
Population: 54.7 million
Gross national product in 1987: (USD/FRF) 877.42/5,275 billion
Per capita GNP: (USD/FRF) 16,041/96,435

**A. 1 Monetary Aggregates**
**1987**

| Items | Absolute USD/FRF (billions) | Per Capita USD/FRF | Percentage of GNP | Number of Accounts (millions) | Number of Accounts per Inhabitant |
|---|---|---|---|---|---|
| Total money supply | 676.4 3,612.1 | 12,366 66,035 | 68.5 | • | • |
| Currency | 41.9 223.8 | 766 4,091 | 4.2 | • | • |
| Transferable deposits* | 586.2 3,130.3 | 10,717 57,227 | 59.3 | 150.1 | 2.7 |

* At year-end 1987.

Note: The exchange rate used to convert FRF into USD for GNP was the average 1987 rate of 6.0119; all other statistical data were converted at the end-of-1987 rate of 5.34.

**France**
**A. 2 Transferable Deposits and Number of Accounts per Category of Institution**
**at Year-End 1987**

| Categories of Institution | Number of Accounts (millions) | Share of Market (%) | Value of Accounts USD/FRF (billions) | Value of Accounts per Capita USD/FRF | Share of Market (%) |
|---|---|---|---|---|---|
| Commercial banks | 33.2 | 22.1 | 210.8 1,125.7 | 3,854 20,580 | 36.0 |
| Savings banks | 39.3 | 26.2 | 107.4 573.5 | 1,963 10,484 | 18.3 |
| Cooperative and rural banks | 49.6 | 33.0 | 179.9 960.7 | 3,289 17,563 | 30.7 |
| Post office | 28.0 | 18.7 | 88.1 470.4 | 1,611 8,600 | 15.0 |
| TOTAL | 150.1 | 100.0 | 586.2 3,130.3 | 10,717 57,227 | 100.0 |

**France**
**B. Points of Entry into the Payment System**

**B. 1 Institutional Framework**
**at Year-End 1987**

| Categories of Institution | Number of Institutions | Number of Branches | Number of Inhabitants per Branch |
|---|---|---|---|
| Commercial banks | 377 | 9,939 | 5,504 |
| Savings banks | 364 | 4,378 | 12,494 |
| Cooperative and rural banks | 190 | 11,175 | 4,895 |
| Sub-total | 931 | 25,492 | 2,146 |
| Post office | 1 | 17,089 | 3,201 |
| TOTAL | 932 | 42,581 | 1,285 |
| Central bank | 1 | 234 | n.a. |

Note: Since 1986 it has not been possible to establish the number of nonpermanent branch offices; as an indication, in 1985 they represented: 15% of the branch offices of commercial banks; 26% of the branch offices of savings banks; 37% of the branch offices of cooperative banks.

**France**
**B. 2 Cash Dispensers, ATMs, and EFT POS Terminals**
**at Year-End 1987**

| Cash Dispensers and ATMs | | | | | EFT POS | | |
|---|---|---|---|---|---|---|---|
| Number of Networks | Number of Cash Dispensers | Number of ATMs | Total Number of Cash Dispensers and ATMs | Number of Inhabitants per Cash Dispenser and ATM | Number of Networks | Number of EFT POS Terminals | Number of Inhabitants per EFT POS Terminal |
| 1 | • | • | 11,500 | 4,760 | • | 70,000 | 781 |

**France**
**C. Relative Importance of Cashless Payment Instruments**
**in the Payment System**
**1987₁**

| Instruments | Volume of Transactions (millions) | Volume per Capita | Percentage of Total | Value of Transactions USD/FRF (billions) | Value per Capita USD/FRF | Percentage of Total |
|---|---|---|---|---|---|---|
| Cheques issued[2] | 4,406.4 | 80.6 | 65.4 | 2,532.6<br>15,225.5 | 46,299.8<br>278,345.5 | 29.9 |
| Payments by credit card[3] | • | • | • | • | • | • |
| Payments by debit card at EFT POS[4] | 530.0 | 9.7 | 7.9 | 27.1<br>163.0 | 495.4<br>2,979.9 | 0.3 |
| Paper-based credit transfers[5] | 128.7 | 2.4 | 1.9 | 5,109.8<br>30,719.4 | 93,415.0<br>561,597.8 | 60.3 |
| Paperless credit transfers[6] | 1,039.5 | 19.0 | 15.4 | 647.6<br>3,893.3 | 11,839.1<br>71,175.5 | 7.7 |
| Direct debits[7] | 637.3 | 11.6 | 9.4 | 153.2<br>921.0 | 2,800.7<br>16,837.3 | 1.8 |
| TOTAL | 6,741.9 | 123.3 | 100.0 | 8,470.3<br>50,922.2 | 154,850.0<br>930,936.0 | 100.0 |

[1] The figures in this table combine the data relating to all payment instruments, irrespective of whether they are routed via "official" circuits or not.

[2] Including postal cheques.

[3] Since transactions of this sort give rise to settlement in the form of a direct debit or, more rarely, a cheque, it has not been possible to isolate them as such.

[4] Of which 45% (by volume) did not give rise to electronic payment.

[5] These figures include credit transfers of a purely interbank nature that have not been possible to isolate.

[6] A breakdown is not available.

[7] Including the universal payment order (superseded by the interbank payment order—TIP— with effect from February 1, 1988).

## Germany
## A. Basic Statistical Data

Territorial area: 248.6 thousand sq.kms.
Population: 61.1 million
Gross national product in 1987: (USD/DEM) 1,125/2,023 billion
Per capita GNP: (USD/DEM) 18,413/33,111

### A. 1 Monetary Aggregates
### 1987

| Items | Absolute USD/DEM (billions) | Per Capita USD/DEM | Percentage of GNP | Number of Accounts (millions) | Number of Accounts per Inhabitant |
|---|---|---|---|---|---|
| Total money supply (M₃)[1] | 703.4 1,112.4 | 11,512 18,206 | 55.0 | | |
| Currency[2] | 78.5 124.1 | 1,285 2,031 | 6.1 | | |
| Transferable deposits[3] | 168.0 265.7 | 2,750 4,349 | 13.1 | 58 | 0.95 |

[1] $M_1$ + $M_2$ + savings deposits of domestic nonbanks at statutory notice.
[2] Excluding banks' cash balances.
[3] Sight deposits of domestic nonbanks (including deposits held at the cental bank) at year-end 1987.

Note: The exchange rate used to convert DEM into USD for GNP was the average 1987 rate of 1.7982; all other statistical data were converted at the end-of-1987 rate of 1.5815.

## Germany
### A. 2 Transferable Deposits and Number of Accounts per Category of Institution
### at Year-End 1987

| Categories of Institution | Number of Accounts (millions)[1] | Share of Market (%) | Value of Accounts USD/DEM (billions) | Value of Accounts per Capita USD/DEM | Share of Market (%) |
|---|---|---|---|---|---|
| Commercial banks[2] | 11.2 | 19.4 | 60.4 95.5 | 988 1,563 | 36.0 |
| Savings banks[3] | 25.6 | 44.4 | 61.7 97.5 | 1,010 1,596 | 36.7 |
| Cooperative and rural banks[3] | 16.4 | 28.4 | 36.6 57.9 | 599 948 | 21.8 |
| Post office | 4.5 | 7.8 | 9.3 14.8 | 152 242 | 5.5 |
| TOTAL | 57.7 | 100.0 | 168.0 265.7 | 2,749 4,349 | 100.0 |

[1] Accounts of domestic nonbanks, partly estimated.
[2] Including mortgage banks, instalment sales financing institutions, banks with special functions, other banks, and central bank.
[3] Including central institutions.

### Germany
### B. Points of Entry into the Payment System

#### B. 1 Institutional Framework
#### at Year-End 1987

| Categories of Institution | Number of Institutions | Number of Branches[1] | Number of Inhabitants per Branch |
|---|---|---|---|
| Commercial banks[2] | 331 | 6,643 | 9,198 |
| Savings banks | 598 | 18,136 | 3,369 |
| Cooperative and rural banks | 3,482 | 19,428 | 3,145 |
| Sub-total | 4,411 | 44,207 | 1,382 |
| Post office | 13[3] | 17,515 | 3,488 |
| TOTAL | 4,424 | 61,722 | 990 |
| Central bank | 12[4] | 201 | n.a. |

[1] Branches = total number of bank offices.
[2] Including mortgage banks, instalment sales financing institutions, banks with special functions, building and loan associations, investment companies, collective securities deposit banks, guarantee banks, and other banks.
[3] Postal giro offices (Postgiroämter).
[4] The Bundesbank as a legal entity comprises the Directorate (in Frankfurt am Main) and 11 Landeszentralbanken.

### Germany
### B. 2 Cash Dispensers, ATMs, and EFT POS Terminals
### at Year-End 1987

| Cash Dispensers and ATMs[1] | | | | | EFT POS[2] | | |
|---|---|---|---|---|---|---|---|
| Number of Networks | Number of Cash Dispensers | Number of ATMs | Total Number of Cash Dispensers and ATMs | Number of Inhabitants per Cash Dispenser and ATM | Number of Networks | Number of EFT POS Terminals | Number of Inhabitants per EFT POS Terminal |
| 4 | • | • | 7,500[1] | 8,147 | 5 | 6,663[2] | 9,170 |

[1] Of which 4,900 in the ec-pool (proportion of ATMs tending to rise). Exact breakdown between ATMs and cash dispensers is impossible.
[2] GZS-POS trial in Berlin and Munich (ec-card): 213 terminals, organised by banks. All Card POS (credit cards and some ec-cards): 450 terminals, organised by nonbanks.
Makatel credit card authorisation with electronic clearing: 1,000 terminals organised by nonbanks.
Eurocard-START association of travel agents, with electronic clearing in paperless exchange of data media: 5,000 terminals, organised by nonbanks.
Eurocard Lufthansa with electronic clearing: approximately 4,000 terminals worldwide, organised by nonbanks. Data not contained in table.
Excluding terminals that are only used for credit card authorisation.

**Germany**
**C. Relative Importance of Cashless Payment Instruments**
**in the Payment System**
**1987**

| Instruments | Volume of Transactions (millions) | Volume per Capita | Percentage of Total | Value of Transactions USD/DEM (billions)[1] | Value per Capita USD/DEM | Percentage of Total |
|---|---|---|---|---|---|---|
| Cheques issued | 545.0 | 9 | 8.6 | 1,886.0<br>3,355.0 | 30,540.0<br>54,910.0 | 18.8 |
| Cheques paper-less collect[2] | (300.0) | (5) | (4.7) | (47.0)<br>(85.0) | (768.0)<br>(1,391.0) | (0.5) |
| Payments by credit card[3] | 38.0 | 1 | 0.6 | 5.0<br>8.0 | 82.0<br>131.0 | 0.1 |
| Payments by debit card at EFT POS[4] | 0.4 | 0 | 0.0 | 0.0<br>0.1 | 0.5<br>0.9 | 0.0 |
| Paper-based credit transfers[5] | 1,805.0 | 30 | 28.5 | 5,795.0<br>10,420.0 | 94,845.0<br>170,540.0 | 58.4 |
| Paperless credit transfers[6] | 1,665.0 | 27 | 26.3 | 1,423.0<br>2,560.0 | 23,290.0<br>41,899.0 | 14.3 |
| Direct debits[7] | 2,285.0 | 38 | 36.0 | 837.0<br>1,505.0 | 13,699.0<br>24,632.0 | 8.4 |
| TOTAL | 6,338.4 | 105 | 100.0 | 9,926.0<br>17,848.1 | 162,456.5<br>292,112.0 | 100.0 |

[1] Partly estimated.
[2] Not included in direct debits in order to avoid double-counting.
[3] Charge cards and bank cards, excluding retail cards; the card companies' settlements with the retailers (normally credit transfers) and payment of the monthly totals by cardholders to card issuers by credit transfer, direct debit, or cheque are contained in the corresponding items.
[4] Only ec-card POS test of the GZS (Common Payment Systems Company) in Berlin and Munich.
[5] Excluding interbank transfers. Interbank transfers via Bundesbank, partly estimated:

|  | Volume of Transactions (millions) | Value of Transactions USD/DEM (billions) |
|---|---|---|
| Local credit transfers | 1.0 | 3,392.0<br>6,099.0 |
| Local clearing house credit transfers | 213.8 | 35,909.0<br>64,571.0 |
| Intercity wire transfers | 0.8 | 2,748.0<br>4,942.0 |

[6] Including customers' paper-based credit transfers that were routed into the paperless procedure (EZU procedure) by the bank to which they were first submitted.
[7] Including cash dispenser/ATM withdrawals made with ec-cards at banks other than that issuing the card.

## Italy
### A. Basic Statistical Data

Territorial area: 301.3 thousand sq.kms.
Population: 56.7 million
Gross national product in 1987: (USD/ITL) 751.5/974,060 billion
Per capita GNP: (USD/ITL) 13,255/17,179,000

### A. 1 Monetary Aggregates
### 1987

| Items | Absolute USD/ITL (billions) | Per Capita USD/ITL | Percentage of GNP | Number of Accounts (millions) | Number of Accounts per Inhabitant |
|---|---|---|---|---|---|
| Total money supply[1] | 709.0 828,770.0 | 12,504.4 14,616,755.0 | 85.08 | | |
| Currency | 43.7 51,125.0 | 771.1 901,675.0 | 5.25 | | |
| Transferable deposits[2] | 267.3 312,542.0 | 4,714.1 5,512,205.0 | 31.09 | 19.9 | 0.35[3] |

[1] Comprises: currency, bank and postal deposits, certificates of deposit, and Treasury bills.
[2] At year-end 1987.
[3] The number of current accounts per household is 1.07.

Note: The exchange rate used to convert ITL into USD for GNP was the average 1987 rate of 1296.1; unless otherwise stated, all other statistical data were converted at the end-of-1987 rate of 1169.3.

### Italy
### A. 2 Transferable Deposits and Number of Accounts per Category of Institution at Year-End 1987

| Categories of Institution | Number of Accounts (millions) | Share of Market (%) | Value of Accounts USD/ITL (billions) | Value of Accounts per Capita USD/ITL | Share of Market (%) |
|---|---|---|---|---|---|
| Commercial banks | 10.8 | 54.3 | 153.3 179,301.0 | 2,705 3,164,284 | 57.3 |
| Savings banks | 5.6 | 28.1 | 67.5 78,949.0 | 1,191 1,393,283 | 25.3 |
| Cooperative and rural banks | 3.0 | 15.1 | 37.5 43,813.0 | 662 773,207 | 14.0 |
| Post office | 0.5 | 2.5 | 9.0 10,479.0 | 159 184,932 | 3.4 |
| TOTAL | 19.9 | 100.0 | 267.3 312,542.0 | 4,717 5,515,707 | 100.0 |

## Italy
### B. Points of Entry into the Payment System

#### B. 1 Institutional Framework
#### at Year-End 1987

| Categories of Institution | Number of Institutions | Number of Branches* | Number of Inhabitants per Branch |
|---|---|---|---|
| Commercial banks | 164 | 7,019 | 8,073 |
| Savings banks | 86 | 4,169 | 13,600 |
| Cooperative and rural banks | 859 | 4,177 | 13,574 |
| Sub-total | 1,109 | 15,365 | 3,688 |
| Post office | 1 | 13,958 | 4,062 |
| TOTAL | 1,110 | 29,323 | 1,932 |
| Central bank | 1 | 97 | n.a. |

* The distinction between branches offering a full range of operations and those with a limited range was abolished by decision of the CICR (Interministerial Committee for Credit and Savings) taken on May 21, 1987. The choice of opening hours for each operating site was thus left to the banks.

## Italy
### B. 2 Cash Dispensers, ATMs, and EFT POS Terminals
### at Year-End 1987

| Cash Dispensers and ATMs[1] | | | | | EFT POS[2] | | |
|---|---|---|---|---|---|---|---|
| Number of Networks | Number of Cash Dispensers | Number of ATMs | Total Number of Cash Dispensers and ATMs | Number of Inhabitants per Cash Dispenser and ATM | Number of Networks | Number of EFT POS Terminals | Number of Inhabitants per EFT POS Terminal |
| 1 | • | • | 4,367 | 12,975 | 10 | 744 | 76,161 |

[1] The data relate to the whole of the banking system.
[2] The figure comprises the POS terminals installed by a sample group of 75 banks that account for approximately 80% of current-account deposits of the entire banking system and those installed by the SIA.

## Italy
### C. Relative Importance of Cashless Payment Instruments in the Payment System
#### 1987[1]

| Instruments | Volume of Transactions (millions) | Volume per Capita | Percentage of Total | Value of Transactions USD/ITL[2] (billions) | Value per Capita USD/ITL[2] | Percentage of Total |
|---|---|---|---|---|---|---|
| Cheques issued[3] | 720.1 | 12.71 | 50.51 | 1,311.4 / 1,699,645.0 | 22,699.9 / 29,421,334.0 | 22.07 |
| Payments by credit card[4] | 12.5 | 0.22 | 0.88 | 1.8 / 2,357.0 | 32.0 / 41,536.0 | 0.03 |
| Payments by debit card at EFT POS | 0.2 | • | 0.01 | • / 19.0 | 0.3 / 342.0 | • |
| Paper-based credit transfers[5], of which: | 612.4 | 10.81 | 42.95 | 4,554.4 / 5,902,906.0 | 80,323.8 / 104,107,690.0 | 76.64 |
| • large value transfers[6] | 1.0 | 0.02 | 0.07 | 2,512.8 / 3,256,861.0 | 44.3 / 57,440.0 | 42.29 |
| Paperless credit transfers, of which: | 53.5 | 0.94 | 3.75 | 57.9 / 75,014.0 | 1,020.8 / 1,322,998.0 | 0.97 |
| • large value transfers[7] | 0.0 | • | • | 0.0 / 0.0 | 0.2 / 282.0 | • |
| • Transfers initiated at ATMs | • | | | • / 16.0 | • / 282.0 | • |
| • Others[8] | 53.5 | 0.94 | 3.75 | 57.9 / 74,998.0 | 1,020.5 / 1,322,716.0 | 0.97 |
| Direct debits | 27.1 | 0.48 | 1.90 | 16.8 / 21,717.0 | 295.5 / 383,015.0 | 0.28 |
| TOTAL | 1,425.8 | 25.15 | 100.00 | 5,942.2 / 7,701,658.0 | 104,372.3 / 135,276,915.0 | 100.0 |

1 The figures for bank payment instruments are taken from a sample group of 75 banks that account for approximately 80% of the current-account deposits of the entire banking system.
2 The conversion into dollars was made on the basis of the mean exchange rate.
3 Includes: bank cheques, banker's drafts, cashier's cheques issued by the Bank of Italy, postal cheques, money orders, and international money orders issued in Italy.
4 Comprises payment transactions effected in Italy and abroad by resident holders of CartaSì, BankAmericard, American Express, and Diners Club cards.
5 Includes: interbank transfers, bank payment orders, domestic and international postal giro operations and transfers to postal current accounts. The last-mentioned are made in cash or by banker's draft; in 1987, 492 million such operations were effected for a total value of Lit. 240,414.
6 Consisting of interbank funds transfers effected by the entire banking system, either directly or via the clearing houses, to the debit/credit of accounts held at the Bank of Italy. Currently such transfers are made exclusively by means of paper forms presented at the Bank of Italy branches. The volume of transactions is estimated.
7 Large-value transfers are currently effected only in a paper-based form (see footnote 6 above.)
8 Comprises the centralised payment transactions effected via the SIA and other automated payments.

## Japan
### A. Basic Statistical Data

Territorial area: 377,835.2 sq.kms.
Population: 122.3 million (as of January 1, 1988)
Gross national product in 1987: USD/JPY 2,385.3/345,010 billion
Per capita GNP: USD/JPY 19,503.7/2,821,013.9

### A. 1 Monetary Aggregates
### 1987

| Items | Absolute USD/JPY (billions) | Per Capita USD/JPY | Percentage of GNP | Number of Accounts (millions) | Number of Accounts per Inhabitant |
|---|---|---|---|---|---|
| Total money supply (M₃ + CDs) | 5,014.0 611,709.8 | 40,997.5 5,001,715.5 | 177.3 | n.a. | n.a. |
| Currency | 261.7 31,926.7 | 2,139.8 261,052.3 | 9.3 | n.a. | n.a. |
| Transferable deposits* | 993.5 121,210.4 | 8,123.1 991,015.7 | 35.1 | • | • |

\* At year-end 1987.

Note: The exchange rate used to convert JPY into USD for GNP was the average 1987 rate of 144.64; all other statistical data were converted at the end-of-1987 rate of 122.0.

### Japan
### A. 2 Transferable Deposits and Number of Accounts per Category of Institution
### at Year-End 1987

| Categories of Institution | Number of Accounts* (millions) | Share of Market (%) | Value of Accounts USD/JPY (billions) | Value of Accounts per Capita USD/JPY | Share of Market (%) |
|---|---|---|---|---|---|
| Commercial banks: city banks, regional banks, long-term credit banks, trust banks | 193.9 | • | 624.4 76,177.5 | 5,105.0 622,823.1 | 62.8 |
| Financial institutions for small businesses: sogo or mutual banks, credit associations, Shoko Chukin Bank, credit cooperatives, labor credit associations | 113.0 | • | 197.8 24,129.3 | 1,617.2 197,279.8 | 19.9 |
| Financial institutions for agriculture, foresty and fishing: Norinchukin Bank, agricultural cooperatives, fishery cooperatives | • | • | 95.9 11,699.3 | 784.0 95,652.8 | 9.7 |
| Post office | 70.6 | • | 75.4 9,204.3 | 616.9 75,260.0 | 7.6 |
| TOTAL | • | • | 993.5 121,210.4 | 8,123.1 991,015.7 | 100.0 |

\*As of the end of March 1988.

### Japan
### B. Points of Entry into the Payment System

#### B. 1 Institutional Framework
#### at Year-End 1987

| Categories of Institution | Number of Institutions | Number of Branches | Number of Inhabitants per Branch |
|---|---|---|---|
| Commercial banks: city banks, regional banks, long-term credit banks, trust banks | 87 | 9,674 | 12,642 |
| Financial institutions for small businesses: sogo or mutual banks, credit associations, Shoko Chukin Bank, credit cooperatives, labor credit associations | 1,014 | 15,047 | 8,128 |
| Financial institutions for agriculture, forestry and fishing: Norinchukin Bank, agricultural cooperatives, fishery cooperatives | 5,912* | 17,975 | 6,804 |
| Sub-total | 7,013 | 42,696 | 2,864 |
| Post office | 1 | 23,158 | 5,281 |
| TOTAL | 7,014 | 65,854 | 1,857 |
| Central bank | 1 | 34 | n.a. |

\* As of the end of September 1987.

### Japan
### B. 2 Cash Dispensers, ATMs, and EFT POS Terminals

| Cash Dispensers and ATMs[1] | | | | | EFT POS[2] | | |
|---|---|---|---|---|---|---|---|
| Number of Networks | Number of Cash Dispensers | Number of ATMs | Total Number of Cash Dispensers and ATMs | Number of Inhabitants per Cash Dispenser and ATM | Number of Networks | Number of EFT POS Terminals | Number of Inhabitants per EFT POS Terminal |
| 61[3] | 24,493 | 37,688 | 62,181 | 1,967[4] | 30[5] | 564 | 216,844[6] |

[1] As of the end of March 1987.
[2] As of mid-April 1988.
[3] Of these 61 networks operated by financial institutions, 9 are nationwide proprietary networks, 51 local joint networks, and 1 a nationwide network. In addition, there are numerous networks operated by nonbanking institutions, including securities companies, finance companies, and department stores.
[4] The number of households per cash dispenser and ATM is 644.
[5] The largest network has 200 EFT POS terminals and the second one has 80.
[6] The number of households per EFT POS terminal is 70,966.

Japan
## C. Relative Importance of Cashless Payment Instruments
in the Payment System
1987[1]

| Instruments | Volume of Transactions (millions) | Volume per Capita | Percentage of Total | Value of Transactions USD/JPY (billions) | Value per Capita USD/JPY | Percentage of Total |
|---|---|---|---|---|---|---|
| Cheques issued | 269.4 | 2.2 | 7.4 | 33,851.2 | 276,788.4 | |
| | | | | 4,129,848.9 | 33,768,184.0 | 67.4 |
| Payments by credit card[2] | 211.9 | 1.7 | 5.8 | 38.3 | 313.2 | |
| | | | | 4,672.2 | 38,202.8 | 0.1 |
| Payments by debit card at EFT POS | • | • | • | • | • | • |
| Paper-based credit transfers | 446.1 | 3.6 | 12.2 | 451.9 | 3,694.7 | |
| | | | | 55,126.5 | 450,748.2 | 0.9 |
| Paperless credit transfers | 869.1 | 7.1 | 23.8 | 15,714.6 | 128,492.3 | |
| | | | | 1,917,181.8 | 15,676,057.2 | 31.3 |
| Direct debits | 1,855.9 | 15.2 | 50.8 | 143.0 | 1,169.7 | |
| | | | | 17,453.0 | 142,706.5 | .03 |
| TOTAL | 3,652.4 | 29.9 | 100.0 | 50,199.0 | 410,458.2 | |
| | | | | 6,124,282.4 | 50,758,898.6 | 100.0 |

[1] Estimated figures.
[2] The figures are composed of 21 bank and nonbank credit card companies, including JCB, VISA Japan, Union Credit, and so forth.

Note: Prepaid cards issued in 1987:

| Issuers | Number of Cards (millions) | Total Value USD/JPY (millions) |
|---|---|---|
| Telephone companies | 228.3 | 1,136.1/138,600.0 |
| Railway companies | 62.2 | 289.4/ 35,301.7 |
| Highway corporations | 0.03 | 3.1/    378.9 |

## The Netherlands
### A. Basic Statistical Data

Territorial area: 37,300 sq.kms.
Population: 14.6 million
Gross national product in 1987: (USD/NLG) 236/434 billion
Per capita GNP: (USD/NLG) 16,163/29,740

### A. 1 Monetary Aggregates
### 1987

| Items | Absolute USD/NLG (billions) | Per Capita USD/NLG | Percentage of GNP | Number of Accounts (millions) | Number of Accounts per Inhabitant |
|---|---|---|---|---|---|
| Total money supply | 182.6 336.0 | 12,506 23,011 | 77.4 | | |
| Currency | 18.1 33.3 | 1,239 2,280 | 7.7 | | |
| Transferable deposits* | 38.5 70.9 | 2,638 4,856 | 16.3 | 15.16 | 1.04 |

* At year-end 1987.

Note: The exchange rate used to convert NLG into USD for all statistical data was the end-of-1987 rate of 1.84.

### The Netherlands
### A. 2 Transferable Deposits and Number of Accounts per Category of Institution
### at Year-End 1987

| Categories of Institution | Number of Accounts (millions) | Share of Market (%) | Value of Accounts USD/NLG (billions) | Value of Accounts per Capita USD/NLG | Share of Market (%) |
|---|---|---|---|---|---|
| Commercial banks | 4.01 | 26.5 | 18.2 33.4 | • | 47.2 |
| Savings banks | 1.57 | 10.4 | 1.6 3.0 | • | 4.3 |
| Cooperative and rural banks | 4.27 | 28.2 | 9.1 16.7 | • | 23.6 |
| Post Bank | 5.31 | 35.0 | 9.6 17.7 | • | 25.0 |
| TOTAL | 15.16 | 100.0 | 38.5 70.9 | 2,638 4,856 | 100.0 |

### The Netherlands
### B. Points of Entry into the Payment System

#### B. 1 Institutional Framework
#### at Year-End 1987

| Categories of Institution | Number of Institutions | Number of Branches | Number of Inhabitants per Branch |
|---|---|---|---|
| Commercial banks | 83 | 2,338 | 6,244 |
| Savings banks | 58 | 1,035 | 14,106 |
| Cooperative and rural banks | 926 | 2,345 | 6,226 |
| Post Bank | 1 | 2,705* | 5,397 |
| TOTAL | 1,068 | 8,423 | 1,733 |
| Central bank | 1 | 12 | n.a. |

* 2,679 of these branches are post offices.

### The Netherlands
### B. 2 Cash Dispensers, ATMs, and EFT POS Terminals
### at Year-End 1987

| Cash Dispensers and ATMs | | | | | EFT POS | | |
|---|---|---|---|---|---|---|---|
| Number of Networks | Number of Cash Dispensers | Number of ATMs | Total Number of Cash Dispensers and ATMs | Number of Inhabitants per Cash Dispenser and ATM | Number of Networks | Number of EFT POS Terminals | Number of Inhabitants per EFT POS Terminal |
| 3 | 450 | • | 450 | 32,444 | 2 | 385 | 37,922 |

**The Netherlands**
**C. Relative Importance of Cashless Payment Instruments
in the Payment System
1987**

| Instruments | Volume of Transactions (millions) | Volume per Capita | Percentage of Total | Value of Transactions USD/NLG (billions) | Value per Capita USD/NLG | Percentage of Total |
|---|---|---|---|---|---|---|
| Cheques issued | 286 | 20 | 19.0 | 18 | 1,258 | . |
|  |  |  |  | 34 | 2,314 | 0.3 |
| Payments by credit card | • | • | less than 0.5 | • | • | 0.0 |
| Payments by debit card at EFT POS | • | • | less than 0.5 | • | • | 0.0 |
| Paper-based credit transfers | 564 | 39 | 37.5 | 400 | 27,385 |  |
|  |  |  |  | 736 | 50,388 | 6.7 |
| Paperless credit transfers, of which: |  |  |  |  |  |  |
| • large-value* | 1 | 0 | • | 4,642 | 317,960 |  |
|  |  |  |  | 8,542 | 585,046 | 77.5 |
| • others | 406 | 28 | 27.0 | 770 | 52,729 |  |
|  |  |  |  | 1,417 | 97,021 | 12.8 |
| Direct debits | 248 | 17 | 16.5 | 160 | 10,944 |  |
|  |  |  |  | 294 | 20,137 | 2.7 |
| TOTAL | 1,505 | 104 | 100.0 | 5,990 | 410,275 |  |
|  |  |  |  | 11,022 | 754,906 | 100.0 |

* Large-value payments: interbank transfers through the central bank's payment system.

## Sweden
### A. Basic Statistical Data

Territorial area: 411.6 thousand sq.kms.
Population: 8.4 million
Gross national product in 1987: (USD/SEK) 159.1/1,008.5 billion
Per capita GNP: (USD/SEK) 18,935/119,900

### A.1 Monetary Aggregates
### 1987

| Items | Absolute USD/SEK (billions) | Per Capita USD/SEK | Percentage of GNP | Number of Accounts (millions) | Number of Accounts per Inhabitant |
|---|---|---|---|---|---|
| Total money supply | 78.940 500.502 | 9,382 59,484 | 49.6 | 28.5 | 3.4 |
| Currency | 8.210 52.043 | 976 6,185 | 5.2 | | |
| Transferable deposits* | 70.730 448.459 | 8,406 53,299 | 44.4 | 28.5 | 3.4 |

*At year-end 1987.

Note:  The exchange rate used to convert SEK into USD for all statistical data was the average 1987 rate of 6.3404.

### Sweden
### A.2 Transferable Deposits and Number of Accounts per Category of Institution
### at Year-End 1987

| Categories of Institution | Number of Accounts (millions) | Share of Market (%) | Value of Accounts USD/SEK (billions) | Value of Accounts per Capita USD/SEK | Share of Market (%) |
|---|---|---|---|---|---|
| Commercial banks | 13.48 | 47.2 | 40.17 254.71 | 4,774 30,272 | 61.9 |
| Savings banks | 11.40 | 39.9 | 21.39 135.59 | 2,542 16,115 | 27.3 |
| Cooperative and rural banks | 2.16 | 7.6 | 5.75 36.48 | 683 4,336 | 7.7 |
| Post Office | 1.50 | 5.3 | 3.42 21.68 | 407 2,576 | 3.1 |
| TOTAL | 28.54 | 100.0 | 70.73 448.46 | 8,406 53,299 | 100.0 |

## Sweden
### B. Points of Entry into the Payment System

#### B.1 Institutional Framework
#### at Year-End 1987

| Categories of Institution | Number of Institutions | Number of Branches | Number of Inhabitants per Branch |
|---|---|---|---|
| Commercial banks | 14 | 1,438 | 5,829 |
| Savings banks | 119 | 1,368 | 6,127 |
| Cooperative and rural banks | 12 | 692 | 12,159 |
| Sub-total | 145 | 3,498 | 2,396 |
| Post office | 146 | 2,200 | 3,825 |
| TOTAL | 291 | 5,698 | 1,477 |
| Central bank | 1 | 21 | n.a. |

## Sweden
### B.2 Cash Dispensers, ATMs, and EFT POS Terminals
### at Year-End 1987

| Cash Dispensers and ATMs | | | | | EFT POS | | |
|---|---|---|---|---|---|---|---|
| Number of Networks | Number of Cash Dispensers | Number of ATMs | Total Number of Cash Dispensers and ATMs | Number of Inhabitants per Cash Dispenser and ATM | Number of Networks | Number of EFT POS Terminals | Number of Inhabitants per EFT POS Terminal |
| 5 | 1,650 | • | • | 5,091 | 2 | 520 | 16,180 |

**Sweden**
**C. Relative Importance of Cashless Payment Instruments**
**in the Payment System**
**1987**

| Instruments | Volume of Transactions (millions) | Volume per Capita | Percentage of Total | Value of Transactions USD/SEK (billions) | Value per Capita USD/SEK | Percentage of Total |
|---|---|---|---|---|---|---|
| Cheques issued | 150 | 18 | 20.70 | 94 | 11,243 | |
| | | | | 600 | 71,285 | 7.57 |
| Payments by credit card[1] | 15 | 2 | 2.07 | 4 | 452 | |
| | | | | 24 | 2,865 | 0.30 |
| Payments by debit card at EFT POS[2] | • | • | • | • | • | • |
| Paper-based credit transfers | 225 | 27 | 31.03 | 473 | 56,240 | |
| | | | | 3,000 | 356,584 | 37.86 |
| Paperless credit transfers | 335 | 40 | 46.20 | 687 | 80,603 | |
| | | | | 4,300 | 511,055 | 54.27 |
| Direct debits | • | • | • | • | • | • |
| TOTAL | 725 | 87 | 100.00 | 1,258 | 148,538 | |
| | | | | 7,924 | 941,789 | 100.00 |

[1] Including transactions by holders of travel and entertainment cards.
[2] The volume of payments at EFT POS is negligible. The figures for payments by debit cards are as follows: volume of transactions: 35 million; volume per capita: 4; value of transactions: SEK 16 billion; value per capita: SEK 1,883.

## Switzerland
## A. Basic Statistical Data

Territorial area: 41,293 sq.kms.
Population: 6.57 million
Gross national product in 1987: (USD/CHF) 200.2/266.3 billion
Per capita GNP: (USD/CHF) 30,473/40,530

### A. 1 Monetary Aggregates
### 1987

| Items | Absolute USD/CHF (billions) | Per Capita USD/CHF | Percentage of GNP | Number of Accounts (millions) | Number of Accounts per Inhabitant |
|---|---|---|---|---|---|
| Total money supply[1] | 242.2 | 36,895 | | | |
| | 322.4 | 49,071 | 121.1 | • | • |
| Currency | 18.5 | 2,825 | | | |
| | 24.7 | 3,758 | 9.2 | • | • |
| Transferable | 41.0 | 6,234 | | | |
| deposits[2] | 54.5 | 8,295 | 2.05 | •[3] | • |

[1] $M_3$; $M_1$: (USD/CHF) 59.5/79.2 billion.
[2] Value of sight deposits at the postal giro accounts: USD 8.6 billion at year-end 1987.
[3] Postal giro account holders: 1.18 million.

Note: The exchange rate used to convert CHF into USD for all statistical data was the end-of-1987 rate of 1.330 (December average).

### Switzerland
### A. 2 Transferable Deposits and Number of Accounts per Category of Institution
### at Year-End 1987

| Categories of Institution | Number of Accounts (millions) | Share of Market (%) | Value of Accounts USD/CHF (billions)[3] | Value of Accounts per Capita USD/CHF | Share of Market (%) |
|---|---|---|---|---|---|
| Commercial banks[1] | • | • | 15.90 | 2,427 | |
| | | | 21.21 | 3,228 | 38.90 |
| Savings banks[2] | • | • | 15.30 | 2,330 | |
| | | | 20.37 | 3,100 | 37.37 |
| Cooperative and rural banks | • | • | 1.20 | 173 | |
| | | | 1.52 | 231 | 2.78 |
| Post office | 1.18 | • | 8.60 | 1,304 | |
| | | | 11.40 | 1,735 | 20.95 |
| TOTAL | • | • | 41.00 | 6,234 | |
| | | | 54.50 | 8,295 | 100.0 |

[1] Five big banks.
[2] Savings, regional, cantonal, and other banks.
[3] Sight deposits.

**Switzerland**
**B. Points of Entry into the Payment System**

**B. 1 Institutional Framework**
**at Year-End 1987**

| Categories of Institution | Number of Institutions | Number of Branches | Number of Inhabitants per Branch |
|---|---|---|---|
| Commercial banks[1] | 5 | 889 | 7,390 |
| Savings banks[2] | 445 | 1,874 | 3,506 |
| Cooperative and rural banks | 2 | 1,242 | 5,290 |
| Sub-total | 452 | 4,005 | 1,640 |
| Post office | 1 | 3,858 | 1,703 |
| TOTAL | 453 | 7,863 | 836 |
| Central bank | 2[3] | 8 | n.a. |

[1] Big banks.
[2] Savings, regional, cantonal, and other banks.
[3] 2 head offices.


**Switzerland**
**B. 2 Cash Dispensers, ATMs, and EFT POS Terminals**
**at Year-End 1987**

| Cash Dispensers and ATMs | | | | | EFT POS | | |
|---|---|---|---|---|---|---|---|
| Number of Networks | Number of Cash Dispensers | Number of ATMs | Total Number of Cash Dispensers and ATMs | Number of Inhabitants per Cash Dispenser and ATM | Number of Networks | Number of EFT POS Terminals | Number of Inhabitants per EFT POS Terminal |
| 2[1] | 1,239 | • | 1,239[2] | 5,303 | 2 | 572 | 11,486 |

[1] Bancomat and Postomat system.
[2] Only cash dispensers.

**Switzerland**
**C. Relative Importance of Cashless Payment Instruments**
**in the Payment System**
**1987**

| Instruments | Volume of Transactions[1] (millions) | Volume per Capita | Percentage of Total | Value of Transactions USD/CHF (billions) | Value per Capita USD/CHF | Percentage of Total |
|---|---|---|---|---|---|---|
| Cheques issued[1] | 42.1 | 6.40 | 13.8 | 96.0 | 14,619.0 | |
| | | | | 127.7 | 19,436.0 | • |
| Payments by credit card[2] | 9.2 | 1.40 | 3.0 | 2.0 | 308.0 | |
| | | | | 2.7 | 410.0 | • |
| Payments by debit card at EFT POS | 1.0 | 0.15 | 0.3 | 0.03 | 3.7 | |
| | | | | 0.04 | 5.0 | • |
| Paper-based credit transfers | 123.7 | 18.80 | 40.6 | • | • | • |
| Paperless credit transfers | 119.4 | 18.20 | 39.3 | • | • | • |
| Direct debits[3] | 9.1 | 1.40 | 3.0 | • | • | • |
| TOTAL | 304.5 | 46.35 | 100.0 | 27,143[4] | 4.13[5] | |
| | | | | 36,101[4] | 5.50[5] | |

[1] Euro-, Bank-, Swiss Bankers Traveller and Postal Cheques.
[2] Rough estimates (American Express, VISA, Diners Club, and Eurocard).
[3] Without payments by debit cards.
[4] Total giro transfers including interbank payments.
[5] In millions of USD/CHF.

## United Kingdom
### A. Basic Statistical Data

Territorial area: 244.1 thousand sq.kms.
Population: 56.8 million
Gross national product in 1987*: (USD/GBP) 669.6/408.5 billion
Per capita GNP: (USD/GBP) 11,789/7,192
* GNP at market prices, 1987.

### A. 1 Monetary Aggregates
### 1987

| Items | Absolute USD/GBP (billions) | Per Capita USD/GBP | Percentage of GNP | Number of Accounts (millions) | Number of Accounts per Inhabitant |
|---|---|---|---|---|---|
| Total money supply[1] | 354.0 187.7 | 6,232 3,304 | 4.59 | | |
| Currency | 26.0 14.0 | 458 246 | 3.4 | | |
| Transferable deposits | 328.0 173.7 | 5,774 3,058 | 42.5 | 133.6[2] | 2.3 |

[1] Includes *(a)* notes and coin held by the general public; *(b)* sight and time deposits of UK private sector, with members of the monetary sector in sterling.
[2] Estimate for sterling retail accounts. Figure includes estimates for accounts with Girobank and National Savings Bank Ordinary Accounts and for ordinary share and deposit accounts with building societies.

Note: The exchange rate used to convert GBP into USD for GNP was the average 1987 rate of 1.639; all other statistical data were converted at the end-of-1987 rate of 1.887.

### United Kingdom
### A. 2 Transferable Deposits and Number of Accounts per Category of Institution
### at Year-End 1987

| Categories of Institution | Number of Accounts[1] (millions) | Share of Market (%) | Value of Accounts USD/GBP (billions) | Value of Accounts per Capita USD/GBP | Share of Market (%) |
|---|---|---|---|---|---|
| Authorised banks | 72.4 | 54.0 | 149.0 79.0 | 2,623 1,391 | 45.4 |
| Building societies | 45.6 | 34.0 | 176.0 93.0 | 3,098 1,637 | 53.6 |
| Post office (NSB)[2] | 15.6 | 12.0 | 3.0 1.7 | 53 30 | 1.0 |
| TOTAL | 133.6 | 100.0 | 328.0 173.7 | 5,774 3,058 | 100.0 |

[1] Sterling retail accounts.
[2] National Savings Bank Ordinary Accounts only. National Savings Bank facilities are available at post offices on an agency basis.

## United Kingdom
### B. Points of Entry into the Payment System

#### B. 1 Institutional Framework
#### at Year-End 1987

| Categories of Institution | Number of Institutions | Number of Branches | Number of Inhabitants per Branch |
|---|---|---|---|
| Authorised banks[1] | 567 | 14,994 | 3,788 |
| Building societies[2] | 137 | 6,967 | 8,153 |
| Sub-total | 704 | 21,961 | 2,586 |
| Post office (NSB)[3] | 1 | 21,211 | 2,678 |
| TOTAL | 705 | 43,172 | 1,315 |
| Central bank | 1 | 5 | n.a. |

[1] Comprises the 567 institutions, other than the Bank of England, which at the end of 1987 were authorised to accept deposits under the Banking Act, 1987. The number of branch offices excludes post offices, at which some Girobank services are provided on an agency basis.

[2] In addition to their branch offices, the building societies have some 19,725 agents (e.g., solicitors, estate agents) where depositors can pay into or withdraw from their accounts.

[3] National Savings Bank Ordinary Accounts only. National Savings Bank facilities are available at post offices on an agency basis.

## United Kingdom
### B. 2 Cash Dispensers, ATMs, and EFT POS Terminals
### at Year-End 1987

| Cash Dispensers and ATMs | | | | | EFT POS | | |
|---|---|---|---|---|---|---|---|
| Number of Networks | Number of Cash Dispensers | Number of ATMs | Total Number of Cash Dispensers and ATMs | Number of Inhabitants per Cash Dispenser and ATM | Number of Networks | Number of EFT POS Terminals | Number of Inhabitants per EFT POS Terminal |
| 21[1,2] | | 12,500 | 12,500 | 4,544 | 23[3] | 13,000[4] | 4,369 |

[1] Comprises banks and building societies that belong to the principal shared networks that are listed in Appendix B of the United Kingdom country chapter. However, this figure does not include the networks that operate in Northern Ireland or the group of 20 building societies and authorised institutions belonging to Funds Transfer Sharing (FTS, which forms part of the LINK sharing consortia (one of the principal networks).
It is understood that the members of the FTS group currently operate some 200 machines.

[2] There are four principal shared networks and three other networks of significance. Again these are listed in Appendix B of the United Kingdom country chapter.

[3] Includes schemes that are at an experimental stage or trial stage.

[4] Comprises: 2,000 on-line data capture terminals accepting debit cards only; 7,000 on-line data capture terminals accepting both debit and credit cards; 4,000 off-line data capture terminals accepting both debit and credit cards.

**United Kingdom**
**C. Relative Importance of Cashless Payment Instruments**
**in the Payment System**
**at Year-End 1987**

| Instruments | Volume of Transactions (millions) | Volume per Capita | Percentage of Total | Value of Transactions USD/GBP (billions) | Value per Capita USD/GBP | Percentage of Total |
|---|---|---|---|---|---|---|
| Cheques issued[1] | | | | | | |
| Town[2] | 5 | less than 1 | less than 1 | 20,025 | 352,552 | |
| | | | | 10,612 | 186,830 | 53.0 |
| Other | 2,963 | 52.0 | 57 | 2,364 | 41,620 | |
| | | | | 1,253 | 22,059 | 6.0 |
| Payments by | 592 | 10.0 | 11 | 36 | 634 | |
| credit card[3] | | | | 19 | 334 | less than 1 |
| Payments by debit card at EFT POS | • | • | • | • | • | • |
| Paper-based | 483 | 8.5 | 9 | 994 | 17,500 | |
| credit transfers[4] | | | | 527 | 9,278 | 2.5 |
| Paperless credit transfers, of which: | | | | | | |
| • large-value | 4 | less than 1 | less than 1 | 13,835 | 243,574 | |
| transfers[5] | | | | 7,332 | 129,084 | 36.5 |
| • others | 678 | 12.0 | 13 | 436 | 7,676 | |
| | | | | 231 | 4,067 | 1.0 |
| Direct debits | 486 | 8.5 | 9 | 239 | 4,207 | |
| | | | | 127 | 2,236 | less than 1 |
| TOTAL[6] | 5,211 | 91.0 | 100 | 37,929 | 667,763 | |
| | | | | 20,101 | 353,888 | 100.0 |

[1] Excluding an estimated 300 million cashed cheques, valued at USD 25 billion (some GBP 13 billion).
[2] Including interbranch cheques.
[3] Excluding transactions by holders of an estimated 9 million charge and budget cards issued by retailers, but including transactions by holders of over 1.5 million travel and entertainment cards.
[4] Including standing orders.
[5] Via CHAPS.
[6] Excluding government payments in cash from post offices against state benefit vouchers.

## United States
### A. Basic Statistical Data

Territorial area: 9.2 million sq.kms. (3.6 million sq. mi.)
Population: 245.1 million
Gross national product in 1987: (USD) 4,488.5 billion
Per capita GNP: (USD) 18,313

### A.1 Monetary Aggregates
### 1987

| Items | Absolute USD (billions) | Per Capita USD | Percentage of GNP | Number of Accounts (millions) | Number of Accounts per Inhabitant |
|---|---|---|---|---|---|
| Total money supply (M$_3$)[1] | | | | | |
| M$_1$ | 751 | 3,065 | 16.7 | | |
| M$_2$ | 2,901 | 11,841 | 64.7 | | |
| M$_3$ | 3,661 | 14,943 | 81.6 | | |
| Currency | 197 | 804 | 4.4 | | |
| Transferable deposits[2] | 547 | 2,233 | 14.1 | 124 | 0.5[3] |

[1] M$_1$ = currency + travellers' cheques + demand deposits + other chequeable deposits.
M$_2$ = M$_1$ + overnight Eurodollar and RPs + money-market mutual funds (general purpose and broker/dealer only) + money-market deposit accounts + savings time deposits.
M$_3$ = M$_2$ + large time deposits (over USD 100,000) + term RPs and Eurodollars + money-market funds (institutions only).
[2] At year-end 1987.
[3] Number of accounts per household at deposit-taking institutions: 1.3; number of households: 92.4 million; number of families: 55.7 million.

### United States
### A.2 Transferable Deposits and Number of Accounts per Category of Institution
### at Year-End 1987

| Categories of Institution | Number of Accounts (millions) | Share of Market (%) | Value of Accounts USD (billions) | Value of Accounts per Capita USD | Share of Market (%) |
|---|---|---|---|---|---|
| Commercial banks[1] | 79 | 64.0 | 462 | 1,886 | 70.0 |
| Savings banks, savings and loan associations, federal savings banks, and mutual savings banks | 27 | 22.0 | 70 | 286 | 20.0 |
| Credit unions | 18 | 14.0 | 15 | 61 | 10.0 |
| Post office | n.a. | | n.a. | | |
| TOTAL | 124 | 100.0 | 547 | 2,233 | 100.0 |

[1] Demand and other chequeable deposits.

## United States
## B. Points of Entry Into the Payment System

### B.1 Institutional Framework
### at Year-End 1987

| Categories of Institution | Number of Institutions | Number of Branches[1] | Number of Inhabitants per Branch |
|---|---|---|---|
| Commercial banks[2] | 14,376 | 62,622 | 3,914 |
| Thrift institutions | | | |
|   Savings & loans | 2,892 | 21,575 | 11,360 |
|   Savings banks[3] | 979 | 8,973 | 27,315 |
| Credit unions | 17,919 | 18,291[4] | 13,453 |
|   Sub-total | | | |
| Post office[5] | 29,344 | 39,270 | 6,241 |
| TOTAL[6] | 36,175 | 105,509 | 2,322 |
| Central bank[7] | 12 | 37 | n.a. |

[1] Total number of offices, including head offices listed in column 1.
[2] 939 multibank holding companies control over 4,000 banks with over 25,000 offices and constitute 73% of commercial bank assets and 70% of deposits.
[3] Includes 370 mutual savings banks; 501 federal savings banks, and 108 cooperative banks.
[4] Estimate.
[5] Not a point of entry into the payment system, except for postal money orders.
[6] Excluding post offices.
[7] Plus the Board of Governors, 11 additional off-site cheque processing centers and two contingency processing sites.

## United States
### B.2 Cash Dispensers, ATMs, and EFT POS Terminals
### at Year-End 1987

| Cash Dispensers and ATMs | | | | | EFT POS | | |
|---|---|---|---|---|---|---|---|
| Number of Networks | Number of Cash Dispensers | Number of ATMs | Number of Cash Dispensers and ATMs | Number of Inhabitants per ATM | Number of Networks | Number of EFT POS Terminals | Number of Inhabitants per EFT POS Terminal |
| 150 | • | • | 76,031[1] | 3,222 | 38[2] | 43,439[3] | 5,640 |

[1] Linda Fenner Zimmer, Payment Services Correspondent, (Marlborough, Connecticut), 1988.
[2] POS News, Barlo Communications (Chicago, Illinois), April 1988.
[3] Does not include either dedicated credit authorisation terminals or retail electronic cash registration terminals.

**United States**
**C. Relative Importance of Cashless Payment Instruments**
**in the Payment System**
**1987**

| Instruments | Volume of Transactions (millions) | Volume per Capita | Percentage of Total | Value of Transactions USD (billions) | Value per Capita USD | Percentage of Total |
|---|---|---|---|---|---|---|
| Cheques issued[1] | 49,200 | 201.0 | 82.9 | 55,917.0 | 228,140 | 16.40 |
| Credit card transactions[2] | 9,100 | 37.0 | 15.3 | 375.0 | 1,530 | 0.10 |
| Payments by debit card at EFT POS | 55 | 0.2 | 0.1 | 0.8 | 3 | <0.01 |
| Paper-based credit transfers | • | • | • | • | • | • |
| Large-value paperless credit transfers[3,4] | 84 | 0.3 | 0.1 | 281,000.0 | 1,146,471 | 82.60 |
| Other credit transfers by ACH and ATM[5] | 613 | 2.5 | 1.0 | 805.0 | 3 | 0.20 |
| Direct debits | 269 | 1.1 | 0.5 | 2,235.0 | 9 | 0.70 |
| TOTAL | 59,321 | 242.1 | 100.0 | 340,332.8 | 1,388,069 | 100.00 |

[1] Includes travellers' cheques (1.4 billion with a value of USD 47 billion) and money orders (0.8 billion valued at USD 70 billion).

[2] *The Nilson Report,* May 1988 (Los Angeles, California). Includes all types of credit card transactions; bank card volume: 2.5 billion valued at USD 165.3 billion. Credit card payment volume and value included in cheque data.

[3] Includes Fedwire volume of 53 million valued at USD 142 trillion and CHIPS volume of 31 million valued at USD 139 trillion.

[4] Approximately 40% of the dollar value of Fedwire transfers are for interbank loans transactions, 10% for Eurodollar transactions, and 10% for commercial transactions. Whereas 55% of the dollar value of CHIPS transactions are for foreign exchange transactions and 28% for Eurodollar transactions.

[5] ACH credit payments: 584 million with a value of USD 803 billion; ATM payments: 29 million with a value of USD 2 billion.

# Selected Bibliography

Akhtar, M.A. *Financial Innovations and Their Implications for Monetary Policy: an International Perspective*. (Economic Paper No. 9). Basle (1984).

Bank for International Settlements. *Payment Systems in Eleven Developed Countries*. Basle: BIS; Rolling Meadows, Ill.: Bank Administration Institute (1985).

Hopton, D. *Payment Systems: a Case for Consensus*. Basle: BIS (1983).

Revell, J.R.S. *Banking and Electronic Fund Transfers*. Paris: OECD (1983).

## CANADA

Bartel, Henry, and Arbuckle, Gavin. *Electronic Banking in Canada and the United States*, Montreal, Québec: Gamma Institute Press (1987).

Binhammer, H.H., and Williams, Jane. *Deposit-Taking Institutions, Innovation, and the Process of Change*, Ottawa: Economic Council of Canada (1976).

Boreham, Gordon F. "The Changing World of Canadian Banking," *Canadian Banker & ICB Review*, Toronto, **90**:3 (June 1983), pp. 6-8.

The Canadian Bankers' Association. *Factbook: Chartered Banks of Canada*, various years.

Canadian Payments Association: *Forum*, various issues. "The Framework for the Evolution of the Payments System," (February 10, 1986); "The Fundamental Elements of EFTPOS"—discussion draft, (October 28, 1987); "Policy Statement on the Use of Pre-authorised Payments," (March 18, 1985).

Canadian Payments System Conference. *Proceedings*, 1985 and 1987.

Craddock, Candace. "Privacy and Equity in EFTS: Some Basic Issues." *Canadian Banker & ICB Review*, Toronto, **88**:1 (February 1981), pp. 10-19.

Crawford, Bradley. "New Laws to Govern EFTS?" *Canadian Business Law Journal*, Aurora, Ont., **5** (1980-81), pp. 37-52.

Crawford, Bradley. "Does Canada Need a Payments Code?" *Canadian Business Law Journal*, Aurora, Ont., **7** (1982-83), pp. 47-72.

David, Guy. "Electronic Funds Transfer—Technological Developments and Legal Issues." *Canadian Computer Law Reporter*, Toronto, Ontario, **2**:4 (February 1985), pp. 65-72; **2**:5 (March 1985), pp. 89-95; **2**:6 (April 1985), pp. 109-114.

Fite, L.R. "Competition and Cooperation in the Evolution of the Canadian Payment System." *The World of Banking*, (July-August, 1982), pp. 25-27.

Kuhlman, Arkadi R. "Canadian Cash Management: Boom or Bust?" *Canadian Banker & ICB Review*, **89**:1 (February 1982), pp. 44-48.

Sinclair, Helen K. "Issues in the Payments System." *Canadian Banker & ICB Review* **89**:5 (October 1982), pp. 10-15.

Touche Ross Management Consultants. *The Impact of Technology on the Canadian Banking Industry*, Toronto, Ontario (December 1984).

Trust Companies' Association of Canada. *General Information Bulletin*, various years.

Vachon, Serge. Remarks by the Chairman of the Canadian Payments Association to the Canadian Payments System Conference, *Bank of Canada Review*, (May 1985), pp. 9-19.

——————— Evolution 1987. Remarks by the Chairman of the Canadian Payments Association to the Canadian Payments System Conference, *Bank of Canada Review*, (October 1987), pp. 9-14.

Valcin, Yvon. *L'argent électronique: position des acteurs*. Québec, Québec: Centre d'information, de recherche et d'analyse sur la monnaie électronique (1985).

Wybouw, George, and Vinet, Françoise. *Le système de paiement électronique au Canada: où en sommes-nous en 1984?* Prepared for the Federal Minister of Communications (1984).

# FRANCE

Administration des postes et télécommunications. *Rapports annuels*.

Administration des postes et télécommunications. *Statistiques sur les services financiers de l'administration des Postes*.

Banque de France. *Rapports du Conseil national du crédit*.

Banque de France. *Rapports statistiques divers* (billets et monnaies, opérations traitées dans les chambres de compensation de province et par les ordinateurs de compensation).

Burgard, Jean-Jacques. *La banque en France*. Paris: Dalloz (1988).

Centre de liaison et d'information sur les moyens de paiement (CLIP). *Annuaire statistique annuel*.

Centre national des caisses d'epargne et des sociétés de prévoyance. *Rapports annuels*.

Centre de recherche économique sur l'épargne (CREP). *Rapports annuels sur les moyens de paiement et les particuliers*.

Chambre de compensation des banquiers de Paris. *Rapports annuels*.

Chemineau, L. *L'argent invisible*. Paris: "Autrement."

Pastre, Olivier. *La modernisation des banques françaises*. Paris: La Documentation Française (1985).

# GERMANY

*Banking in Germany*. 7th ed. Frankfurt a.M. and London: Peat, Marwick, Mitchell (1986).

*The Banking System in Germany*. 15th ed. revised by J. Stein, *et al*. Cologne: Bank Verlag (1987).

Judt, Ewald. Zahlungsverkehr—eine Literaturübersicht. Teil I. *Österreichisches Bank-Archiv,* Vienna (June 1987), pp. 375-381.

——————· Zahlungsverkehr—eine Literaturübersicht. Teil II. *Österreichisches Bank-Archiv,* Vienna (July 1987), pp. 477-490.

Stand und weitere Entwicklung der Automation des unbaren Zahlungsverkehrs bei der Deutschen Bundesbank. *Monatsberichte der Deutschen Bundesbank,* Frankfurt a.M. (August 1985), pp. 47-51.

Werthmöller, Ottomar. Die Entwicklung des Zahlungsverkehrs aus der Sicht der Bundesbank, in *Rationalisierung und Personalmanagement in Kreditinstitutionen*. Frankfurt a.M.: Fritz Knapp (1983).

Zur Rolle der Deutschen Bundesbank im unbaren Zahlungsverkehr. *Monatsberichte der Deutschen Bundesbank,* Frankfurt a.M. (March 1982), pp. 31-33.

# ITALY

Banca d'Italia. *Il sistema dei pagamenti in Italia: progetti di intervento*. Rome (April 1988).

Banca d'Italia. *White Paper on the payment system in Italy*. Rome (April 1988).

Barucci, P. I nuovi sistemi di pagamento. *Bancaria,* Rome (February 1987).

Ciampi, C.A., Dini, L., and Padoa-Schioppa, T. L'evoluzione del sistema dei pagamenti. *Banca d'Italia Bollettino Economico,* Rome, no. 8 (February 1987), pp. 29-50.

Giannini, C. L'evoluzione del sistema dei pagamenti: una sintesi teorica. *Moneta e Credito,* Rome, no. 162 (June 1988).

Indagine sui sistemi di pagamento. *Lettera Marketing (Associazione Bancaria Italiana),* Rome, no. 5 (September-October 1985).

Il marketing dei nuovi strumenti di pagamento offerti dalle banche alla clientela privata. *Lettera Marketing (Associazione Bancaria Italiana),* Rome, no. 5 (September-October 1985).

Padoa-Schioppa, T. Sistema bancario e sistema dei pagamenti. *Banca d'Italia Bollettino Economico,* Rome, no. 7 (October 1986), pp. 55-67.

——————————·Credit Risks in Payment Systems: the Role of Central Banks. *Banca d'Italia Economic Bulletin,* Rome, no. 6 (February 1988), pp. 64-69.

## JAPAN

*Payment Systems in Japan.* Tokyo: Federation of Bankers Associations of Japan, 1988. (This publication is only available in Japanese.)

*The Japanese Financial System,* edited by Yoshio Suzuki. New York: Oxford University Press; Oxford: Clarendon Press (1987).

## THE NETHERLANDS

Bankgirocentrale. *Annual reports.*

Ministry of Finance. *Notitie inzake het elektronische betalingsverkeer in Nederland,* The Hague (November 1988).

Peekel, H. and Veluwenkamp, J.W. *Het girale betalingsverkeer in Nederland,* PCGD/RPS, Amsterdam (1984).

Wolf, H. *Betalen via de bank—van verleden tot heden,* Bankgirocentrale, Amsterdam (December 1983).

## SWEDEN

Conversations with Bank Giro, Centre, Postal Giro, and Kontocentralen.

Swedish Bankers Association. *Computerisation of our Payments Systems,* Stockholm (1986).

## SWITZERLAND

Granziol, M.J. Notenbankpolitische Aspekte des Zahlungsverkehrs. *Geld, Währung und Konjunktur, Quartalsheft der Schweizerischen Nationalbank,* Berne, **4**:4 (December 1986), pp. 263-269.

Haeberli, H. Im Sog der Börsenelektronik. *Schweizer Bank,* Zurich, no. 2, (1988), pp. 36-38.

*Handbuch des Geld-, Bank- und Börsenwesens der Schweiz.* Edited by E. Albisetti, *et al.* 4th ed. Ott: Thun (1987).

Hess, M. Die Rechtsgrundlagen des Swiss Interbank Clearing (SIC). *Wirtschaft und Recht,* Zurich, **40**:1 (1988), pp. 31-49.

Lehmann, G.D. *Zahlungsverkehr der Banken.* Zurich: Verlag des Schweizerischen Kaufmännischen Verbandes (1986).

Marbacher, J. *Das Zahlungsverkehrssystem der Schweiz.* Berne: Haupt (1977).

Portmann, P. Der Schweizerische Postzahlungsverkehr. *Bank und Markt,* Frankfurt a.M., no. 9 (1987), pp. 5-11.

Schweizerische Nationalbank. *75 Jahre Schweizerische Nationalbank.* Zurich (1981).

*Das schweizerische Bankwesen im Jahre 1987.* Zurich: Schweizerische Nationalbank (1988).

Schweizerische PTT-Betriebe. *Statistisches Jahrbuch 1987,* Berne (1988).

SOFFEX. *SOFFEX Management Summary,* Zurich (1987).

Spahni-Klass, A. *Cash Management im multinationalen Konzern.* Thesis, Berne (1988).

Vital, Ch. Das elektronische Interbank-Zahlungsverkehrssystem SIC: Konzept und vorläufige Ergebnisse. *Wirtschaft und Recht,* Zurich, **40**:1 (1988), pp. 9-30.

Vital, Ch., and Mengle, D.L. SIC: Switzerland New Electronic Interbank Payment System, *Economic Review,* Federal Reserve Bank of Richmond, Richmond (November, December 1988).

## UNITED KINGDOM

Annual Survey of ATM Installations. *Banking World.* London (November 1987), pp. 45-57.

*Bank of England Banking Act report for 1987/1988.* London (1988).

*Bank of England Quarterly Bulletin.* London, various issues.

Central Statistical Office: *Financial Statistics.* London, various issues.

Committee of London and Scottish Bankers. *Abstract of Banking Statistics 1988.* London (1988).

Department for National Savings. *Annual Report 1987-88,* London.

Information from the Building Societies Association.

Information from the Northern Ireland Bankers' Association.

Members of the Bankers Clearing House. *Payment Clearing Systems: Review of Organisation, Membership and Control.* London: Association for Payment Clearing Services (APACS), (1986).

National Consumer Council. *Banking Services and the Consumer.* London: Methuen (1983).

Price Commission. *Banks: Charges for Money Transmission Services.* London: HMSO (1978).

"Recent Developments in UK Payment Clearing Systems." *Bank of England Quarterly Bulletin.* London (August 1987), pp. 392-394.

United Kingdom. *Banking Act 1987.* Ch. 22. London: HMSO (1987).

United Kingdom. *Building Societies Act 1986.* Ch. 53. London: HMSO (1986).

*United Kingdom National Accounts [Blue book] 1987.* London: HMSO (1987).

*Whitaker's Almanack [1988].* London: Whitaker (1987).

## UNITED STATES

The ACH in a New Light. *Federal Reserve Bank of Atlanta Economic Review,* Atlanta (March 1986), complete issue.

*American Banker.* New York, various issues.

American Bankers Association. *1987 Retail Deposit Services Report,* Washington, D.C. (1983).

*Annual Statistical Digest 1987.* Washington, D.C.: Board of Governors of the Federal Reserve System (1988).

Association of Reserve City Bankers. *Risk in the Electronic Payments Systems,* Washington, D.C. (1983).

The Automatic Clearing House Alternative: How Do We Get There from Here? *Federal Reserve Bank of Atlanta Economic Review,* Atlanta (April 1986), complete issue.

Avery, Robert B., Dudley, William, and Snyder, Eugene. *Social Security Check Float.* Washington, D.C.: Board of Governors of the Federal Reserve System (January 1984).

Avery, Robert B., Elliehausen, Gregory E. *et al.* Changes in the Use of Transaction Accounts and Cash from 1984 to 1986. *Federal Reserve Bulletin,* Washington, D.C. (March 1987), pp. 179-196.

———————————————————————— . Financial Characteristics of High-Income Families. *Federal Reserve Bulletin,* Washington, D.C. (March 1986), pp. 163-177.

———————————————————————— . Survey of Consumer Finances, 1983: A Second Report. *Federal Reserve Bulletin,* Washington, D.C. (December 1984), pp. 857-868.

———————————————————————— . The Use of Cash and Transaction Accounts by American Families. *Federal Reserve Bulletin,* Washington, D.C. (February 1986), pp. 87-108.

Avery, Robert B., Elliehausen, Gregory E., and Kennickell, Arthur B. Change in Consumer Installment Debt: Evidence from 1983 and 1986 Surveys of Consumer Finances. *Federal Reserve Bulletin*. Washington, D.C. (October 1987), pp. 761-778.

Baker, Donald I., and Penney, Norman. *The Law of Electronic Fund Transfer Systems*. Boston: Warren, Gorham and Lamont (1980).

*Bank Network News*. Chicago: Barlo Communications, various issues.

*Bank Operations Bulletin*. Washington, D.C.: American Bankers Association, various issues.

Berger, Allen M., and Humphrey, David B. *The Role of Interstate Banking in the Diffusion of Electronic Payments Technology*. Rev. ed. Washington, D.C.: Board of Governors of the Federal Reserve System (July 1985).

Berger, Allen M., and Humphrey, David B. "Interstate Banking and the Payments System." *Journal of Financial Services Research*, **1** (January 1988), pp. 133-45.

Board of Governors of the Federal Reserve System. *Controlling Risk in the Payments System*, Washington, D.C. (August 1988).

Board of Governors of the Federal Reserve System. *Credit Cards in the US Economy: Their Impact on Costs, Prices, and Retail Sales*. Washington, D.C. (July 27, 1988).

Board of Governors of the Federal Reserve System. *The Federal Reserve System: Purposes and Functions*. 7th ed. Washington, D.C. (1984).

Board of Governors of the Federal Reserve System. *Functional Cost Analysis*. Washington, D.C. (1986).

Board of Governors of the Federal Reserve System. *Planning and Control System Expense Report (PACS)*, Washington, D.C. (1987).

Board of Governors of the Federal Reserve System. Large-Dollar Payment System Advisory Group. *A Strategic Plan for Managing Risk in the Payment System*. Washington, D.C. (August 1988).

*Corporate EFT Report*. Potomac, Md.: Phillips Publishing, Inc., various issues.

Displacing the Check (special issue). *Federal Reserve Bank of Atlanta Economic Review*. Atlanta (August 1983).

Dudley, William. *A Comparison of Direct Deposit and Check Payment Costs*. 2nd ed. Washington, D.C.: Board of Governors of the Federal Reserve System (June 1983).

Dudley, William C. The Tug-of-War over Float. *Morgan Guaranty Survey*, New York, (December 1983).

*Economic Report of the President January 1988*. Washington, D.C.: U.S. Government Printing Office (1988).

*EFT Report*. Potomac, Md.: Phillips Publishing, Inc., various issues.

Federal Reserve Bank of Atlanta. *A Quantitative Description of the Check Collection System*, vols. 1 & 2, Atlanta (1981).

Felgran, Steven D., and Ferguson, R. Edward. "The Evolution of Retail EFT Networks. *New England Economic Review*. Boston (July/August 1986), pp. 42-56.

*Funds Transfer Report*. Westport, Conn.: Bankers Research Publications, various issues.

Humphrey, David B. *Future Directions in Payment Risk Reduction*. Richmond: Federal Reserve Bank of Richmond (February 1983).

Humphrey, David B., and Berger, Allen N. *"Market Failure and Resource Use: Economic Incentives to Use Different Payment Instruments"* in David B. Humphrey, ed., *U.S. Payment Systems: Efficiency, Risk, and the Role of the Federal Reserve*. To be published, 1989.

Humphrey, David B. "The US Payments System: Costs, Pricing, Competition and Risk." *Monograph Series in Finance and Economics*, New York: New York University, Monograph 1984-1/2.

Jackson, D. Mark. *1986 Survey of the Electronic Funds Transfer Transaction System*, Rolling Meadows, Ill.: Bank Administration Institute (1987).

*The Nilson Report.* Los Angeles: HSN Consultants, Inc., various issues.

*Payment Systems Newsletter.* Tampa, Fla.: Payment Systems, Inc., various issues.

*POS News.* Chicago: Barlo Communications, various issues.

The Revolution in Retail Payments (special issue). *Federal Reserve Bank of Atlanta Economic Review,* Atlanta (July/August 1984).

Table 5: Components of Money Stock, Liquid Assets, and Debt. *Federal Reserve Statistical Release H.6.* Washington, D.C.: Board of Governors of the Federal Reserve System, September 1, 1988.

Table 9: Operations in Principal Departments of Federal Reserve Banks, 1984-87, *Federal Reserve Board Annual Report 1987.* Washington, D.C. (1988), p. 237.

Trans Data Corporation (Salisbury, Md.), various reports.

van der Velde, Marjolijn. *Consumer Checking Accounts: Debits, Credits, and Balances.* 2nd ed., rev. Rolling Meadows, Ill.: Bank Administration Institute, 1987.

Zimmer, Linda Fenner. "ATMs 1988: The Light at the End of the Tunnel." *Bank Administration,* Rolling Meadows, Ill., **64** (May 1988), p. 23.

# Subject Index

# Subject Index